THE PLOTTERS

By *JOHN ROY CARLSON*

THE PLOTTERS
UNDER COVER

THE PLOTTERS

by

Derounian, Arthur

JOHN ROY CARLSON

1946 · E. P. DUTTON & COMPANY, INC. · NEW YORK

The author gratefully acknowledges the permissions granted him for reprinting excerpts from the following books and articles, copyright as follows:

1941: Atlanta *Constitution,* news story on Governor Eugene Talmadge.

1943: Simon and Schuster: *One World* by Wendell Willkie. 1944: New York *World-Telegram:* Henry J. Taylor's interview with Joseph P. Kennedy. 1945: Reynal and Hitch-cock: *The New Veteran* by Charles G. Bolte; The Pamphlet Press: *The Truth About Unions* by Leo Huberman; *Collier's* magazine: Walter Davenport's article, "Savior from Texas." 1944: The *Commonweal,* John C. Cort's article on the PAC.

1946: *Life* magazine: "The U.S. Communist Party" by Arthur M. Schlesinger, Jr.; Station WJZ, one of Drew Pearson's broadcasts; Cleveland *Press:* articles by Eugene Segal; New York *Times:* Harold B. Hinton's interview with J. T. Karam, story on the Klan Kavalier Klub; *The Grizzly:* Tom Powers' report on the Klan; *PM:* article on Herbert von Strempel, Tom O'Connor's story on Helen Bell; New York *Post:* James A. Wechsler's interview with O. John Rogge; New York *World-Telegram:* Charles T. Lucey's article on Bilbo; Mutual Broadcasting System for Hodding Carter's comments on Bilbo; Atlanta *Journal,* editorial; United Features Syndicate: several columns by Thomas L. Stokes.

The illustrations were assembled and prepared by the author

American Book–Stratford Press, Inc., New York
⬥ 55

Fair criticism of political figures, whatever their shade of politics or field of work—labor, economics, religion, public information—in no way reflects upon their Americanism or good faith. Besides exposing anti-democratic elements, *The Plotters* discusses and mentions other groups, constructive and destructive. No charge, direct or implied, of disloyalty or un-Americanism is made or inferred against any person, group or organization mentioned in this book, except when so specified in the text.

Those who are mentioned as being under indictment are so as this book goes to press.

DEDICATED TO MY BROTHERS

STEVEN AND JOHN

AND TO THE MILLIONS OF OTHER AMERICAN VETERANS OF
WORLD WAR II WHO FACED THE ENEMY'S BULLETS
ABROAD AND LIVED TO RETURN HOME

Author's Preface

> What constitutes the bulwark of our own liberty and independence? It is not our frowning battlements, our bristling sea coasts.
> ... Our reliance is in the love of liberty which God has planted in us. Our defense is in the spirit which prized liberty as the heritage of all men, in all lands everywhere.
>
> *Abraham Lincoln*

THE PLOTTERS is a personal adventure report covering America's first year of "peace," and is based almost exclusively on undercover activity since V-J Day. I have gathered a considerable proportion of the material since January 1, 1946. Unlike *Under Cover*, in which I narrated my experiences over a five-year period as an investigator of Nazi and Japanese agents in this country and of their collaborators and dupes, *The Plotters* strikes deep into the rash of poisonous political and social growths blossoming from our native soil.

In their native quality lies their greatest danger to our democracy. Whether one is concerned with the tactics of the American Communist Party or the endless array of extreme nationalist elements symbolized by Gerald Smith's America First Party, their foreign genesis and financing are now difficult to trace. The finger of public scorn can no longer be pointed at the non-citizen, the accented agent, the display of the swastika. These symbols of an alien philosophy have disappeared from public view.

Not so, however, the ideas they represented. Adapted to the United States, they are being faithfully propagated by transmission belters as native to America as the rattler, and just as restful to our national community. Alien philosophies now bear the trademark "Made in America." Ideas which we once regarded as "alien" and "un-American" are now being propagated by American agents in modified form, under guises acceptable to native-born Americans, and promoted with American dollars. Nazi agents have done their work and departed, but so far as psychological propaganda against our democracy is concerned Hitler is by no means dead. Hitlerism in our country is a sinister and expanding reality.

vii

One of the forms Hitlerism takes is that of *extreme* nationalism. The word "nationalism" to many Americans means a healthy love of their country and includes the concept of neighborly love and mutual respect between nations. But the new extremist nationalism, engendered by Hitler's worldwide agents and supported now by Americans who secretly admired him, is a perversion of the usual concept, much as "Christianity" and "Americanism" have been perverted by bigots and false patriots. *The new "nationalism" is the negation of democracy and of our traditional philosophy of government by all and for all.* It excludes from the democratic fraternity the non-"Aryan" and non-Anglo-Saxon and sets up the concept of a master race, master philosophy, master culture. It unleashes dynamic and fearful emotions—hate and brutality—which, when galvanized among the unschooled and easily led masses of the people, become unstoppable and ungovernable.

The slogans "America First" and "America for the Americans" are warning signs of the indoctrination of some Americans with this alien philosophy. They are the counterparts of Hitler's slogan "Germany for the Germans," which presaged Germany's doom. Unfortunately, I have found that many Americans who truly love their country are innocently drawn within the orbit of those who under the guise of "Christianity," "nationalism" and "America First" incite hate and disunity and wish to "preserve the Constitution" by methods identical with Hitler's.

I have written this book primarily to expose the methods, appeals and objectives of fanatical extremists of the Right and Left and of their fellow travelers. Their most important objective is to capture postwar America's most precious prize: the mind of the veteran. That is why in my investigations for *The Plotters* I have posed as an "Anglo-Saxon" veteran, whereas in the work described in *Under Cover* I posed and lived as an Axis-minded Italian American.

The extent and viciousness of the hate movements I have been asked to join as a "veteran" have astonished me. I had thought myself inured to the display of prejudice, but even I was alarmed at the scope of anti-Catholic, anti-Semitic, anti-Negro, anti-foreign-born bigotry which I discovered. Its vicious quality seems unnatural to the America I have known and loved for twenty-five years. The conclusion is inescapable that while we have won a war of democracy over fascist evil abroad, we have allowed hate and prejudice to gain a firm foothold at home.

I have rediscovered that these poisons in the national blood-stream are by no means confined to so-called "crackpots" or to the politically naïve. They have made themselves felt in the Congress. They have infected influential and moneyed "Park Avenue" Americans, and reached segments of our middle classes. The grim fact is that they have infiltrated into the warp and woof of American life.

Those who insist that a psychological or political Pearl Harbor could never "happen here" are either naïve or ignorant of the sinister undertow tending to carry our democracy toward the shoals of an American type of "fascism." Anyone tempted to laugh off the "crackpots" with their crude but insidious ideas as mere "lunatic fringers" forgets that fascism requires mass support. Fascism is a mass revolutionary movement, rooted in ignorance and fear and propelled by hate. There can be no successful fascism without a civilian army of gullible adherents such as Hitler cultivated to give body and weight to his extreme nationalist revolution. The American "Nationalist" hierarchy therefore encourages the so-called "crackpot" and welcomes his raucous support. And, in a subconscious attempt to emulate Hitler, it's making a particular bid for the veteran.

Postwar instability is only one factor in the strong undertow mentioned above, which may be attributed to four main underlying causes:

Economic: The rise of labor as a powerful voice in national and world politics, which has alarmed and angered those who traditionally dominated the field;

Social: The social advances of the New Deal, which aroused the hate of those who thought of the "American way" as something exclusive and limited to members of an Anglo-Saxon economic and social "aristocracy," and who could not become reconciled to the change;

International: The upsurge of the USSR as the second power in the world, threatening the established order, has brought new problems, fears and suspicions;

Religious: The gross treatment by the USSR of religious values and church dogmas has set in motion a strong reaction against such excesses, which in turn can go too far in the opposite direction.

With war restraints and wartime inhibitions lifted, each of these four major groups—powerful and gifted in the art of public conversion—is engaged in grinding its ax, individually and collectively.

It is bombarding America with a wild barrage of counter-propaganda bullets. Each sincerely believes its way is *the* way to economic, social, international and spiritual salvation. The kettle is boiling furiously as each group pours in its venom—in the name of humanity, patriotism, civilization or religion—to eliminate the faction it dislikes most.

Meanwhile there has arisen an aggressive empire-nation, its bold challenge fired by its own missionary zeal to make its philosophy supreme, and convinced that Western capitalism has failed.

The United States is a major battleground for the global revolution of ideas and the war of nerves. It is a tugging clash between an established order which, finally admitting some of its shortcomings, is trying to reform and keep the machinery working before it breaks down under pressure from within and without, and an arising giant impatient to be heard, suspicious of others, and fearful that a delay will stifle its voice.

This explosive new power has courted the same fears which in an earlier day it courted among certain powerful German classes. We have the same classes here. They are American, and they are frightened, as were the Germans. While I have never held any brief for Communism, as an investigator I cannot overlook the sinister fact that some of our methods of "fighting Communism" bear a close parallel to the methods resorted to by moneyed German classes.

I have asked myself: Will these nearly identical tactics lead to nearly identical ends here? Will they result in the cry for the need of a "strong man" to "save America from Communism"? Will this "savior" on horseback be a veteran of World War II? Like Hitler, will he gather around him veterans of World War II and repeat in America the tragedy which overtook Germany—and the world—as an aftermath of World War I? Or will it be an American "superman" with an even newer, more dynamic appeal?

With Europe reduced to a shambles, and the appeal both of the führer-principle and of anti-Semitism as a demagogic device snuffed out in most areas for the present, those who tried to make fascism permanent in Germany, Italy, Norway, Austria, Poland and other countries are now flocking to the Western Hemisphere to renew their satanic efforts. The Americas are in danger of becoming the repository for those who deserted the sinking ship and want to go back to the evil business all over again. To those who still doubt the creeping approach of the fascist cancer to the shores of this hemisphere I submit the grim invitation of Dr. Santiago M. Peralta, Director of Migration of Argentina, for "1,000 Quislings" from Norway as "superior types" in order to breed an Argentinian "super race" in fifty years. The dregs of Hitlerism are finding refuge in our own back yard. America may become the final battleground between democracy and resurgent fascism, for these imported Nazis will eventually creep up from Argentina, through Mexico, into the United States. As America goes, so may go the world.

In *Under Cover* I tried to explain these forces as they functioned in the early years of the war. Those who approved the exposure in the book of the activities of Nazi and fascist enemies of the war effort, and their gullible dupes, became my staunch friends. Those who opposed it became an enemy army who stopped at nothing to smear me out of existence. I was called almost everything and charged with committing all manner of crimes. The pseudonyms which I had to use in the course of my investigations, since there was no other way for me as a reporter to get the hidden facts, became sinister "aliases." I was falsely charged with having a criminal record.

I was then called a "Communist," when as a matter of fact I have always strongly expressed my opposition to Communism and have always believed in the political middle road. Army Intelligence, I'm confident, checked on me with the FBI and conducted their own independent investigation before allowing me to lecture extensively for Army Air Force orientation courses, at hospitals and elsewhere for the Army. My topic was "The Enemy Within." Contrary to rumors that *Under Cover* had been permanently banned by the Army, I found the book prominently displayed on Army library shelves.

My enemies made a great issue of my "foreign birth." It's quite true that I was born in Europe, in 1909, of Armenian ancestry. Love of freedom and devotion to the Christian faith have been historic characteristics of the Armenian people. This background is the main motivation for my work against bigotry. With my parents, I came to America in April, 1921 and was immediately enrolled in public school at Mineola, L. I., N. Y. I was graduated from the School of Journalism of New York University in 1932. I have been an American citizen since 1926. I have never made a secret of the name with which I was born, but for personal reasons contingent on the security of others, I prefer not to use it in connection with my undercover work or writings. John Roy Carlson is my pen name. As to my draft status, my draft board is satisfied and so is my conscience.

Let me add that no "secret" group of any type has ever sponsored any of my writings. Mr. Walter Winchell, like many other Americans, believes in fighting for our democracy, but he does not do my writing, as charged. I do my own writing and my own thinking. Neither I nor my publishers, E. P. Dutton & Company, Inc., have ever made any "deals" with anyone, anywhere, as was darkly hinted by the bigots.

I am indebted to a number of persons for their part in making *The Plotters* possible, though the opinions expressed in the book are reserved as strictly my own.

To Morton Levy, American Legion and Jewish War Veterans member, who arranged for me to receive correspondence and literature, un-American and otherwise, under my guise as a "veteran," I owe a profound debt of thanks.

Once again I am grateful to the Reverend L. M. Birkhead for extending to me the facilities of the Friends of Democracy Library for such help as I needed.

To the Most Reverend Bernard J. Sheil, Auxiliary Bishop of Chicago, and Eric Johnston, former President of the United States Chamber of Commerce, I am grateful for permission to quote from their inspiring addresses.

I am indebted to the officers of the National Better Business Bureau in New York and the Better Business Bureaus in Boston, Chicago, Kansas City and San Antonio for their aid. Splendid documentary material has been made available to me by Better Business Bureaus throughout the country and I regret that limitations of time and space have prevented my using more of it.

I wish to thank Jean for her voluntary and deeply appreciated help, and my thanks also go to Gus and Michael.

To my various friends throughout the country, I'm grateful for the timely help which came to me in the form of investigational leads, news clippings and direct assistance whenever I needed it.

And finally, I wish to pay tribute to the loving inspiration of Marie, Robert and Elyse, without which I would not have had the incentive to carry on with my undercover activities.

August 14, 1946

John Roy Carlson

Contents

THE PLOTTERS

CHAPTER ONE

Goons on the Rampage

America must choose one of three courses after this war: narrow nationalism, which inevitably means the ultimate loss of our own liberty; international imperialism, which means the sacrifice of some other nation's liberty; or the creation of a world in which there shall be an equality of opportunity for every race and every nation.

Wendell Willkie, in "One World" *

Today we stand on the threshold of a new world. We must do our part in making this world what it should be, a world in which the bigotries of race and class and creed shall not be permitted to warp the souls of men.

President Truman

SEPTEMBER 2, 1945 was V-J Day. Victory won, nearly ten million GIs, sailors and marines, many of them scarred by enemy bullets, have returned home only to find themselves facing enemy bullets all over again. They are bullets of new design, made of paper—hate bullets, poisoned-propaganda bullets, fired by expert marksmen camouflaged as in pre-Pearl Harbor days in star-spangled patriotic colors. A paper bullet can be just as disruptive mentally as live ammunition is destructive physically. One maims a man's body, and he is lucky if it can be patched together again. The other tears his mind to bits so that he cannot think straight. The victims of both are equally casualties of war, whether of the military or psychological war makes little difference. In the life and death of nations the paper bullets may well be the more deadly variety.

The war that ended militarily when Nazi Germany surrendered at a Rheims schoolhouse and when the Japanese signed the surrender agreement aboard the U.S.S. *Missouri* in Tokyo Bay is still being waged ideologically on democratic American soil in the name of a spurious "Americanism."

* Reprinted from *One World* by Wendell L. Willkie, by permission of Simon and Schuster, Inc. Copyright 1943 by Wendell L. Willkie.

1

Propaganda bullets sprayed by breeders of hate and plotters against democracy are finding new victims. The times are ripe for perverted nationalism and crusading un-Americanism. Our ex-GIs have not escaped the attacks of hate-mongers on the home front. War is a social earthquake, inevitably followed by dislocations in personal, economic and political life. Strikes and the atom bomb have confused a lot of Americans and made some of us hysterical. The woeful shortage of housing, inflationary prices, the pains of re-conversion—all have helped embitter both veterans and stay-at-homes. Having sweated it out overseas, the former expect to get a better deal at home. And they're right!

They deserve better than $25 jobs. They deserve better than the run-around some of them are getting. They deserve homes where they can be with their wives and children. The raw deals and run-arounds were not included in the Great Promises made to them before they got into uniform. But it's not always easy to convince the ex-GI of the valiant efforts of the Veterans Administration. It's hard to explain the combined attempts of labor and some industrial leaders to guarantee a year-round livable wage and decent working conditions. Government efforts to keep prices down and wages high enough to meet living costs are apt to be overlooked completely.

Some veterans, having stepped more or less directly from school into the Army, find it especially hard to understand it all. They are apt to be easy marks for the demagogue who has all the wrong answers and explains the ills of the world by blaming them on some scapegoat minority. Such veterans make good targets for the sharp-shooter with the nationalist propaganda gun and the endless supply of paper bullets.

A hate meeting I went to after V-J Day was intended for such victims. It was a Saturday night, October 6, 1945—just 61 days after the first atom bomb burst over Hiroshima and 34 days after the "Aryans" of the Far East surrendered unconditionally to Allied non-Aryan democracy. It had rained all day. Toward dusk the downpour stopped, but the New York streets were still sleek with water and the gutters flowed noisily.

It was an important evening for democratic citizens of the borough of Queens, former stronghold of the notorious Christian Front, the Coughlinite organization, seventeen of whose members were tried for plotting to overthrow our government. More than fifteen civic, religious and veterans' groups had banded together as the Citizens of Queens United for Democracy. They were meeting in Andrew Jackson High School to hear Principal Ralph W. Haller, Dr. Dan Dodson of the Mayor's Committee on Unity, Rev. L. M. Birkhead of the Friends of Democracy, Mary Margaret McBride, the radio star, myself and others speak on democracy. It was an American meeting and the audience was a cross section of the borough population. Their circulars read:

The Fight's Just Begun To Keep What We've Won
No Fascism in Queens!
Give Your Pledge to Veterans
to Safeguard the Democracy They Fought For

Down in a small park adjoining the Long Island Railroad station, another meeting was scheduled that night. Preparations had been carefully made for it in New York, Chicago and Philadelphia. I attended this meeting just before going on to the high school, where I was scheduled to speak late in the program. As I walked toward the little park I recalled an "Anti-War Mass Meeting for Patriotic Christian Americans" I had attended in precisely the same spot, almost exactly four years earlier. That was back on September 26, 1941, when the regular Christian Front was still operating openly. The chairman was A. Casimir Kudelski, führer of the Christian Front Minute Men. Kudelski was better known by his alias—C. Daniel Kurts.

It had rained that day, too, I remembered, and the rain had stopped about seven o'clock. Kurts had advertised the meeting, announcing as speakers Kurt Mertig, Chairman of the Citizens' Protective League, a Yorkville outfit at whose meetings Hitler was adulated and democracy belittled, and Rev. John C. Fitting, Union City, N. J., clergyman associated with the German-American Bund (*Deutscher-Amerikanischer Volksbund*); a naturalized American citizen, Fitting later lost his citizenship in proceedings brought by the Department of Justice and in 1945 was interned as a dangerous enemy alien. Edward James Smythe, a member of the Bund and the Ku Klux Klan, was on the program. Fitting and Smythe did not show up, but Joe McWilliams, the Yorkville führer (who together with Smythe is, at this writing, under indictment for seditious conspiracy, charged with corrupting the morale of our Armed Forces) was there with his goons and their baseball bats, ready for any "emergency."

I could still see Kurts as he got up, brandishing a huge white-painted cross made of three-inch-wide fence boards. Clutching the cross in his massive fist, he shook it menacingly aloft as he orated. In his hands, and used to emphasize his words, the cross became a white-painted club.

"God is with us!" he bellowed. "It was raining all day, but the rain stopped an hour before the meeting! God watches over us nationalist Americans! See? No more rain!"

Then came the miracle. Within five minutes—no more—the heavens burst open and the waters poured in rivulets. The nationalists ran for protection from the downpour and took refuge under the railroad trestle. Kurts still clutched his profaned cross. The meeting was washed out.

In the four years that followed, God showed further whose side He was on.

Reaching the same lot four years later, I saw that a crowd of several hundred had gathered. It was dotted with service men and women in uniform. I noticed a lot of others wearing their discharge buttons. The police were there, too, ringing the outer fringes of the mob.

A burly figure in a rumpled suit was setting up the speakers' stand just off the sidewalk. I recognized him. It was C. Daniel Kurts. He was raising the flag when the cross fixed atop the staff slipped off and fell into the gutter. C. Daniel Kurts bent down. Two decorated marines were watching with me.

"Hey, you're letting that flag touch the gutter!" one of them snapped.

Kurts didn't seem to hear. With a smirk he picked up the cross, replaced it and set the flag up. Water mixed with mud dripped from its folds.

The brazen incongruity of the man and the scene struck me deeply—the beefy, perspiring "Minute Man," the mud-soaked flag in his hands, the crowd of servicemen, veterans and civilians waiting to hear the vicious program. I had a good idea of the rank poison which would be pumped into them.

As dusk settled over the scene Kurts mounted the speakers' stand.

He took off his coat, revealing a shirt that was wrinkled and discolored. He opened his mouth wide and yammered:

"The war is over—and we're gonna have meetin's again all over the country! There ain't nothing and nobody to stop us now. Take that, you guys who don't like us! This is a meetin' of the Christian Front—not so-called, but *The* Christian Front. This is it! The speakers who come after me are all Christian, one hundred percent patriotic Americans! I personally guarantee you that! As you listen, you'll think you have been transported back to July the fourth, 1776; you'll imagine you are present in the Cradle of Liberty or when the Declaration of Independence was proclaimed."

He introduced Patriot No. 1, who mounted the stand, a thick, fleshy man with a mouthful of gold-capped teeth. He was Ernest F. Elmhurst, born Herman Fleischkopf. A defendant in the Washington wartime sedition trial, Elmhurst, as this is written, is still under indictment. He is the former head of the Pan-Aryan League. He was a delegate to the Nazi International Congress at Erfurt, Germany, in 1937. His literary works include a Jew-baiting book which was published by Silver Shirter William Dudley Pelley, in jail for sedition, and a Pan-Aryan booklet decorated with the swastika (there is nothing subtle about Elmhurst). He was the mentor of a Brooklyn Christian Fronter imprisoned for draft evasion.

Elmhurst launched into a harangue on the sedition trials, picturing himself and the other defendants as martyrs, hounded and persecuted for daring to oppose a plot to capture America engineered by the Communists and the Administration.

"The sedition trial is persecution of Christianity!" he told the audience in thick, guttural English. "It is Communism in action. It is persecution of real Americans by the New Deal. It is unconstitutional and un-American!"

Elmhurst was followed on the stand by another "patriot" with whom he has long been associated. He was a squat, thick-jowled man with a crew haircut, none other than the same Kurt Mertig who was scheduled to speak at the drowned-out anti-war meeting of 1941. Still Chairman of the Bund-type Citizens' Protective League, Mertig is a familiar figure in the American Nazi underworld. He was once employed by the Hamburg-American Line, and his meetings in Yorkville before the war were rallying points for nationalists. The professed purpose of the League was to place German members in the New York City Government. Mertig had a large mailing list and was a prolific letter and article writer for nationalist publications. Since the war ended Mertig has served as a leading apologist for Nazi war crimes, and tried to bring together various pro-Nazi societies under a new cloak of patriotism.

The crowd listened curiously as Mertig, in thick accents, denounced the policy of the Department of Justice in de-naturalizing and deporting Nazis like Fritz Kuhn.

"The Department of Justice," he yelled, "is un-American! They are persecuting good Americans. We are innocent. We are doing nothing wrong. We are one hundred percent correct Americans!"

Patriot No. 3 was thirty-three-year-old Homer Maertz of Chicago. He was a pal of Gerald L. K. Smith, at one of whose meetings Maertz advocated the sterilization of Jews. Maertz was organizer of the Bundist German-American Alliance (*Deutsche-Amerikanische Einheitsfront*) and a storm-troop outfit known as the Silver Shirts whose chief was seditionist William Dudley Pelley. On December 29, 1939 Maertz was sentenced to the penitentiary in Chicago for organizing a gang of hoodlums with whom he painted swastikas on Jewish stores and smashed their windows—Nazi style. When Maertz was arrested William Wernecke, Nazi agent and Bund leader, paid his bail. On his release, Maertz went back to his patriotic endeavors, founding the Pioneer News Service, a vicious nationalist agency. In the fall of 1941 a raid on Maertz' residence by Congressional investigators yielded a half ton of "anti-Semitic, pro-fascist, pro-German and pro-Japanese literature," in addition to numerous pictures of Hitler.

Maertz read passages from *Jewish Ritual Murder*, a fantastic, inflammatory book by Arnold S. Leese, former leader of the Imperial Fascist League of London. Leese served six months in jail for selling the book. Maertz had it published over here for mass American consumption, and distributed it from coast to coast at fifty cents, through a network of nationalist agents. The "Jewish ritual murder" theme was a favorite topic of Julius Streicher, the notorious Nazi sadist.

Most of the servicemen and veterans listened quietly as Maertz blared that America was "run by Jews." One marine cupped his hands and shouted:

"I heard that over the Berlin short wave!"

The cops eased him away.

Dour-faced Mrs. Catharine V. Brown, head of a Philadelphia nationalist group known as National Blue Star Mothers of Pennsylvania (it is not to be confused with the praiseworthy Blue Star Mothers), had come up from Philadelphia bringing a gang of "Crusading Mothers" with her.

A friend had given Mrs. Brown the inside dope.

"The Japanese Ambassador in Washington," she screeched, "tried to deliver the declaration of war the day before Pearl Harbor, but the State Department wouldn't let him come in. Who can say that the attack on Pearl Harbor was not planned deliberately by Washington?"

Someone shouted, "You're a liar!" and was escorted away by police.

Kurts blared a long-winded introduction of the fifth speaker, Frederick Kister, stating that Kister had come all the way from Chicago and implying that as a veteran he had a message of particular significance.

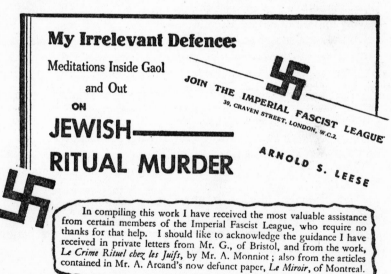

Imperial Fascist League führer Leese acknowledges the sources of his fantastic book. Homer Maertz published it verbatim; he omitted only the large swastika and peddled the Nazi poison as "American."

"Men like him," Kurts yelled, "will save our country! They're the hope of America. Here he is—a hundred percent American!"

A pale-faced, zealous-looking young man, discharge button in his lapel, mounted the stand. He fingered the flag at his elbow, stared about, then let loose a barrage of star-spangled intolerance:

"I am the founder of the Christian Veterans of America. I had a good job, but the Jews made me lose it. The refugees have all the jobs now! I fought for a Christian America! I am for Christians First, for America First—for my country first, last, and all the time! I am a nationalist!"

There was no denying this, for Kister, too, had an interesting pedigree. An America Firster before being drafted, Kister was an ex-employee of *Scribner's Commentator*, semi-highbrow, pro-Nazi monthly (in no way connected with *Scribner's Magazine*, once published by Charles Scribner's Sons). One of the editors of *Scribner's Commentator*, Ralph Townsend, went to prison as an unregistered Japanese agent, after pleading *nolo contendere*, while its Douglas M. Stewart, one of its publishers, was held in contempt of court and jailed for refusing to divulge the source of $30,000 he admitted receiving under mysterious circumstances.

On the outskirts of the crowd, distributing hate literature from a car loaded down with pamphlets and books, was Patriot No. 6, Eugene R. Flitcraft, Chicago editor of *The Gentile News*. Hawkers passed out copies of *The National Record*, published by ex-Senator Robert R. Reynolds, who once said, "Hitler and Mussolini have a date with destiny, so why not play ball with them?" They sold copies of *Jewish Ritual Murder* and other Nazi-inspired poison to be taken home and absorbed.

The gathering had unforeseen results before the night was over. Police hauled Elmhurst, Mertig and Maertz to the lockup and booked them on charges of "distributing false, malicious, vicious and inflammatory literature calculated to disturb and cause breach of the peace." Eventually they were sentenced to from six months to a year each in the workhouse for "unlawful assembly."

Such are the phony "patriotic" rallies to which the general public and the veteran are being invited and which they're attending in increasing numbers. The Queens rally represented an attempt to

start things with a bang. One "big shot" hate-monger is enough for a drawing card. Here seven of them presented a unified brain trust. So far as I know it was the first postwar affair to bring together nationalist leaders from America's three largest cities, New York, Chicago and Philadelphia. Most of the poison literature sold at the rally, I later discovered, was shipped by Maertz from Chicago.

Few Americans have the experience to detect the bogus patriot readily. His camouflage is too expert. On the battlefield, the soldier could spot the enemy by his weapons or uniform. He got onto him through briefing sessions and reconnaissance. But the enemy at home looks like every other American; he wears no special dress and can cover up even subversion so well that the law can't touch him. The racketeer in patriotism wants the citizen's most precious possession: his mind. At his hands the returning veteran or almost any of us may get an injection of something he never bargained for: the virus of hate, pumped into him by an unregenerate crew of ex-Bundists, jailbirds, hate-mongers, followers of numerous "front" and "shirt" movements, America Firsters and others of an unholy squad who have come out from hiding to carry on from where they left off on Pearl Harbor morning.

We've won the military war abroad but we've still got to win the democratic peace at home. Hitler is dead, but incipient Hitlerism in America has taken on a completely new star-spangled face. It follows a "Made in America" pattern which is infinitely subtler and more difficult to guard against than the crude product of the Bundists. It is found everywhere at work in our nation. It's as if living embers had flown over the ocean and started new hate fires here while the old ones were dying in Europe.

Returning veterans who tuned in on Axis Sally, Tokyo Rose and Lord Haw-Haw get the same poison here. "Now that the war's over, we've got the green light," one nationalist said at a meeting I covered. The word "nationalism" can mean patriotic devotion to one's country and among decent, democratic Americans it still does. But America's hate-mongers and saboteurs of democracy call themselves "nationalist" to deceive the unwary. Throughout the book I use the word in both senses, depending on the type of group or individual discussed. The extreme American "nationalist" movement stands for the same poisonous brand of autocratic, minority-hating politics

known in Hitler's Germany and Mussolini's Italy as fascism. Hitler's, Mussolini's and Tojo's were all extreme nationalist governments, as is Franco's régime.

"I am counting on the returned servicemen," another "patriot" wrote me. And Frederick Kister said in his April, 1946 bulletin:

The next three years will witness a tremendous struggle to capture and control the opinions of the American people—and particularly the millions of veterans of World War II. It is the veteran that will have the fate of the nation in his hand. Our ability to keep him informed on the facts will depend on money, work, and organization.

Hitler started off with a gang of disillusioned World War I veterans meeting in a beer hall, saying they were fighting only for "God and Country" and "against Communism." They scraped together enough pfennigs to buy a duplicating machine with which to print hate literature. They held street meetings because they couldn't afford a hall. They kept their money in a cigar box. They were laughed at and ridiculed. They were called crackpots and lunatic fringers and sometimes clapped—temporarily—into jail. When the American nationalists are called the same things, I cannot forget that many smart people laughed in 1921 when Hitler talked as the nationalists do now. They laughed for twelve years, while he laid the groundwork for his revolution.

American nationalism likewise is still in the groundwork-laying period. Its hierarchy need a broad base on which to build their pyramid of hate. Young, impressionable, war-trained men can potentially be stirred up into an ugly mood and regimented into automatons. Hence the efforts of the nationalists to woo the veteran. The role reserved for him in the grim projected drama is to do the dirty work—in the name of "God and Country."

Such blatant rabble-rousers as Frederick Kister and his friend Gerald L. K. Smith may be comparatively small fry, but they are part of a movement working today on every level of American life and even extending into the Congress. Our hate-mongers and some who back them have some such schemes for America as the National Socialists planned for Germany. They won't go about them the same way. They won't talk in foreign terms. Those who most want an American form of fascism will denounce Hitler's fascism.

allayed suspicion by turning Anglo-Saxon and operating as Robert Thompson, Jr. The name is almost as common as Jones, but I chose Thompson because it was the surname of a close boyhood friend of mine. The "Jr." was tacked on so that, when necessary, I could also assume the character of the father, Robert Thompson, Sr. My name had to be as versatile as the roles I was called on to undertake. To achieve greater force in a letter, sometimes I added the signatures of two imaginary "buddies," "Charles Roberts" and "Lawrence H. Wayne." "Miss Roberta Thompson" was a WAC or WAVE as the occasion demanded. In several instances I also corresponded as Mrs. Roberta Thompson.

Thompson and his buddies needed a "home" somewhere outside of, yet convenient to, New York City where I worked. The person who received my mail had to be thoroughly trustworthy. I found the ideal man in Morton P. Levy of Buffalo, N. Y.

An American born in Buffalo, Mort Levy is a member of Edward M. Daly Post No. 1130 (Police Post) of the American Legion, and Americanism officer of the Jewish War Veterans Frontier Post No. 259. His fight against America's bogus patriots began as far back as 1933 when he opposed the Friends of the New Germany, who later merged with the German-American Bund. Mort also clashed with Robert Minor, Communist official, and reported to Federal officials meetings at which Ella Reeves Bloor ("Mother Bloor"), William Z. Foster and Israel Amter spoke. In 1938 Mort and the American Legion ran head on into Bundists holding "Americanism" meetings at near-by Bund Camp Porterville. The Legionnaires next went after Gerald L. K. Smith and his goons. They kept Smith's effectiveness as hate-monger at absolute minimum in Buffalo. Among Mort's Legion associates and friends is school principal Paul Wamsley, winner of the highest award of the Legion, the Lewis B. Rosensteil Prize of $1,000 for achievements in Americanism and for outstanding, unselfish community service.

Mort is a spark plug of patriotic activity. He keeps watch on nationalists in the western New York area. There is nothing fancy or pretentious about Mort. He is a humble, hard-working tailor. A fearless fighter for democracy, he is my idea of a useful American because he knows that nowadays the duties of a citizen go beyond voting and paying taxes. J. Edgar Hoover, who thinks equally well of Morton P. Levy, wrote him on March 28, 1946:

I want to take this opportunity to express my personal thanks for the valuable assistance you have given this Bureau on frequent occasions. We sincerely appreciate your fine spirit of cooperation and want you to feel free to call upon us at any time we can reciprocate.

In the fall of 1945 I had a close call. The danger, that time, was not physical. What is equally harmful to an investigator, one of my effective pseudonyms was almost discovered. It happened when I went to Washington to interview Robert Rice Reynolds, who as Senator was Chairman of the important Military Affairs Committee and a strong isolationist and America Firster. He was a darling of American fascists and of the Nazi press abroad. Both praised his views volubly. After he refused to run for re-election, Reynolds became a professional nationalist. He organized the American Nationalists' Committee, American Nationalist Party, Nationalist Federation and similar enterprises. As I entered Reynolds' Washington office I saw two women typing at their desks. The one on my left was gray haired and had a thin, scrawny face. The other looked like a Spanish ballerina. It was lucky for me that I introduced myself to her.

"The Senator will see you in a few minutes," she said.

I found a seat and began to survey the room. Once more my eyes fell on the elderly woman. Our eyes met for a fleeting moment, then I bowed my head forward in a desperate attempt to give my face an angle which would prevent her from recognizing me—if she hadn't already, for I was less than ten feet away. I recognized her as Mrs. Lois de Lafayette Washburn, a notorious nationalist who was under indictment for seditious conspiracy. I had met her at a "patriotic" convention in 1942 about which I wrote at length in *Under Cover.*

I had often wondered what I would do if I met one of my ex-"pals" while investigating new nationalists. "I'll cross that bridge when I come to it," I'd said to myself—and now I *had* come to it.

I crossed the bridge by sitting tight and making it difficult for Mrs. Washburn to get a direct look at my face. I accomplished this by continuing to bend over my newspaper and wiping my brow constantly, as if afflicted with the itch. Between my fingers I kept watching Mrs. Washburn. While she typed she shot quick glances at me but gave no indication of recognizing me. Just then she passed a note to the other woman. My heart sank. Was it intended to warn Reynolds? I watched the woman's every move. To my momentary relief, she took the note to the office marked "Wesley E. McDonald," Reynolds' associate. But doubts crept up again. Suppose the note had asked McDonald to phone Reynolds about me.

I was sweating it out when Reynolds finally came out of his office. I waited till he was up to me, then I rose to greet him, keeping his husky, well-padded frame between me and Mrs. Washburn. In shadow fashion I followed him to his room. I wasn't comfortable. Had McDonald warned him? Was Mrs. Washburn waiting till I was with Reynolds before exposing me—or were some of "the boys" being gathered for a little "reception" to their ex-pal?

I went ahead with the interview. I found Reynolds to be a voluble talker, an easy man to interview. He talked with sweeping gestures, as if delivering a speech. His sentences were repetitious but rhetorical and uttered in a deep, resounding voice, with a charming Southern accent. Reynolds must seem attractive to those women who like the type. He was a modern version of the old-fashioned gallant, with puffy eyes, florid face, waxed mustache. He was graying, but the mustache was yellowish-brown. He was wearing a blue sleeveless shirt and speckled bow tie.

On Reynolds' desk was a copy of Rev. Winrod's *Defender*. I asked him about his political plans. He said he planned to issue a nationalist weekly and someone had promised $50,000 worth of printing equipment. Reynolds predicted that the issue in 1948 would be "nationalism versus internationalism." "It's got to be," he said. "Lindbergh will come back. Nye, Wheeler, Fish—they will all have their day. The country will go nationalist. It can't help it."

I asked what the attitude of industrial concerns was toward nationalists.

"They are internationalist now because they don't want to get in trouble with the government," Reynolds answered. "They're afraid to give money now because somebody will find out and expose them. They're nationalists at heart. As for me, I'll never change. I've always been a nationalist. I'm against all immigration. I'm against foreigners coming to America."

"What do you think of the Jews, Senator?" I asked bluntly.

"My best friends are Jews. Why, I was raised with them. Somebody once picked on a Jewish schoolmate of mine and I beat him up. I love the foreign born. I'm tolerant, I am. Why, the Finkelsteins and the Pollacks down in North Carolina, they're my best friends. They helped me get elected Senator." It was true. Some "Jewish money" went into the campaign to elect the nationalist führer. It's more proof that so-called "Jewish solidarity" is a myth. Except for a united front against such a universal enemy as Hitler, Jewish groups fight one another bitterly, like most people. I know this from personal observation over a period of years. Feuds between German-born and Russian-born Jews are particularly acrimonious.

I wanted Reynolds' answer to my next query before Mrs. Washburn burst in on us.

"What do you think of John Roy Carlson, Senator?" I asked.

Reynolds looked at me for a moment. I looked back. With a wave of the hand he began: "Why, Carlson told the truth about me in his book. He said I am for America first, and I am. He said I was a nationalist. I am. He said I did my best to keep America out of war. I did. He don't make me mad with his book."

I had said more than that, of course—particularly about his intimate collaboration with Gerald L. K. Smith. I hadn't forgotten Reynolds' by-lined article in Hitler's personal newspaper, *Voelkischer Beobachter,* in February, 1939, in which Reynolds said, in part: "I am happy to state without the least hesitation that I am absolutely against the United States waging war for the purpose of protecting Jews anywhere in the world." Reynolds skipped all that. Since I was posing as a fellow "nationalist" it would have been imprudent of me to remind him.

It had been a fruitful interview, and I decided to leave. Reynolds rose to escort me out. "I'll go that way," I said, pointing to his private door which led into the hallway. "It's locked," Reynolds said. "Well, can't it be unlocked?" I asked. Although my opinion of his nationalist views was low, Reynolds proved a gentleman to the last. He unlocked the door and bid me a gracious good-bye.

Once on the street, I made sure I wasn't followed. To make absolutely sure that the gray-haired woman was Mrs. Washburn and that she hadn't recognized me, I phoned Reynolds.

"I'd like to speak to Mrs. Lois de Lafayette Washburn," I said in a disguised voice.

"Just a minute," Reynolds answered, and I was switcned to her.

I told her I was "Mr. Williams" from out of town and wanted to call on her for a special reason. "I must make absolutely sure you are Mrs. Washburn before I discuss the patriotic matter with you," I said. "Are you the one mentioned in *Under Cover?*"

"Yes, yes. I am the one," she said. "That Carlson viper wrote about me."

"Where is Carlson these days?" I asked. "We don't want him around."

"Carlson is hiding," Mrs. Washburn assured me. "He doesn't dare go around the way he used to. I know him and I'm watching out for him."

We agreed to meet, but of course "Mr. Williams of Albany" never showed up.

I interviewed Reynolds just after his fund-raising racket had been exposed nationally by Eugene Segal in the Scripps-Howard newspapers. Segal disclosed that Reynolds' New Jersey representative, one John S. Gillmeier, "was arrested in Newark on charges of grand larceny in 1934 and open lewdness in 1938, but both charges were dismissed." A New York representative was John Scott, publisher of an obscure "money-reform" magazine, a speaker at Kurt Mertig's meetings, who shortly after V-J Day said: "Now that the war is over we have the green light."

J. Victor Malone was Reynolds' Public Relations Director. Malone was once employed by Harry E. Prettyman of Chicago, about whom the New York Better Business Bureau stated:

Prettyman . . . has a history of "promotions" in Florida and the Mid-West. In the late 20's, a Florida court revoked the license of his realty concern, in connection with complaints that he was selling swampy land. Last year [1944] his project was a "Chicago Aeronautical Association" which he abandoned when it came under investigation (according to the Chicago *Sun*).

Malone also served Reynolds as a fund-raiser. He kept forty percent of contributions collected from businessmen on the pretext that he was "fighting Communism." Malone engaged Prettyman and also the unsavory Joseph McWilliams, führer of the Christian Mobilizers. Joe worked under the alias of Jack Williams. His territory was Cleveland and Boston. It was arranged that when Joe got a contribution he could keep thirty percent, while Malone got ten percent and Reynolds received the rest to carry on "against Communism." Collecting in Boston was a mysterious Ralph Forsland who remained several days at the Hotel Statler, then suddenly disappeared.

Malone claimed that he had "made a deal" with the American Democratic National Committee, whose former chairman was Dr. Gleason L. Archer, president of Suffolk University, Boston. Archer is on the advisory board of the Committee for Constitutional Government (sponsored by Frank Gannett, newspaper owner). Another of its members, Malcolm McDermott, Duke University Professor, also served on the American National Democratic Committee. This was a Republican-backed group of disgruntled Democrats, and Republicans posing as Democrats. Intended by its strategists to split the regular Democratic Party, it endorsed regular Republican Party candidates in the 1944 elections.

When I wrote to Reynolds—as Thompson, Jr., the nationalist veteran—he sent me a stack of literature urging me to "become a political leader" for his Nationalist Party. It espoused "American nationalism pure and simple" and urged, "Keep America American and save America for Americans." Reynolds explained the basis for organizing the Third Party in a 34-page booklet, "Here's How You Can Become a Political Leader in Your District." It gave full instructions for organizing cells of ten members each. "This number is restricted to ten for the reason that in a unit every member will be personally acquainted with his fellow unit members." In true conspiratorial fashion Reynolds explained that "meetings may be held in the homes of one of the members."

The unit-cell idea was patterned after Father Coughlin's instructions in 1938 to members of his Christian Front hooligans, whom he goaded to fight "in Franco's way." I used to belong to a Coughlinite revolutionary group which drilled in New York City in preparation for civil warfare. It was called The Phalanx. A chapter was devoted to the experience in *Under Cover*. Our purpose was so sinister that, except for our own cell members, we knew few others. The reason was obvious. "If we are caught," our Commandant instructed, "all you say is that you know only the members of your own unit. You don't know anybody else."

That Reynolds had long-range plans for his Nationalist Party was boldly announced in his booklet:

It is apparent that the Republican Party is dead; it cannot be rejuvenated, its past history, evidencing a lack of backbone, and defeats have relegated it to the junkheap. The Democratic Party was first taken over by the New Dealers; then by Communists through Earl Browder, and by the PAC through Sidney Hillman. . . . If in 1948 there is not an avowed candidate for the Presidency . . . who sees eye to eye with American Nationalists then THE NATIONALIST PARTY will place its own candidate in the field.

When I wrote to Reynolds a second time and asked about his veterans' organization, he answered from Palm Beach, where he went every winter. He suggested that I get in touch with his New York State Chairman, Joseph E. Nelligan. He gave Nelligan's phone number as "Murray Hill 2-1234, Extension 32." The number is the office phone of the New York *Daily News,* isolationist newspaper. The extension is in Brooklyn, where Nelligan is employed as a guard. This wasn't news to me, because John Scott had printed the information in his paper, *Money:*

So I am working at present with the Nationalist Party, and I have been appointed Temporary Publicity Director for the Party in New York . . . Get busy organizing your first ten unit. Teach the other nine to go out and organize new units while you also get a new ten started. New York State readers contact Mr. Joseph Nelligan, care *Daily News,* 700 Pacific Street, Brooklyn 17, N. Y. . . . They believe in America First.

I wrote Nelligan, Commander of the National Veterans' and Ex-Servicemen's Organization of America, as Robert Thompson, Jr., "nationalist veteran." Of the four answers I received up to May 16, three begged for funds. Adjutant James W. Barnett, World War II veteran, wrote on May 10: "I send this letter to you as an appeal for funds. . . . You must instill in the minds of your membership the fact that it costs a great deal of money to finance an organization like this. So far the burden has been placed on the shoulders of eight men, including myself." A few days later Nelligan urged: "You will please send your contribution . . . to me."

I sent him four dollars, representing a fifty-cent contribution each from me and seven supposed "buddies" who had "joined" his outfit. Nelligan, a World War I veteran, appointed me "County Commander." The titles bestowed on my "buddies"—I just made up the seven names—ranged from "First Vice-Commander" to "County Judge Advocate." The platform of the National Veterans' and Ex-Servicemen's Organization of America is patterned on Reynolds' nationalist program of "keeping America American and America for Americans." In addition, Nelligan wants "immediate state and Federal bonuses" and "immediate pensions for all honorably discharged veterans."

After the four dollars were sent in, Nelligan and Barnett forgot all about the Buffalo Post of the National Veterans until I reminded them. Then on June 14 Nelligan wrote: "Those GIs who would shy away from an organization because of its political aspects will be clamoring for such an organization before many years. The principles for which we stand must be preserved by the removal from office of those responsible for the present state of affairs."

Barnett wrote, enclosing a page from the New York *Daily News,* which had printed Nelligan's resolution to the Congress, opposing the British loan in the name of his nationalist veterans. Barnett's letter added: "We are, as you know, backed by the New York *Daily News,* and in the enclosed you will find our resolution, printed in part, taking a stand on the British loan."

Questioned about Barnett's claim of backing by the *Daily News,* F. M. Flynn, general manager of the paper, denied any connection between the *News* and Nelligan's and Barnett's veterans.

During the years when I worked under cover as George Pagnanelli, Major General George Van Horn Moseley, U. S. Army, retired, was the hero of America's Bundists. At nationalist meetings which I attended the name of the ex-Commander of the Fourth Corps Area was cheered together with those of Hitler, Mussolini and Franco. General Moseley meant well, but he was a dupe of Nazi and nationalist propaganda.

On his retirement from active service in 1939, the New York *Herald Tribune* published an editorial entitled, "A Disgrace to the Army Uniform," in which it quoted Secretary of War Harry Woodring's branding of Moseley's political views as "flagrantly disloyal to his Commander-in-Chief." In 1940 Moseley said, "Democracy, hell! It's nothing but Communism. We don't want the mob rule of democracy." To Joseph McWilliams, the pro-Nazi speaker at Bund meetings and führer of the Christian Mobilizers, General Moseley

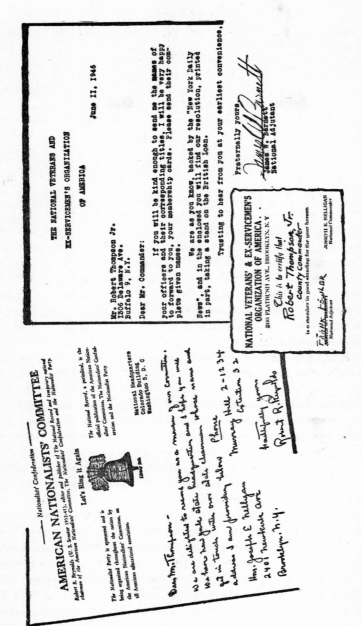

Barnett claimed that the New York *Daily News* was backing his nationalist veterans. The *Daily News* denied this.

wrote: "I am deeply impressed with you, your character, your energy, and your ability. I want to be in the same camp."

The fascist underworld looked upon Moseley as a prospective "man on horseback." They hoped he would lead them to the promised land of nationalism—by the military method if necessary.

I was extremely anxious to meet General Moseley. I wanted to know to what extent, if any, he had changed since 1939, and to learn what his plans were for the future. Was he still the potential "man on horseback"—this time to lead veterans down the nationalist road?

In the spring of 1945 I met General Moseley by appointment at the Biltmore Hotel in Atlanta. He was a hard man to see. He seldom answered letters and he saw only those who came well recommended. I had recommended myself over the telephone, however, mentioning truthfully that I knew Colonel E. N. Sanctuary, with whom, during the Pagnanelli years, I had been well acquainted. Sanctuary, the publisher of many hate pamphlets and who is under indictment for sedition, is a close friend of General Moseley's.

"I've just met Gene Talmadge," I added. "He spoke very well of you and asked me to give you his regards." This was also the truth.

In the lobby I shook hands with the General, a man with small, beady blue eyes and deeply furrowed face. Dressed nattily in a brown suit, he did not look his seventy years. He had a fine posture, his movements were quick, and he used his hands energetically while talking. I asked him first about Eugene Talmadge, Klan hero recently re-nominated by the Democrats for Governor of Georgia, whose "white supremacy" program is on a par with that of Rankin and Bilbo. I had just finished interviewing Talmadge. Moseley said:

"Mr. Talmadge is an intimate friend of mine. I stopped in to see him the other day at his office, but he was out and I left word for him. Yes, I know Talmadge well; he's a good friend of mine."

I asked whether he knew Atlanta-born Lawrence Dennis, best known as America's number one intellectual fascist. A former Army lieutenant and State Department aide, Dennis is the author of fascist books and formerly advised many nationalist figures. His application for active service as an Army officer in World War II got nowhere. Dennis, who has denounced democracy and advocated American national socialism as a substitute, is at this writing still under indictment, charged with sedition. Moseley answered without hesitation:

"Yes, I know him. I met him first at one of my speeches in New York. He came up to see me. I corresponded with him up to the time of the sedition trial in 1944. I stopped then—I had to."

Once I had gained the General's confidence I was surprised at the ease and fullness with which he answered my questions. I asked him about seditionist William Dudley Pelley's ex-lieutenant, Gerald L. K. Smith. The General's exact words were:

"He's a very capable man and has great ability, but he'll have a terrible time fighting against the things that are set against him. He just won't be able to do any good because of the smears against him."

Moseley's views on the Jews were more than I'd bargained for. "The Jews own this town!" he said passionately. (Of Atlanta's 500,000 population, only 15,000 are Jewish.) He told how, in a speech at New Orleans, he had advocated "the sterilization of refugees entering America." Then he elaborated: "The white race cannot go on with foreign elements in it—the Jews. We sterilize cattle—why not human beings? But I suppose," he added resignedly, "nothing will be done in America until the flood of cripples and syphilitics becomes too much for the taxpayers. Then they'll do something about it."

The General knew many Park Avenue-type members of America's native nationalist underworld. "Merwin K. Hart?" he said. "Yes, he's a fine man. I've met him." (Hart has denounced our democracy as "Communist" and volubly praised Franco's Falange.) I asked about ex-Senator Reynolds, who was pampered in the Nazi press during his visit to Germany and for a time was considered by our American fascists as second only to General Moseley as a potential führer.

"Oh, yes, I know Reynolds well," Moseley replied. "I had a letter from him only the other day. He's fine."

Throughout our conversation Moseley spoke contemptuously of President Roosevelt, always referring to him as "that man."

Moseley has no present plans for getting back into nationalist politics. "I have to be careful," he said. "I'm on pension. But I keep up with everything. I know what's going on. I'm putting my private papers into shape. I've destroyed some letters but I've saved many and some day I'll publish my memoirs. When you get back to New

York," he urged, "tell everybody you found me fit as a fiddle."

On parting, I asked Moseley's advice on the formation of "patriotic" groups, and he said: "What you ought to have is not a large, central organization, but a central coordinating party which will direct patriotic activity all over the country and let the local ones make adjustments to local conditions."

Something in my tone must have been unconvincing, for all at once the General became suspicious: "You're not a writer, are you?" he asked. "We've talked confidentially, of course!"

It was too late for the General. As soon as I left him I made full and detailed notes of my two-and-a-half-hour interview.

Let me say for the record that I interviewed Moseley as a civilian visitor to Atlanta and not as a veteran.

Wanting a confirmation of Moseley's views on paper, I wrote him a letter which was signed with the name of Robert Thompson, Jr., and countersigned by my "buddies," Charles Roberts and Lawrence H. Wayne. It was a high-powered, carefully written letter—a tirade against Communism, unions and "this equality business." Moseley answered in less than a week, confirming the major points he had made in the Atlanta interview.

In June, 1946, Moseley publicly broke his silence since his retirement in 1939. In an article in *The* [Atlanta] *Advertiser* entitled "The Whipping Post—a Deterrent to Crime," Moseley advocated the revival of the old-fashioned whipping post for "certain classes of male criminals, old and young, white and negro." He claimed it "would reduce crime almost to the vanishing point."

Moseley sent me two copies of his article, responding to my letter as Thompson on August 3. "I am enclosing the article you requested," he wrote, "also another on a different subject."

This latter proved to be a most amazing document. It was a mimeographed letter which Moseley had had printed in *The Advertiser* on July 5, 1946. Moseley explained the revival of the Klan by contrasting its post-Civil War causal factors with those today. "The only difference now," he said, "is that the present-day tragedy is nation-wide and the carpet-baggers have come very generally from Europe, if not recently, within a few years . . . Especially is Christian America in jeopardy today."

While asserting he was "not aware of ever knowing a member of the Ku Klux Klan," and stating that he was not defending the Klan, nonetheless, Moseley affirmed:

The Ku Klux Klan will again fade away when we return to real majority rule in the United States and give proper respect to the Constitution; when we have the willpower and the guts to curb un-American groups and minorities that would destroy us; . . . I am convinced that the Ku Klux Klan has no aims against such a grand organization as the Catholic Church or against any really Christian group or organization. . . . We are constantly being misled by the press when it attempts to warn us. . . .

Let us stop worrying about the Ku Klux Klan. Let us clean house at home so that there may be no reason for the existence of such an organization. If the Ku Klux Klan could, in some perfectly lawful way, rid the country of two or three columnists who are a pest, a menace and a national disgrace, it would win in the hearts of millions of our good people sincere commendation, and we might then forgive the Klan for all the crimes and misdeameanors it may have committed in the past.

Do these initial releases presage a "comeback" by the former would-be "man on horseback." Is Moseley again destined to become a major nationalist hero? The Atlanta *Journal* cracked down on the whipping post idea:

One can easily understand why Ku-Kluxers and other Nazi-minded secret groups would relish a whipping post. Old adepts themselves in the black art of flogging helpless victims, they would feel immensely complimented if Georgia adopted their favorite form of torture as a legal practice. The heavier the lashes fell, the more the blood came, the more the victims writhed and groaned, the keener would be the satisfaction of such spectators.

Encouraged by the response from General Moseley, I began sending out other letters in which I assumed the identity of Robert Thompson, the nationalist, one hundred percent American veteran.

Soon afterward a development occurred which underlined the special effort Nazi-inspired nationalists are making today to get backing and money from veterans. I received from Washington a copy of a four-page newspaper, the organ of a group calling itself the United American Veterans, Inc.* Thomas Dixon was its National

* Not to be confused with the United American Veterans in Boston, Mass.

Adjutant. C. H. Whitsey was Commander, and Elmer J. LaGue, Secretary. The publication, entitled *United American Veterans' Commentator,* gave as the aims of the outfit:

To foster and preserve the ideals of Americanism; to aid and assist all veterans in securing employment; to adjust all legal claims to which he may be entitled; to strive for a better understanding between nations, that peace and good will may prevail; to cherish and preserve the memories of our military association; to aid and assist worthy veterans, their widows, their orphans and their dependents.

At first glance, the *Commentator* and United American Veterans seemed typical of hundreds of such mushrooming groups. Its shrill cry against "Communism," however, and its labor-baiting references demanding that the charters of striking unions be revoked, made me suspicious. The phrase "immediate action in destroying all foreignisms on American soil" was another tip-off to the organization's true character.

The *Commentator's* masthead listed Thomas Dixon as editor. On the opposite page was an article, "Happy Hunting Ground," by Chief New Moon. These names betrayed the guiding genius of United American Veterans, for Dixon and the Chief are the same person. Dixon, a Cherokee Indian, was a familiar figure in the prewar Bund and Christian Front circles amongst which I worked under cover from 1938 on. I remember the Chief: a tall, swarthy man with high cheekbones, sleek, black hair and a flair for rabblerousing. In the American Nazi underworld he was called Chief New Moon, and was rarely known as Thomas Dixon.

Dixon spoke for the Bund. He was a friend of *Bundesführer* Fritz Kuhn, and in the summer of 1939 accompanied him to Chicago. When Kuhn was arrested and New Moon's real name made public, he lost his job. After that, he became a regular wheelhorse for the hate-mongers. He spoke for the Crusaders for Americanism, Inc. The chairman of that organization, George A. Van Nosdall, in 1939 looked upon Hitler as "the greatest man since the time of Christ." Dixon also spoke under Joe McWilliams' auspices. On August 13, 1940 the Chief was convicted for disorderly conduct and sentenced to serve twenty days on charges arising out of an inflammatory street meeting.

Now New Moon was offering to assist veterans, and editing a

paper which purported to be in their behalf. To check once again on his identity, I compared notes he wrote me on August 10 and 22, 1939, with his signature in 1946, and found the handwriting the same. In order to leave no doubt, I wrote him as Thompson, Jr., inquiring about his background as a "nationalist." With no more hesitation than grammar, New Moon replied:

I am the principal organizer of the United American Veterans. . . . From 1934 to the present time I have been fighting Communism, at every oppuertunity. I and the United American Veterans is 100% for Senator Reynold and Rep. Rankin. I have spoken several times for the America First [Committee]. As a matter of records, a few years ago my picture appeared in Life Magazine * with Senator Reynold [Ex-Senator Robert R. Reynolds] Father Coglin [Coughlin] and several other Orators. One of the principal object of this organization is to combat Communism. . . . I will gladly give . . . space to any organization who will help to combat Communism. If you and your friends agree with the above, we will be very glad to have you start a Post in Buffalo.

* *Life,* March 6, 1939.

United American Veterans

OFFICE OF
THOMAS DIXON
NATIONAL ADJUTANT

WASHINGTON 3. D. C.

C. H. WHITSEY
NATIONAL COMMANDER

ELMORE J. LAGUE
NATIONAL SECRETARY

ELPHEGE DESGRES
GENERAL COUNSEL

Dear Comrade: February 16, 1946.

From 1934 to the present time I have been fighting Communism, at every oppuertunity. I and the United American Veterans is 100/% for Senator Reynold, and Rep. Rankin. I have spoken several times for the America First. As a matter of records, a few years ago my picture appeared in Life Magazine with Senator Reynold, Father Coglin, and several other Orators. One of the principal object of this organization is to combat Communism.

July 12,46.

I expect to go to Chicago about the end of August and I would like to meet Mr. Fredrick Kister, if you can get me his address I will be very thankfull to you, and I will make arrangement to see him while in Chicago.

I have herd of the Christian Veterans of America, and our Organization is anxious to co-operate with any patriotic Organization, THAT IS THE ONLY WAY WE CAN EVER HOPE TO THROW THE COMMUNISTS OUT OF AMERICA.

Yours in Comradeship.

Thomas Dixon

Dixon expresses the desire to save America by teaming up with the dubious Christian Veterans of America.

Chief New Moon seemed a reincarnation from the musty past. My last meeting with him was in August, 1939, at a bar where New York's Christian Fronters gathered. The Chief was a sorry figure. Disheveled and surly, his hair in disarray, his eyes bloodshot, he was on the warpath against the Bund, which had turned against him because he was no longer useful to them.

"Ten or twelve dollars a week isn't much," he wailed, "but it's enough to keep a fellow going. When I see Fritz Kuhn he tells me, 'Tomorrow, come tomorrow.'"

Shorn of a meal ticket by an ungrateful Bund, New Moon had decided to go into the patriotic business on his own and to this end was organizing the Union of Patriotic Americans. His scheme, he explained, was to pose as a defender of Democracy and milk "gullible Jews." He would spend twenty-five percent of the income for promotion, and pocket the rest. New Moon invited me to serve as chairman. The prospectus he displayed was the epitome of "one hundred percent Americanism." It opened with the Preamble to the Constitution and urged "Courageous Americans" to unite and "help save America." A "To Whom It May Concern" letter certified that Chief New Moon was authorized to collect funds. It was signed "Thomas N. M. Dixon."

"The idea was given to me by the Bund," Dixon said.

Dixon claims that he fought in World War I and was a charter member of the American Legion in Paris. As adjutant of the United American Veterans, he is urging that $10,000,000,000 be spent on a public works project to benefit veterans. He sent me copies of a letter which he said was from Senator Walter F. George, expressing interest in the Chief's grandiose ideas. "We get RESULTS," Dixon boasted.

Dixon's background hardly qualifies him to run a democratic organization, but he's in the business, hustling up members at five dollars a head. I wrote him I would try to organize a post in Buffalo but later told him I couldn't carry on. On May 21 New Moon wrote again, saying that the Veterans Administration "have given us full recognition. . . . We are invited to set in and voice our opinion in all matters pertaining to the future welfare of the veterans."

I regard the United American Veterans as one of hundreds of booby traps being set for unsuspecting GIs who want to join a

World War II veterans' outfit. It represents only one of the various types. Let's look at another.

Deep down in Bryan, a city of 20,000 rugged Texans, Claude Mitchell edits *"The National Veteran,* organ of the Order of the Golden Eagle." "As we see it," he wrote me, "the answer to a great number of our questions is the organization of a United Veterans Political Party. We have done this. It is called the Order of the Golden Eagle."

Mitchell explains in his monthly bulletin how his Veterans Political Party will function: "behind closed doors we will meet as comrades and turn a searchlight of inquiry upon the activities of our towns, counties, states, nation and the world. . . . The SECRET work will not be discussed in this column for obvious reasons but will be given to the members as needed."

Why the Klan-like secrecy?

Mitchell's other idea to benefit the veteran is to establish and set up a vigilante committee to preserve peace, as follows:

This money will be used to send keen intelligent observers to the various countries in whom we are interested. If Germany hires too many policemen, if Japan attempts to buy scrap from Mars, if Italy tries to make Rome the capital of the world again, we are going to know about it together with various other bits of information and we are going to tell our readers about it. . . . This is going to take a lot of money. If you believe in this set-up, send us any amount you want to, we will put it with ours. . . .

Another way in which Mitchell raises money is through memberships in the Golden Eagle. He solicits $5 memberships and $100 life memberships. "Mothers, Wives, Daughters and Sisters of Veterans" can join the Auxiliary by sending in $5 a head. Mitchell's most ambitious project, however, is the establishment of a Veterans Bank. He says it's going to be one of the largest in America. Its capital stock will be $125,000,000, and it'll do most of its business by mail. Mitchell is now offering five million shares at $25 each. In May, 1946 he had reservations for 2,000 shares. Travis B. Bryan, President of the First National Bank of Bryan, doesn't think much of the scheme. He wrote Mitchell in a letter published in *The National Veteran:*

Maybe I am wrong but I do not think it is a good idea. I do not think that it would stand much chance of success. I do not think there is any need of it, and that a better way would be to use the 15,000 banks of the nation, to use the personal neighborly contact of veteran and banker . . . rather than set up a new organization with its attendant necessity of trying to handle a very difficult job . . . *by mail.*

Mitchell is not discouraged and is hustling at a hot pace. "Any investment you see fit to make in the Veterans Bank," he wrote me, "will be guaranteed by the undersigned. Should you see fit to write to The Merchants' Credit Association of Bryan . . . it is believed you will find the writer is in a financial condition to do this. Believe it or not, I am not working this organization to make money but to render service." I wrote the Bryan Credit Association. "We cannot furnish you with this report," they said, and suggested that I "get in contact with the Better Business Bureau."

Mitchell operates from P.O. Box 1107. He explains: "The Box number has no connection whatever with a crap game."

Let's take another example. In December, 1935 Capitol Hill rocked with the sensation of a Congressman being sent to prison for conspiring to sell a cadetship to West Point for $1,000. A Washington Federal Jury found Representative John H. Hoeppel of California and his son, Charles, guilty of the charge and Justice Daniel W. O'Donoghue sentenced them to from four months to a year in jail.

It required almost a year to get them behind bars. The two resorted to all sorts of delaying tactics. Father and son became fugitives from justice and with the help of a disbarred lawyer hid in a Virginia tourist cabin. In an ironic ending to the bizarre case, the doors of Washington District Jail closed on them on Thanksgiving Day, 1936. As newsmen tried to photograph his son, Hoeppel, Sr. growled, "Leave him out of it. I'm the guilty one."

On his release in May, 1937, Hoeppel, Sr. told newsmen he was going to Arcadia, California, to start a veterans' magazine. He did. *National Defense* is one of the most vicious all-round nationalist hate sheets in the country. Hoeppel, judging by his magazine, hates nearly everything and everybody except Hoeppel and *National Defense.* He's a bonus fiend. He pleads for money and more money. His hate-inciting articles parallel those of the Bund organ, *Deutscher*

Weckruf und Beobachter. Here's Hoeppel on Congress (issue of August, 1945):

From what is now taking place in the Congress . . . it is a safe assumption that our Congress, knowingly or unknowingly, is composed of Zombies. They articulate and move about. They even legislate but they are irresponsible for their actions because they are mentally dead. They are the typical Zombies whose souls have been deadened. . . .

The patriot of Arcadia on "racial superiority" (April, 1946):

We read in the press also how the British are employing thousands of German scientists. . . . We read how . . . our Nation is taking forcibly from the Germans their patents and inventions. . . . It would appear that the Germans must be a superior people. . . . As we personally converse with returning soldiers . . . it would seem to indicate that perhaps after all we are giving approval to the reported claim [by Hitler!] that the Germans are a superior race.

In April, 1946 Hoeppel told why Anglo-American democracy was all wrong:

Capitalism has been held up by the hand *of the false* prophets of Christianity in our so-called Christian England, and America. Our church leaders have been nothing other than stooges for the private money monopolists. . . . We are being undermined because there is no *honor* or *honesty,* there is no justice or humanity in the hearts and minds of our so-called industrial and political leaders—who are leading us to economic and cultural ruin with the *blessings* of our so-called Christian leaders.

The same month he set the record on European atrocities straight —six thousand miles away:

We read of the atrocities committed through the *forcible* moving of millions of Germans from their ancestral homes, in the dead of winter. . . . The Czechs are performing other *acts of inhumanity* directed against people of German ancestry. The alleged persecution of the Jews by Hitler pales into insignificance compared with the atrocities which we today are committing against men, women and children because they are of German blood.

As long ago as May, 1944 Hoeppel showed masterly understanding of the psychology of minorities:

If the minority groups continue to advance their own selfish interests above our national welfare, then we may well say that the CIO, the Negroes, the Jews (with the aid of hundreds of thousands of foreign compatriots) and other minority groups, through their selfish attitude must be held responsible if national collapse is ours.

Such are the poison pellets which Hoeppel, Sr. feeds his veteran readers. Hoeppel brands the American Legion "lower than [a] dung-hill." Former Secretary of State Hull is a "hypocrite." As for Pearl Harbor, Tojo and his sword-rattlers are exonerated. Hitler is absolved. "We lay the blame into the lap of Churchill who apparently controlled the Squire of Hyde Park," says Hoeppel. In the March, 1946 issue of *National Defense* he ranted:

The piano player in the White House is no better than the departed scoundrel of the New Dealers; he has vetoed the bill passed by Congress, but then he wants to make payments to all the loafers in the U.S., give them $25 a week for 26 weeks. . . . We have no Statesmen, only crooked politicians, such as Byrnes, Barkeley [*sic*], Wallace, etc., and it will never improve the present conditions until the "New Stealers" are out of Washington. This piano player was not elected by the people, but was fostered on us by a Russian Jew, Sydney [*sic*] Hillman.

Hoeppel loves only "real" Americans such as Representative John Ellsworth Rankin of Mississippi, whom he proposes for President. "Rankin is the man of the hour and it is men of his calibre, his ability, and stature *who* will rally to their support other *real* Americans and *save* our Nation from the *menacing danger* of Communism and un-American *control* of this nation." Another Hoeppel hero is Representative William Lemke (R.–N. D.), 1936 Presidential candidate of Father Charles E. Coughlin's party, the National Union for Social Justice. A third is Senator William Langer (R.–N. D.), isolationist, Britain-hater, and darling of America's nationalists.

A fourth Hoeppel favorite is Tyler Kent, former decoding clerk at our London Embassy. In 1940 Kent turned over vital State Department secrets involving 1,500 cablegrams between Churchill and Roosevelt to a foreign agent named Anna Wolkoff. Through her, the information reached the Nazis in Berlin. In the presence and with the consent of U. S. Embassy officials, Scotland Yard detectives examined Kent's room and found highly incriminating evidence against Kent, resulting in Kent's and Wolkoff's conviction under the Official Secrets Act. On October 28, 1940 Kent was sentenced to seven years in British prisons. After serving five years he returned home on December 5, 1945. Disregarding Kent's shameful betrayal of our national secrets, Hoeppel compared him to Nathan Hale and called him "inspired with patriotism." The nationalist vermin press from coast to coast regards Kent as a "persecuted hero."

Tyler Gatewood Kent is a linguist and was educated in several universities. He is a descendant of old-line American parents and his father distinguished himself in our diplomatic service. An explanation of the cause of Kent's actions was given by Ambassador Joseph P. Kennedy to Scripps-Howard correspondent Henry J. Taylor. According to Taylor's story of September 5, 1944, Kennedy said:

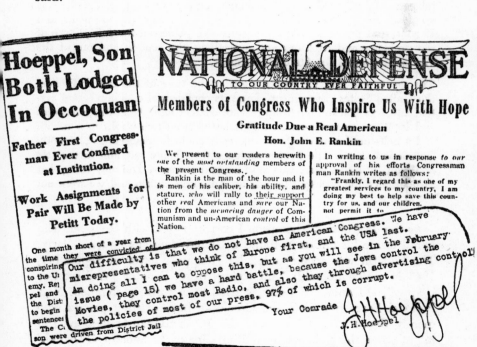

Hoeppel admires John Rankin; he damns Congress, which he left in 1936 to begin a prison term.

As to why Kent did what he did . . . Kent seems to have built up a terrific anti-Semitic complex, and I am convinced that this attitude was the driving power for his behavior in London. When Kent was arrested I asked him how on earth he could break trust with his country and what he must be thinking about its effect on his parents. Kent never batted an eye. He played up and down the scale of an intense anti-Semitic feeling, showing no remorse whatever except in respect to his parents. . . .

When we searched his room we found in a locked box 1500 copies of "unbreakable" cables, both incoming and outgoing, dating back to October, 1939, which Kent had deciphered. And while we were there, a telephone call to Kent from the Italian Embassy put us on the trail of his Italian outlet to Germany.

That night America's diplomatic blackout started all over the world. I telephoned the President in Washington, saying our most secret code was no good any place, and I told Mr. Roosevelt that the Germans and Italians, and presumably the Japanese, had possessed the full picture of the problems and decisions and everything else sent in and out of the White House and the State Department. . . .

The result was that for weeks, right at the time of the fall of France, the United States government closed its confidential communication system and was blacked out from private contact with American embassies and legations everywhere. . . . This lasted from two weeks to a month and a half—until a new unbreakable code could be devised. . . . Nobody "railroaded" Kent. The British sentence that finally put him in the Isle of Wight for seven years was mild beyond measure. The only thing that saved Kent's life was that he was an American citizen and we were not yet at war.

As the disgruntled Thompson I corresponded with Hoeppel, who bared to me his efforts to found a United Veterans Political Party. The bulletin was accompanied by Hoeppel's letter of September, 1945 in which he said: "Am trying to get Senator [Wilbert Lee "Pappy"] O'Daniel [of Texas] started to organize a complete New Political Party free from the Crooks in both existing parties who merely dance as the Jews and the Internationalists dictate. You might stress this yourself by writing directly to Senator O'Daniel."

"Veterans should organize on a purely political basis," Hoeppel's revolutionary prospectus reads. "There should be no pussy-footing as to their objective. They should loudly proclaim that their main objective is to wreck the two political machines—Democrats and Republicans—and convert them into museum pieces." Hoeppel's party would "combat Communism" and followers must be inoculated and impregnated with one thought, to wit: "America, first, last, and always."

I asked Hoeppel about his veteran status, and on May 20 he replied that he had "served 19 years as an enlisted man" and "almost two years as an officer" in World War I. "West Point does not make an officer," he added. Hoeppel complained that he was "a victim along with millions and millions of others of our corrupt economic system, which prevents the average human from enjoying the fruits of his labor."

Hoeppel's convictions and aspirations equip him as the potential führer of an American National-Socialist Party. His activities show how the minds of some veterans can be bought through the highly developed art of bonus-begging. "All for the veteran," is Hoeppel's cry. In return for promises of enrichment, hopeful ex-servicemen have to absorb Hoeppel's poison. He dupes the unwary by glorifying himself as a "former member of Congress." It's only half of the truth about ex-Congressman Hoeppel and ex-convict No. 107702, Lorton Reformatory. Patriotic phonies thrive on the dissemination of lies and half-truths.

The case of Edward James Smythe—a big, paunchy man with a beet-red complexion—in many ways parallels Hoeppel's. Smythe has lived National-Socialist politics. An importer of Nazi literature, he described Naziism as "Protestantism in action, the highest form of Christianity." A caustic speaker against Catholics and Jews, he has been a member of the Bund, the Christian Front and the Ku Klux Klan. I was present at the joint meeting of the Klan and the Bund which he arranged at Bund Camp Nordland, near Andover, N. J., in 1940.

Smythe heads the Protestant War Veterans of the United States, Inc., organized in 1937. The incorporators were James T. Blakeley and Donald Shea. A few days after the incorporation, Shea organized his Gentile War Veterans, with Smythe as a director. Both men belong to the coarser fringe of nationalists. Both have expressed their pro-Nazi sentiments, and I have a photograph of Shea giving the Nazi salute.

Shea, according to his own statement to me, was once a member of the Klan. He spoke at Italian Fascist meetings in Baltimore. At Bund Camp Nordland, according to the New York *Herald Tribune* for October 13, 1943, he wore a black overseas cap, lettered 'American Fascist." He began his address with "Viva Mussolini" and "Heil Hitler" and went on to announce a plan for a national Gentile boycott of all Jews and firms employing Jews. In October, 1943 General Hugh A. Drum barred him from various military areas, including seaboard states. He settled in Chicago, where he kept up his "patriotic" activity during the war. His Gentile War Veterans is at present dormant, but Shea is still active. He has cooked up a new enterprise called the Legion for Law and Order, which is "opposed to Rasputinism and injustice" and devoted to "perpetuating a Constitutional government." On July 17, 1946 he wrote me:

Now for your record the above org [the Legion for Law and Order] is going over the top—reports very encouraging and the Stalin Stooges will experience rough and tough times ahead. The range to Moscow is just a short run via Rocket. Communist cattle asked for it. The Klansmen are rallying around the Fiery Crosses—Klaverns springing up here and else-wheres—Wouldn't be amazed too see daylight parades here.

Edward James Smythe has been spouting patriotism since I met him in 1939. He puts up an impressive front. His gaudy letterhead lists eleven "affiliated organizations" and two "official publications." They're phony letterhead fronts and he has established no magazine of any kind. "For God, for Home and Country" is one of his slogans, followed by "Honor Our Heroic Dead by Helping the Wounded." He sent me a lurid red-white-blue leaflet with the screaming head-line: "Persecution of [in bright red] Protestant War Veterans of the United States MUST STOP! [in blue] AND WILL STOP!" [in red] He added, in red: "OR WE WILL STOP IT!"

Smythe has the answer as to what's wrong with New York:

Three million Protestants in the City of New York, and eight million Protestants in the State of New York are Civic and Political OUTCASTS. . . . Because of an unholy alliance between the Roman Catholic con-trolled Tammany Hall machine (Democratic) and the Jew-Communist controlled Republican machine under Governor Thomas E. Dewey.

Smythe makes much of his anti-Communism: "We will fight these DIRTY, STINKING COMMUNISTS in the streets if necessary." His panacea is to rid the nation of the Catholics, Communists, Jews, Negroes, labor leaders and aliens and leave it to men of his ilk as well as such "patriotic and outstanding Americans" as Representative Rankin and Senator Theodore G. Bilbo. For $2 he will send you the dope on who is "Raping the Protestant South" and tell you all about the "Negro Communist Republic." If you're interested in joining his Thomas Jefferson Post No. 1776, the initiation fee is $5, plus $3 dues, making $8 payable in advance. With Smythe, patriotism is strictly a cash-on-the-line proposition.

In Washington he shared a one-room office with a disbarred lawyer and induced the telephone company to give him "National 1776" as a phone number. Smythe and an associate arranged to reprint the GI Bill of Rights for sale to industrial firms at $35 a hundred. (Any GI can get it free from the Veterans Administration.) They sold "victory" stickers. Smythe hoodwinked a Washington bishop into selling stickers for him at the church's annual May festival, but he was exposed before the festival started.

Switching his attentions next to New York's heavily Teutonic Yorkville district, where he once used to parade with the German-American Bund, Smythe tried to encroach upon an organization known as the German-American Veterans of World War II, Inc.

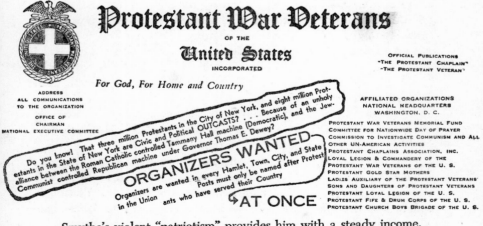

Smythe's violent "patriotism" provides him with a steady income.

The group, organized in late 1945, is interesting. Its headquarters are at the Hansa Bar, a long, dim-lighted Yorkville beer joint. Here the Veterans meet in a back room. Albert J. Daubach, 40, short, stocky, pugnacious in manner, was formerly their commander. I met Daubach at the trial, in January, 1946, of Christian Front "patriots" Elmhurst, Mertig and Maertz. After sentence had been passed, Daubach, Kurts and others gathered in angry little knots in the courthouse corridors. Newspapermen and I heard Daubach declare, "This is not the end! It's only the beginning for us. We're just starting to fight." He wore an Army officer's coat and his discharge button. I went over to him.

"Do you intend to fight as veterans?" I asked.

"I've already talked too much," Daubach said, and sulked away.

After the trial, Daubach was asked to resign. He was replaced by Albert Dreyer as Commander of the German-American Veterans. Herman Schwoerer became Secretary. My requests for the military ratings of the officers brought evasive letters, written in a Germanic scrawl, from Schwoerer. These letters tend to bear out confidential reports that many members are more Germanic than American.

"It's an odd veterans' bunch," one undercover investigator observed. "The men are mostly past 40. They don't seem to be veterans of World War II. . . . Conversation is carried on mostly in German. If I didn't know German, I'd be lost."

Many of the German-American War Veterans' growing membership of about 500 in New York alone are innocent of any nationalist activities. But former members of the Bund have bored into their ranks. Apologizing for Hitler and blaming the war on us are common topics of conversation. Anti-Semitism is bitter and widespread. At a meeting on April 1, 1946 one member suggested affiliating with the American Legion. He was voted down because the Legion was declared to be "mostly Jewish."

The surest way of being admitted to membership is to be okayed by a short, mousy little man named Eugene Brand. His small, shifty, suspicious eyes are constantly on the prowl. He is thin to the point of gauntness. His face is pasty, and he wears a dirty gray fedora pulled tight over his eyes. Brand screens applicants in his cramped newspaper store in the heart of Yorkville. Before Pearl Harbor I used to buy the *Deutscher Weckruf, Social Justice* and seditionist Pelley's hate sheets there. Brand's carried a full line of propaganda imported from Germany. After Pearl Harbor, to those he trusted, Brand sold pencils marked "Jew Money and Jew Deal and New Deal Means War." He bought them from Lee R. Finehout of Indianapolis.

The shop is still a clearing house for un-American poison. If he knows you, Brand will quietly slip you Maertz' magazine, *Dispatch.* Openly on sale is *The Broom,* an inflammatory hate sheet published in San Diego by a dishonorably discharged ex-soldier named Constantine Legenopol, alias C. Leon de Aryan. Defender of Nazi agents and Bundists, De Aryan was formerly under indictment for sedition. He was indicted on sedition charges in Washington in 1942 but was dropped from a later indictment. Brand himself frequently contributes articles. The front page of *The Broom* for March 25, 1946 carried an article by Daubach on the German-American Veterans.

Into Brand's hole-in-the-wall shop come ex-Bundists, Christian Fronters and other goons of the postwar hate fraternity. They get from him instructions on secret meetings. They buy tickets for closed "socials" which are used to disguise conclaves of yesterday's revolutionary agitators. Sometimes the tickets are slipped inside a newspaper. Brand, a suspicious man, has been known to fly into a rage and yell "Spy!" at innocent nationalist customers. On the other hand, in more talkative moments, Brand has sometimes unwillingly made startling admissions to undercover investigators posing as enthusiastic shoppers.

Late in May, 1946, when nationalists from coast to coast were organizing voters for the fall elections, I received a letter with Brand's name and address rubber-stamped on the envelope, which was addressed in an immature scrawl. Inside the envelope was a yellow slip on which the following notice was typewritten:

Please take notice that the next meeting will be on Monday May 27 8 pm in the Hindenburg [probably the bar-restaurant in Yorkville] 1 floor. Proposed By-Laws of the Alliance will be dicussed [*sic*]. Chicago, California, Oakland and Winona, Minnesota already have Voters Leagues for American [*sic*] of German ancestry. One group published a newspaper. It is time for Americans of German ancestry here in New York to make their existence known.

Sincerely
Voters Alliance.

Circumstances pointed to the conclusion that Brand had fallen heir to Kurt Mertig's list of the German-American Republican Voters League and was carrying on "patriotically" while Mertig, Elmhurst and Maertz were in jail.

On August 5, I received notice of a meeting of the Voters Alliance for Americans of German Ancestry at the Cafe Hindenburg in Yorkville. Accompanying it was a leaflet sponsored by the Alliance, a section of which was devoted to a long nationalist statement by Otto L. Fricke, addressed to "Americans of German Ancestry." Fricke is a Cleveland attorney and former president of the *Stadtverband* (United German Societies) which included Bundists in its membership. In 1939 Fricke managed the Cleveland branch of the American Fellowship Forum, which was initiated by Nazi agents George Sylvester Viereck and Friedrich E. Auhagen, and promoted a "subtle Nazi propaganda technique." In 1945 Fricke headed a German relief society and called on everyone of "German blood" to protest against the "persecution and destruction of our immediate kin" in Germany.

The Alliance leaflet stated its "protest against the low level of integrity to which American domestic politics has been brought by the New Deal Democratic Administration" and the alleged "inhuman and barbarous treatment of the German people." These fancied wrongs would be righted by making "the vote of Americans of German ancestry effective in elections," by urging "Americans of German ancestry to take an active part in the political life of the country," and by making their "influence" felt against alleged "persecution" of Americans of German ancestry.

It resembled the old cry of "persecution" which was aired by the Bund, and which Hitler and Conrad Heiden exploited in Czechoslovakia. Signatories of the declaration included Emil Russ, Otto Bochow, Frederick Drager. These names are new to the Germanic-nationalist scene. Two others I knew well. They were Eugene Brand and Conrad Grieb, former member of the Coast Guard, of whom I write in detail in Chapter Six.

CHAPTER THREE

Klansmen on the Prowl

There is no doubt in my mind that patriotic organizations will carry on after the war. They will come up. . . . It might be a reorganized KKK or made up of the former America First Committee.

Imperial Wizard James A. Colescott

You can't destroy the Klan. You can't destroy the Bible. You can't destroy the Truth. The Klan will never die!

Grand Dragon Samuel H. Green, M.D.

ᴐᴘʀɪɴɢɪɴɢ ᴜᴘ from underground even before the war ended, night-riding bigotry is on the rampage. In Georgia, Florida, California, Tennessee, Michigan and other states, press dispatches report outrages perpetrated by the "Invisible Empire" of a resurgent Ku Klux Klan. Kluxers have been linked with murder, flogging, house burning, fiery crosses and are reported to have actually threatened death to public figures who dare oppose them. Statistics from inside sources show that numbers of recently discharged veterans are doffing their uniforms only to don the hood and bedsheet. And the

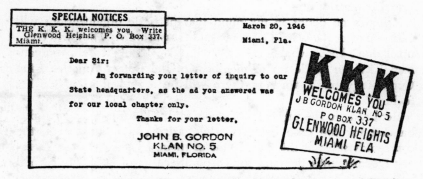

The Klan extends the glad hand. *Right:* Roadside sign near Miami.

41

postwar Klan is a streamlined, flexible proposition, with organizations like the Society of Forward Men and the United Sons of America to accommodate the more polite bigots who prefer to avoid actual violence and to carry the "white supremacy" and anti-union torch in better-cut clothes.

To investigators of America's nationalist hate-mongers, the resurrection is no surprise, though the Knights of the Ku Klux Klan, Inc. had publicly "disbanded" as a nation-wide organization on April 23, 1944. Their charter, paid up through 1946, is still on file in Atlanta.

In January, 1945 I interviewed their last Imperial Wizard, James A. Colescott, at his home in Miami. For the occasion, I posed as an Anglo-Saxon tourist with anti-Semitic views.

Suspicious at first, Colescott gradually loosened up as we talked. His dog, more intuitive, continued to bark and growl at me. Colescott was a big man of about 50, with a large, rotund face, big, glistening bald dome, and a chewed-off left ear. Otherwise he was not unusual in looks or manner. There was nothing about his green sweater, his rimless glasses or his well-modulated voice to suggest that he was capable of issuing hate edicts in Klan mumbo jumbo to "all Genii, Grand Dragons and Hydras, Great Titans and Furies, Giants, King Kleagles and Kleagles, Exalted Cyclops and Terrors, and to all Citizens of the Invisible Empire, in the name of the valiant and venerated dead." The Imperial Wizard looked normal.

Since the war was on, I started by expressing fears for the future of the nationalist "patriotic" movement in America—Colescott's brand of patriotism.

"There's no doubt in my mind that patriotic organizations will carry on after the war," Colescott said reassuringly. "They will come up. I don't know what form they will take. It might be a reorganized KKK, or made up of members of the former America First Committee, but I am sure there will be a revival of nationalist feeling."

Returning to the present, Colescott said: "The Klan has been disbanded for the time being. Certain arising situations made the course advisable at this time." One of them, I knew, was the Treasury Department's demand for corporate taxes of $685,305, earned between 1919 and 1926 and unpaid since then. "It doesn't mean that the Klan is dead. It can be revived at any time we think it necessary. I still have my title; so have the other officials." I asked about the membership lists. "They were destroyed," he said, then added significantly, "Of course, some might be around." Colescott was steering a crafty course, speaking slowly and measuring every word. It was obvious that the Klan had gone underground merely for the duration.

Colescott had sold his property in Atlanta and settled down in Miami where, he said, he was looking for "something to do." I asked about his friends. He spoke fondly of Governor "Gene" Talmadge, exponent of "white supremacy," and ex-Senator Reynolds, both of whom he said he knew personally. I asked if Martin Dies of the House Committee to Investigate Un-American Activities was a Klansman. Colescott replied evasively. "I liked some of the things he did, but didn't like others," he said, adding that Dies had once fought the Klan. This safe reply didn't refute persistent reports that Dies was sympathetic to the KKK or explain his whitewash of them in a brief two-hour hearing which Colescott himself instigated. The results were not made public. After this farcical "investigation," the Imperial Wizard launched a campaign urging Klansmen to support "the work of the Dies Committee."

Colescott, a veterinarian, had been in Klan work 23 years, taking over as Imperial Wizard from Hiram W. Evans in 1939. Evans claimed that his Klan was a "legitimate successor of the 'original genuine' Ku Klux Klan and the Knights of the White Camellia of the Reconstruction Period." This is false. The modern Klan is a far cry from the Confederate bands, first founded by six veterans in Pulaski, Tenn., in 1865, to counteract the influence of the "carpet-baggers" from the North and prevent excesses by the newly liberated slaves. The movement spent itself and disappeared. The hate racket bearing the name of the Klan was incorporated in Atlanta on December 4, 1915 by William Joseph Simmons. It had an elaborate ritual and mystic appeals. In 1922 Simmons sold out for $90,000 cash to Evans, who made it a money-making and political racket.

Florida

I thought of Colescott when a year later I learned that the Klan had been officially revived in Florida, causing R. A. Gray, Secretary of State, to declare: "Almost as if there had been no war fought for the rights of man, the Klan is again recruiting neighbor to fight neighbor, race to fight race, and religion to fight religion." Its incorporators on September 7, 1944 were listed as A. B. Taylor of Orlando; A. F. Gilliam of Clarcona; H. F. McCormack of Apopka.

I thought of Colescott when the fiery cross was burned in a Miami Negro neighborhood and a few days later the torch was put to the home of Will White, a harmless Negro. I thought of Colescott when a road sign brazenly appeared on the outskirts of Miami, inviting the bigoted to join the ranks of the postwar hate klan. I thought of Colescott when the Miami *Herald,* a fine and democratic newspaper, on February 24, 1946, unwittingly ran an advertisement: "The KKK welcomes you. Write Glenwood Heights. P.O. Box 337, Miami."

The Imperial Wizard's prophecy had come true. Bigotry was on the march!

I wrote P.O. Box 337 as the native-born, Protestant, one hundred percent American, Robert Thompson, Jr. In reply came a letter dated March 20, 1946, and bearing a green rubber stamp: "John B. Gordon, Klan No. 5, Miami, Florida." It was a mere acknowledgment, stating that my letter had been forwarded to "State headquarters, as the ad you answered was for our local chapter only." I did not hear from State headquarters. Writing from Buffalo, I doubt if I ever will. In order to avoid payment of corporate taxes, the Florida Klan has severed its links with the national body and operates only within the state. A Federal agency cannot prosecute the Klan unless the hooded members begin interstate activity.

My subsequent research disclosed that at least four Klan Klubs meet in Miami. Meetings are held in the lodge rooms of the Knights of Pythias at 2726 Flagler Street. To a question by a reporter on the number attending these meetings, a Klansman answered: "You'd be surprised how many veterans we have. We fought for the right to join things like this."

My confidential sources state that the Klan today is using "horror stories of social equality" to get veterans to join. According to these sources, which I regard as highly dependable, at least fifteen percent of the membership in Georgia and Tennessee is veteran. And recruiting has only just begun.

Is Imperial Wizard Colescott, World War I veteran, behind the Klan network? Do cross burnings in cities as widely separated as

Birmingham, Ala., Charleston, S.C., Trenton, N.J., Big Bear, Cal., Chelsea, Mich., Stone Mountain, Ga., lead to him and his Kleagles? Is the Klan again determined to grow to an estimated 6,000,000 members and assert itself politically as in 1924? How many veterans, disillusioned with postwar America, will be sucked into the dragnet? Has the former horse doctor finally found "something to do"?

Georgia

The distinction between the old national and the new state Kluxer setups was explained to me by Grand Dragon Samuel H. Green, M.D., in the "Imperial City of Atlanta," "on the Deadly Day of the Weeping Week of the Appalling Month of the Year of the Klan LXXVIII"—that is to say, 1945. I interviewed Green immediately after my talk with General Moseley.

"The Knights of the Ku Klux Klan, *Inc.* are dead," Dr. Green said coldly. "But the Knights of the Ku Klux Klan are far from dead! They're almost as strong as they ever were. They're meeting all over the country right now." From his thin, bloodless lips came these fanatic words:

"You can't destroy the Klan. You can't destroy the Bible. You can't destroy the Truth. The Klan will never die!"

I talked with Grand Dragon Green in his office in the Peters Building. His patients waited in the reception room while the Doctor and I talked "patriotism." I came well recommended, for Dr. Green will neither write to nor see strangers. I found him a short, stocky man with compressed lips, pale face, straight, unruly hair and rimless glasses. He had a curt, sandy-red Hitlerian mustache. He left me with the impression that I was facing a cold, calculating, fanatical advocate of "white supremacy" and kindred evils.

I started by telling Green of my meeting with Colescott. "Why, I used to sit side by side with him," he said, a sour smile breaking the austere lines of his face. "I still correspond with him." Beyond this admission, Green was too tight lipped to mention any other associates. I asked him about the attitude of the Klan toward Jews and Catholics. He answered in double talk. "We're for America! *If these people do not try to destroy our country,* we have nothing against them. We want to keep America American. We are for the

Constitution and want to bring America back to the principles of the Constitution."

Green alleged that former Attorney General Francis Biddle was a Catholic * who had appointed "a Catholic priest, two Jews and two Communists" to censor wartime "patriotic" literature. As a result of this, Klan literature had been banned. He referred to Bishop Gerald O'Hara of Savannah as "a fine citizen who would be as good as any white Protestant American if he stepped out of his Catholic collar." It has been my experience that every "patriot" knows at least one "good Jew" or "good Catholic" or "good nigger" (Bilbo and Rankin love only "good" Negroes) whom he parades to refute the charge that he is against a minority. Father Coughlin's Jew-baiting articles always made an exception of such "good Jews" as George E. Sokolsky. Watch out for those who bray, "My best friend is a Jew" or "a Catholic."

I asked Green about Martin Dies. He began by denouncing Jerry Voorhis of the Dies Committee as "a violent Klan hater. You couldn't get anywhere with him." Toward Dies, Green was much more gentle. He said Dies had filed an unpublished report which had completely cleared the Klan of charges of un-Americanism!

"Mr. Colescott went up to Dies himself and asked to be investigated," Green confirmed.

As I left, the Grand Dragon of the Georgia Klan warned, "Don't get the idea the Klan is not meeting. We are busy."

He was right. My investigations disclosed that secret Klan meetings were held in Georgia all during the war. Five months after my talk with Green a huge cross, visible for many miles, was burned on Stone Mountain. On May 8, 1946 the Klan held a Klon Klave (convention) in Atlanta, followed two days later by another cross-burning ceremony on Stone Mountain. Members were armed with blackjacks and pistols. About 400 new members joined. A news story reported: "Members of the Atlanta police force who are members of the organization were instructed to direct traffic at Stone Mountain, 14 miles east of Atlanta."

Grand Dragon Green estimated that in October, 1945, 20,000 Klansmen were loose in Georgia alone. Members pay an initiation fee of $10; dues are $6. Other fees make it a profitable racket for the führers of the bedsheet empire. Green declared in the fall of

---

* Actually Mr. Biddle is a member of the Protestant Episcopal Church.

Lynch Mobs Roar Through Hamlet; Leader and

The Fires of Race Hate Blaze Again

America first, last, and always

Talmadge Wins Against Georgia's Will

Knights & Women of the
KU KLUX KLAN

NEGRO DEATH LAID TO MISSISSIPPIANS

Grand Dragon Finds

SINCE SHERMAN SHERMED SIXT-SIX
THE KU KLUX KLAN
Has been riding and will
continue to do so as long as
the WHITE MAN liveth.

Fun In Klan Job, Not A Living

Klan Flogged Negro Vet, Georgia DA Charges

KLAN TERRORISTS LINKED TO KILLING

AFL CHARGES KLAN KIDNAPPED NEGRO

Green Reports Georgia Worker Was Beaten After He Refused to Resign From Union

Georgia Agents Report Boast of Murder—Negro Veteran of Navy Is Flogged

INVISIBLE EMPIRE

Klan Hangs Everything on the CIO;
That's the Way Outfit Hopes to Grow

WHITE SUPREMACY

What does the Klan stand for?

No one can doubt the true Americanism of the Knights of the Ku Klux Klan. It is at the top as America's No. 1 Patriotic organization.

Bilbo Urges Whites to Bar Negro Vote by 'Any Means'

Sweet Land of Liberty

BILBO VOTE TOPS OPPONENTS BY 4,102

KLAN IS ACCUSED OF A REVOLT PLOT

Georgia Charges It Seeks to Take Over Key Agencies—Sues to Revoke Charter

Georgia Mob of 20 Men Massacres 2 Negroes, Wives; One Was Ex-GI

$10,000 Offered for Lynchers
Police Inquiry Thwarted

Georgia Sues To Strip Klan Of State Charter

Charges Terrorism, Murder, Plot to Seize Police Agencies

1945 that "the Klan has as much right to exist as the Masons, Rotarians or any other organization." He insists that "the Klan is fighting Communism." It purports to be protecting the "chastity of white womanhood." It regards itself as the "exemplification of a pure patriotism to the United States, its Constitution and its flag."

One of the strongholds of the Klan continues to be East Point, Atlanta suburb. It was there that Klansmen in 1940 flogged to death Ike Gaston, a helpless barber who refused to leave town. The Klan also bravely flogged to death Tom Parker, a World War I veteran. When Georgia justice finally brushed aside the staying hand of its pro-Klan Governor Talmadge and convicted three floggers, Talmadge threatened to pardon them. An aroused citizenry poured out its protest. On November 19, 1941 Talmadge calmly told a reporter of the Atlanta *Constitution:* "The trouble with those fellows was that they had good motives, but went about them in the wrong way. I can sympathize with them. They thought they were doing right, but they just went a little crazy. I was in a thing like that one time myself, but I got mine out in the daytime."

This statement—probably enough to cause some direct action by the people in certain states—wasn't the only time Talmadge has spoken on behalf of the Klan. How the cancerous growth had eaten its way high into the hierarchy of state officialdom was revealed by the Covington (Ga.) *News* on December 16, 1943 in a story promptly reprinted by the enlightened Atlanta *Constitution.*

This was an astonishing account of a get-together dinner held by the Porterdale, Ga., Klan in a memorial gymnasium in that Eden. Judging from the write-up the *News'* impressed reporter gave the affair, it went off with all the gushing respectability and air of civic righteousness you'd expect at a Ladies' Aid supper. After stowing a roast turkey banquet dished up by the Business Girls Club, the gathering of about two hundred business and professional lights of the county applauded an amazing speech by Talmadge. Gene was joined on the program by Imperial Wizard James A. Colescott, who had come on, and George Hamilton, State Treasurer of Georgia.

Grand Dragon Samuel Green, M.D., and two Exalted Cyclopses— of Porterdale and East Atlanta—were among those present, as were former State Game and Fish Director Zach Cravey and the ex-head of the Georgia State Troopers, Johnny Goodwin. He was the same Goodwin who joined Talmadge himself in forming The Vigilantes,

Inc., a "secret Fraternal, Benevolent, Social and Patriotic" organization patterned on the Klan.

Talmadge's remarks at the affair were a medley of prejudice-confirming nationalist theme songs, attacking refugees and the war-time Administration, urging "Christian" democracy, higher protective tariffs and, needless to add, White Supremacy. The Klansmen then pumped Talmadge's hand, according to the account, and the town band and a group of young lady songbirds rendered Christmas carols and patriotic military music, conducive to national unity.

"We didn't hold any public meetings during the war, because we didn't want to stir up any feelings," Grand Dragon Green has said, not bothering to count things like the goings-on at Porterdale. Then he added, "We're not at war now!"

Regular Kluxer meeting places in the Atlanta region are at Oakland City, near Atlanta, and in the Red Men's Wigwam in the heart of the "Imperial City." Another Klan dive was disclosed through an intercepted meeting notice:

> Feb. 10. 1945
> Box 122 Sta A
> Atlanta Ga.

Esteemed Klansman—

There is Work to be done—are you doing your Part? Do you Know what happened Friday Night Feb 2nd. on Ormond Street and on Grant St.? Would you have been ready if Called?

There Will be a Special Klonklave of your Klan, Thursday Night Feb 15th 7:30 P.M. in your Klavern, 1173½ Lee St. S.W. *Be There, Duty Calls*

> Yours Itsub [*sic*]
> G. T. Brown
> Exalted Cyclops
> Klan #297

Repeated authoritative reports indicate that the Klan has a dangerous foothold in the Atlanta Police Department. An Associated Press dispatch reported an address on June 13, 1946, by Dan Duke, Assistant State Attorney General, who charged that one meeting of Atlanta's Klan Post No. 1 was attended by 38 uniformed police officers. Moreover, Mr. Duke said, an Atlanta policeman had promised at a recent Klan meeting that the hooded organization would be allowed to handle in their own way any race riots in the city. A New York *Times* report on June 20 stated that in addition to Dr. Green, Grand Dragon of the "association of Georgia Klans," the charter lists S. W. Roper as an officer. Roper, who under Talmadge's administration headed Georgia's Bureau of Investigation, is identified as Exalted Cyclops of Post 297 in East Atlanta. Also named.as officers are B. G. Otwell, Exalted Cyclops of Post 213 in East Atlanta, and G. T. Brown, now Grand Titan of the Fifth Province of the Georgia Realm.

Addressing Governor Ellis Arnall in his regular broadcast June 9, 1946, over Station WJZ, Drew Pearson said:

In your probe of the Ku Klux Klan please investigate the meeting of Atlanta Klavern No. 1, June 3. You will find that attending that meeting were 11 policemen of the City of Atlanta—in uniform. That may explain, Governor, why the murder of an Atlanta taxi driver, Porter Turner, stabbed to death by the Ku Klux Klan, has been so wantonly neglected by Atlanta Police.

Anonymous letters from Klansmen, Pearson said, had been threatening him "with all sorts of dire consequences, including death."

A New York *Times* dispatch, datelined June 7, 1946, tells of the reopening by the Georgia Bureau of Investigation of an inquiry into the slaying of Turner near Atlanta in August, 1945. The move came "after secret State agents working inside the Ku Klux Klan reported that members of [the] Kavalier Klub, its strong-arm squad, were boasting they had killed a middle-aged Negro taxi driver. . . . Turner was stabbed to death and his body was dumped on the lawn of a physician in De Kalb County near the Atlanta city limits. De Kalb police records show the case marked unsolved."

According to the *Times*, Georgia's fighting Assistant Attorney General Daniel Duke, "asserted that the members of the Kavalier Klub numbered about fifty and were picked for their brawn and willingness to go out on terroristic raids."

Duke, who sent seven Kluxers to prison for flogging in 1941, was authorized by Governor Arnall in June, 1946 to crack down on the Klan. In addition, State Attorney General Eugene Cook has filed a suit in the Georgia Superior Court to revoke the Klan charter. The State charged that the Klan intended to "organize police officers, cab drivers, truck drivers and others in key positions" so that it could "seize" parts of the State government charged with protection of citizens. Should these efforts fail, Arnall has said that he may call a special session of the Legislature to "de-hood" the nightshirters.

Following these courageous measures to cope with the Klan, Arnall received threats upon his life. "Anonymous callers tell me that the Klan is not accustomed to having public officials interfere with its activities in Georgia. They say they are going to 'get' me," Arnall said. Then on June 21 he announced, according to the Associated Press, that the FBI, which had been quietly carrying on its investigation, had uncovered a "well-organized plot" under which two members of the Klan would be "given the job of taking care of me." Mr. Arnall quoted an FBI undercover agent as reporting that the Oakland City Klavern had instigated the plot by having the names of Klansmen drawn by lot from each klavern to "rub him out."

"From these names," Arnall said, according to an AP dispatch, "the Grand Dragon is to draw two and the Federal Bureau of Investigation advised me that these two, unknown to each other and to anyone else, except the Grand Dragon, are to be given the job of taking care of me." Arnall's charges were denied by Grand Dragon Green.

Under Governor Arnall, the fight has been joined between crusading State executives and the deep-rooted hate and terror of the Georgia Klan. But Arnall's term is about up. The man who as Democratic nominee looks like Georgia's next Governor is the orator who thrilled the Klan jamboree at Porterdale.

"The Man" and Klan in Mississippi

Mississippi has its full share of the Klan-minded, and not only is Senator Theodore Gilmore Bilbo, sometimes called "The Man," a symbol of Klan-like bigotry, but he is a self-admitted member of the cowardly shirt order. Bilbo admitted this in August, 1946 when interviewed by newspaper and magazine correspondents on the Mutual Broadcasting System's "Meet the Press" program. To the question, "Are you or have you ever been a member of the Ku Klux Klan?" Bilbo replied:

"I have. I am a member of the Ku Klux Klan No. 40, called Bilbo

Klan No. 40, Mississippi. I attended one meeting and have not attended it since, because I was not in sympathy with some of the things in it."

When asked if he had ever left the Klan, Bilbo answered, "No man can ever leave the Klan. He takes an oath not to do that. Once a Ku Klux, always a Ku Klux."

Bilbo was queried about news stories quoting him to the effect that the way to keep Negroes from voting was to visit them the night before. He reiterated, "The best time to keep a nigger away from a white primary in Mississippi was to see him the night before. . . . We thought, under the law, he had no right to vote, and the best thing was to see him and advise him the night before and tell him that he had no right."

Bilbo was reminded of Article 15 of the Constitution which says, "The right of the citizens of the United States to vote shall not be denied or abridged by the United States or by any State on account of race, color, or previous condition of servitude."

Bilbo's brazen reply was, "Notwithstanding the fact that the 14th and 15th Amendments were adopted through fraud, I did take an oath to uphold it, and I am upholding it. I have not violated it."

During the primaries Bilbo exhorted Mississippians, "If you never voted for me before, vote for me now. Let me go back to Washington. I'll represent you in the Senate so that you'll be proud and never regret it. I'll fight and fight and fight, and I'll kill and kill and kill,' reported Scripps-Howard writer Charles T. Lucey.

The quotation typifies Mississippi's führer and its blackguard Klan. Only uncontrolled hate can so shrivel the soul.

A distinguished Mississipian, Hodding Carter, publisher of the *Delta Democrat-Times* of Greenville and winner of the Pulitzer Prize for editorial writing, declared in a radio broadcast:

I believe it may be a good thing that Bilbo has been returned to the Senate. . . . He can do Mississippi less harm in Washington than he can at home. He left it bankrupt, its universities in disrepute, and blacklisted . . . its institutions in political and moral chaos. . . . In the larger sense it may be a good thing for this Nation to have one Bilbo among the 96 men who sit in the Senate. For he sits there as a horrifying warning of what the combined forces of bigotry and anger and fear can produce in a democracy.

Tennessee

At a Klan meeting held during the war on Market Street in Chattanooga, Kleagle J. B. Stoner wheeled on his crippled foot and with blazing oratory told the Furies, Cyclops and other goons present how the Klan terror would operate in postwar America. Administering the oath of allegiance to a new member who expected his draft notice shortly, the little, five-foot-tall Kleagle gloated over the fact that the new Kluxer would soon be in the Army, learning to fight. When he and the many other Klansmen in service from all over the country got back, Stoner said, they would be better trained to serve the Invisible Empire in fighting the Negroes. Stoner climaxed his flaming speech with the promise that "vigilante" squads would be recruited from veterans. It was no empty boast. Vigilante squads *were* organized in Chattanooga, as strikebreakers.

I wrote Stoner but received no response. Following up with an-

The native born American is the salt of the earth—and the ranks of the Ku Klux Klan are open only to men born in the United States.

The Knights of the Ku Klux Klan stand for "America First" — first in thought, first in affection, and first in the Galaxy of Nations.

J. B. STONER
KU KLUX KLAN ORGANIZER
204 TEMPLE COURT BLDG.
OFFICE HOURS: THURS.-FRI.-SAT.
11:30 A.M. to 1:30 P.M. — 3:30 to 6 P.M.

CHATTANOOGA 2, TENN.

Dear Sir:
  In reply to your letter to Byerley.
  I am the local Klan Kleagle (Organizer).
  Notify me when you expect to be in town next and let me know your local hotel and I will call on you.
  If you come to town unexpectedly, you may telephone me at either my apartment or my office. However, it would be best to notify me in advance of your coming because, otherwise, I might be out of town.
  I would appreciate a prompt reply enclosing any references you have xxx available. As you probably know, I need to know something about anybody I talk with.

                              Yours truly,

                              J.B. Stoner
                              Kleagle

other letter throbbing with "Americanism" and dripping with super-patriotism, I got a cordial answer from Stoner, who introduced himself as "the local Klan Kleagle" (organizer). The envelope announced that "J. B. Stoner, Ku Klux Klan Organizer," held office hours on Thursdays, Fridays and Saturdays from 11:30 to 1:30 and from 3:30 to 6:00. He invited me to let him know when I was next in Chattanooga, but cautiously requested references.

An enclosed card invited applicants "to join a secret organization that stands primarily for WHITE SUPREMACY." I filled out the card and enclosed a dollar bill. I heard nothing further of my application, however, and my repeated letters brought no response. Stoner wouldn't operate across state lines.

I wrote Stoner again under another name. He replied that he was no longer a Klan organizer, but was "now engaged in distributing anti-Jewish literature." In a fanatical diatribe against the Jewish people, he told about his work to help build up a "national anti-Jewish political party" to function by the Presidential election year of 1948. His party, he wrote me, is "very strongly for White Supremacy and America First." Stoner also tried to sell me a copy of the *Protocols* for two dollars. It's a steep price. I can get the book from the "finest" fascist hate shops for fifty cents—less in wholesale lots.

Another Tennessee Klan organizer, according to New York *Times* correspondent George Hatcher, is Rev. A. A. Haggard of Maryville. According to Hatcher's story on June 23, 1946, Haggard, an Evangelist minister, admitted membership in the Klan, and had been principal speaker at a recent Kluxer rally in Knoxville. Haggard said he was not a Klan leader but roughly estimated the Order's total membership in Tennessee at 10,000.

One of the most fantastic documents I have read in my career as investigator came from Chattanooga. It is the Ritual of the United Sons of Dixie, incorporated in Tennessee in 1943 as a "fraternal and political club." How the Ritual fell into my hands is a long story, entailing many months of exhaustive investigation and correspondence. Suffice it to say, I received it from a highly reliable source. The secret terrorist group seemed determined to exterminate the Negro by the direct use of bullets. In this respect its mission seemed similar to that of the Christian Front "Sport Clubs" of Bundist days, to one of which I belonged. The proposed victims then were the "Jews" and "Communists." The United Sons of Dixie concentrated on the Negro as a scapegoat.

According to the Ritual, the conferring of its second, or White Legion Degree, began by demanding a satisfactory answer to the following queries from those awaiting membership:

Do you believe that the negroes should have better treatment in the U.S.A.?

Do we want another Pearl Harbor from the negro in this country?

Will you fight to make the U.S.A. a white man's country?

Pledged to absolute secrecy, the prospective member was then subjected to a ritual in which the President called for volunteers for a lynching party, saying, "They have asked for 150 men. We ought to send 300 members if possible. I am going!"

The Chaplain was required to state, "I will be there and ready."

The Sergeant-at-Arms' line was, "I, for one, will be there and ready to do my part. I only wish I had a tommy gun and plenty of shells."

After this, the prospective candidate submitted to a lecture by the President of the United Sons of Dixie. Following are verbatim transcripts from the Ritual. I have selected them for the sake of clarity and speed in reading:

America faces a crisis that cannot be avoided by the mere closing of our eyes. . . . The negroes are demanding more privileges every day. They want social equality with the white race. . . . They want to be able to step out with your mother, wife, daughter or sweetheart. Men, we will not stand for this here in the South—here in Dixie. . . .

. . . Why shouldn't we organize? We will not be spectators in a war between the whites and negroes. . . . It is our liberty that is at stake. I am sure you will realize that and I am sure that you will, as all of us are, put everything you have into the job of getting the South organized and ready for the trouble when it comes. We . . . must be ready and waiting when it comes for it will surely come soon. The negroes are now talking of the GREAT BROWN RACE OF TOMORROW—so, let us be ready and see that there is no tomorrow for them.

Whipping prospective candidates into a white-supremacy frenzy, and again reminding them of their solemn oath of secrecy, the President then delivered the final call to arms to "save the white race." These are his blood-chilling words:

There are two solutions. First, inter-marry and help build up the "Great Brown Race of Tomorrow" of which they are talking. Second, get ready for a racial war that will surely come, and very soon. It may be a month, a year or five years—but it is coming.

We must nominate and elect members of our Order and put them in State, County and City public offices. These men will be able to put laws on our statute books which will help us. They can also help us to get arms and ammunition in order to defend ourselves and the White people of the United States.

. . . The negro is quietly arming himself. We want 15,000,000 members in the United States, and every one of them with a good gun and plenty of ammunition—ready to fight when it starts. This is plain talk, Brothers, but we must face the facts. Let us prepare now before it is too late and be ready to protect our loved ones from the negro, whatever the price. Eventually, we must eliminate the negroes in this country.

You have obligated yourself to provide yourself with a gun and ammunition and it is your duty to get them as soon as possible, for you may need them at any time. We hope to have rifle teams and a rifle range, where our members can practice to qualify for sharpshooter—because the best shots live the longest and we want you to live a long time. You should do all you can to promote our social entertainment and sports program. Take an active part whenever you can.

We do not want the public to know what is behind the First Degree of the United Sons of Dixie. Let them think it is only a social, fraternal and political order. We are military minded. We are preparing for the future as we see the handwriting on the wall. So, my Brother, live up to your OATH. Prepare now before it is too late. Be ready to fight for your Honor, your Home and the Master White Race of white people and white supremacy here in the United States of America—our country. . . .

California

The spectacle of a Klansman speaking in a high-school auditorium under the sponsorship of an American Legion Post may seem unbelievable. It happened on March 26, 1946, at the resort town of Big Bear Lake in Southern California, when Col. Harry Graham, commander of Big Bear Lake Post 584 unwittingly invited Rev. Wesley Swift to "explain" what the Ku Kluxers stood for. Graham said he was alarmed and wanted to know. According to Tom Towers of *The Grizzly*, the newspaper which broke the story, Swift explained the "Americanism" of the Klan to about fifty Legionnaires and their wives. *The Grizzly* reported that Swift was flanked by the American and Legion flags and a service flag bearing fifty blue and three gold stars as he yammered, "The Klan is here in Bear Valley to stay. We intend to form restrictive covenants here and elsewhere in order to hold the line of pure Americanism."

Launching into a heated tirade against international Jewry, Swift blamed Pearl Harbor on President Roosevelt, who, he alleged, had "provoked the attack just to find an excuse to send our boys overseas." This fantastic lie is a favorite nationalist canard.

Swift's speech climaxed a series of cross burnings in the township, during which anti-Semitic feeling flared up. Eleven-year-old Deanna Di Renzo was called "Jew" by her classmates, the Los Angeles *Daily News* reported. An anonymous voice phoned Charles Di Renzo and snapped: "Jew shop." When the Di Renzos—Americans of Italian descent—moved into a new home, a rock crashed through their window.

"There is no anti-Catholic feeling in the Klan and there won't be any," *The Grizzly* reported Swift as saying. Stating, according to the newspaper, that he was an "admirer of Father Charles E. Coughlin, Monsignor Fulton J. Sheen . . . and many other Catholic leaders throughout the country," Swift divulged the new "party line" of the Northern Klan:

The KKK of the present day—a symbol of Christianity on the march—is no longer like the Klan of old when bigotry and prejudice caused a cleavage line between Catholics and Protestants. Today the goal was pure American nationalism and nothing else . . . The KKK has a big job to do, particularly in the coming elections.

Sealing the unholy bond between the Klan and the Christian Front, Rev. Swift in 1945–6 accompanied Gerald L. K. Smith on a hate-inciting speaking tour across the country. I heard them speak at Celina, Ohio, and again at Detroit's Northern High School. I can't easily forget that meeting in September, 1945. Smith pointed his finger in my direction (without actually recognizing me) and bellowed something about "pitching the Carlsons feet first right out of this auditorium!" (I was seated in the third row, under Smith's nose.) The audience booed my name. I booed, too. The woman at my right hissed, "I wish I could lay my hands on Carlson. I'd scratch his eyes out!"

"I've heard Carlson speak," I said to her. "I felt like punching him in the eye, but he had ten bodyguards."

I looked at her. She was elderly and white haired, with a rather cold, brutal face. I felt sure the vixen could undoubtedly carry out her threat. As I made detailed notes of the meeting, the harridan became suspicious, and I finally whispered: "Shh . . . I'm taking this down for a nationalist paper in Chicago." It quieted her.

I had sat up close so I could observe Rev. Swift. He was short and pudgy, with a pasty face and black brows. His mouth was surly, his lips thick. He wore a dark blue suit and blue tie. He was introduced as a preacher from Lancaster, Cal. Swift made a short political speech which passed off as a "prayer." Its delivery was emotional and set the tone for Gerald Smith, who spoke for two hours. Smith posed as the defender of Catholicism against "anti-Catholics." He claimed Catholic priests had commended his "patriotism" and mentioned Father Edward F. Brophy, speaker at Brooklyn Christian Front meetings. Time and again Smith implied that his views had been sanctioned: "The Catholic Church knows that Gerald L. K. Smith is the enemy of their greatest enemy, the Christ-hating enemies of Christ." Klansman Swift aped the hate führer, Smith, when he spoke at Big Bear Lake.

"The worst thing that could happen with unemployment prospects and racial tension would be the revival of the Klan," said Attorney General Robert W. Kenny of California. "We intend to smash the organization before it gets started."

A deputy sheriff at Lancaster, Cal. was charged with being over-friendly with Swift, and questioned. Constable Coy Brown also was ordered to appear at the Attorney General's office. State investigators staged a series of raids on klaverns. One on a downtown auditorium in Los Angeles unearthed Klan robes and hoods—outlawed in the city eighteen years ago—thousands of Klan pamphlets and an eight-foot "fiery cross." Mr. Kenny sent me samples of the Klan poison. They attacked Jewry and immigration. The membership application form was identical with those used in Florida and Georgia.

Mr. Kenny's swift action may have checked Klan growth, although reports persist that more than 100 Klan Klubs flourish in Southern California and are working jointly with former Bund interests. Klan depredations have been renewed. On May 20, 1946 Temple Israel in Los Angeles was desecrated. The Holy Scroll was ripped from its Ark and the Synagogue walls defaced with painted swastikas and the words "Der Juden Parasite." Shortly thereafter, a cross was burned on the lawn of Zeta Beta Tau, a Jewish fraternity. The vandals defaced its walls with the painted letters "KKK."

New York

New Yorkers who smugly point the finger of scorn at the South were shocked to find major Klan units operating in their own back yard.

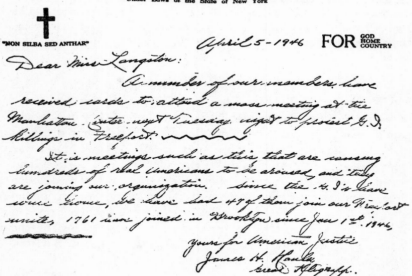

Klan hate is not confined to the South alone. A New York group organized in 1921 as the Alpha Pi Sigma fraternity, later changed to Knights and Women of the Ku Klux Klan, Inc.

A letter received in early April, 1946 by Miss Dorothy Langston, Executive Secretary of the New York Committee for Justice in Freeport, L. I., from one James H. Hanley, Great Kligrapp of the Knights and Women of the Ku Klux Klan, Inc., gives some indication of the postwar growth of Klan units and the enrollment of veterans in Brooklyn, N. Y., and Freeport, L. I. Hanley's letter was on the stationery of the Klan group, but no address was shown; it came in an envelope bearing the name of a publication with offices on lower Fifth Avenue in Manhattan. Hanley, apparently, was disgruntled about plans announced by the Committee for a meeting of protest over a tragedy which had, so far as is known, no connection with the Klan. The incident in question was the killing in Freeport in February, 1946, of Pfc. Charles Ferguson, a Negro, and his brother Alphonso, and the wounding of a third brother, a Navy ship's cook, by a rookie Freeport policeman, Joseph Romeika.*

The Hanley letter, dated April 5, 1946, read:

It is most unfortunate that the collored people should line up with a bunch of rabble rousers like those on the list of your speakers. . . . It is meetings such as this, that are causing hundreds of real Americans to be aroused, and they are joining our organization. Since the GIs have come home, we have had 47 of them join our Freeport unite: 1761 have joined in Brooklyn since Jan. 1st, 1946.

The receipt of this letter stimulated investigation of the Knights and Women of the Ku Klux Klan, Inc. The initiative was taken by the *Daily Worker*, Communist Party organ, but all New York newspapers published the subsequent developments. It was disclosed that on September 7, 1923 a fraternity called Alpha Pi Sigma was incorporated by J. Archibald Wilson, Horace A. Demarest and others. Two years later, on October 10, 1925, the society filed notice of its intention to change its name to Knights and Women of the Ku Klux Klan, Inc. Horace A. Demarest's name appeared only in the original incorporation papers, not in those relating to the change of name. Besides being one of the incorporators of the front organization, Demarest was one of three persons named in the certificate as directors of the fraternity. Since Demarest had meanwhile

* A grand jury declined to indict the policeman. Later Governor Dewey, after a further investigation, dismissed a petition to name a special prosecutor to reopen the case.

become a well-known Republican leader and, when the history of the Klan group was probed, held the post of Deputy Commissioner of Motor Vehicles in Queens County, his connection with Alpha Pi Sigma aroused publicity.*

While I do not subscribe to the politics of the *Daily Worker* or to the one-party, one-voice, so-called "democracy" the Communists want in America, in this instance the Communist daily rendered a public service by initiating the investigation of the Knights and Women of the Ku Klux Klan, Inc.

On the night of September 19, 1940 I attended a meeting of Klansmen and Klanswomen in Brooklyn, in the premises of what was described to me as the Yale Republican Club, in the Ridgewood section. I went with a Klansman from Queens whom I had met at the joint meeting of the Klan and the German-American Bund at Bund Camp Nordland, on August 18, 1940. He manufactured "medicine" which he alleged was a cure-all for such diverse and unrelated diseases as diabetes, pneumonia and gonorrhea!

That evening the Ridgewood Klan presented its affiliate, the "Women's Mayflower League," with an American flag and a "Christian" flag—the latter white, with a blue corner bearing a red cross. The ceremony over, the speech-making began. The first speaker was a convert from Catholicism, and obviously of Italian origin. He was obsessed with anti-Catholic phobia. He recited alleged murders committed by "the Borgia Pope." The next speaker, one Terence Magowan, delivered an anti-Catholic address which was as inaccurate as it was frenzied. "I hate the Church from the bottom of my heart for what it does to innocent minds," he said, using gestures effectively. He had been making anti-Catholic speeches since 1928, when Al Smith ran for President.

Someone in the crowd of about forty men and women shouted that the Jews were "just as bad as the Catholics."

"Go fight the Jews yourself if you know them so well!" Magowan invited. "I know the Catholic Church. I have yet to see a Jew set

---

* Demarest emphatically denied that he was a member of the Klan, or that he knew anything about the change of name. He explained that in September, 1923, while a mere "investigator for a firm of attorneys," a Klan attorney whom he identified only as Noah had offered him a chance to make a few dollars. Demarest agreed, whereupon Noah suggested, "Suppose you just be one of the incorporators for a little fraternity I'm organizing." Demarest signed his name. On May 6, 1946 Demarest was dismissed from the state service.

himself up as King on Earth, and Emperor of Heaven! I have yet to see a Jew claim he was the infallible disciple of God. I have yet to see a Jewish organization enslave the minds of its followers!"

Magowan kept up his barrage of religious intolerance for an hour under the folds of the American and so-called "Christian" flags.

On July 29, 1946, the sensational announcement of the banning of the New York State Klan was made by Attorney General Nathaniel Goldstein. Thus New York established the lead contemplated by New Jersey, Kentucky and other states in outlawing the Klan. A fine of $10,000 and imprisonment may be imposed for violation of the court order dissolving the corporation.

The disclosures upon which the Court's decision was made were based on the magnificent undercover investigations of a New York detective whom Mr. Goldstein identified only as "Mr. Bauer." Bauer turned in the names of 1,100 Klan members and identified 15 units in metropolitan New York alone. He gained the confidence of Klansmen by posing as a former member of the Ridgewood unit. When asked where he worked Bauer truthfully stated that he was employed at the District Attorney's office. He added the fiction that he was secretly in sympathy with the Klan and intended to "double-cross Mr. Goldstein." Delighted at their valuable contact, Klansmen regularly phoned Bauer at the District Attorney's headquarters. All their conversations were recorded.

Goldstein named Wilson D. Bush, a ghost writer, as the Exalted Cyclops of the Bronx and the key figure in the State. Bush informed Bauer that he had maintained close contact with the Georgia Klan and as late as May, 1946 had visited Georgia to get advice on how to proceed with Klan reorganization. James Wagner was revealed as the Kligrapp or secretary of the Richmond Hill unit. Clarence Herlth was Grand Titan and as such the New York State representative of the national organization. According to Mr. Goldstein, Herlth worked as steward for the Knights of Columbus and reported on their activities to Klan units. Unit 38, in Jamaica, was the largest, it was disclosed. Others functioned in Richmond Hill, Glendale, Queens Village, the Bronx and Staten Island. The American Krusaders Kamp No. 1 was at Flushing. Richmond Hill had a women's unit; another was known as the Molly Pitcher.

Interviewed by the New York *Post*, Grand Titan Herlth denied the Klan was anti-Negro, anti-Catholic or anti-Jewish.

"We don't hate the Negro," he said. "We just believe in white supremacy." The Klan had no feelings against Catholics—"except that they get dictation from Rome and worship idols and statues." As for the Jews, the Klan doesn't dislike them, either. It's just that "there is a strong element of low class Jews in New York City in the Red movement; there is a majority of Jews over here now and we believe in no foreign element having power in this country." Herlth denied spying on the Knights of Columbus for the Klan, too.

The Klan's "principles of hate, intolerance, bigotry and violence have no part in the American way of life," Mr. Goldstein said. "It should be stamped out whenever and wherever it raises its ugly head." For the time being at least, the New York Klan seems to have been checked. Has it been completely eradicated? The resistance of hate-groups is made of sterner stuff. I predict that the New York Klan will come back under another guise or front, as "American" and "innocuous" as the Alpha Pi Sigma fraternity. One group to be watched is the White Collar Action Committee, Inc., incorporated May 9, 1946. One of its directors is Horace A. Demarest.

Michigan: The United Sons of America

In April, 1946 thirty-five cars formed a circle on a deserted farm at Chelsea, Michigan, forty miles from Detroit. More than 100 Klansmen in full regalia stood stiffly at attention while the Grand Cyclops lit the cross in the center of the circle. Angry flames licked into the sky, heralding the rebirth of the Klan in Michigan. Most of the Klansmen were Detroiters.

In 1942, while investigating the National Workers League,* I spent more than three weeks in Detroit, ostensibly working as an "organizer" of the notorious pro-Nazi, intensely nationalist "fraternity." During that investigation of the League, which is reported upon in detail in *Under Cover*, I frequently heard the name of Charles J. Spare. Popularly known as "Nightshirt Charlie," Spare was Detroit's No. 1 Klansman and former Grand Klailiff of Michigan. His name cropped up in the investigation of the Black Legion,

* This, in brief, is its pedigree. Three of its leaders are under indictment for sedition. One of them had dealings with a Nazi spy. Its members included Klansmen, Black Legion gangsters, Silver Shirts and other American Nazi hoodlums.

a Klan offshoot which imported strikebreakers from the South and was found responsible for many murders.

To meet "Nightshirt Charlie" I was directed to a house at 89 West Forest Avenue, on the fringe of Detroit's shabby section. Vigilante groups, hired as "action committees" to break the United Automobile Workers' strike against General Motors late in November, 1945, met at this address.

It was a haunted-looking, three-floor frame house, unpainted and ugly. City records showed that the house was held in the names of Spare, John Hosmer and Thompsie C. Nations. It adjoined a parking lot. Its rear porch overlooked a factory. On the front was a sign labeling it as a meeting place of "Townsend Club No. 42, formally No. 8." My instructions were to "go in the back way." I walked past an elderly attendant by telling him I was an "organizer for the National Workers League" and found myself in a large, empty meeting room. I hurried past a series of closed doors and up a staircase to a second-floor room containing a desk and chairs and lined with files. "Nightshirt Charlie," however, was not in. After several other attempts to see him I gave up in order not to arouse suspicion by my insistence.

That was my last contact with 89 West Forest Avenue until on March 16, 1946 I received a letter from R. R. Roberts, National Secretary of the United Sons of America, mailed from the same address. The United Sons of America was the new mask for the old Detroit Klan, which was among the first to change its name to the super-patriotic one of the new organization. Detroit nightshirters underwent the transformation gradually. In 1941 the Kleagles and Titans were replaced with Marshals, Captains, Lieutenants and Corporals, and under military discipline continued in modified form the strikebreaking tactics of the Black Legion. The United Sons of America was the next step for the Detroit Kleagles. Emphasis was placed on veterans, who were recruited on the promise of getting them jobs. They were told that the USA had "connections" with industrial concerns.

The Articles of Incorporation for the USA were filed in Michigan on March 19, 1943. The incorporators were listed as E. E. Maxey, Howard Clark and David Cole.

On March 13, 1946, as the veteran Thompson, I wrote the United Sons of America a carefully prepared letter which began: "I lived in the South up to ten years ago. I was born and raised in Tennessee. My father was a Kleagle, but he is now dead. We had to move up here to live with relatives. I live with my mother." I went on to denounce labor, Communism and the PAC, and signed the letter "Fraternally." I had a warm answer within a few days. Secretary R. R. Roberts urged me to organize fifty of my "buddies" at $5.00 a head:

We are a fraternal group [he said] and instead of having Posts as the veterans have we call our individual groups Circles. . . . We have a ritualistic initiation. We are interested in getting Protestant, white Americans organized for the protection of the United States of America.

The application form contained forty-eight questions, such as whether the prospective recruit was married by a "priest" or a "preacher," his parents' religion, and whether his children (if any) attended "public" or "parochial" school. A USA organizer has been quoted in an interview as stating that Jews, Negroes and former parochial-school students are barred from membership. "Will you faithfully practice spending your money with Americans?" another question demanded. This could only mean "Buy Christian"—an obviously anti-Semitic policy pursued vigorously by the Bund and the Christian Front. Under its false mask, the United Sons of America carries on the ugly traditions of the Klan. That the revised Klan can organize nationally under its new guise is made clear in a letter to me from Roberts:

We are organized under the laws of Michigan as a National organization with the privilege of establishing circles in any State in the United States. We are inclosing one of our Creeds which will give you information concerning the operations of our order and the things we stand for.

The Creed of the USA—"A fraternity dedicated to America"— covers not four but *eleven* "freedoms." It has everything, including a claim that the outfit stands for "freedom from persecution because of Race, Creed or Color!" The Creed is designed to appeal to veterans and union men. An ex-soldier or unionist could honestly subscribe to every word of it, unaware that its professions of Americanism and Christianity are merely window dressing for a Klan rebaptized under another name but still continuing its business of promoting hatred against Negroes, Catholics, Jews and foreign-born.

Latest confidential information from Detroit is that the United Sons of America is still concentrating its efforts upon veterans, baiting the hapless ex-GI with the lure of a well-paying job in a non-union plant. Meanwhile, USA-type "Circles" have been operating as the "Old Glory Clubs" in Florida, Tennessee, Kentucky, Alabama and Indiana. Membership must be large, though exact figures are not available. The purpose of these Clubs is everywhere the same: to inject the Klan spirit into labor relations. The five states just mentioned, like Michigan, have large industrial labor populations. Strikebreaking through the use of thugs and the Black Legion having failed, the same elements are now attempting to bore from within under patriotic guise.

The United Sons of America is one of many groups of roughly similar mold which, taken together, wield considerable influence and form a militant wing of the anti-labor movement.

Kentucky: The Mason-Dixon Society, Inc.

The story of the Mason-Dixon Society, Inc., "A National Association for the Advancement of White People," is one of racial hate doled out with a flavoring of refinement. Membership is "restricted to white citizens." The Society denies being anti-Semitic or anti-Catholic and insists that it cannot be compared with the Klan. Indications are, however, that it is another Klan-type organization, minus only the bedsheets, the mumbo jumbo and the tar and feathers.

The Mason-Dixon Society, Inc. was founded by L. J. Dooley of Covington, Ky., for many years a Washington representative of Kentucky firms. Front man and President was Beecher Hess of Norwood, Ohio, who served as "legislative agent" for Dr. F. E. Townsend's old-age pension movement. He was employed for two years by the Republican National Committee, according to Robert L. Riggs, correspondent for the Louisville *Courier Journal*. The Society's headquarters are in Covington, home town of all its incorporators except Hess.

"Our broad purpose is to form a strong, white voting group to protect the majority of our citizens against un-American legislation," a Society leaflet reads. With this aim the Society sent a deputation to Washington to "help defeat" the "infamous" Fair Employment Practices Committee, which it denounced as "100 percent Communist." The Society bellows the holy cry of "white supremacy" and advocates the "segregation" of Negroes. It opposes loans to England, Russia, "or any other foreign country," and the "establishment of a Jewish State in Palestine" with U. S. aid. A subtle anti-Semitic tone is betrayed in one passage:

We are opposed to modern "carpet-baggers" who are attempting to obtain by law something that others earn through merit. The worst enemy of minority groups of a certain character is that group of intellectual nobodies who put themselves up as a modern "Moses," who, for a profit, will lead their paid members out of the wilderness.

Complacently, the Mason-Dixonites say:

Many of our radio commentators are constantly shouting about racial intolerance and religious intolerance. Where is this religious and racial intolerance? There is very little racial or religious intolerance in the country today. Where it does exist you will find the white carpet-bagger inciting it.

Letters under various names brought no response until I wrote Dooley as Thompson, the veteran. Two days later came a consignment of Society literature and the suggestion that I organize a Mason-Dixon Club with twenty like-minded veterans. I was surprised to read:

Our principal officers are veterans, members of the American Legion, Veterans of Foreign Wars and Disabled Veterans. Our Secretary [Virginia Bayard] is a member of the DAR.

The Society has not been the success its founders hoped. Writing the Society at its Washington branch, I received an answer from Beecher Hess on the letterhead of the Good Government Association. He explained that "the name Mason-Dixon did not lend itself to a national program" and that he had "resigned as trustee and President. Immediately a group of influential people assisted me in organizing the Good Government Association, whose objectives are much the same as those of the Mason-Dixon Society."

Hess' letter of December, 1945 enclosed a leaflet addressed to hotel and restaurant owners, exhorting them to oppose the FEPC, and urging the formation of Good Government Clubs, his own patriotic group patterned on the Mason-Dixon model. Lengthy instructions on how to organize were included. "We are seeking to give a voice to that great, unorganized majority (some 80 percent of our population) who have no representation in Washington or in State legislatures," I was informed. It seemed a large order, but apparently Beecher Hess could take it in his stride.

District of Columbia: The Society of Forward Men

Another organization resembling the Ku Klux Klan in its political objectives, though not in methods of operation, is the Society of Forward Men, organized and headed by Captain Frank S. Flynn of Washington, D. C. Still comparatively new, the Society bears a striking resemblance to the old American Cavalcade, a prewar nationalist group Captain Flynn used to conduct. Here's another instance of standard nationalist poison under a new label.

I first met Flynn when I interviewed him on July 17, 1941 aboard his large, comfortable houseboat anchored in the Potomac River at Washington. Flynn lived on the boat all year round. He was not a hermit, however, and he received a fairly comfortable monthly pension for disabilities he suffered in World War I. ("I am classed as unfit for military service now," Flynn had written me, "but I will be in the front ranks when the clean-up comes over here to reclaim this country.") On the cabin walls hung autographed pictures of Huey Long, with whom Flynn worked at one time, and Ham Fish. Flynn claims he is a direct descendant of Patrick Henry and John Marshall "of the Colonial Days." He was once associated in an editorial capacity with the political magazine *Plain Talk*.

Flynn has praised Father Coughlin and Gerald L. K. Smith in a signed article as "dynamic and able leaders." He himself is one of the most accomplished Jew-baiters I have encountered in my seven years as an investigator. Describing how a drunken driver once fractured eight of his ribs, Flynn blamed the accident on the Jews. They are also responsible, of course, for our various wars and depressions. "Asiatic Jews" have "conquered" the United States and placed Christian Americans "in subjection and under absolute domination." As führer of the American Cavalcade, Flynn urged his followers: "The stranglehold that Asiatic Jews have on Christian Americans must be broken. The influx of Asiatic Jewish refugees being dumped into every city, town and hamlet must be stopped." °

Before Pearl Harbor, Flynn circulated four pages of excerpts from *Communism in Germany,* an official Nazi document printed in Berlin, which were prefaced with a quotation from Hitler. He also peddled *War, War, War,* one of the most vicious anti-Semitic books ever published in America. His letter to me of January 22, 1941 gives an idea of his dyed-in-the-wool nationalist friends: "I am very well acquainted with George Deatherage and get a letter from him once in a while. I am acquainted with most of the leaders all over the country, Jim True, Jenkins, Lyman, Edmondson, McGuire . . . and many others, including General Moserly [*sic*]." †

Five years later, on March 28, 1946, Captain Flynn again wrote me—this time as Thompson. Flynn came forward with the Society of Forward Men. Its pledge and purposes were similar to those of the prewar American Cavalcade. The membership applications of the Cavalcade, on the other hand, were almost exactly identical with the Klan's. Flynn demanded that members be "White Gentile,"

° Statistics compiled by the U.S. Immigration and Naturalization Service show that from 1932 to 1945 about 593,000 immigrants entered the United states legally. About one third were Jews. Immigration for 1944–45 totalled 93,465. Statistics by religious preference were not kept. Our laws state that no immigrant may become a public charge: support must be guaranteed by a responsible relative or friend.

† Deatherage is under indictment for seditious conspiracy; he advocated a red-white-blue "American" swastika. True, ardently pro-Bund, is also under indictment. Newton Jenkins, now deceased, was hero of Chicago Nazis and called "Führer of the Third Party" by them. Robert Lyman, hate pamphleteer, is also under indictment. Robert E. Edmondson, strongly pro-Nazi, is under indictment. McGuire was a pal of True's.

believing "in the maintenance of White Supremacy and the principles of 'Real Americanism.' "

Among the objectives of his Society, Flynn advocated:

That all immigration to the United States shall be barred for a period of ten years.

That no foreign loans shall be made at the expense of American taxpayers.

That Communism shall be abolished and all alien Communists deported.

That no person other than native-born Americans shall hold an elective or appointive position in any Federal, State or city government in the United States.

That all of the 3,500,000 refugees that entered the United States since 1932 shall be deported to the country from whence they came.

Flynn's letter spoke of a "rich Jew of New York who has for the past several years raised several millions of dollars each year from the suckers, both Gentiles and Jews, to plant Communistic propaganda into our churches, schools. . . ." Etc, *ad nauseam* "Our organization is not only for veterans but for all red-blooded Americans," he wrote. "I am certain that if the proper men will get behind this movement and will work sincerely for the good of the country, we can whip the Jews in a very short time." His Society of Forward Men would take care of that! Flynn's letter to me went on to say:

Why, in the past few weeks . . . they have had a get-together of all religious bodies Protestant Catholic and Jewish . . . and put over the radio the speeches extolling the virtues of the Jewish race and an appeal of racial tolerance. . . . Our "Baby" in swaddling clothes is growing into a good size boy now and the outlook is very bright that he will grow into a giant before very long as the "Winds of the four corners" are carrying the message all over the U. S. and the people are just awaiting leadership and are ready for action.

I did not mention Flynn in my former book, disliking to report on a man of his professed heroism in the first World War. But his attempts to entice veterans into his hate cause make him somebody worth watching.

Tennessee: Free White Americans, Inc.

June 28, 1945 was literally "Bilbo Day" for the United States Senate. While an entire Appropriations Bill waited, the watchful lawgiver from Mississippi rode roughshod over the Senate floor in a filibuster against the appropriation for the Fair Employment Practices Committee. Denouncing Jews, Negroes, Communists, liberals, "rotten Catholics, Methodists, Baptists," and the FEPC, Bilbo applied the "Communist" smear brush to anybody who favored the Committee. "Here is a hot letter from Jellico, Tennessee," he shouted. "Not from Jericho, but Jellico. 'We most earnestly urge you to use every means at your command to block the vicious FEPC bill.' . . . It comes from C. E. Mills, National President, Free White Americans, Inc."

Bilbo's interest suggested that something was definitely wrong

American Cavalcade

To the COMMANDER-In-Chief, KNIGHTS of the AMERICAN CAVALCADE:

I, the undersigned, a native born, true and loyal citizen of the United States of America, being a white male gentile person of temperate habits, sound in mind and a believer in the tenants of the Christian religion, the maintenance of White Supremacy and the principles of "pure Americanism" fully understanding and concurring in the purpose and ideals of the AMERICAN CAVALCADE, do

most respectfully apply for membership, through Division No. ....

APPLICATION FOR CITIZENSHIP
IN THE
INVISIBLE EMPIRE

Knights of the Ku Klux Klan
(INCORPORATED)

To His Majesty the Imperial Wizard, Emperor of the Invisible Empire, Knights of the Ku Klux Klan:

I, the undersigned, a native born, true and loyal citizen of the United States of America, being a white male Gentile person of temperate habits, sound in mind and a believer in the tenets of the Christian religion, the maintenance of White Supremacy and the principles of a "pure Americanism," do most respectfully apply for membership in the Knights of the Ku Klux Klan through Klan No. ...., Realm of ....

I guarantee on my honor to conform strictly to all rules and requirements regulating my "naturalization" and the continuance of my membership, and at all times a strict and loyal obedience to your constitutional authority and the constitution and laws of the fraternity, not in conflict with the constitution and constitutional laws of the United States of America and the states thereof. If I prove untrue as a Klansman I will willingly accept as my portion whatever penalty your authority may impose. The required "klectokon" accompanies this application.

Signed.. Applicant

Endorsed by   Residence Address ....
Kl..   Business Address ....
Kl..   Date ...., 19

Note the almost identical wording in the application blank for membership in Capt. Flynn's American Cavalcade and that of the Ku Klux Klan.

with the Free White Americans. Hoping to find out what it was, exactly, I wrote them as Thompson, advocate of "white supremacy." Thomas Parrott, National Secretary, shot back an answer by air mail. The Free White Americans, Inc. were all out for "the Fifth Freedom—Freedom from indiscriminate, unwise, and unnecessary mixing of the white race with other races." They urged "the deportation of all other-colored races except the American Indian"—which meant that they wanted not only to ship thirteen million Negroes back to Africa but also to deport all Puerto Ricans, Filipinos, Chinese and others of non-Caucasian stock. "This is the only solution to our race problems," Parrott explained in his letter.

Despite these declarations, the Preamble of the Free White Americans' Constitution stated that their aims were "to encourage the daily living of the Golden Rule in all human relationships; to encourage better race feeling and cooperation; to promote peace and good will on earth!" There were some other long-range objectives, too, but by this time I was discouraged. For professional purposes I became a member of the Free White Americans; life membership costs $100 (and is certainly cheap considering the scope of the program), regular membership costs $10—the usual levy demanded by the old Klan, while for veterans only, the FWA had established a special rate of $5. Such was the desire for veteran support, or such was the group's generosity toward veterans—free, white veterans—that this was again slashed to $2.50—an unheard-of bargain price for a Klan-type body. "The national emergency now existing because of the activities of the radical elements of race, religion and politics," Parrott wrote me March 9, 1946, "requires a streamlined organization of real Americans to defeat such groups. . . . We find veterans eager to join Free White Americans."

Parrott later wrote me that "probably 50 percent" of the FWA's membership were veterans. His letter of April 16 said:

We have a Veterans committee that has no duties except to look after the welfare of Veterans. Local Posts accept Veterans at half the usual entrance fee. In all things they receive special consideration. . . . Some posts have special Veterans groups for Patrol units, etc.

. . . We are making a special effort to obtain as many veterans in our ranks as possible. . . . We mean to use every legal, peaceful, economic and political method at our command to gain our objectives.

A copy of *The Practice of Klanishness,* "First Lesson in the Science and Art of Klancraft," shows the kind of gibberish of which members of the nightshirt empire are victims. "Imperial Instructions Document No. 1, Series AD 1924, AK LVIII" (Year of the Klan) is explained as "Being Official Instructions in K-uno in the border Realm of Karacter from the one who traversed the Realm of the Unknown, wrested the solemn Secret from the grasp of Night and became the Imperial Master of the great lost Mystery."

The gent who did this and "who out of Mystic Darkness brings Light" was Hiram W. Evans, second Imperial Wizard, who bought the Klan in 1922 for a cool $90,000. The Klan Kreed gives instructions in "Physical, Social, Moral, Vocational, Patriotic, Domestic, Racial, Imperial Klanishness." It ends with:

Catch the Vision! You are no ordinary man. You are a K-L-A-N-S-M-A-N! Let this thought obsess you, then when the portal shall be opened to admit you to the Peerage of Knighthood in the Invisible Empire you will be found worthy to enter therein, pass the great K-duo in the Mystic Realm of Kourage and take your place in the greatest Order of Chivalry in all history. Ponder well all these things which I have spoken to YOU as coming from the hidden recesses of a soul unselfish communing with its God for the betterment of its fellows. . . .

Done in the Aulik of His Majesty, the Imperial Wizard, Emperor of the Invisible Empire in the Imperial Palace, in the Imperial City of Atlanta, Commonwealth of Georgia, United States of America, this the Third day of the Sixth Month of the Year of Our Lord Nineteen Hundred and Twenty-four, and on the Dismal day of the Woeful week of the Gloomy month of the Year of the Klan LVIII, and of the Year of the Reincarnation IX. Officially uttered, inscribed, signed, sealed, communicated and committed to you in the sacred unfailing bond.

H. W. Evans

Evans' and Colescott's Klan with its tar and feathering and lynching orgies is gradually emerging into a modern, "nationalist" counterpart stressing an "America First" policy. The ultra-modern Klansman will not publicly admit that he is anti-Catholic, anti-Semitic or even anti-Negro. He will shout that he stands for "pure" Christian, American, Protestant "white supremacy." He advocates "pure nationalism."

The South alone should not be blamed for the Klan. Men like Rankin, Bilbo, Eastland, Talmadge and O'Daniel give the South a blacker eye than it deserves. Talmadge himself, for example, has been criticized for serving the interests of Northern absentee power, textile, and railroad concerns which, in carpet-bagger fashion, have helped to impoverish the South. Writing of Talmadge's victory in the Georgia Democratic primaries in July, 1946, Thomas L. Stokes points out:

Big interests generally want a low wage economy and subservient workers. They don't want workers organized, which makes them more independent economically and politically. Nor do they want the franchise spread to Negroes, as it was in this election by Gov. Arnall's staunch stand backing up the Supreme Court's edict against the white primary.

So Talmadge raised the racial issue crying "nigger, nigger" all over this state, appealing to prejudice and ignorance, and also howling about Yankee interference. It never seems to get through to so many that the industrial overlords who represent Yankee interests are using them as dupes.

Some old-style industrial "barons" are still inclined to treat the South as a colony for the production of raw materials. Discriminatory railroad rates have added to its burden. The South is finally waking to a realization of its strength and of factors which have weakened it. Governor Arnall's successful action in obtaining a reduction of railroad rates is one of the many signs of a renaissance. Reforms are slow, however, and the habits of generations do not change overnight.

There are those who consider it profitable to divide the South so that it cannot rise up in strength. No more effective way of dividing a people has been discovered than through the creation of fear, hate and prejudice. Take a man of normal, humane instincts and instill all three into him, and you have made a Klansman of him.

That is partly why the complexion of the Klan is strongly anti-union, why in coming months it will organize vigilante squads and terrorize AFL and particularly CIO organizers in answer to their plans to organize the South. The Klan can be expected to crack the heads of many Americans of all creeds whom they label "Jewish, Communist, alien agitators," and to oppose sorely needed economic and political reforms.

Early in June, 1946, for example, Willie Dudley, AFL member employed in a clay pit at Gordon, Ga., was abducted by four masked and armed Klansmen and severely beaten with a rubber hose for refusing to resign from the union. According to a news report, "they told Dudley they intended to keep Negroes from joining the union and for him to tell the union representative they would get him next." The union had succeeded in getting an eight-cent raise, establishing a fifty-cent hourly wage.

Booker T. Washington said: "One cannot hold another down in the ditch without staying down in the ditch with him—and in helping the man who is down to rise, the man who is up is freeing himself from a burden that would also drag him down."

Only the extension of democracy can lift the South from its poverty. Keeping Negroes away from the polls helps drag whites down. On the eve of the Mississippi primaries in June, 1946 Senator Bilbo made one of the strongest "white supremacy" statements of his career, calling on every "red-blooded, Anglo-Saxon man in Mississippi to resort to *any means* to keep hundreds of Negroes from the polls. And if you don't know what that means, you are just not up on your persuasive measures."

Bilbo's statement came after Etoy Fletcher, a Negro veteran attending Jackson College under the GI Bill of Rights, charged in an affidavit that he had been flogged after going to the Circuit clerk at Brandon, Miss., and asking to register to vote. A United Press dispatch reported that Fletcher was threatened with death if he made another attempt to register.

Not to be outdone by Bilbo, Rankin—member of a Congressional committee to investigate un-Americanism—urged Negroes to forsake their Constitutional rights. "I appeal to the law-abiding Negro to refrain from attempting to participate in the white primaries," he said.

The reason is obvious. Once the Negroes vote, Rankin, Bilbo and their ilk stand to be voted out—to the betterment of the South, the Congress and America at large. The Klansman's lash keeps the Bilbos in office, as the Gestapo whip did Hitler.

According to Walter White, Secretary of the National Association for the Advancement of Colored People, repeated instances of mob violence which, peculiarly enough, seem directed at Negro veterans, are due to a systematic attempt to cow the Negro. "Evidence in-

creasingly points to a well organized and determined drive to terrorize . . . Negro veterans in an effort to make them believe that they
must not expect or demand any change in their status from that
which existed before they went overseas to defend and preserve
democracy," Mr. White said. "I fear that we are in for increasingly
dark days unless the Federal government, prodded by an aroused
public opinion, stops talking and actually does something to curb
these outbreaks which, unless curbed, will spread like a prairie fire."

Colescott knew that the Klan would carry on after the war. "I
don't know what form it will take," he said. The form is suggested
by Parrott's phrase: "streamlined organization" to defeat "radical
elements of race, religion and politics."

Streamlined hate, streamlined white supremacy, streamlined
bigotry!

To all this the veteran who fought hate and bigotry side by side
with his Negro buddies is now exposed. Together they faced fascist
bullets overseas. Together they are now facing fascist-inspired bullets at home. The "American" bullets are not manufactured in hard
copper casings. They come marked "Made in America." They are
wrapped in red-white-blue cellophane.

CHAPTER FOUR

Marching as to War

Americans, I turn to the America First Party as the only hope of salvation for a free America. I was a member of the Ku Klux Klan and I expect to renew my membership at the earliest possible date. . . . Both the Democratic and Republican parties seem to be under Jewish control. Therefore we must have a new party line in America.

Rev. William L. Blessing

MY "FAN MAIL" in March, 1944 included the following provocative letter:

This is from a soldier in the army of the U.S.A. I don't have a colledge education but I have had a grade school and Night School education and I beleive I know right from wrong . . . Your not fit to lick the boots of some of the people you slandered and lied about in your article [meaning the book *Under Cover*].

Mrs. Elizabeth Dilling is a personal friend of mine and if it were possible to meet you face to face I beleive I would receive a great deal of pleasure out of kicking in your teeth. That is not a threat, it is simply a wish.

Pvt. J. F. McManoman, Camp Shelby, Miss.

Ten months later his father, Frank McManoman, wrote me an abusive letter. He didn't think me "fit to lace the boots" of such "good Christian Americans" as Father Coughlin and Mrs. Dilling. Father and son aroused my curiosity. I wanted to know if the father was responsible for the behavior of his son and whether the son would carry through his wish to kick my teeth in.

On the night of February 1, 1946 I rang the doorbell of their home in Waukegan, Ill. I was alone and unarmed. I had never been afraid of the worst of the Nazi underworld goons. After eight years it's a bit late to begin being afraid.

77

I announced myself as Carlson.

"Wait here, I'll get Jim," Mrs. McManoman said. While she went inside, I waited in the living room. It had inexpensive furniture but it was neatly kept. "Here he is," Mrs. McManoman said, following her son in.

Jim was a husky, strongly built youth in his early twenties, wearing woolen Army trousers with the cuffs pulled into large rubber boots, and a leather windbreaker which increased his bulk. As soon as he saw me he began to take off his gloves. His face took on a surly look. He put the gloves under his left arm and I noticed his hands—large, red, bony and raw. I kept watching McManoman's eyes. What does one do when confronted by a husky youth who wants to kick your teeth in? You just stay there, alert for any move.

I broke the ice. "Why did you write me that letter?" I asked.

The answer came in a throaty voice: "Because you told lies about Father Coughlin and Mrs. Dilling." Despite his austere appearance, Jim wasn't a mean guy. I could see he was just gullible.

Mrs. McManoman proved to be the pepper pot in the household. She dominated the interview while Jim sat back and watched the fireworks. A short, plumpish woman in her forties, she snapped at me: "That man Birkhead of the Friends of Democracy that you work with—he's a Red Communist skunk, that's what he is." I reminded her that Rev. Birkhead was a minister of the Unitarian Church, a man who had no sympathy whatever with Communism.

"He ain't no Christian. And neither are you. I don't care how often you go to church, you're no Christian."

"What do you think of Mrs. Dilling?" I teased, to test her reaction.

"She's the greatest Christian woman in America," she burst out.

"But she's under indictment for sedition."

"That's because of the likes of you. That's why. You put her there." Her anger was mounting.

"Why blame me? I had nothing to do with it. The Department of Justice indicted her after two years' investigation. Go tell them. Don't jump on me."

From the kitchen came the voice of Mr. McManoman, Sr. "If that's Carlson have nothing to do with him! Throw him out!" he shouted to his wife. But McManoman didn't come out. Mrs. McManoman held the fort. With that acid tongue which characterizes many Coughlinites, she lashed at everyone who criticized "the greatest Christian woman in America."

"They hung men like Pétain [she confused him with Laval] and let skunks like you and Birkhead live. Where's justice in that?"

Mrs. McManoman ranted on about "good Jews like that man Henry Klein who is defending Sanctuary at the sedition trial. But the Jewish leaders," she declared, "they're no good. Take it from me!"

I cut my visit short. I had come to give Jim McManoman the opportunity to carry through his wish and to see what made him that way. I had my answer. Jim stood by while his mother elaborated on her views. His parents meant well in their own way, but themselves were victimized by the cleric whose portrait hung on the wall: Father Coughlin. Through his Christian Front and *Social Justice*, both of which wielded enormous influence, Father Coughlin has poisoned more good Christians than any other American fascist. I am reminded of this sinister force whenever I meet simple, impressionable, politically uninformed folk like the McManomans.

Wanting to find out whether Coughlin was going to "come back," I wrote him in a rough scrawl as Thompson, the "Christian veteran" who used to read *Social Justice* every week "before I went into the Army." I also corresponded with him from another city under the name of an imaginary civilian. In July, 1945 Coughlin sent me a medal "for my brother" in the Army.* Accompanying the leaflet, "St. Sebastian, the Soldier Saint," was the information I wanted:

I am only too happy to send you particulars regarding membership in the St. Sebastian Brigade. It means the boys in service are enjoying mementos in all our special prayers and Masses for their safe return. It also means that over seven hundred school children (of this parish) include them in their prayers. . . . There is no set fee for these enrollments but we do receive contributions.

Through his St. Sebastian Brigade, Coughlin has piled up a list of several hundred thousand servicemen. From his Church at Royal Oak, Mich., he keeps in touch with them directly or through their parents.

* Actually, I have two younger brothers who served overseas, one as sergeant, the other, who was decorated twice, as a captain.

Will Coughlin someday organize the St. Sebastian Legion, patterned after his Christian Front hoodlums? I tried to find out. Writing to me as "Dear Bob," he denied any present political plans and said he couldn't return to the radio as petitioned to do by his friends.

I have not corresponded with Mr. Gerald Smith nor have I had occasion to talk to him. Without knowledge to me, my name was placed on the leaflet. Mr. Smith neither investigated the possibilities of my returning from a political angle, from a financial angle, nor did he look into the ecclesiastical angle. . . . I do not want to appear to be ignoring your other inquiries, but I must advise you that I cannot discuss political problems in my correspondence.

Coughlin asked me to join his League of the Little Flower, into which he was channeling his veteran friends like McManoman. This is the same League for which Coughlin collected thousands of dollars prior to Pearl Harbor. Coughlin never lacked funds for "Christian" hate work and the formation of his political party, the National Union for Social Justice.

Is Coughlin eventually planning a comeback? Indications are that he may do so "at the right time." Coughlinites are urging that his name be kept alive. Monsignor Osais Boucher, for example, told a Boston audience who had gathered to celebrate Coughlin's birthday in 1945: "I congratulate you on your loyalty to Father Coughlin and his principles. Let me give you some advice—always remind people of him. We don't have enough men of that type."

Certainly Father Coughlin is hard at work cultivating veteran good will. One of his letters to me ended: "Write me often, Robert, and let me know how things are going with you. I shall be looking forward to your mail." On July 11 Father Coughlin acknowledged receipt of my contribution to the League of the Little Flower and expressed the comforting thought that I would "be remembered in the weekly masses offered on Calvary Hill, Jerusalem."

Father Edward Lodge Curran, priest of St. Joseph's Church in Brooklyn and President of the International Catholic Truth Society, has been referred to in many articles and speeches as the "Father Coughlin of the East." In 1940, when seventeen Christian Fronters were arrested and charged with a plot to overthrow our government, Father Curran spoke at meetings held in their defense. I heard him speak on February 2, 1940 at Columbus Hall, Brooklyn, at a meeting sponsored by the Parents Defense Fund of the Christian Front. Curran spoke together with Jack Cassidy, ringleader of the revolutionary Christian Front "Sports Club" and John Henihan, Jr., Bronx leader of the Christian Front. The bigoted, so-called "Christian" Front, which was founded by Father Coughlin in 1938, may be described as a private army of American storm troopers, certain units of which were trained in the use of violence and exhorted to fight against democracy "in Franco's way." Many of Curran's special articles and speeches were reprinted in Coughlin's *Social Justice*.

On February 11, 1941, and again on November 15—just three weeks before Pearl Harbor—Curran addressed members of the Holy Name Society of Our Lady of Perpetual Help in Richmond Hill, N. Y. The Brooklyn *Tablet,* official diocesan organ, quoted him:

The Lend-Lease Dictatorship Bill . . . is unconstitutional in its entirety and in its parts. It is unconstitutional . . . in its entirety because it is a dictatorial and unwarranted demand by the President.

The war party in Washington does not dare . . . explain the provocative words which have been constantly hurled against Japan. What, then, is the reason for all the manufactured trouble with Japan? There is only one answer. . . . Our foreign policy of provocation is immoral!

In the last six years I have heard him speak, I have never heard him advocate world cooperation. The average Curran speech has included an array of diatribes against "internationalism" and pleas for nationalism. On January 31, 1942 he was reported shouting from the stage of a Knights of Columbus meeting in Boston: "I'm still an isolationist!" On November 25, 1944 he wrote in *The Gaelic American:* "Any American political leader who would rush the American nation into any postwar world security organization . . . is a traitor to Americanism." He has decried the Bretton Woods Agreement, the San Francisco Conference, the United Nations.

After Pearl Harbor, Father Curran continued to speak at functions held for Father Coughlin's financial benefit, mainly in Boston. In February, 1944 he spoke at the Chicago Citizens U.S.A. Committee whose chairman, Earl Southard, had also sponsored Gerald Smith meetings and was a leading figure in Smith's America First Party. The audience of Chicago nationalists applauded Curran wildly. In March, 1945 Gerald L. K. Smith reprinted a part of his speech, calling it a "dramatic and intelligent address." Smith considers Father Curran a "distinguished" man.

In November, 1945 Father Curran participated in a so-called "Save America Rally" called in defense of Tyler Kent. Among those present I recognized many faces familiar to me from meetings of the old Christian Front. The meeting was arranged with the help of John Henihan, Jr., World War II vet and the former Bronx Christian Front leader, who sat in the same box with Father Curran at the Friends of Frank Fay rally in January, 1946. It's reported that Henihan is being groomed for leadership "at the right time." At the "Save America" meeting I heard Father Curran denounce world cooperation and the UN as the work of "internationalist dreamers." He opposed a loan to Britain, France or "any other European country." He blamed Churchill for "getting us into the war," but remained mum on Tojo and Hitler. After a blistering attack on Russia, he alleged that "Reds run our State Department"; he wanted them "cleaned out." He also wanted Stalin tried as a "war criminal."

I have noticed that whenever Father Curran speaks in the presence of his superiors he is politically well behaved. Such an instance was his address before the Knights of Columbus in New York City on January 17, 1941, with Monsignor Martin Fitzpatrick present. Again, at the Laymen's Retreat League dinner in Brooklyn, on October 23, 1940 when Bishop Thomas J. Molloy was present, Curran was a model speaker. I attended both meetings.

No one denies Father Curran the right to speak his mind. As a priest, however, he has certain moral obligations. I do not believe that the preachment of defeatism, disunity, hatred toward our Allies, and derision of efforts for world cooperation is the proper function of a Christian cleric. I emphasize that I have no quarrel with Father Curran as priest. My quarrel is with the political views of Edward Lodge Curran. By the same token, I have no quarrel with any priest or minister mentioned in this chapter. I object to the politicians who carry on in His name.

Coughlin denies having any political plans, yet, among the currents in American political thought, Coughlinism—with its fanatical nationalism, its racial intolerance, its adoration of Franco, its fear of organized labor, its distrust of international collaboration—flows on unabated. Indeed, cities like St. Louis, Philadelphia, Detroit and New York are witnessing its sinister resurgence.

Like the intolerance of Father Coughlin, anti-Catholicism kept alive by artificial methods reaches out in the name of Christ, preaching hate in the guise of love. Los Angeles is headquarters for the Christian War Veterans of America, Inc. It's an ultra-religious, evangelistic, Fundamentalist group. Applicants are required to attest that they "believe in the Scriptures of the Old and New Testaments as having been supernaturally inspired of God, and that they were inerrant in the original writing and are the supreme and final authority in faith and practice."

Belief in the absolute authority and "literal" interpretation of the Bible represents one basic distinction between the Fundamentalist Protestant and the modernist who takes a broader attitude. Most modernists accept the scientific explanation of evolution. They regard the story of the "six days," with God resting on the "seventh day," as symbolic of a process which required millions of years. The Fundamentalists pride themselves on taking the Scriptures literally, yet elaborate and ingenious interpretations of obscure passages sometimes buttress their theology.

America's Fundamentalists may be roughly divided into two categories. Perhaps we may call them, for the sake of convenience, the "Moderates" and the "Extremists." By Extremists I refer only to that bigoted fringe who brazenly teach that the Roman Catholic Church is "false" and "anti-Christian." Their un-American intolerance and disregard for fact make the subject an unpleasant one to discuss. As a believer in the basic American doctrine of freedom of worship, however, I feel compelled to face this particular form of intolerance in a book dedicated to the cause of tolerance for Americans of all races, national backgrounds and creeds.

This chapter does not apply to the moderate Fundamentalists. To draw another distinction for the sake of clarity, the Moderates feel that "salvation" of the Jews and other non-Christian peoples can be achieved through missionary endeavors. The Extremists seem to consider such methods a waste of time and to assume, tacitly or openly, the attitude that the Jews' souls can be "saved" only through persecution and slander. Politically, the Extremists incline toward nationalism and some of their clergy and laity labor busily in the political vineyard, cultivating the grapes of wrath. The Extremist wing includes Rev. Gerald B. Winrod and others. Most rank-

and-file Extremists are impressionable folk, living largely in the Midwest and the "Bible Belt."

References to Fundamentalists from this point are to the Extremists. They do not reflect in the least upon the clergy or members of those Fundamentalist churches which, more truly Christian, believe in the Golden Rule and the philosophy of "live and let live." Our argument is with un-Christian Extremists who spread religious and racial intolerance. It is also with those who, ridiculing democracy, wish to substitute for it political authoritarianism not dissimilar to European brands. Democratic Americans reject both as thoroughly un-American. Religious dogma obviously has no place in our political institutions. That politics must be distinct from religion and from the Army is a fundamental of the American way.

As Thompson, the Protestant veteran, I corresponded with National Commander George C. Little and Assistant Adjutant N. C. Parsons of the Fundamentalist Christian War Veterans of America. In his letter of October 16, 1945 Parsons explained that only those could join who could furnish satisfactory evidence of being "born-again" Christians "according to the third chapter of John."

"We are not bigoted," he said smugly, "for we realize there is but one crowd going to Heaven and they are those who come to Him on His terms, not their own or through church ritual."

Commander Little was explicit in his ill-advised views on Catholics:

I, personally, am alarmed at the seeming hold on national affairs the Catholics seem to be getting. For instance, they have news in the papers all the time, and it is next to impossible for our organization to get news printed. . . . As yet the Christian War Veterans of America has not done anything to "curb their power," but one thing we are doing constantly is to pray and tell of the saving grace of Jesus Christ. The time may come when we feel that a definite course of action must be taken, but until then work, testify, and pray is all we are doing. . . .

The CWVA has been heartily endorsed by the *Congregational Beacon,* Extreme Fundamentalist monthly which subscribes to Gerald Smith's *Nationalist News Service.* The *Beacon* has published advertisements of *The Constitutionalist,* whose columns are filled with Jew-baiting articles, of *The Converted Catholic,* bitterly critical of the Roman Catholic Church, and the books of anti-Catholic Rev. L. J. King.

I attended the convention of the CWVA at the Calvary Baptist Church in New York, in March, 1946. About sixty "born-again" veterans were present, including four women. A "born-again" Christian resembles any other Christian or Jew. You can't tell the difference until he begins to talk. Then you find yourself confronted with a zealous missionary determined to "win" your soul. The convention was like a revivalist meeting. Speakers gave "testimony" on how they had been "born again" and how they had accepted personal salvation. Some spoke as if in a trance. The CWVA was termed "an organization that's out and out for Christ, organized to bring Christians together again." Satan was damned all over the lot.

One of the speakers was a member of the Aaron Post 788, American Legion, Chicago. He said the Legion hadn't satisfied him spiritually; the other Legionnaires were "too worldly," an "ungodly crew." He and some kindred spirits had founded the Aaron Post where they now met in "true Christian fellowship." All were "born-again Christians." The Legion, the speaker admitted, had been unwilling to give them a charter because of some members' attitude toward Catholics. But nevertheless he naively explained, "Anyone can join the Aaron Post—Negroes, Jews, Catholics—as long as they are 'born-again' Christians." He laughed. "The Legion didn't know what to make of it so they let us have the charter anyway!"

Major J. D. Pinkerton edits *The Gospel Fundamentalist,* Extremist magazine published in Leesville, La. In 1945 I wrote him while he was still in the army. He replied as follows:

As far as I am concerned Popery has corrupted the truth, persecuted the saints of God, advanced arrogant and blasphemous claims, assumed universal dominion, and adopted the principles and practices of a great harlot. Up to the present time I have not felt safe in saying too much about it . . . due to my military connections. But I am expecting the day to come soon when I can really speak out against it.

After being released from active service, Pinkerton lost no time in going into Pope-baiting. I learned this when I wrote him again as Thompson, the Extreme Fundamentalist veteran. He sent me a copy of his magazine and a long, revealing letter:

I have just been released from military duty after more than five years service as an army finance officer paying troops and for supplies and services. . . . I started *The Gospel Fundamentalist* a year ago in my spare time while I was performing full military duty, and have had to be rather careful what I published so as to avoid trouble with the military authorities. But now that I am again a civilian I hope to open on both the Communists and the Pope via sermons by some high calibre writers.

Major Pinkerton's magazine is filled with the usual Extreme Fundamentalist articles. A "Prayer Request Department," by Brother Henry, claimed that Mrs. Bessie B. Bopp's broken rib was healed in three days. (Mrs. Bopp's photograph was printed.) An "anointed cloth" sent by mail assertedly cured a woman of *cancer!* Others suffering from gall-bladder trouble, "tormenting spirits and diarrhea," were fixed up by Brother Henry's ministrations. And, too, a wife-deserter returned home!

The Gospel Fundamentalist, well filled with advertising, carried a half-page ad by Dr. Dan Gilbert, Director of the Christian Press Bureau. Headquarters of the Bureau are the Washington offices of the *National Republic* magazine, edited by super-patriot Walter S. Steele.* Side by side with Gilbert's ad were those of three vitriolic

* Fundamentalist Gilbert solicits subscriptions for the *National Republic,* which Steele calls "a magazine of fundamental Americanism." Steele has recommended Rev. Curran as an "expert on Communism," and defended Father Coughlin and his Christian Front. He regards most progressive, non-Communist Americans as "Reds," and has collaborated closely with Mrs. Dilling in the publication of "patriotic" books.

Steele testified before the Dies Committee on "Communism." One of his fund solicitors exploited that testimony, according to the Kansas City, Mo. Better Business Bureau. Its bulletin of October 26, 1942 charged that Steele's "representative, V. W. Carrington," in selling subscriptions to *National Republic* and other "patriotic" Steele literature to businessmen, also stated that the literature had the approval of Dr. Harold C. Hunt, Superintendent of Schools. Businessmen could subscribe in the following amounts: $7.50, $22.50, $45 and $75. Subscription to the magazine is $2 a year.

According to the Better Business Bureau release, Carrington solicited funds in units of $7.50, each unit to pay for the mailing of Steele's literature to a public school teacher in the Kansas City system. Dr. Hunt strongly denied authorizing Carrington to use his name, stating that he had only had an interview with the solicitor. Following complaints about Carrington's methods, the Kansas City Police Department investigated. The Bureau report stated: "In a special meeting of the . . . Welfare Board, October 21, a resolution was passed commending the Police Department for stopping the unlicensed and unauthorized solicitation."

Robert E. Stripling, chief investigator of the Dies Committee, wired the Better Business Bureau on October 14: "There is no connection between this Committee and the *National Republic* of Washington, D.C. No individual or agency is authorized to solicit funds under the pretext that they are aiding the Dies Committee."

foes of Catholicism: Rev. L. J. King, Toledo; *The Sword and Shield,*
a paper edited by Dr. Wallace Winford Bradley in Portland, Ore.;
and Dr. J. A. Lovell, Los Angeles. Major Pinkerton offered subscribers a booklet by Rev. Harvey H. Springer, Colorado "Cowboy
Evangelist," another Protestant on the warpath.

Evangelist L. J. King describes himself as an "Ex-Romanist, formerly of New Brunswick, Canada—Champion and Defender of the
Protestant Christian Religion." His Protestant Book House in Toledo issues an amazing variety of such works as *Popery, the Devil's
Masterpiece.* It handles books in the literary tradition of the long
since discredited Maria Monk, heavy in lurid tales of grisly goings-
on in convent and monastery. "Priest Poisons Roman Widow and
Son. . . . Rome and Ruin." A four-page tract advertises King's "new
book," *House of Death, or Convent Brutality,* promising in breath-
less style "Horrible and blood-curdling revelations of convent life.
. . . Poison, Murder, Rapine, Torturing and smothering babies"—all
for $1.50. It's a book—

Exposing Rome's Heathen, Pagan, Un-natural, Un-American Convent
System. . . . See nun bound hand and foot, gagged lying in dungeon
because she refused to obey a priest. See the nun who struck priest with
an ax . . . and killed him. Cincinnati nunnery. See photo of nun shot by a
Roman thug, bullet passing through her hat—riding in carriage under
guard. . . . Read of two nuns who crawled nearly a mile in sewer under
City of Detroit; captured and forced back into "House of Death" again.

THE GOSPEL FUNDAMENTALIST!

expose the papal system and all its evil doings. As far as I am
concerned Popery has corrupted the truth, persecuted the saints of
God, advanced arrogant and blasphemous claims, assumed universal dominion, and adopted the principles and practices of a great harlot.
Up to the present time I have not felt safe in saying too much about
it in my new gospel magazine, The Gospel Fundamentalist, due to my
military connections. But am expecting the day to come soon when I
can really speak out against it.

        Yours for God and humanity,
                                        J. D. Pinkerton, Editor

King has political ideas, too. "Get the book and read it," his leaflet urges, "then go to the polls and vote this Romish curse out of the land. . . . In Jesus' name move quickly." Canada, King complains in the leaflet, has barred the book from the country.

King contributes articles to *The Sword and Shield*. Dr. Bradley, its editor, is "utterly opposed to the diabolical teaching" of Catholicism. I wrote him, asking which Protestant veterans' group I should join. Bradley replied by asking whether I felt "a call to the ministry and would like a fellowship with a Protestant fundamentalist organization of ministers." I hadn't felt any such call, but as Thompson I could adapt myself to almost anything, so I played along and asked Bradley for more information. Bradley wrote back enthusiastically. He needed a "young man to assume the responsibility of circulation and advertising manager of our publication."

I wrote that I didn't think I'd better leave home. I thought it best to stick to the ministry. "I used to teach Sunday School" I said, and while in the Army "used to hold prayer services." This must have pleased Dr. Bradley, for he wrote me on stationery of The Federated Full Gospel Assemblies of the U.S.A., Inc., and offered to make me an honest-to-goodness minister overnight for only $6.

I was amazed at the ease with which I could have been ordained as a "licensed minister" of the Federated Full Gospel Assemblies. I should only have needed to pay $6, start using the title of "Reverend" or "Pastor," hire a hall and start preaching and taking up collections. And I'd have been exempt from most taxes: all religious groups are. I wouldn't have had to report my earnings, expenses or other business to anyone. Had I decided to throw in my lot with the intolerant brethren, the Be-a-Minister-Quick scheme could easily have led me to get-rich-quick schemes. (These daydreams imply no reflections, naturally, upon real, qualified ministers of the Gospel.)

Dr. J. A. Lovell's advertisement in Major Pinkerton's *The Gospel Fundamentalist* carried a letter from the "wife of a serviceman" reading: "*The Kingdom Digest* makes me feel so much closer to our Lord and inspires me to be a better Christian. I send clippings from your magazine to my husband and I know he gets help and guidance from them." I've never been able to understand how anyone can get "inspiration" and comfort from Dr. Lovell's *The Kingdom Digest*, which prints such bigotry as:

Someone speaks of the Roman Catholic Church as a "great branch of the Christian Church." I deny it. It is not Christian: it is anti-Christian. It is not of God: it is of the devil. It is not of heaven: it is of hell. Call it "Christian?" Never. . . . I repeat, there is no language too strong to exaggerate the evil of this thing, and when you admit for a moment that the Roman Catholic Church is a Christian institution, you have surrendered the field. It is not!

Dr. Lovell has numerous GI and ex-GI readers. He quoted a letter from a GI in Italy who spent his spare time "reading and enjoying your literature." A Navy man wrote: "I enclose $20 as a token of my appreciation, and that of my buddies, for your splendid magazine." Dr. Lovell's poison pellets had really taken hold of the GI who wrote, "If you could be here in Italy and see how the people have been held in subjection, you would preach with more force the interpretation that holds that the Catholic Church is anti-Christ." Lovell didn't need to make the trip. His veteran readers were treated to this double-barrelled attack against Jews and Catholics:

The Federated Full Gospel Assemblies of USA, Incorporated
PORTLAND 6, OREGON

Dear Brother Thompson,   January 22, 1946

We have your letter of January 18th and in reply thereto briefly will say that we could give you a license as a licensed minister. This only costs $6.00 a year and includes a years subscription to our paper as well. You would not be required to take any course of instructions or study as long as you are a born-again christian and feel led to do some work for the Lord in the way of teaching, witnessing, or even preaching to some extent.

Yours in Christ,

THE FEDERATED FULL GOSPEL ASSEMBLIES OF USA, Inc.

W. Bradley

General Secy-Treas.

Dr. Bradley offers to issue a license to practice as a minister for only $6. The bargain price includes a year's subscription to the anti-Catholic magazine, *The Sword and Shield*.

In reality they [Jews] are the Black Sheep of the House of Israel, the Problem Child, stiff-necked and rebellious, and as a thorn in the flesh of God's Chosen People. . . . The very name "Vatican" itself reveals that the Roman Catholic System, through its titular head, the Pope, actually represents the system, or people, responsible for slaying or killing the mighty prophet, Jesus, the Christ. Instead they have instituted their own false church, thus they are called the whore, or the mother of harlots. Legally, it was the Romans who crucified the Lord. Actually, it was the Jews. Both bear the responsibility.

But Lovell modestly insists: "I am not anti-Semitic, nor am I anti-Jew, for I have love and a respect for all races, creeds and colors. . . . I have many Catholic friends. I am very tolerant, kind and charitable."

He is also influential. In six years Dr. Lovell has distributed 350,-000 copies of his *Kingdom Digest* and tons of leaflets, brochures and tracts. He lectures widely. He speaks over a network of radio stations. In 1945, according to figures given in *The Kingdom Digest* for January, 1946, his organization conducted 535 fifteen-minute radio broadcasts. They got responses from listeners in 33 states. Approximately 60,000 attended their 131 local church services. A fund-raising appeal in the same issue stated, "Our budget is approximately $4,000 a month."

Lovell is highly veteran conscious. When I wrote him as Thompson he answered promptly, offering to send me *The Kingdom Digest* free. There is a reason for Lovell's saccharine attitude toward veterans. His editorial, "Veterans to Run the U.S.A.," asked that "when the veterans take over" they "demand a housecleaning of all subversive activities." One can glean what Lovell wants from his standards of "Americanism." Together with Klansman Swift, Dr. Lovell served on the Committee of California Pastors, which backed Gerald L. K. Smith's meetings to promote a new, totalitarian "America First" political party.

In Los Angeles, the tolerant and super-patriotic Dr. Lovell directs the United Israel Fellowship. It follows the teachings of the Anglo-Saxon—British-Israel movement, one of the craziest of the religious and racialist cults. The leadership of this fantastic movement is primarily vested in the Anglo-Saxon Federation, with headquarters in Haverhill, Mass. It holds that the Anglo-Saxons are the Israelites, chosen by God to lead other nations. The Jews, it seems, are not

Israel at all, but a bastard mixture of Edomites, Hittites, Canaanites, etc., who weren't included in God's scheme.

The Anglo-Saxon Federation bases its beliefs on its own distorted interpretation of the Bible, the passages in the Great Pyramid, the stars and the "science of numerics." Its director, Howard B. Rand,* expounds the fiction that Christ was not a Jew. "As a matter of fact," he throws in, "neither were Abraham, Isaac, Jacob, Joseph nor Moses Jews." Never—they were Anglo-Saxon Israelites! The Twelve Apostles, with the exception of Judas, weren't Jews either. The distinction between "Jews" of the Judas tribe and "Israel" provides a convenient excuse for blistering attacks against Jewry. That Jews are Communists, and vice versa, is also among the most sacred directives of the cult. The implication is that Anglo-Saxons, being true Israel, can't be Communists.

All this mumbo jumbo is intended to prove the "superiority" of the Anglo-Saxons as a "chosen" Aryan people with the exclusive right to enter into a covenant with God! No other people are entitled to such an aspiration.

Spearhead of the Federation is dour, bald, fiftyish Howard B. Rand, who edits its magazine, *Destiny*. The Federation has carried on quietly since 1928, selling the *Protocols* and an enormous volume of other literature. Since V-J Day its screwball philosophy has mushroomed to an amazing extent throughout the country. It regards itself as a "religion," but is not a religious institution in the ordinary sense. Howard Rand seems hardly more a churchman than a hustling salesman. Actually, the Federation is engaged in espousing a new "Master Race" theory manufactured in America. This

---

* Rand has accused me of making misstatements in *Under Cover* against his cult's teachings. When I urged him, in two registered letters, to provide proof of his charge, Rand refused to amplify.

Anglo-Saxon Federation of America
NATIONAL HEADQUARTERS
HAVERHILL, MASSACHUSETTS 7233
This is to Certify that *Robert Thompson, Jr.*
of *Buffalo, N. Y.* has paid the Annual Fee
for Regular Membership in the
Anglo-Saxon Federation
of America
for Year ending *August 1947*
NATIONAL COMMISSIONER

Membership Certificate
1946
This certifies that
Robert Thompson, Jr.
is a member of
The United Israel Fellowship
A National Organization, for more effectively Spreading the Gospel of the Kingdom
(This in no way obligates the bearer, nor interferes with his membership elsewhere) I A LOVELL, *President and Founder* Los Angeles 53, California

myth has attracted some extremely wealthy patrons and considerable numbers of "Park Avenue" fascists. *Destiny* is an expensively
printed magazine. In addition, Rand publishes a number of books,
some of which sell for as much as $8.25—with plenty of buyers
among the master-racialists.

Rand looks upon the FEPC as a device "to elevate aliens to positions of control over industrious Americans by means of Gestapo
methods." Rand has prophesied the doom of democracy, which he
has denounced (as did the Nazis) as "mobocracy." "The present
conflict," he wrote before Pearl Harbor, "is in the plan of God, for
the purpose of completely smashing democratic forms of government for all time! . . . When the present conflict ends, democracies
will be a thing of the past, never again to be restored as a form of
human government." After Pearl Harbor he insisted that "true democracy is the predecessor of tyranny and suppression." He is no
gentler and no more accurate on the Catholic Church, regarding it
as putting forth "blasphemous pretensions worse than Imperial
Rome did in pagan days. . . . The Cardinals kiss the feet of the
Pope. . . . This is nothing else than paganism baptized and is blasphemous in the sight of God."

Rand's widely advertised book, *Study in Revelation*, was one of
the volumes recommended to Veteran Robert Thompson, Jr., by
N. I. Simons of the Federation. "We are interested in your appraisal
of conditions from the standpoint of a former serviceman," Simons
wrote, "and no doubt you will be reading the editorials contained
in *Destiny* with interest."

Rand's formula is simple: damn democracy, damn the Jews and
the Catholics, damn anybody you don't like and ascribe it to "the
plan of God." Master-race theorists elsewhere carried the argument to its extreme.

The followers of one school of Anglo-Saxon thought include Rev.
Gerald B. Winrod of Wichita, Kan. Rev. Winrod is under indictment for seditious conspiracy. It doesn't bother him; and it doesn't
seem to bother most of the church congregations and other audiences he harangues on Fundamentalist religion and regressive politics on his long speaking tours about the country. He blames the
indictment on persecution by conniving "Communists" who, he
charges, instigated the New Deal and control the Department of
Justice. His followers believe it.

Winrod's attacks on the Jews as the alleged instigators of "Communism," of depressions, of wars, and finally of a world plot to "destroy" Christianity run parallel to his attacks on the Roman Church. Winrod is a leader of the cult which believes that Jews cannot be converted to Christianity by peaceful, missionary methods. He harbors the dogma that they must be browbeaten into salvation. At one time Winrod was a leading peddler of the *Protocols*, which used to be regularly advertised in his magazine, *The Defender*.

Winrod with rare modesty describes *The Defender* as "dynamic, evangelical, a prophetic voice crying in the wilderness, deeply spiritual, rigidly patriotic, courageous, constructive, inspiring, informative." "Hate-mongering" would describe it better. Winrod once wrote that Naziism and Fascism "stood for life, happiness and prosperity." He has published articles by Gerald Smith, Mrs. Dilling and ex-Senator Reynolds, and advertisements of books by jailbird William Dudley Pelley. Among its examples of anything but spiritual prose, *The Defender* has described the Roman Catholic Church as a "harlot woman" and the "Scarlet-Colored Beast" of the Bible.*

In October, 1945 the magazine published an article that paralleled the worst from Herr Doktor Goebbels' *Der Angriff*:

Nero, a sadistic maniac, played his violin while Rome burned. Franklin Roosevelt played with his stamp collection, waiting for Pearl Harbor to be bombed. Nero, a crowned wretch, as silly as he was cruel, imagined himself to be a great artist and conceived the idea of writing a poem on the destruction of Troy. To get inspiration, he caused Rome to be set on fire, and watched the flames roar upward from the palace roof.

Franklin Roosevelt imagined himself to be the greatest military strategist of all time and conceived the idea of involving his country in a war that would eventually make him President of the World. He watched the conflagration from the vantage point of the White House, in a wheel chair.

* In the 17th Chapter of the Book of Revelation the decadence of Babylon is symbolized as a scarlet woman "with seven heads and ten horns" . . . "having a golden cup in her hand full of abominations" . . . "drunken with the blood of the saints," etc. Winrod and other Extremist Fundamentalists say the scarlet woman represents Rome and the Papacy. It's a convenient device for Catholic-baiting, just as the forged *Protocols of the Learned Elders of Zion* serve as a convenient tool for anti-Semites.

No wonder *World Service,* notorious Nazi organ, endorsed *The Defender,* which has a circulation of about 130,000.

Winrod is a big-time "patriot" operator, one of the most influential Pied Pipers of all the Extremist preachers. He broadcasts over a chain of stations and maintains numerous missions. Winrod tells hearers and readers his work is "spiritual," but the record shows him to be part of the web of nationalist intrigues stretching from coast to coast.

Another "spiritual" nationalist, Rev. Harvey H. Springer, of Englewood, a suburb of Denver, calls himself "the Cowboy Evangelist" and dresses the part. Winrod contributed an introduction to Springer's book, *Termites,* which Major Pinkerton used as a premium. Winrod described affectingly how Springer walked to the pulpit "wearing boots, garbed in a flaming shirt and flowing tie, [and] carrying a five-gallon hat in his hand." Brother Winrod and Brother Springer form a mutual-admiration team and when Winrod hits the soul-saving trail for a missionary tour, Springer sometimes tags along.

In October, 1945 Winrod, Gerald Smith and nationalists from coast to coast high-pressured the Rankin Committee to investigate the Friends of Democracy and its national director, Rev. L. M. Birkhead. Springer aped the Wichita witch-hunter by devoting an entire issue of his *Western Voice* to assailing the Friends of Democracy. The nationalist faithful flooded Rankin with letters. The attempt misfired. Committee members (other than Rankin, whose bigotry and callous indifference to nationalist hate-mongers are scandalous) saw no cause for investigation.

Springer is a disciple of Winrod's kind of Christianity. One of his pet lines—we'll hear this one often—is that President Roosevelt and the New Deal invited the Jap attack. Tojo and Hitler are nowhere on Springer's guilt list. His stand on Catholicism matches Winrod's and Lovell's. The Roman Catholic Church, says the Cowboy Evangelist, started not in Rome, but supposedly in ancient Babylon, together with other "false" religions. His erudite article in the July 5, 1945 issue of his magazine concluded:

Mystery, Babylon the great, the Mother of . . . abominations of the earth. . . . As a matter of conclusive identity between the paganism of Old Babylon, the references in Jeremiah, the prophecy of Revelation,

and Roman Catholicism as it exists today, we are reminded of Pope
Leo XII and his famous "cup." Whenever nations have sipped from the
"cup" of Romanism, those nations have become intoxicated on the wine
of paganism.

Springer, who also works closely with Gerald Smith, has eleven
assistants and claims his Englewood Tabernacle is the largest Baptist church in Colorado. That's only part of his layout. He has a
160-acre youth camp in Jarre Canyon in the Rockies. His Ninth
Annual Rocky Mountain Bible School in 1946 attracted many thousands of Extreme Fundamentalists. The main drawing card was
Rev. Gerald B. Winrod. One of those who attended said, "Everybody was thrilled and spirit-filled, having had a triple-distilled good
time." Rev. Springer is enlarging his business and has established a
new printing plant in Englewood. Veterans picketed the building
in January, 1946, when it was under construction, carrying placards
reading:

> What are YOU doing ABOUT HOUSING?
> We can't live in FOX HOLES Here
> SPRINGER'S $28,000 LIE FACTORY would make HOUS-
> ING FOR 100 VETERANS

"I have always held the opinion that preachers should not mix in
politics," Springer said in May, 1946. But early in June, Springer
was in Fargo, N. D., thumping for Senator William Langer's re-
election. Springer is a close friend of Langer's and the May 23,
1946 issue of his *Western Voice* carried the headline "Sen. Langer
Supports Fundamentalists." Langer's politics match Father Curran's.
At the "Save America Rally" his topic was "England—the Enemy of
Humanity." Amid applause he boasted: "I am very happy to say
that I was the only one to vote against Lend-Lease." Langer cast
one of only two votes against ratifying the United Nations Charter.
He voted against the Arms Embargo Act and Bretton Woods. And
in September, 1944 Langer delivered a lengthy defense of the persons who were then on trial for sedition and called them all "innocent." This should indicate where his sympathies lie.

Springer formerly broadcast from Denver, and frequently attacked
the highly respected Federal Council of the Churches of Christ in
America. These attacks were one reason why officials of Station
KLZ refused him further radio time. Springer set up a howl, blam-

ing it all on the Communists, the PAC and the CIO, who have had nothing to do with it, even remotely. Springer said they had acted on supposed "orders from New York." Screaming "Communism" and "persecution," Springer ran down to Washington and was received with open arms by Representative Rankin, who promised a "thorough" investigation. Springer has been elected Chairman of a Radio Emergency Committee to protest against "un-American" radio stations which refuse to permit hate to be broadcast over the air as freely as it is dispensed from some Extreme Fundamentalist pulpits.

Springer has a disciple in Kenneth Goff, former Communist Party member, who claims that he and his wife saw "the Christian light" after four years in the Party. Goff disclosed that on December 17, 1943 some 350 pastors and youths, meeting in Springer's Tabernacle, decided that the Communists were causing juvenile delinquency. Thereupon The Christian Youth for America was organized and Goff was elected Chairman, with Sgt. Richard Morris as Executive Secretary. Springer and Gerald Smith are grooming Goff as their newest crusader. The trio claim that their Christian Youth is killing two birds with one stone: "fighting" Communism and, *ipso facto*, juvenile delinquency.

Goff's idea of combating Communism is to blame it on the Jews and arouse class, religious and race hate. His poison sheet, *The Pilgrim Torch*, reprints articles from other nationalist organs. A booklet, *Pearl Harbor Exposed*, by John T. Flynn, purports to give the low-down on "the most diabolical conspiracy to plunge the world into war to satisfy the lust of a few power-mad politicians." To "nationalists" and other hate-crazed partisan readers, that spells President Roosevelt and his aides. Springer, Winrod, Smith and many other "nationalists" propagated the myth. Each relied upon and quoted heavily from Flynn's books blaming President Roosevelt and not Tojo, *et al*, for Pearl Harbor.

In January, 1946 Goff passed a rubber check and was hauled off to jail. He pleaded *nolo contendere* (no contest of charge). The amount was small and his sentence was deferred for one year. Although Goff wrote and passed the check, he blamed the incident on a mysterious plot by Moscow agents. Not many years ago he was a Communist bedfellow. He tells of his conversion to the opposite extreme in a 48-page book.

The anti-Catholicism of Springer, Winrod and company is shared by a Fundamentalist preacher whose main missionary work was at Army and Navy bases—Raymond T. Richey, President of the Richey Evangelistic Association, Inc., of Houston, Tex. Richey's full-page advertisement in *The Defender* read in part:

Our ministry in Army camps and Army and Navy hospitals continues with wonderful results. . . . No part of the program is more important or nearer my heart personally, than the preaching, teaching and colportage work in the Army camps and hospitals. Thousands of returning veterans are discouraged, downcast and despondent—in need of spiritual rehabilitation. Our workers are busy going from camp to camp. I have personally visited 267 training centers [as of April 1, 1946].

Anxious to know the quality of his "Evangelistic and Bible-teaching work," I wrote Richey as veteran Thompson and asked bluntly: "I would like to know how you stand on the Catholics." I also asked about the 17th Chapter of Revelation. Here is Richey's answer: "With reference to Revelation 17, many eminent Bible scholars are agreed that this applies to apostate Christendom, whether Catholic

KENNETH GOFF IN JAIL

Englewood, Colorado
January 24, 1946

        The news I want to give you is one of the most diabolical plots to defame a Christian's character that was ever promoted by the anti-Christ gang in Denver.

        I called the local police station and an officer came and took me to the Chief. He told me that some detectives from the D.A.'s office had a warrant for me. He called them on the police radio. They arrived in a few minutes and drove me to the police department in Denver. Then they took pictures of me with a prison number pinned on me. I was finger printed four times, then cross questioned on my past life. Following this, I was taken on the elevator to the ground floor where members of the Rocky Mountain News were waiting for a story. Escaping this crowd of red reporters by quick action on my part, I was taken to the County jail. Then they stripped me of my clothes and examined my wooden leg to see that there were no concealed weapons on me.

When Goff's rubber check bounced, he issued a special bulletin and blamed it not on himself but on a "diabolical plot" which included "red reporters."

or Protestant, but will probably be 'headed by the Papacy.' This, of course, is the ecclesiastical Babylon."

From Herrin, Ill., one day in January, 1945, I received a collection of tracts from an ex-Catholic named Rev. S. L. Testa. He wrote: "I am opposed to the Roman Church on religious grounds—99 percent, and only one percent on political grounds." Rev. Testa had sent thousands of leaflets to Italy, where they reached GIs and officers. "Two of these soldiers, one an Assistant Chaplain and the other a school teacher," he wrote, "have learned to love the Italians so much that they have decided to become missionaries. On their return to America they will prepare themselves for their life work." Wanting to find out how one went about preparing himself as an anti-Catholic missionary, I wrote Testa in the name of Thompson, asking him which "Christian" veterans' group I ought to join. I received an answer from John E. Miller:

Mr. Testa has just asked me to answer your letter. I have also just been discharged from the Army, and the regular veterans' organizations don't appeal to me either. I returned from Italy, and am now taking missionary instruction under Dr. Testa in methods of dealing with Roman Catholic Italians. The heathenism and spiritual darkness in Italy was so evident and heart-rending, that God spoke to my heart to tell the Italian people about Jesus Christ.

Miller sent me a copy of "Why I Am a Protestant and Not a Roman Catholic," a booklet by Testa. His next letter was from Portland, Oregon:

How glad I am to hear that you are interested in how to deal with Roman Catholic people who are under such a bondage of religion. . . . I am now attending the Multonah School of the Bible, Portland . . . and what a blessed experience it is to study the word of God. . . . Wouldn't you like to go to a Bible School for a while?

Miller practiced his proselytizing on me. He enclosed a batch of leaflets and urged me to read a rabidly anti-Catholic tract, "Scriptures for Use with Roman Catholics," in order to answer Catholics "when you are discussing the Lord Jesus Christ."

Another missionary school, the Fundamental Bible Institute in Los Angeles, advertised itself as the "Veteran's choice." "A number of ex-servicemen are in training," it boasted. Again curious, I wrote in. M. H. Reynolds, Superintendent, answered:

As far as the Roman Catholic Church is concerned, their efforts to dominate the political situation should, along with the preaching of the gospel, be exposed; however, we must recognize that the time is at hand when the false church is coming into power, and that through political influence . . . etc., etc.

Reynolds made a statement which startled me: "GIs, under the GI Bill of Rights, have an opportunity of being trained in our school at Government expense." That the GI Bill of Rights could be used to train anti-Catholic missionaries at the taxpayers' expense was, I'm sure, never dreamed of by our Congressmen who drafted the law!

Reynolds' Institute was advertised in the *Christian Beacon,* Fundamentalist, anti-Catholic weekly published in suburban Collingswood, N. J., by Rev. Carl McIntire, pastor of the Bible Presbyterian Church. He is a former member of the regular Presbyterian clergy who was deposed from that ministry after refusing to resign from an independent board for Presbyterian foreign missions. McIntire, with Springer, Winrod and other extreme Fundamentalists, as well as Christian Front-type clerical fascists like Coughlin, are the spearhead of a concerted attack on the Federal Council of the Churches of Christ in America. The Council exercises a democratic influence over more than 140,000 member churches. It supplied the Armed Forces with more than 6,000 chaplains who served all GIs regardless of their faith. It has roundly condemned hate-mongering and has worked closely with the Conference of Christians and Jews, which, of course, is added reason for its being smeared as "Communist" by the Extremists.

McIntire has two pet phobias. One is the Federal Council of Churches, which he calls "apostate, Communist and Modernist." The Council, he proclaims, is plotting to destroy the Christian faith. In this McIntire follows Winrod, whose introduction to Springer's booklet (distributed by Major Pinkerton) damns the Council as the "Protestant Papacy" and a "powerfully financed bureaucracy." McIntire's other phobia is the Roman Catholic Church, on which he sees eye to eye with Winrod and Springer.

McIntire has denounced Bishop G. Bromley Oxnam on two counts: the Bishop is not only President of the Federal Council, but he has actually said: "Roman Catholic and Protestant worship the same God, adore the same Christ, and are inspired by the same Holy Spirit." To a Fundamentalist who believes the Roman Catholic to be a "false" church, this statement seems heresy. McIntire declared:

Instead of convincing people that Romanism is fundamentally wrong and contrary to the teachings of the Bible, Bishop Oxnam has declared that Roman Catholicism is fundamentally right. . . . As we enter the postwar world, without any doubt the greatest enemy of freedom and liberty that the world has to face today is the Roman Catholic system. . . .

McIntire is a friend of Merwin K. Hart, President of the "Park Avenue"-type nationalist body, the National Economic Council, Inc. Both have opposed the Federal Council of Churches. The reactionary coalition of businessmen symbolized by Hart, who apparently fear the spreading influence of the Federal Council, has contributed to the nation-wide, relentless smear attack against it.

McIntire's influence is growing. His church budget of $57,000 for 1946 was oversubscribed by $2,350. His parish has some 1,800 Presbyterians belonging to the Extreme Fundamentalist sect. (Extreme Fundamentalists claim membership in Baptist, Methodist and many other denominations.) He is constantly called upon to speak away from his church in Collingswood. In May, 1946 he spoke together with Springer in Knoxville, Tenn. McIntire, too, is an addict of Rev. Springer's interpretation of Revelation 17. He preached a series of sermons defaming the Catholic Church as "the Harlot Church and the Bride of the Anti-Christ" and selected the Christmas season of 1945 to circulate them among readers of his *Christian Beacon.*

Last of the self-styled "Christian" preachers is a slight, balding veteran of World War I, Rev. William L. Blessing, whose bailiwick is the Barnum area of Denver. He works hand in hand with Springer, Winrod, Goff and Smith. Blessing runs a magazine called *Showers of Blessing* and a church, "The House of Prayer for All People." These are deceptive names. They camouflage a Jew-and-Catholic-baiter of extraordinary talents. Blessing spouts hatred of other faiths in hysterical language. Here's Blessing excoriating the Jews.

Jews are a hissing, . . . a curse, a reproach, . . . evil figs, very evil, . . . false religionists, evolutionists, atheists, broken cisterns, . . . synagogue of satan anti-Christ, killers of the prophets, murderers of Christ, children of the devil, serpents, vipers, contrary to all men. . . . Will Henry Ford and Montgomery Ward be put out of business and will their business be given to the Jews???

Like Lovell, however, Blessing blithely disclaims being anti-Semitic. He also says he isn't anti-Catholic, but writes:

Atheistic Communism at least does not control a man after he is dead, but the Pope owns the child before it is born, all of its life and after it is dead. He is a pseudo-God of heaven, earth and hell. No dictator on earth ever had or ever claimed even half the power that the Pope claims and that he has.

Blessing damns the Federal Council. It's worst than Communism, he says:

Today organized religion under the Federal Council of Churches is a menace more threatening to civilization than atheistic Communism. Why? Because they would enslave the world under one religious head. They would mix the races to produce a third race. They would put Communism and Americanism together to produce a third Government. *Down with all Denominations.*

Blessing is not a man without friends. "It was my privilege," he writes, "to be entertained at dinner on October 10 [1945] by Mr. and Mrs. Gerald L. K. Smith, Mr. and Mrs. Kenneth Goff, and Mr.

"SHOWERS OF BLESSING"

All that the Jews want with Palestine is to establish an international bankers headquarters (a headquarters for Jewry similar to the Vatican of the Catholic Church at Rome) The Bible only gave the true tribe of ancient Judah—the Judahites one-twelfth of Palestine. That's all that the true Jews ever were allotted in the land, but Lo, and Behold, these modern imposters, "the synagogue of Satan," "children of the devil" want all of Palestine and dumb senators and governors want to give it all to them.

Americans, I turn to the AMERICA FIRST PARTY as the only hope of salvation for a free America. I was a member of the Ku Klux Klan and I expect to renew my membership at the earliest possible date. Truman has ordered Eisenhower to put Germans out of their homes and move the Jews in. Will Henry Ford and Montgomery Ward be put out of business and will their businesses be given to the Jews???

Both the Democratic and Republican parties seem to be under Jewish control. Therefore we must have a new party in America.

A sample of Blessing's patriotism.

Wesley Swift. I have never met a finer group of Christians in all my life than these people, and I can say the same thing about Charles Bartlett Hudson [Hudson is under indictment on sedition charges] who was a guest at dinner in my home, and Mr. and Mrs. Gerald Winrod of Wichita, who were my guests in my home a year ago."

I exposed Blessing in an article published in *The American Mercury* for April, 1946. There may be no connection, but then perhaps there may be, between that and the following item which appeared shortly afterward, on April 23, in *Showers of Blessing:*

From February 23 to March 22, 1946, I received 298 first-class letters, of which 100 were requests for *Showers of Blessing* and 198 contained money totaling $1788.00. From March 23 to the present time, April 17, I have received only 58 letters and only $149.00.

Blessing is a self-styled authority on Revelation 17, and has written a booklet on it, illustrated with crude drawings. He has given the "Papal Beast" a number—666. How he arrived at it, or why, and what he plans to make of it, aren't explained. Blessing belongs to both the Legion and the Veterans of Foreign Wars and claims to have been State Chaplain of the Legion, as well as an honorary member of the Denver police. Like Capt. Frank S. Flynn, he takes refuge in ancestry, claiming that two of his great-great-great-grandfathers fought under George Washington. If this is so, they must be spinning rapidly in their graves, considering the plans their great-great-great-grandson has today for the United States of America:

Americans, I turn to the America First Party [Gerald L. K. Smith's] as the only hope of salvation for a free America. I was a member of the Ku Klux Klan and I expect to renew my membership at the earliest possible date. . . . Both the Democratic and Republican parties seem to be under Jewish control. Therefore we must have a new party line in America.

Neither in World War I nor World War II did America fight for Gerald Smith's fascist party or the propagation of the Klan. The Democratic and Republican Parties are American parties. Blessing's "new party line" can only be a call for an un-American Third Party, "American" in its outer shell, but fascist at the core. So-called men of the Gospel are leading gullible American citizens down that nationalist road to revolution and ruin—in His name!

CHAPTER FIVE

Pattern for a Fascist Veterans Party

> My time will come in the post-war period. The candidate will
> not be me; it will be a young veteran of this war, but I'll be
> behind him. If business conditions are bad—inflation, widespread
> unemployment, farm foreclosures—then my candidate will be
> elected. . . . Then the flame will spread, and the extreme na-
> tionalist will come to power. . . . When chaos comes, I'll be the
> leader.
>
> *Gerald L. K. Smith*

THE PURPOSE of this chapter is to show in American terms, in an
American locale, how a group of disgruntled veterans under fanatical leadership, with the mass support of nationalists and the help of
short-sighted financial angels could make it "happen here," and
how we Americans can recognize the warning symptoms so that
perverted "nationalism" can never gain a permanent hold. The
Chairman of the American Veterans Committee, Charles G. Bolte,
writes sagely in his book, *The New Veteran* *:

Men do not go fascist of themselves, in most cases. But recent Italian
and German history, where two disgruntled ex-soldiers led some of their
similarly disgruntled comrades in the vanguard of the fascist movements,
should be enough warning of what could happen. Some veterans may
very well allow themselves to be formed into an irresponsible political
power if they find a jobless America, an America torn by racial, religious
and economic strife.

My story begins with my trek in September, 1945, by train, bus
and hitchhike, to arrive in time to hear Gerald Smith, Carl H. Mote,
Klansman Wesley Swift, Legionnaire Harry A. Romer and Smith's
Charlie McCarthy veterans, George Vose, Frederick R. Kister, and

* Copyright 1945 by Reynal and Hitchcock.

Paul Meinhart, stage a "patriotic meeting" in the Mercer County Fair Grounds at Celina, Ohio. The town nestled in lush, fertile farm country.

I took a 3 A.M. train from Cleveland and at 6:30 arrived at Sydney, Ohio. I was still about 40 miles from Celina. It was Sunday and bus service was bad. The only way I could get to Celina on time was to hitchhike. I had brought the coat of my old George Pagnanelli suit for good luck and also—together with other devices—to help me look like a farmer. On the outskirts of Sydney I was picked up by a toolmaker who told me disgustedly that oil workers at Lima were on strike. We talked about labor. He admitted that his CIO union had done him a lot of good, but he kept on damning unions.

"Are the dues too high?" I asked.

Naw. The better wages we get make up for that."

"Then what have you against unions?"

"Guess I can't get used to 'em," he said, scratching his ear. "Never belonged to one before. Say, what one do you belong to?"

"None," I said. "Don't belong to any."

"What the hell do you do for a livin'?"

"I'm a farmer," I answered.

"You got a white shirt, and with them glasses you don't look like no farmer to me," the toolmaker said. "What the hell work do you do?"

I stuck to my story. "I was graduated from Ohio State Agricultural College," I said. "Took up scientific farming."

"One of them book farmers, hey?" he laughed. "Guess these here colleges polish off you guys so you don't even talk like farmers."

After this rebuff, I decided to give up "farming." The meeting was sponsored by the United Farmers of America, which operated under the thumb of Mote, its President, before he died in April, 1946. Among real farmers I'd stand out like a sore thumb. If I were asked again I decided to say I was a clerk in a grain-and-feed store.

The toolmaker took me as far as St. Mary's, where a well-dressed man wearing the Legion cap picked me up. He was headed for the Celina meeting.

"What do you think of Gerald Smith?" I asked, anxious to know his leanings.

"I don't think much of him," he said. "I want to know how he gets away with it. I want to learn who's behind Smith, who pays him, what he's aiming at. I'm going to the meeting to report to the Americanism Committee of the Legion."

I took down his license number and later learned he was Allan Tarshish from Columbus, Ohio.

The Celina Fair Grounds were like those at Mineola, L. I., where I was raised as a boy. A high, white fence enclosed acres of woodland. A grandstand overlooked the race track. At 1:30 P.M. the tunes of a hillbilly band came over the loud-speakers. The farmers, who had spread their lunch on the grass, headed toward the grandstand. At the entrance was Patriot No. 6 at the Queens meeting—Eugene Flitcraft. He was overcharging 10 cents for copies of *Gentile News.* I bought the September issue. It carried the forged *Protocols,* a column by Rev. Blessing's friend Charles Hudson, Smith's Nationalist News Service report, and vicious anti-Semitic articles. A Chicago *Tribune* editorial was praised and a front-page article was headlined, "Upton Close Chides Jews."

Handbills advertising the rally were worded to appeal to the veteran. Their come-on message followed the familiar, almost sure-fire formula of the Townsend Plan and other unsound bonus movements: enlist gullible followers by appealing to their pocketbooks. The dodgers read:

Mr. Smith will announce plans for the organization of a great nation-wide crusade in behalf of Veterans, Unemployed, Farmers, Workers and Small Businessmen. This new organization has in it the best features of Father Coughlin's "Social Justice," the Townsend Plan, the Farmers' Guild Program and other popular movements, based on the principle of America First, Constitutional Money and the principle of Free Enterprise. The time has come to run the money changers out of the temple and constitutionalize our money system so that we can provide adequately and fully for . . .

1. VETERANS	5. WORKERS
2. UNEMPLOYED	6. AGED
3. FARMERS	7. INFIRM
4. SMALL BUSINESSMEN	

This financial lure adapts the psychology of the confidence man to national politics.

Copies of ex-Senator Robert R. Reynolds' *National Record* were being given away free. It was the September, 1945 number, carrying an article by Hubert H. Heath of the Hot Springs, N. M., *Herald,* a cartoon from the Chicago *Tribune,* and a futile attempt to refute Eugene Segal's articles in the Cleveland *Press* against Reynolds and his crew. Gerald Smith's *The Cross and the Flag,* which I bought, gloated: "The war is over now, we can say what we please." I picked up a copy of *The X-Ray,* a semi-literate weekly issued by an ex-bootlegger and ex-Klansman of Muncie, Ind., named Court Asher. He was once under indictment for sedition.

A uniformed sailor stood guard at the entrance. Other servicemen were in the audience.

I kept away from Gerald Smith lest I be recognized and booted out. Suddenly, I saw Carl H. Mote less than ten feet from me. Mote owned the Northern Indiana Telephone Company. He was wealthy and gave liberally to the fascist cause. His articles appeared in seditionist Pelley's *Roll Call.* His own magazine, *America Preferred,* was one of the most vicious hate sheets in the nationalist fold. Luckily I spotted Mote first. I ducked just in time, after which I hastened to a seat and buried myself between a burly farmer in shirtsleeves and a fat woman in a green gingham dress. I looked around at about 1,500 farmers and their spouses, thrifty, hard-working, tough-fibered men and women. The crowd impressed me as being politically inexperienced and probably easily led by a spellbinder who knew how to play on their prejudices. Most of the menfolk wore suspenders and wildly colored shirts. (I was uncomfortably conscious of my white shirt.) Few had coats on. Most of the women wore gaudy, shapeless print dresses.

Later I learned that Mercer and Darke Counties, known as the "Holy Belt," are peopled largely by "low-speaking" Germanic farmers who are fanatical worshippers of Father Coughlin. He carried these counties with his political ticket in 1936.

As the hillbilly band swung into religious music, some in the mob began to chant and laugh loudly in accompaniment. They swayed and rocked. They yelled "Hallelujah!" and "Amen!" When the speakers came, the mob was already in a state of self-hypnosis, stamping, yelling, and screaming hysterically. My mind went back to the mob rallies addressed by Hitler, Goebbels, Kuhn, Coughlin, Joe "McNazi" McWilliams and Winrod. I saw the same religious frenzy here, the same mesmerism induced by rabble rousers, the same hero worship, the same bilious mob and, potentially, the same ugly consequences.

The meeting started with the Pledge of Allegiance to the flag, led by Harry Romer, vice-presidential candidate of Smith's America First Party in 1944. Romer didn't seem very familiar with the Pledge; he incorrectly said: ". . . with liberty and freedom for all." Romer was followed by the Kluxer, Wesley Swift. "God is with us," Swift said unctuously, "or He wouldn't have given us this beautiful day!"

Romer then spoke again and damned the Farmers Union as "Communist." He damned Dayton newspapers (except the *Independent*) as smelling "worse than manure and of less use to the farmer." The mob guffawed. Romer wanted Coughlin back on the radio and "them slobbering foreign-language speakers off the air." He demanded "more radio time for such great Americans as Lindbergh, Gerald Smith, Hamilton Fish, Senator [Burton K.] Wheeler, Senator [Wilbert Lee] O'Daniel, Congressman [Clare E.] Hoffman, Mrs. Dilling and [ex-Senator Gerald P.] Nye."

MAMMOTH RALLY
Mercer County Fairgrounds
CELINA, OHIO
FREDERICK KISTER
Gerald L. K. Smith
CARL H. MOTE

The "Master" Race

"HITLER, I guess, has practically lost the war, so we ought to be able to speak out more freely. I am ashamed to be an American. Properly considered, the war has fully demonstrated one thing, and that is that the Germans are superior to Americans and English physically, intellectually, aesthetically and morally. They are the master race all right, if "master" means superior. I think it is about time to tell the ignorant Americans something about the greatness of the Germans, at this time when some Americans are counting on sending some of our folks to teach the Germans something about morality and other things. It is to laugh. *C'est a rire.*

"One only has to look at the photos of German prisoners, to study their faces, to see how much superior in looks they are to us Americans. I think in things cultural that the composite German man excels the composite American, just about as much as the composite American excels the African Negro."

THIS IS A CALL TO ACTION!   NO SOFTIES NEED APPLY

It is a call not to the weak, not to the vacillating, not to the bootlickers, not even to the man who loves his job more than his liberty - - it is a call to the understanding Christian American Veteran, regardless of his particular creed, who is tired of being kicked around by bureaucrats, smear artists, refugees, alien-minded propagandists, Communists, plug-uglies, whip crackers and other varieties of un-American vermin who infest our beautiful America.

Speakers at the Celina, Ohio, rally in September, 1945, and excerpts from publications sponsored, respectively, by Mote and Kister. *Upper left:* Portion of handbill announcing rally. *Upper right:* Portion of an "international lawyer's" letter in the May, 1945 issue of Carl H. Mote's magazine, *America Preferred*. *Bottom:* From the big red-white-blue leaflet announcing Kister's Christian Veterans of America.

Mote, short, bald and nervous, ridiculed international coopera-tion. He yammered about the Bretton Woods "Steal," the Dumbar-ton "Hoax" and the San Francisco "Sell-Out." "There's no difference between the two major parties," he bellowed. "A Third Party is what we need—the Christian America First Party!" *

Finishing an hour later, Mote next introduced Gerald L. K. Smith as "a loyal servant of Christ." Since Coughlin's banishment from politics, Smith has taken over the flock. His headquarters are in De-troit, where he lives on Seyburn Avenue and on occasion receives mail under the name of Rosemary Lawrence. Pompous, barrel-chested Smith has been in the hate business for fourteen years and knows it intimately. Once minister of the Fundamentalist First Christian Church, Shreveport, La., he was closely associated with Huey Long and was an organizer for Pelley's Silver Shirt Legion of American storm troopers, of which he was member No. 3223. Führer-at-large of the America First Party, the Committee of One Million, the Post-War Recovery Commission and other hate groups dedi-cated to the cause of leading America in the direction of extreme "nationalism," Smith gets along well with such diverse elements as Klansmen, Christian Fronters, economically selfish labor-baiters, and Extreme Fundamentalists.

One of our loudest trumpeters against "Reds," Smith can bellow with the power of a hog-caller. Almost any American who does not breathe, eat and drink Smith's perverted "nationalism" is a "mangy Red" or "Communist Red rascal." Thus Frank Sinatra and Bill Mauldin are dyed-in-the-wool Reds, according to Smith, especially Sinatra who starred in the inter-faith film short, *The House I Live In.* Smith's monthly dope sheet, *The Cross and the Flag,* has been running articles screaming that "Hollywood Communism" is "rap-ing" America.

Never short of funds, Smith keeps up appeals to the faithful for money, giving the impression that almost before his begging letter can be received he may have been assassinated by Reds. Consider-able circumstantial evidence indicates that he still receives money

* Mote's will bequeathed two thirds of his estate to "revive, restore and per-petuate the American way of life . . . especially American Constitutional government, which in my lifetime I have learned to describe as American nationalism." The balance was left to his secretary and a friend. Mote's surviv-ing children, two sons and a daughter, have contested the will, charging that Mote was "of unsound mind" and under "undue influence" when he made it.

from "big business" sources. When he ran for Senator from Michigan in 1942 Smith got more than 100,000 votes, no small feat. He claims a following of several millions. His supporters, ranging from hysterical devotees to lukewarm adherents, may conservatively be estimated at somewhere around 250,000.

Smith is a master of mob psychology. Using extremely simple language to incite prejudice, he aroused the farmers to spasms of emotional hysteria.

"The nicest fair grounds, the best hotels, the best restaurants, they all belong to us," he boomed into the loud-speaker. "Why shouldn't we enjoy them? Who enjoys them now?"

"The Jews!" the Coughlinites yelled.

"Yes, and if the Jews don't like our country, they can go back where they came from! We'll even buy 'em a one-way ticket!"

Straining for humor, Smith asked the mob if it knew the difference between a bull and a steer. The shapeless woman on my left giggled. He outlined his various hate projects: "I'm sponsoring mothers' groups, veterans' groups, youth groups, Christian groups, money-reform groups! We now want farmers to join our bandwagon from coast to coast! Nationalism is going to town and people like you are going to help our plans come true!" He appealed to their short-sighted sense of thrift: "Instead of giving away money on Lend-Lease to those Rooshians and English internationalists, I say give it to our own boys. Veterans should get $1,000 mustering-out pay."

In the audience Smith pointed out Mrs. David Stanley of the United Mothers of America; Mrs. Katherine M. Sutter, American Mothers, Pontiac, Michigan; and Mrs. Bertha Glebe, Friends of the Constitution, Dayton, Ohio.* Each, loudly dressed, took a bow.

"I carried a petition 150 feet long," Smith ranted, "to have Holly-

---

* The main phobia of this small-time "patriot" is that the U.S.A. will become part of a "world government." "Get on your hind legs, America! Put a stop to it!" she warns in lurid leaflets. Another phobia is the Federal Council of the Churches of Christ, which is allegedly furthering that "conspiracy." A third phobia is that she will unwittingly correspond with John Roy Carlson. To forestall this she demands references, affidavits, etc., of all her correspondents. I know this because we've exchanged letters. Mrs. Glebe sent me a copy of "The Jewish Problem," an article in the Anglo-Saxon Federation's *Destiny* hostile to the Jews, and a large packet of similar tripe. She's an inveterate writer to the "Letters to the Editor" columns of Dayton newspapers, and a leading nationalist there.

wood investigated as the new American Moscow, and put it in the hands of that great, Christian American patriot, John E. Rankin. Friends, it's coming to this: you're either going to join up with the internationalist Wall Street bankers and the atheistic Communists, or you're going to follow the way of Jesus Christ, Jefferson and Lincoln. Call my plan the Lincoln plan! That's the road I'm taking! Give me a hand if you agree!" A thundering ovation roared across the fertile Ohio farmlands.

It was time for Smith's veteran trio to make an appearance. George Vose, former führer of Smith's Nationalist Veterans of World War II and now Secretary of the Christian Veterans of America, and Paul Meinhart, Chairman of the Philadelphia chapter of CVA, were introduced, after which both resumed their seats abruptly.

"We are going to put the veterans first in our nationalist crusade as we move across the country," Smith said. "I want you to meet an up-and-coming nationalist leader, Frederick Kister, Chairman of the Christian Veterans!"

The short, blond Kister, whom I had last seen at the Queens rally, jumped into high gear and screamed hysterically in a high-pitched voice: "How many of you know that Stalin has a five-year plan for America? Do you know that in five years he wants to make America a Soviet Republic? Who is behind the Communists? I'll tell you who! Certain elements who live in New York and Palestine. We veterans fought for the Four Freedoms, but pro-Communist, Jewish groups deny us the right to work. Is that justice? Is that Americanism? Are you going to take it sitting down? *We're not!* We Christian Veterans are organized to fight it!"

His words left their impact on the simple-minded mob. They swallowed his poison.

I met Kister after the meeting while he, Vose, Meinhart and the sailor were distributing lurid red-white-blue leaflets which screamed, "Christian Veterans, AWAKE!" In them Kister wailed that upon his discharge (after serving eight months as a private) he found America "flooded with refugees who had come to take jobs vacated by my buddies." He blamed the loss of his job on a "Jewish-Communist Editor," and alleged that he had suffered "tortuous persecution" at the hands of "venomous enemies of America." A "Red, revolutionary plot" was afoot to smear all Christians like himself. "What is the veterans' answer?" he finally asked. "ORGANIZE! . . . NO SOFTIES NEED APPLY."

It sounded like a Bund storm-troopers' call to action.

Kister's ham-and-egg scheme was to advocate a "cash bonus of $2,500 for every honorably discharged veteran." * Nothing was said on how this was to be done. Nor did Smith's protégé offer a program, outside of such generalities as the supporting of "national defense, free enterprise, labor unions, sound leadership."

The meeting over, the mob poured out. I noticed that some of the goons had surrounded two clean-cut young men. A tall, burly Coughlinite was slapping the smaller of the two repeatedly. It was infuriating to watch, but it was typical of the cowardly tactics everywhere used by Christian Front bullies. The two American youths (members of the CIO in Dayton and the Greenville, Ohio, Farmers' Union) had been distributing leaflets denouncing Smith as a Hitlerite. The mob followed the defenseless pair, punching them at every step and yelling:

"Rooshians! That's what they are! Git! Git, you Rooshians!"

A frowzy woman, with disheveled hair, screamed hysterically above the noise: "Hang 'em! Plenty of trees here! Git the rope! Hang them Rooshians!"

It was all typical "Christian" Coughlinism.

Outside the Fair Grounds students of Antioch College handed out anti-Smith leaflets, amid the jeers and threats of nationalist goons. The possibility that, should things go wrong, the hate-filled goons rather than the clean-cut students might control America's future was a chilling thought. I longed to take my place with the students, but an undercover reporter must deny himself many pleasures until his work is done.

Shortly after, walking to the bus along Main Street in Celina, I came face to face with Mr. and Mrs. Court Asher. Both had met me. In *Under Cover* I wrote at length on Asher. Both gave me a quizzical look.

I decided to take the offensive. "Meester Asher, I sure am glad to see you, friend!" I said. "Meester Smith introduced you at the

---

* Kister is a piker compared to Joseph McWilliams, former führer of the pro-Nazi Christian Mobilizers. Joe's super-bonanza Servicemen's Reconstruction Plan offered the veteran $7,800 in 3¾% interest-bearing bonds.

meetin' and I sure wished I wuz there sittin' right by ye to shake your hand." I pumped it.

Mrs. Asher wasn't convinced, "Aren't you . . . er, Italian?" she asked.

I laughed aloud. "I'm German—German as they make 'em. Name is Hoffmaier. Eric Hoffmaier from Dayton."

"Come and see me when you're in Muncie," Asher finally invited. But Mrs. Asher kept eyeing me until I got into the bus.

When I returned to New York I looked up Kister's background in the files of the Friends of Democracy. He was born on December 24, 1914 and was graduated from East High School, Rochester, N. Y., in June, 1934. Investigation showed that his school grades were somewhat below average; on graduation he stood 155th in a class of 189. Kister's ambition was to join the stage. He spent some time in dramatic school and the management of small plays, but didn't make a mark in the theatre world, so turned to the political theatre.

Kister's "nationalistic" training was at meetings of Chicago's Citizens USA Committee, which were addressed by such "patriots" as Lawrence Dennis and Carl Mote, a financial agent of the nationalist movement. "It is entirely fitting and proper to consign to hell anyone who breathes the word 'democracy' or palavers about the 'democratic way of life,' " Mote wrote in his magazine, *America Preferred*. "I say *fie* on all melodrama that exalts the so-called 'rights of minorities.' "

Kister also went to meetings of the Constitutional Americans at which anti-Semitic fanatics like Mrs. Dilling spoke, and was a friend of Joe McWilliams. He was employed as an editorial assistant by *Scribner's Commentator,* and is still friendly with Douglas M. Stewart, who was one of the *Commentator's* publishers. Stewart went to jail for contempt of court rather than divulge the source of a large sum received by the magazine. *Scribner's Commentator* pleaded for appeasement of Hitler and followed a strong pro-Axis course.

To study the potential young führer further, I decided to interview Kister openly. He avoided me at first but I finally collared him on November 10, 1945 at his home in Chicago. As witness I brought along a newspaperman from the Chicago *Sun.* I found the Kisters living in a small, neatly furnished home. It was strangely bare of books. But the one book which stood upright on the table spoke volumes. It was large and thick, with a light blue jacket. It was

Hitler Germany, by Cesare Santoro, published by Internationaler Verlag, Berlin, in October, 1938. I had obtained my own copy while investigating the German Library of Information in 1940. *Hitler Germany* glorified the Reich for nearly 600 pages.

In the room beside Kister were his wife, a small woman with blazing eyes and snapping tongue; a tall, baronial man who was introduced as Douglas M. Stewart. It was Stewart who refused to tell the Washington Grand Jury the inside story of his magazine's finances, and was sent to prison for contempt. He "explained" that $15,000 was once hurled through his office window; another $15,000 was left mysteriously on a table in his home. Stewart also wanted us to believe that someone in a New York crowd slipped several thousand dollars into his hand to help with the financing of the pro-Nazi magazine.*

Kister and Stewart were mild mannered and willing to talk freely, but Mrs. Kister constantly interrupted her husband to warn him against answering questions. "Now, Fred, dear," she would interrupt, "do be careful, dear. Don't answer that!"

Kister tried to clear himself of complicity with Homer Maertz by

---

* *Scribner's Commentator* echoed the Nazi propaganda-line by urging America to remain disarmed and unprepared. We were the war-mongers. Hitler *et al.* wanted peace.

Scribner's Commentator published an article by Yakichiro Suma, official Japanese spokesman, in which he said: "It was on more than several occasions that the Japanese Government declared that Japan had, and has, absolutely no designs toward conquering China or any other nation or people in East Asia. On the contrary, Japan has proposed to achieve a neighborly solidarity among the nations and the peoples of East Asia."

Townsend, who accepted money from Jap interests but didn't tell the State Department, wrote in an article in *Scribner's Commentator:* "We do more business with Japan than with all the other countries of Asia combined." He was worried lest *we* provoke war and lose "this profitable trade." His article was titled "Japan—our Commercial Prize."

Scribner's Commentator called convicted Quisling Pétain "one of the great characters in the world today." It praised Nazis, saying that churches in Germany were as "free as anywhere in the world." Another contributor was Boris Brasol, a Czarist Nazi who introduced the *Protocols* to the United States in 1916.

Aping *Scribner's Commentator* was *The Herald,* a weekly edition of the same type of poison. Stewart was editor, Kister an assistant. *The Herald* called Hitler's invasion of Russia a "Holy Crusade." Both magazines used mailing lists compiled by the Italian Fascist Library of Information. Both sent bulk shipments to Army and Navy installations in the Pacific. They were among many such publications which lulled us into a false sense of security and contributed to our being caught napping at Pearl Harbor.

saying that he hadn't known Maertz was to be at the Queens meeting.

"But you drove to the meeting with Maertz and Flitcraft, didn't you?" I asked. He hesitated. His wife cautioned him against replying, but Kister, with a whipped look, nodded, "Yes. He knows the answer, anyway."

Stewart and Mrs. Kister defended Ralph Townsend and denounced the Department of Justice for "persecuting" the "innocent" Japanese propagandist.

Kister told me that he had spent a year at the University of Rochester. University officials have written me they have no record. Kister brazenly denied any collaboration whatsoever with Smith and protested, "I'm not against the Jews." For once Mrs. Kister did not interrupt.

"You don't know him very well," Stewart said. "Kister is not an anti-Semite. If you are a Jeffersonian Democrat or in any way express nationalist instead of internationalist sentiments you are called a fascist." On his own behalf Stewart said: "I can't be a fascist because my ancestors were here in the 17th century. I am, goodness knows, how many generations back one hundred percent American. I'm a democrat. I talk with everybody."

Stewart forgot that William Dudley Pelley, an old-line American, was in prison for sedition, that the name of Vidkun Quisling, a "pure" Norwegian and a major in the army, stood for those who betray their country in the name of patriotism. The one hundred percent American-born Klan is the most un-American of the lot.

I turned to Kister. "Are you working?" I asked. He hesitated.

"Yes, he is working," Mrs. Kister answered.

I asked Kister why he was engaged in hate work.

"I gotta make a living, don't I?" he answered. It was a damaging reply. The stock answer of most "patriots" is that their work is a labor of love.

The continuing Kister-Stewart friendship was highly significant. After he came out of a Federal jail, Stewart went under cover and wasn't heard from. Many wondered what had happened to him. The answer was apparent: Stewart was still a "nationalist" and still in close contact with other "nationalists."

Newspapermen who had speculated on the source of *Scribner's Commentator's* mysterious income were interested in the testimony of Herbert Von Strempel, former First Secretary of the German Embassy in Washington. *PM* carried the story in its June 2, 1946 issue. According to the news report, Von Strempel testified at the Nuremberg war criminals trial that he had personally handed "between $10,000 and $15,000" to Stewart and George Eggleston, *Scribner's Commentator* editor, "around the middle of 1941," in New York. Von Strempel added: "Before their meeting with me, Stewart and Eggleston had had conversations with Baer and Kapp," German Consuls General in Chicago and Cleveland. "Their negotiations already had reached an advanced stage."

Von Strempel was interrogated by Sam Harris, member of the U.S. prosecution staff. The testimony was introduced into the trial as U.S. Exhibit 880, Document 3800-PS, as part of the prosecution's case against Rudolph Hess. When *PM* reporters tried to reach Eggleston in advance of publication he was unavailable. Later Eggleston issued a formal denial through Pendleton Dudley, Special Adviser to the editor of *The Reader's Digest*. In a letter to me, bearing Kister's return address, Stewart has also denied Von Strempel's allegations.

George Vose, secretary of the hate veterans, is a big fleshy man from Kalamazoo, Mich. A report from school authorities stated: "Attended Central High School. Left January 17, 1935, when in the 11th grade. No diploma received." While in the Army, Vose, according to creditable informants, was tried before a general court martial on May 3, 1943 at Ft. Sheridan, Illinois, and convicted of violating Article 84 of the Articles of War, specifically, selling army shirts; and of violating Article 96, AOW, specifically, selling passes to enlisted men, while serving at Camp McCoy, Wisconsin. He was sen-

CHRISTIAN VETERANS OF AMERICA

	CHICAGO 90. ILLINOIS	
FREDERICK KISTER National Chairman		PAUL J. MEINHART Chairman, Philadelphia Chapter
GEORGE VOSE National Secretary	**LARRY ASMAN** <small>Eastern Vice-President CHRISTIAN YOUTH FOR AMERICA Director CHRISTIAN VETERANS INTELLIGENCE BUREAU</small>	JAMES PIGOTT Chairman, Denver Chapter
REV. ARTHUR W. TERMINIELLO National Chaplain	<small>Subject</small> "RED TREASON" TIME: 8 P.M., Monday, June 17, 1946 PLACE: First Baptist Church, 3195 So. Broadway AUSPICES: CHRISTIAN YOUTH FOR AMERICA	LORENCE ASMAN Chairman, Detroit Chapter

This nationalist gang—including two court-martialled ex-GIs and a suspended priest—work together intimately. The church Asman addressed is Rev. Springer's, in Englewood, Colo.

tenced to six months hard labor at the rehabilitation center at Ft. Custer, Mich. The conviction and sentence were approved by the Major General in charge at Ft. Sheridan.

Vose did not serve sentence. He was medically discharged on August 17, 1944, after which he ran for lieutenant-governor as the candidate of Smith's America First Party.

Paul J. Meinhart, Chairman of the Philadelphia chapter of the Christian Veterans of America, served as a private during the war. A former iceman, he lives in a small bungalow in Lester, Pa. I visited him there one night in February, 1946, tramping through six inches of snow. I found Meinhart a tall, thin fellow in his twenties, dressed in a collegiate sweater, blue shirt and sporty socks. On investigation I found his school record undistinguished, his grades mediocre and his recorded I.Q., 87. His home was neat though inexpensively furnished. Meinhart's parents impressed me as humble American folk who were getting uncomfortable at the notoriety of their son, though they had relished it at first.

The odd hour, and the attacks against him by Philadelphia newspapers, had put Meinhart on guard. He maintained stolidly, in a monotone, that only Christians could join the Veterans, and warned me, "We have ways of checking up on people." I gave him a fictitious name and Philadelphia address and said good night. Though Meinhart was reluctant to say much to me during my visit, he readily answered a letter from "Thompson":

Received your welcome letter of Jan 27 and I must say their are still some good American's like yourself. who are with me in organizing Christian Veterans. If we Christian Veterans stick together we will have not fought in vain. Inclosed you will find some pamphlet's pretaining to our organization. Hoping to hearing from you I am for Christ, Country and Home

> Paul J. Meinhart
> Chairman Phil. Chapter

Director of Kister's "Intelligence Bureau" is Lorence Asman, Detroit Chairman of the Christian Veterans and Vice-President of the Goff-Springer-Smith-inspired Christian Youth for America. Born in Michigan twenty-two years ago of German parents from the Ukraine, Asman is an explosive combination of political fanaticism, religious frenzy and an intense hatred of Communism. He drew anti-war cartoons in 1941 for the America First Committee and toured Michigan with Smith in 1942 when the latter ran for senator. The following year, Asman himself has revealed, he penned the following letter to President Roosevelt:

Just as Judas betrayed Christ, so you have betrayed America, and just as Judas went out and hanged himself, so you should have done many years ago. If you continue to destroy our wealth and our treasury, and if you continue to promote Jewish Communism, and if you continue to shed the innocent blood of our sons on foreign battlefields, then we, the 100,000,000 Christians of America, will rise up in righteous anger and tear down your tower of Babel and get you.

Drafted in 1943, Asman boastfully describes his Army experiences in the February, 1946 issue of Goff's *The Pilgrim Torch*. Talmadge of Georgia, he writes, recommended him for assignment to Military Intelligence, but he was turned down for that and Officer Candidate School. Asman was assigned to the 1800th Engineers Battalion, stationed in Tennessee. He declares the unit was filled with "America Firsters, Christian Front leaders, Silver Shirt members, Bundists, ex-members of the Nazi Party and German Army, Ku Klux Klan members," and others considered "dangerous, disaffected, disloyal, subversive and pro-Nazi."

Court-martialled for "disrespect to a superior officer," Asman goes on, he was sentenced to six months' hard labor and partial forfeiture of pay. The Army didn't treat him right, he complains. Misunderstanding his "Christian philosophy," investigators persecuted him and called him "fanatic."

Removed to Camp Shelby military prison, Asman continued zealous efforts to gain support from sympathetic Congressmen. He claims the friendship of Senators Wheeler and William Langer and Congressmen Clare Hoffman and Fred L. Crawford, who, he says, received him at their offices and appealed to the War Department on his behalf. Asman also has a good word for Rankin, and boasts that the Mississippian used anti-Communist material of his in a Congressional speech.

Asman wrote me that the Christian Veterans Intelligence Bureau would be the "Gestapo of the nationalist movement," meaning a "counter-spy system to the Reds in America." He boasted that he had "agents" in more than thirty cities. If most of his correspondents and his so-called agents are investigators, like myself, Asman won't get to first base. Asman also claimed that Talmadge had used some of his tracts. He ended his letter by saying that he was leaving for the South to lay the foundations for a campaign against Senator Pepper.

A fascist international, the Western Hemisphere Committee Against Communism, has been founded by Asman under Smith's guidance. It was born in May, 1946 in Detroit as the result of a resolution by Don Lohbeck, editor of Smith's hate sheets, and seconded by Lawrence Reilly, director of the Lutheran Research Society. Purpose of the Committee is to represent "the South American republics, Mexico, the United States and Canada for the purpose of fighting Communism." The meeting was addressed by Norman Jaques, member of the Canadian Parliament whom Smith calls an "outstanding crusader against internationalism, Communism and Zionism" and a "world-famed Christian nationalist." Jaques is a devotee of what he described as the Canadian "Social Credit Movement." It was the first time in my memory since Adrian Arcand, the Canadian Nazi, crossed the border to address a Bund meeting in 1939, that a Canadian nationalist had openly thrown in his lot with United States fringers. Jaques' topic was "Christian Liberty Versus Communist Bondage."

Jaques spoke again in Chicago in July, with Kister as chairman. The cream of Chicago's nationalist underworld came to hear Jaques discourse on "The Red Plot to Destroy Christian Civilization." The mob of about 500 super-patriots included Ellis O. Jones and Mrs. Dilling, both under sedition indictment, and others of their ilk. Jaques ascribed "all the terrible convulsions and upheavals in the world" to "aliens," waxed hot against Zionism, and drew comparisons between Jews and Christians. As may be surmised, the Jew emerged second best on the grounds that "spiritually, the Jew is faced with an impossible task, for in spite of all his efforts he can never pay to his account the debt against him, which must go on increasing forever."

Jaques' ultimate conclusion surprised even a case-hardened investigator like myself. The Jew, according to the Canadian MP:

. . . must earn his own salvation—he must work for his living. Hence his fanatical belief in the policy of full employment. The fact that a power age could largely displace human labor, and that therefore full employment is not a reasonable policy, does not affect the Jew since it agrees with his religious faith. The Christian, on the contrary, denies his faith when he applies it to the economic plane and, by supporting the policy of full employment, adopts that of the Jew, and submits himself to the servitude which it entails. By so doing he denies his Christian heritage of freedom, and violates at once his reason and faith.

Whatever this jumble meant, the Chicago nationalist mob loved it, for Jaques was "giving hell to the Jews." That's all that counted.

Returning to the same theme, Jaques ascribed sinister motives to our Atomic Development Authority: in the chairmanship of the distinguished Bernard Baruch, Jaques saw sinister implications and a dark plot by the "Hidden Hand" (that means Jews in "nationalist" parlance) against Christian civilization.

Jaques' merger with American nationalism may eventually result in the merging of United States and Canadian forces, and a unified program of hate-collaboration stretching from Argentina to Quebec, both of which are already hotbeds of nationalism. The dark outlook is that fascist forces which tried unsuccessfully to enthrone a totalitarian hierarchy in Europe are extending that evil scheme to these shores in a final attempt to internationalize fascism. Like vermin

---

This card will admit bearer and one friend to hear . . .

The Honorable NORMAN JAQUES
Member, Canadian Parliament

KIMBALL HALL
CHICAGO, ILLINOIS

MONDAY, JULY 29, 1946 — 8 P. M.

Subject:

THE RED PLOT TO DESTROY CHRISTIAN CIVILIZATION

Note: Mr. Jaques is one who fought World Government, Bretton Woods, Union Now, and helped bring about exposure of the Red plot to steal atom bomb secrets in Canada.

Auspices: Western Hemisphere Committee Against Communism
FREDERICK KISTER, Chairman — Chicago Committee

Norman Jaques, Canadian nationalist, joins hands with the American variety. They will fight Communism—à la Hitler.

which desert the sinking ship, they have made America their new
spawning ground. And America may well become the ultimate battlefield between decency and democracy on the one side, and
authoritarian bondage on the other.

In addition to two court-martialled veterans and an apparent
semi-illiterate, Kister's ménage contains a Catholic priest suspended
by his bishop for activities "detrimental to the church and the unity
of our country." Widely ballyhooed as the "Father Coughlin of the
South," Rev. Arthur W. Terminiello of Birmingham, Ala., Chaplain
of the Christian Veterans and organizer of the Union of Christian
Crusaders, is one of Gerald Smith's most vocal and useful associates.
The orders of Bishop T. J. Toolen suspending Terminiello from the
priesthood on November 27, read as follows:

Rev. Arthur W. Terminiello having refused to obey the orders of his
Bishop to cease sending out literature which we feel is detrimental to
the church and the unity of our country, resigned his pastorate at Sacred
Heart Church, Anniston, and is no longer considered a Priest in good
standing in the Diocese of Mobile, nor has he the right to use his facilities
as a Priest nor is he considered a Priest of the Diocese.

Terminiello, born in Boston in 1906 and trained for the priesthood
at St. Mary's Seminary, Baltimore, is a short, pale-faced, balding
man with buck teeth and an obsession to be a second Coughlin. He
longs to become a political martyr. Ordained a missionary in 1933,
he was assigned to work in Alabama among poor white and Negro
farmers. He helped establish St. Teresa's Village, near Bolling, Ala.,
a cooperative farming enterprise for the needy. In 1939 he aped
Social Justice by publishing *Rural Justice*. Its last issue carried articles by Carl H. Mote; Earl Southard, Chairman of the Citizens
USA Committee and a leading America Firster; and David Gordon, a Jew turned Catholic, who published racy magazines simultaneously with *Catholic International*, a religious hate sheet. *Rural
Justice* had a claimed circulation of 15,000, but Terminiello's editorial attacks on the New Deal and Britain displeased many Southerners. He gave up the magazine, the co-ops and missionary work
in 1943.

In June, 1944 Terminiello began a series of sensational broadcasts
at Novena services at the Church of the Visitation, in Huntsville,

Ala. Utterly defeatist, he pleaded for a negotiated peace and hinted that Hitler's atrocities were mere "propaganda." He printed the sermons in a booklet entitled *Our Victory.*

At the midnight mass on Christmas Eve, 1944 Terminiello outdid his Novena utterances in a scathingly un-American sermon, entitled "Santa Claus or Christ?" In phrases dripping with hate, he showered abuse on our Allies. He denounced our war effort. He blamed the White House for Pearl Harbor. Hitler emerged as having been goaded by atheistic Russia, imperialistic England and our own secret diplomacy. Terminiello made the prediction: "Tonight I repeat with greater assurance that Russia will NEVER enter German territory for the purpose of conquest, for German territory is territory FRIENDLY TO Russia. . . . The Russo-German war is a phony war."

I was interested in learning who paid for the broadcasts and the enormous amount of printing. My personal inquiries at Huntsville disclosed that Terminiello seemed to have considerable money, seldom discussed prices with printers, and paid bills promptly. One printer told me that Terminiello had paid half of a bill of his with a personal check, the other half with a check of the Church of the Visitation, of which he was pastor.

After V-J Day Terminiello became bolder. He claimed to have obtained 20,000 signatures to a petition to the Senate urging an investigation of the circumstances leading to Pearl Harbor. These petitions were distributed by various isolationist and defeatist groups. Terminiello induced Senator Langer to speak in his behalf on the Senate floor and demand an investigation of the "criminals" who "caused Pearl Harbor." Not the Nazi and Japanese war lords— but "those in Washington." After their "speedy punishment," Terminiello planned with his goon followers a bloodthirsty "March of Death" on Washington:

To make sure there will be no technical escape we are going to have proposed a Federal WAR CRIMINAL ACT which will call for hanging for those who led this country into war and who create an "incident" which will lead us to war. Begin now to organize your CRUSADE CITADELS for this MARCH OF DEATH to the traitors. . . . We will meet on the same day—and bring such men as John Roy Carlson, Walter Winchell and Harry Monsky * with us to stand trial.

* President of B'nai B'rith, a Jewish benevolent organization.

Dixie's Coughlin claims a law degree from an Alabama law school. He feels that the State of Alabama is unfair to him. The passing grade for its Bar Examination is 70. Terminiello received 67 when he took the exams to practice law. He has sued the State Board of Law Examiners to restore his papers so he can check on their marking. The case is still pending.

For a man who indiscriminately smears anyone he doesn't like as "Communist," who loosely applies the label of "traitor" to Jewish organizations, who denounces American Jewry, collaborates with some of America's most notorious hate-mongers, and has been suspended as a priest by his own Bishop, Father Terminiello is unusually sensitive to criticism. The impression he creates is that he can dish it out, but he can't take it. Terminiello is ready to sue at the drop of a hat. He has filed two suits. One is against the Huntsville, Ala. *Times* for $100,000 for alleged damage to his reputation as a "patriot." The other is against the Birmingham *News* and *Age-Herald* for $500,000. Terminiello drew up the complaint himself when various Birmingham lawyers turned him down as a client. He has stated that Maximilian St. George of Chicago will handle his case in court. St. George served Joe McWilliams in the sedition trials and later defended Gerald Smith in Chicago. Chicago nationalists claim him as one of their own.

Terminiello's tactics made him unpopular and he was transferred from Huntsville to the Sacred Heart Church at Anniston. Terminiello continued his barrage of defeatist, hate-inciting literature. He denounced Masonry and Zionist propaganda as seeking the "destruction of religious unity," inaugurated *The Crusader*, organ of his Union of Christian Crusaders, travelled to Boston to speak at a banquet tendered by Coughlinites.

Back in Alabama, Terminiello again aroused criticism in Anniston and went to Birmingham. Here he intensified his hate crusade. Homer Maertz, publisher of *Jewish Ritual Murder*, visited him in Alabama, Maertz told me at the time of his trial in Queens. Terminiello's propaganda assaults reached such intensity and attracted so much unfavorable attention that he was suspended from the priesthood. He set up shop independently in Birmingham, opening the Unique Publishing Service. His headquarters are a clearing house for a large list of nationalist and isolationist literature, which is sold mainly to nationalists north of the Mason and Dixon line. By the end of 1945 his Union claimed 40,000 enrolled Crusaders. Terminiello disapproves of my writings, but he corresponded with "Thompson," who wrote as a Christian veteran for "truth-telling" literature. He answered on red-white-blue stationery carrying his emblem, a cross, and the legend, *In Hoc Signo Vinces* (By This Sign Thou Shalt Conquer), encircled with a cord. The letterhead proclaims *"Deus Vult* (God Wills It): Union of Christian Crusaders." On October 31, 1945 Terminiello thanked me for my "encouraging letter." He had received others like it from "a cross section of the best people of our country"—meaning nationalists. He ended:

Under separate cover you will receive literature explaining what I believe to be the solution for these evils and outlining a plan of action for all of us who are more interested in preserving our way of life than in perpetuating our "handout" economy at the expense of the blood of our boys. We cannot allow irresponsible rabble-rousers at home to be successful in their plans for revolution and chaos. Wishing you God's choicest blessings, I am,

> Yours for Christ and country,
> A. W. Terminiello

Shrewdly, Terminiello declared he would send no literature "construed as seditious" to members of the Armed Forces. But he will send it freely to anyone else. The diet he mailed me included the Midnight Mass sermon, *Santa Claus or Christ?*; a leaflet entitled *The Double Deal Steps to the Cross of War*, which ridiculed the Atlantic Charter and heaped scorn on Roosevelt and Churchill; and one entitled *Zionism Is Treason*. Another sermon, *The Cross of War* (it is said to have passed the million mark), justified the Jap attack. "We gave the Japs a REASON to attack us," Terminiello declared in this amazing sermon, which he preached and published during the war. Branding "victory" as a sham and mockery, he exhorted:

We must stop joining the refrain—"We must win the war." Let us examine first whom they mean when they say "WE." Who is going to win the war? Is it the boys who are doing the fighting and dying? Is it their parents, their children, their wives? . . . There are some things worse than defeat, and one of them is to prostitute our flag and our democratic way of life on behalf of a foreign tyranny. If by winning the war we mean taking cities like Berlin—that too would be a false victory. Berlin is a beautiful city. But we should not pay one cent for it. . . . We have enough big cities of our own.

Terminiello originally delivered the sermon to his parish from the pulpit of the Church of Visitation on October 22, 1944.

Late in 1945 reports came that Terminiello planned to join forces with Smith. Not wanting to arouse his suspicions by inquiring bluntly, I wrote and asked whether his Crusaders included a "special veterans unit," and whether he planned to speak in "Thompson's" home town, Buffalo, where Smith maintains a unit of Coughlinites. The "Coughlin of the South" replied: "Your veteran unit is a good idea. Probably we could arrange it. How many vets do you know who would be interested? I certainly look forward to your active support. I expect to speak in Buffalo with Gerald L. K. Smith soon. Hope I see you."

A friendship by mail had been growing between the two men. On January 31, 1945 Smith wrote Terminiello a significant letter which reveals the strategy behind their association:

Dear Reverend Terminiello:

I cannot begin to tell you how much I appreciate your letter of January 25. It is almost too good to be true to discover one like yourself in a position of importance and trust who seems perfectly willing to throw caution to the winds and dive in with abandon for the salvation of our beautiful America and our Christian way of life.

The Jews and the British are attempting to cripple the Nationalist Movement by introducing anti-Catholic bigotry. You and I, from the South and North, joining hands, can do much to stem this awful attempt being made on the part of the anti-Christian elements. You will be interested in knowing that the second half of your historic address [*The Cross of War*] will appear in the March issue of *The Cross and the Flag*. . . .

I just returned from Washington, D.C., and only wish I could see you personally to tell you some of the good things I learned while there. . . .

Sincerely yours for Christ and America,
Gerald L. K. Smith

This friendship ripened when the two met in New Orleans early in January, 1946. Shortly afterward the "Alabama Coughlin" accepted the Chaplaincy of the Smith-promoted Christian Veterans of America. On January 18 Terminiello spoke in Philadelphia at the first of a series of appearances at Coughlinite meetings in Northern cities which were to end in his arrest and conviction for rioting. He appeared in the City of Brotherly Love under the auspices of the "Crusading" National Blue Star Mothers of America (a different group from the praiseworthy Blue Star Mothers) led by Mrs. Catharine V. Brown, Patriot No. 4 at the Queens Christian Front rally. In Philadelphia they play host to Meinhart's unit of Christian War Veterans. Permission to use a Catholic hall being refused by Church authorities, they entertained Terminiello at the headquarters of their Current Events Club. Investigators present said the audience of some 300 included about 125 young men from about 18 to 25, many of them in uniform or wearing discharge buttons.

Deus Vult

Union
of

Christian Crusaders

REV. A. W. TERMINIELLO, M.A., LL.B., SECRETARY

United for the cause of freedom of speech, the press, religion and assembly

OCT 31 1945

Dear Mr. Thompson:

Many thanks for your encouraging letter. This fine spirit of loyalty to God and country is evident in the thousands of letters we are receiving in response to this movement. Representing, as they do, a cross section of the best people of our country, we may have some hope that even at this late date it is possible that the forces of evil and corruption rampant in our land will not prevail.

Under separate cover you will receive literature explaining what I believe to be the solution for these evils and outlining a plan of action for all of us who are more interested in preserving our way of life than in perpetuating our "handout" economy at the expense of the blood of our boys. We cannot allow irresponsible rabble-rousers at home to be successful in their plans for revolution and chaos.

Wishing you God's choicest blessings, I am

Yours for Christ and country,

(Rev.) A. W. Terminiello

Terminiello greeted the Coughlinites in the audience. He denied "any anti-Semitism," but went on, "I do say I am an American, thank God, and when I mention Jews, I mean Zionist Jews, and I don't want any truck with either of them." Announcing that he had accepted the Chaplaincy of the Christian Veterans, he urged ex-servicemen to join "this new Christian Crusade." There was resounding applause from the Mothers and their friends.

Paul Meinhart, next on the program, assailed the leading veterans' organizations as "pro-Jewish" and urged all vets to join Kister.

Moving on, in the next few days Terminiello addressed large audiences in Cleveland, Pittsburgh and Detroit. More than 200 picketed the Cleveland meeting. *The Pittsburgh Catholic,* official diocesan organ, carried on its front page Bishop Toolen's declaration suspending Terminiello from his rights and duties as a priest.

In Detroit, on February 5, 1946 I heard Rev. Terminiello speak before a packed house of better-dressed nationalists in the swanky ballroom of the Book-Cadillac Hotel. He was sponsored by Gerald Smith. Unleashing a brand of anti-Semitism I had not heard from a priest since Christian Front days, Father Terminiello spoke for more than an hour. He admitted that eight lawyers in Birmingham had refused to represent him in bringing suit against Birmingham papers for alleged libel. "Why?" Terminiello shouted. "Why, because of the fear of the Jews!" Later he declared that "Jews" had become "brazen." "You and I are going to make up our mind. We can't take it any more. We must oppose every attempt to dilute Christianity with their paganism, oppose every attempt to democratize our Republic, to Sovietize our Christian home, to fertilize with American boys the Zionist empire!" Wildly applauded by the crowd, Terminiello yelled, "Now, take F. D. R.! Some people do not think he's dead. Some think he's in Palestine!"

After the meeting Smith announced that those who wanted to help Father Terminiello financially could make their contribution while shaking his hand. Dozens of the faithful lined up and slipped into his hand bills of undisclosed denomination. This is one way in which the nationalist movement is financed—through cash donations which leave no tell-tale marks. As the flock of faithful were occupied in that task I picked up copies of Maertz' *Dispatch* and the Jew-baiting *The X-Ray* which I found strewn on the seats.

Two nights later a crowd estimated at more than 1,000 people picketed the Chicago club where Terminiello spoke under Christian Veterans auspices. The audience of about 800 jammed aisles and balcony. Many were turned away. Sharing the platform with Terminiello were Mrs. Dilling, her co-worker Ellis O. Jones, Kister, Flitcraft and many other nationalist big-wigs.

The blunt quality of Terminiello's speech is indicated by these amazing excerpts, taken from a report on the proceedings: ". . . don't ever use that word 'democracy' again. This country is a Republic . . . when we degenerate to the so-called Red democracy, we are degenerating to the level of the howling mob on the outside." Making the fantastic assertion that President Roosevelt and Henry Morgenthau were behind a plan for the starvation of babies and pregnant women in Germany, Terminiello declared President Roosevelt had refused to control infection there. This led up to the equally incredible charge of atrocities practiced against the Germans, according to Terminiello, by persons of a certain "kind" in the service:

You will know who is behind it when I tell you the story of a doctor in Akron, Ohio. He boasted to a friend of mine . . . while he was in the service of this country as a doctor, he and others of his kind made it a practice—now, this was not only one man . . . to amputate the limbs of every German they came in contact with, whenever they could get away. . . .

. . . Someone reminded me of the plan to sterilize them. The nurses, they tell me, are going to inject diseases in them, syphilis and other diseases. . . . F. D. R. told us one time—how well I remember that—"Things don't just happen that way. They are planned."

Coming to the postwar period, Terminiello stated, "We have gathered together what we call the peace-loving nations of the world, and the only ones that are not in this peace are the nations that have been at peace. The only ones eligible for membership are warring nations."

As a result of rioting which broke out outside the hall between pickets and nationalists, a number of persons, including Smith, Terminiello and Kister, were arrested and taken to the police station. A jury, composed, as it chanced, largely of Catholics, found Terminiello guilty of inciting to riot, and he was fined $100. Smith was sentenced to 60 days in jail for contempt of court; his assistant, Don Lohbeck, got 30 days. All have appealed. Kister's case is pending.

The July, 1946 issue of Terminiello's *Crusader* carried a sinister item: "Confidential sources reveal that Vigilantes are being organized in the United States. One man is being chosen for every precinct who can recruit from 10 to 1,000 men on short notice to put themselves at the disposal of the law enforcement agencies." Can this be a budding storm troop movement patterned on the Christian Front? Are the Vigilantes to be patterned on the Christian Front Sport Clubs which were secretly organized to help preserve "law and order" and "fight against Communism"?—the first with brass knuckles, the latter with guns and bullets?

On May 28, 1946 "patriot" leaders gathered under Gerald Smith's wing in a solemn "Christian" convention at St. Louis. The event brought together the largest postwar assembly: some Jew-baiters, some poison peddlers, and others, nationalists of various shadings. The list included:

Norman Jaques of Canada
Gerald L. K. Smith
Mrs. David Stanley (Coughlinite
    leader)
Rev. Arthur Terminiello
Frederick Kister
Lorence Asman
Kenneth Goff
Kirkpatrick Dilling (son of Mrs.
    Dilling)

Harry Romer
Leo Stammen
Frank J. Liette

Smith's personal entourage
{
Mrs. Gerald L. K. Smith
Miss Renata Legant
Don Lohbeck
Stephen Goodyear
Rev. L. L. Marion
    (Smith's pastor)
}

The mob ran into rough weather when civic-minded organizations observed that municipally owned Kiel Auditorium—which had been engaged by the "patriots"—could only be used for events "which shall be of benefit to the city." The groups ran a full-page advertisement in St. Louis newspapers protesting the rental of the city-owned property to Gerald Smith "or any other bigot." It was sponsored by:

Gold Star Mothers of World War II
State Americanism Commission, Veterans of Foreign Wars
State Americanism Commission, American Legion
AF of L Central Trades and Labor Union
Jewish War Veterans of St. Louis

St. Louis Industrial Union Council, CIO
Jewish Community Relations Council
State Department AMVETS (American Veterans of World War II)
American Veterans Committee

Chief of Police James J. Mitchell was alarmed that the nationalist mob might cause the usual rioting, and forbade the meeting. The next day, however, he relented. Gerald Smith and his mobsters were extended that privilege of democracy which they are trying to destroy.

Smith, Terminiello and Kister all deny being "fascist." Each goes to great lengths now to denounce fascism. They fulfill Huey Long's prophecy, "Fascism will come to America in the name of anti-fascism." It may start with a group of disgruntled veterans who find a fanatical leader. A suspended priest or a Klansman like Swift can help equally to arouse the passions of the mob. Once the mob is aroused the rest comes easy, *if* another essential ingredient is present—economic disaster. We can survive the Smiths and Kisters, as the body survives many toxins in its blood stream. But America may be unable to survive them in combination with unemployment, poverty, disillusionment, mass frustration. Under such circumstances they and their adherents command an ominous power, as did Hitler's Brown Shirts, who were jeered at and belittled as mere "crackpots." Gerald Smith bellowed in 1944:

My time will come in the post-war period. The candidate will not be me; it will be a young veteran of this war, but I'll be behind him. If business conditions are bad—inflation, widespread unemployment, farm foreclosures—then my candidate will be elected. . . . Then the flame will spread, and the extreme nationalist will come to power. . . . When chaos comes, I'll be the leader.

Smith may be a Hitler-type crackpot. An economically and politically healthy nation can survive many such goons. But when we get another depression some Huey Long will inevitably arise to "save America" from "Communism," unions, Jews, Masons, Negroes, Catholics, Winchell, internationalism, immigrants, aliens, the CIO, the PAC, or what not. The "Franco way" or the "Hitler way" may be offered as a remedy. Or it may be something entirely new and "American," but rooted in the un-American hate pattern. One cannot foretell the exact form of American nationalism while it is developing, or the precise mob appeals which will prove most effective. I can only indicate the process roughly.

In all instances hate is induced at the expense of an imaginary "enemy" by cleverly playing upon prejudice, narrowness, selfishness and discontent. Hate is the main propellant of the nationalist revolutionary movement—consuming, overpowering hate which can blind reason so completely that even the sincere American becomes a pawn of the demagogue. Though anti-Semitism will be an integral part of it, here as in Germany certain Jews will kneel to the Jew-baiter in a deluded attempt to save their own necks. Fascism is a disease which can attack anyone, regardless of his race or creed. It victimizes most easily those in whom fears and doubts can be quickly aroused.

When the hate has grown sufficiently in fury and the success of the nationalist mob spirit is assured, then it will become safe for labor-baiting, democracy-hating "big-money" boys to give openly instead of feeding the revolutionary underground surreptitiously. Whatever faction first arouses mob hate and directs it, that faction, or more likely a coalition of anti-democratic factions, will rule America—through the veteran. That is the hope and strategy of our Smiths and Terminiellos.

"It is the veteran that will have the fate of this nation in his hand," Kister writes in his bulletin. "Our ability to keep him informed on the facts will depend on money, work, and organization." Going into a tirade against "Communism," he urges help—financial and moral help—from those who "have the most to lose in material wealth and culture."

Kister alone is a nonentity. In pre-Hitler Germany there were countless misguided youths like him. Should it "happen here," Kister himself may already have been forgotten. But Kister and his henchmen are symbols. They illustrate the process by which the nationalist wave is seeking to gain tidal proportions. Kister and his fellow goons are ripples. The conscientious American will watch them, as the meteorologist watches every shifting wind, every moisture-laden cloud bank, every fluctuation of the barometer. They tell him tomorrow's weather.

CHAPTER SIX

Nationalist Boosters, Inc.

> The veterans of our latest war of abominations already are de-
> claring their disillusionment. A mighty storm of protest, of anger,
> of resentment, of vengeance is in the making. These returning
> veterans have been trained to kill their enemies. If they decide,
> after an inspection of the home front, that their most deadly
> enemies have been the politicians at home, a personal account-
> ing will be the next order of business.
>
> Carl H. Mote, 1946

IN HIS BULLETIN, Frederick Kister boasts that the Christian Veterans
of America are endorsed by "practically every patriotic group in the
country." That is, his kind of "patriots." The Kisterites also have
less notorious boosters and admirers. The extreme nationalists
would get nowhere without the support of respectable Americans
—people who are less crude than the Gerald Smiths, better dressed,
who eat at clubs and vent their hates behind locked doors. The
friends of the so-called Christian Veterans and their leaders present
an amazing cross section of American life which takes us far from
the humble bleachers of the Celina Fair Grounds.

Chaplain Arthur W. Terminiello has been congratulated on his
"courage" by a self-styled "Gentleman from Indiana." Letters addressed to this gentleman in Indiana are, somehow, often answered
from New York. He is a member of the Advisory Board of the
powerful, super-conservative New York group, the Committee for
Constitutional Government, founded by Frank Gannett, wealthy
newspaper publisher, of which Dr. Edward A. Rumely * is Secre-

---

* Rumely, former Executive Secretary of the Committee for Constitutional
Government, was convicted on December 18, 1920 of using German funds for
carrying on Kaiserite propaganda and failing to report the funds to the Alien
Property Custodian, as required by law. For the full story of Rumely's association with Imperial Germany's agents see *Under Cover*.

tary. The man "from Indiana" is former Congressman Samuel B. Pettengill.

On March 2, 1945, while Americans were fighting and dying in Germany and the Philippines, Pettengill ordered from Terminiello 100 copies of his infamous *The Cross of War* sermon. It denounced our war effort and urged nationalists: "We must stop joining the refrain, 'We must win the war.'" Pettengill suggests in his writings that he is a hundred percent American. He is the author of a book on the Constitution and speaks volubly on Americanism. Pettengill screams "Communist" at those displaying a progressive philosophy; however, he buys Terminiello's poison wares. On March 2, 1945 he wrote Terminiello:

Herewith my check for $3.00 for which please send me 100 copies of "The Cross of War." I congratulate you upon your courage.

The Gerald L. K. Smiths and their brothers in the same cause would wither on the vine except for the moral support of those on a higher social and political plane whose mental processes apparently resemble theirs.

Certain Congressmen have accepted the support of notorious nationalists. The relations of super-isolationist Representative Clare Hoffman of Michigan with Homer Maertz in the fall of 1944 are a case in point. A copyrighted story in the Chicago *Sun* on November 2, 1944, by William I. Flanagan, charged that Maertz and Hoffman conferred "frequently and openly in the lobby of the Hotel Vincent" during Hoffman's campaign in Benton Harbor, Michigan. Maertz accompanied Hoffman to campaign meetings and also "spied" on the opposing Democratic candidate, Flanagan said.

Hoffman denied he knew Maertz, asserting, "I have no connection with Maertz or any organization he represents. He's taking no part in my campaign. I never saw the man before he came here."

As for Maertz, the notorious pro-Nazi führer of the *Deutsch-Amerikanischer Einheitsfront* also denied any links with Hoffman. "I'm not really campaigning for Hoffman," he told Flanagan. "I'd like to, but I think I'd do more harm than good."

Maertz' statements are belied by his own letter to Mrs. Lyrl Van Hyning postmarked "Benton Harbor, Mich. Nov 3 1944—1:30 PM," written in his handwriting on the stationery of the Hotel Vincent—

where he and Hoffman had registered. Maertz wrote Mrs. Van Hyning, Chicago nationalist Mothers leader, as follows:

You probably would like to hear about events from the spot itself. The campaign is hot. White hot.

My prediction is that Hoffman will win. When the Col. & I came here it looked mighty bad. We went to work and really put everything we had behind it. Now the lies circulated about Hoffman are being corrected. (By counter leaflets, adds [*sic*], etc.) Hoffman is so honest and orthodox that he wouldn't fight fire with fire. However, we found a few top men here that would and are.

. . . You deserve all the credit in the world for what you and through you the women are doing for Anderson * and your gesture to help Hoffman. That will not be forgotten. At least as far as I'm concerned. You'll see. With best of personal wishes

Your correspondent
Maertz

"THE GENTLEMAN FROM INDIANA"
SAMUEL B. PETTENGILL

UNION TRUST BUILDING
SOUTH BEND, INDIANA

SHOREHAM BUILDING
WASHINGTON, D. C.

Room 405,
205 East 42nd Street,
New York 17, N. Y.

Father Terminiello,   March 2, 1945.
Box 556,
Huntsville, Ala.

Dear Father Terminiello:

Herewith my check for $3.00 for which please

send me 100 copies of "The Cross of War".

I congratulate you upon your courage.

Sincerely,

SAMUEL B. PETTENGILL

"INSIDE YOUR CONGRESS"
— TWICE A WEEK

This letter needs no caption!

* In 1944 Charles J. Anderson, Jr., of Chicago was Republican candidate for Representative from the Sixth Congressional District. He lost. On April 9, 1945 Chicago papers reported him arrested, "charged with assault to commit murder" upon a 15-year-old boy whom he caught tying the bumper of his car to that of another automobile as a prank. Anderson is out on bail.

With Maertz' and the mysterious colonel's help, Hoffman won. Two years later, when Hoffman was renominated in the primaries, Gerald Smith crowed that it was "the most outstanding victory of his public career." Maertz could not help Hoffman this time. As of July, 1946 he was serving time in the New York City prison.

As Thompson, I sent a "patriotic" form letter to Upton Close (Josef Washington Hall), author and former radio commentator for Lumbermen's Mutual Casualty Company. I did not expect to hear from him. I am used to being shocked. But even I was jolted when Close wrote back praising Kister and enclosing Kister's viciously intolerant leaflet, *Christian Veterans, Awake*. Close wrote:

Your good letter of March 7 has been in my briefcase ever since it was handed to me in Detroit. I have waited until I returned to Hollywood, because of the matter which I am enclosing [Kister's leaflet]. I am referring you to this organization of Mr. Kister's—because just at present it is the only one on our side which is really "under way" and doing something constructive. About election time there will no doubt be other groups which will be organized—but I have every faith in this one, and the young chap at the head.

When I wrote Close a second time I did not mention my correspondence with Kister, but asked what he thought of Kister "as a leader." I had heard reports that Hart was organizing a veterans' group and wanted to know more. I waited anxiously for the answer, and it came. Close was friendlier than in his first letter:

In my opinion Kister is an excellent leader. As a matter of fact, he won't need boosting so much as he might tend to need a little holding back. But I think you need have no fear about his leadership.

So far as Merwin K. Hart's organizing a group of veterans, [sic] I know nothing about it.

Copies of Close's radio scripts came in. His radio programs at this writing are being sponsored by the National Economic Council. Its director, Merwin K. Hart, works in friendly cooperation with the Gannett-Rumely-Pettengill triumvirate. Hart has sneered at "democracy" and offered Franco's Falangism as substitute. He was called "pro-fascist" by Supreme Court Justice Robert H. Jackson.

A bitter isolationist, staunch America Firster, ardent Russophobe, Close has also consistently expressed opinions unusually favorable to the Japanese:

March 4, 1941: I can see much more constructive future in letting the Japanese wear out what remains of their empire-building frenzy, and it's nearly worn out, I can tell you. . . . And nobody can quite accuse me . . . of being pro-Japanese.

Jan. 30, 1944: The crime against the heroes of Bataan did not begin with the Japs. It began with our people and Congress and the Administration, who put those boys out there. . . . Their desperate resistance angered the Japanese and brought on them brutal reprisals.

Sept. 3, 1945: The Japs will be able to offset the proved instances of atrocities by other instances of relative mercy. It seems now that the captured Doolittle fliers were not executed.

On March 25, 1946 Close revealed himself as an ardent nationalist:

Had Commander Stassen put his campaign on a base of proclaimed nationalism of the highest type instead of the crumbling base of Willkie one-worldism, Stassen might have walked away with such national leadership. Our veterans just out of uniform are hungry and thirsting for new leadership with political sex appeal.

Close's concern is not restricted to Japs only. He is very fond of Sam Pettengill. His bulletin, *Closer-Ups,* on September 10, 1945 endorsed Terminiello's correspondent as follows: "Sam Pettengill you all know. I don't want you to forget him. His excellent column 'Inside Your Congress' is getting into many of our smaller city, but very influential papers. His address is 205 East 42nd Street, New York." Close's bulletins have endorsed John T. Flynn—intimate friend of Hart—who follows the "nationalist" line that *we* caused Pearl Harbor, not the Japs. Close has also championed Tyler Kent, the decoding clerk who betrayed our state secrets.

On March 4, 1941 Close deprecated the sympathy for England and hatred for Germany displayed by "the Anglophiles and the Jewish people on the umbilical coast, east of the Hudson River." Later, on February 11, 1945 Close's broadcast scolded the "Protestant chiselers" and "Jewish opportunists" for calling attention to the rise of racial and religious prejudice. Close does not consider himself a biased man, and he once offered a $1000 War Bond "to the person who will bring the first authentic quotation from my writings or broadcasts which is 'anti-British' or 'anti-Russian' . . . [and] to any person who will produce anything I have ever written or said in public that is anti-Jewish." Close apparently reserved to himself the right to serve as judge and jury.

In March, 1946 Close spoke in Pittsburgh and praised Governor Edward Martin. The Governor rejected Close in these bold American terms:

I have never accepted, nor will I ever accept, the support of those who seek to breed discord or strife among the American people. We reject as unwelcome and unwanted in the Republican Party those who spread the unwholesome and corrupting doctrines of hate, intolerance and bigotry, no matter which party banner they flaunt to disguise their false representations and their destructive motives.

UPTON CLOSE
JOSEF WASHINGTON HALL

March 19, 1946

Mr. Robert Thompson, Jr.
1306 Delaware Ave.
Buffalo 9, New York

Dear Mr. Thompson:

Your good letter of March 7 has been in my briefcase ever since it was handed to me in Detroit. I have waited until I returned to Hollywood, because of the matter which I am enclosing.

I am referring you to this organization of Mr. Kister's -- because just at present it is the only one on our side which is really "under way" and doing something constructive. About election time there will no doubt be other groups which will be organized -- but I have every faith in this one, and the young chap at the head.

As you know, I am trying in every way I can to inform people about communism, and just at present I'm doing all I can physically. However, I am keeping your letter on file -- and when the right time comes, I'll surely let you know!

In the meantime, why not find out about Mr. Kister's organization?

Sincerely,

Upton Close

April 18, 1946

Mr. R. Thompson, Jr.
1306 Delaware Ave.
Buffalo 9, New York

Dear Mr. Thompson:

Thanks so much for your letter of April 10. I'm sorry that I haven't got around to answering it sooner -- but I can only plead pressure of work. You know that excuse well, though, so I won't use it any more!

In my opinion, Kister is an excellent leader. As a matter of fact, he won't need boosting so much as he might tend to need a little holding back. But I think you need have no fear about his leadership.

So far as Merwin K. Hart's organizing a group of veterans, I know nothing about it. At least he hasn't told me anything about it at all.

Please excuse my briefness, Mr. Thompson -- but I'm going to rush off to my 600 acre ranch in the San Jacinto Valley and commune with the horses!

Write again, won't you?

Sincerely,

Upton Close

A super-patriot steers a likely recruit to a nationalist "leader."

I emphasize these undeniable facts because of a recent meeting in Western Pennsylvania at which ideas and opinions were expressed by a speaker who had no regard for the truth when he professed adherence to the principles of the Republican Party. I warn the citizens of Pennsylvania to be constantly on their guard against the evil influence of persons who masquerade under whatever guise best serves their unholy purpose, which is to undermine the structure of our liberty and endanger the future of America.

Close's manager, who distributes his news letter and has charge of his speaking engagements, according to Eugene Segal of the Cleveland *Press,* is Leo F. Reardon, former confidential adviser to Father Coughlin.

Smith and his goons would starve were it not for friends like the late Carl H. Mote. The Indiana nationalist was contemptuous of Jews and of the Catholic hierarchy. He called Cardinal Mundelein a "half Jew" and the Most Rev. Bernard J. Sheil, Auxiliary Bishop of Chicago and a liberal Catholic, a "garrulous humbug." Mote was also a violent man. I saw him smash his fist at one of the youths at the Celina Fair Grounds. His speeches were filled with references to ropes, hangings, revolution, vengeance. Speaking in 1941, he declared: "Unless there is a shortage of rope, at the end of five years human necks will be more talked about than bottlenecks. . . . If and when a Caesar appears, he is likely to come from the Army, the Navy, the Air Force, the Marines."

While the war was on Mote published in his magazine, *America Preferred,* an "extract" from an amazing letter entitled *The Master Race,* which he credited to an unnamed "international lawyer": "I am ashamed to be an American . . . the war has fully demonstrated one thing, and that is that the Germans are superior to Americans and English physically, intellectually, aesthetically and morally. They are the master race all right, if 'master' means superior. I think it is about time to tell the ignorant Americans something about the greatness of the Germans. . . ."

I wrote Mote as Thompson and he answered: "I want you to write Mr. Frederick Kister, identify yourself with his organization (tell him you are doing so at my suggestion) and keep in touch with me." Mote helped in the founding of Kister's veterans and was Chairman of Gerald Smith's America First Party. He was a friend of Lawrence

Dennis, the "intellectual fascist" who is under indictment for sedition. *

A former Illinois Commander of the Veterans of Foreign Wars spoke for Kister in Chicago, in November, 1945, on the "problems" facing the new veteran. He is Earl Southard, a kingpin of the Chicago nationalists. Together with William J. Grace, past State Commander of the VFW and the American Legion, † Southard directed the Citizens Keep America Out of War Committee. Its objectives were identical with those of the America First Committee. Dennis spoke for it. During 1941 the Committee sent out photographs of flag-draped coffins marked "Bundles FROM Britain."

For these and kindred "patriotic" deeds, including his advocacy of "no obedience" to the Lend-Lease Act, Southard was suspended on August 16, 1941 as State Commander of the VFW, pending court-martial by the organization for alleged "disloyalty to the United States and disobedience to the Constitution." ‡ Southard lashed back verbally at the "little Joe Stalins" in the VFW. Grace acted as his attorney. Delegates to the VFW convention refused, by a vote of 2,225 to 261, to permit Southard to sit as a delegate. Southard was found guilty of disloyalty § by the court-martial, but reinstated as Commander of the Illinois Department by the retiring Commander-in-Chief, Dr. Joseph C. Menendez, who revoked the suspension with a warning to Southard to conduct himself "in a manner to be worthy of membership in the Veterans of Foreign Wars."

After Pearl Harbor, however, Southard and Grace renamed their

* In *Dynamics of War and Revolution,* Dennis expressed his outlook: "I do not believe in democracy or the intelligence of the masses. I am in favor of the revolution here. . . . This book is addressed not to the masses but to the elite or to the ruling groups, actual and potential. It is the governing minority of wealth, prestige and power, economic and cultural, present and future, which determines whether, when, where, how, and whom we fight." Dennis greatly influenced nationalists.

† No reflection on the Americanism of the Veterans of Foreign Wars or the American Legion is intended. Neither group bars a veteran because of his political affiliation. Even Communists manage to join. The presence of nationalists in the Legion and VFW reminds us that a few bad potatoes may influence a barrel of good ones. Legitimate veterans' groups can best serve America's postwar needs by watchfulness in selecting their leadership.

‡ According to the New York *Times* of August 17, 1941.

§ According to the New York *Times* of August 30, 1941.

Citizens Keep America Out of War Committee the Citizens USA Committee. Throughout the war they held defeatist meetings, denounced rationing, our Allies and our national leadership and—in the name of patriotism—generally did their utmost to impair morale. Citizens USA Committee meetings became rallying points for the nationalist political underworld in Chicago. Smith, Mote, Father Curran and Rev. C. O. Stadsklev, Minneapolis Anglo-Saxon theory preacher who attends J. A. Lovell's conventions, spoke in an endless parade. Frederick Kister served, before being drafted, as an usher at these meetings.

In the summer of 1945 Grace and Southard parted company. Southard carries on under the Committee for American Independence. He sells, on a commission basis, nationalist literature issued by the country's foremost poison peddlers, and publishes his own under the imprint of Citizens Press. Southard and Grace are still friendly. They attended a "secret" banquet on March 4, 1946, in Chicago, at which Kister, Smith, Mrs. Dilling and Terminiello were present, with a concentration of the city's most ardent nationalists. Arrangements for the affair were made by Lorence Asman. So secret was this function supposed to be that guests were screened three times to prevent anyone not a "friend" from getting in. Some of my friends got in too, however, and I have a lengthy report on exactly what happened.

The study of Kister's friends and boosters led me next to Pittsburgh. There I interviewed at his home Charles Madden, former Legion Post Commander and a follower of Smith and Coughlin. Instead of posing as Thompson the nationalist, I made Thompson appear the "doubting Thomas," and decided to test Madden's reaction by calling Kister a "radical."

"Well, it's always a radical man with a lot of nerve that gets things done," Madden said. I asked whether I ought to join Kister's Veterans. "He has a right to organize," Madden replied. "The only way you can have liberty is to give it."

From members of the American Legion in Buffalo, N. Y., I learned that in 1944 Madden had telephoned a Buffalo hotel and arranged to use its facilities for a meeting, giving the impression that it would be a Legion affair. The hotel announced it as such. When Paul Wamsley, Dr. Joseph Hawn, Mort Levy and other Buffalo Legionnaires heard, with surprise, about the unexpected

"Legion" meeting, they turned up unannounced and found Madden on the platform with Gerald Smith. Madden then delivered an innocuous talk on the Declaration of Independence. His appearance with Smith, however, told heavily against his candidacy for the State Legion command. I have, incidentally, a leaflet announcing Madden as a co-speaker with Smith in Buffalo in May, 1944, but Madden kept away from the meeting.

On the Sunday when Pearl Harbor was bombed, Madden was chairman of an America First meeting in Pittsburgh at which he and the then Senator Gerald P. Nye expounded the familiar line that the New Dealers—not the Japs—were the war-mongers. Told by a reporter that Pearl Harbor had been struck, Nye shrugged.

"It sounds terribly fishy to me," he said. "Is it sabotage, or is it an attack? I am going to withhold comment until I can find out what this is all about." He then switched into a denunciation of the President.

When the audience was informed of the bombing, one of the assembled patriots shouted, "Throw the President out!"

Before leaving Madden, I asked whether he knew Mrs. Marie I. Lohle, leader of the Coughlinite clan in Pittsburgh. "Yes, I know her," Madden said. "She lives on Squirrel Hill. You go up the street and take car No. 60."

A kindred spirit in Pittsburgh, and also a friend of Mrs. Lohle, is F. H. Smith of the War Veterans Association of America, a paper organization. I wrote Smith for information about the group, using the stationery of the Friends of Democracy, but Smith replied curtly: "We do not wish you to meddle into affairs that are no concern to you . . . thus I am forced, as real American to deny you the information you want." I wanted to know if Smith was linked to Kister. I got the information by writing him as the "veteran," Thompson. This time Smith answered: "I suggest that you get in touch with Frederick Kister. . . . He has a wonderful movement in line with the ideals of the America First program. He will see that you are active in Veterans affairs in your area. Let me hear from you soon."

If only a few Southards and Smiths were attempting to spread nationalism among veterans, the movement would probably be ineffectual, but the entire extreme rightist political underworld, from coast to coast, is bombarding the ex-serviceman with insidious paper bullets. For the present, all are backing Kister. Should his flame die before reaching major proportions, they will promote any new-comer. Their common objective is to poison the veteran's mind.

Take William Kullgren of Atascadero, California, self-styled expert in "Astrological forecasts, all phases of prophecy, health, economics, current problems." One of his prophecies was that Hitler in "a lightning stroke" would reach Moscow—in 1940! In Kullgren's astrological chart, the stars always favored the fascists and never smiled on the democracies. When things went wrong, the Jews were blamed for influencing the outer cosmic world. Kullgren—who was once indicted for alleged sedition—attended J. A. Lovell's United Israel Fellowship conclave in 1945. "It was the most enjoyable convention I ever attended," he wrote.

Kullgren's newspaper, *America Speaks*, publishes the sentiments of Mote and Pettengill. In April, 1945 he reprinted Pettengill's pet work by Terminiello, *The Cross of War*. I wrote Kullgren as Thompson, asking his advice on a nationalist veterans' group. He answered:

As far as I am concerned, there is only one worthy of serious consideration, and that is the one headed by Frederick Kister of Chicago. This one is fundamentally sound, Christian, and American; and frankly I am expecting great things of it, and would suggest that you throw your lot with this Christian Veterans' organization. I am advising all my readers who are veterans to join up; not only join up, but contribute financially to its support. I believe in this organization so much that I am giving them one page in *America Speaks* for their own page.

One of Kullgren's busiest correspondents is Hubert H. Heath, publisher of a coarse dope sheet, known as *The Herald*, in Hot Springs, N. M. One of his editorials reads: "Some of the reddest and most radical internationalists have been registered as Republicans all their lives, and the Democratic Party is no more responsible for the reds kept in power than is the Republican Party for internationalists like Stassen, Dewey, Willkie and scores of the same ilk." Heath reprints articles by Winrod, Senator "Pappy" O'Daniel and Pettengill. In answer to my letter as to which veterans' group "Thompson" should join, Heath sent me one of Kister's lurid leaflets and enclosed an article of his own. Printed on cheap, yellow paper, it was headlined "Caste System Dangerous and Thoroughly Un-American":

Do away with the dangerous and un-American caste system that West Point and Annapolis borrowed directly from the Prussian warlords. . . . Let us be American in heart and soul and return to our Constitutional system, and ship . . . Mr. Sidney Hillman and his radicals back to Russia where they belong.

How Hillman could ever have influenced West Point was not explained.

Fred Dyster of Los Angeles was another Kister-booster who endorsed his Veterans. Dyster's book, *America's Tomorrow*, urges that "foreign-born citizens should not be privileged to vote or hold office, or be placed on the payroll in domestic affairs." "True nationalism," Dyster says, "demands that we rid our country of *all* foreign influence in whatever form it may exist. Keep America for Americans!" That's "pure nationalism"—the brand evolved by Hitler and his sadistic Brown Shirts. They rode to power on the slogan "Germany for the Germans!"

Dyster hasn't learned the lesson of history. Have the rest of us learned?

Kister's Veterans have attracted their full share of women nationalists as supporters. One of the keenest is Mrs. Elizabeth Dilling of Chicago. A friend of the Kisters, Mrs. Dilling has denounced as Communist the YMCA, the Quakers, members of the Catholic hierarchy, and the University of Chicago.

I have met Mrs. Dilling on many occasions. Far from being those of a "lady patriot," as she styles herself, her manners in public have impressed me as incorrigible. Her abusive language and cheap histrionics have endeared her to the crackpot mob everywhere. A clergyman, in writing to her, described her attacks on the Jews as "positively nauseating." Here's how the "lady patriot" writes about people she doesn't like:

Harold Laski, #%, the little half-pint British atheist Communistic Jewish counterpart of his close friend, Felix Frankfurter, °#%, the Austrian-born-miniature-sized Red Rasputin of the Jew Deal.

Mrs. Dilling has worked with Bundists, with Winrod, Kullgren, Pelley, Mote, Gerald Smith (like Smith she's always begging for money), Dennis and others.

On March 10, 1945 John T. Flynn spoke in Chicago. Mrs. Dilling listened avidly. After the meeting she introduced herself and congratulated Flynn on his talk. Flynn warmly shook her hand and the two discussed "Communism"—Mrs. Dilling adding her bit in her usual voluble way. Looking around, I was later told, Flynn said suddenly:

"I'm surprised that guy Carlson isn't around to take a picture of us together!"

I wasn't there, but one of my friends was!

Mrs. Dilling thinks well of Bundists Gerhardt W. Kunze, August Klapprott, Herman Max Schwinn and Hans Diebel—all under indictment with her on sedition charges—and of Nazi agent George Sylvester Viereck. She regards them all as "gentlemanly, scholarly men" and "refined individuals." It helps explain why the Nazi *World Service* highly recommended her "patriotism." Mrs. Dilling refers to the FBI as the Federal Bureau of Intimidation.

In a letter to me (as Thompson), Mrs. Dilling enclosed Flynn's booklet, *The Final Secret of Pearl Harbor.* She wrote that she was sending me "part of my October bulletin on the Communistic orientation course in the United States Army." Her fantastic 18-page bulletin is crammed with an amazing web of distortions and ridiculous conclusions. I know a little about the courses because I lectured before many Army groups on "The Enemy Within." I had long talks with the officers in charge. The courses were an earnest attempt to stimulate thinking and encourage GIs to take an interest in current affairs. They tried to make servicemen *participate* in the affairs of our country and to offset some of the intellectually deadening effects of Army routine. Their aim was to make more enlightened citizens through a program of information and education. Mrs. Dilling didn't think so. She branded them RED. Even the educational Public Affairs Committee Pamphlets were branded RED Communist. Her bulletin also denounced John Dewey, dean of American educators, as a "tireless, atheistic Red." After 12,000 weary words, Mrs. Dilling came up for air and under the headline "Traitors to America" took a final crack at the Army:

The entire Army compulsory "orientation" program is a glorification of the Red Atheist Soviet State's inefficient collectivism and brutal totalitarianism. . . . Those responsible for this are traitors to the Constitution they are sworn to uphold and to the taxpayers whose liberty and system of government they are deliberately undermining. They are war criminals of the lowest and most treasonable order.

Between the United States Army's alleged disloyalty to our own country and "Liz" Dilling's alleged patriotism, I'll side with the Army.

As Thompson, I wrote to another inveterate booster of Kister's hate cause—Mrs. Lyrl Clark Van Hyning, head of We, the Mothers Mobilize for America, Inc., in Chicago. Mrs. Van Hyning sent me 26 separate pamphlets—all free—ranging from defenses of Tyler Kent and booklets by Earl Southard, to others attacking our leadership, Allies, minority groups, political and economic systems. Mrs. Van Hyning's own monthly scandal sheet, *Women's Voice*, denounced the Democratic and Republican Parties as "The Two Party Fake" and urged a third "nationalist" party to take over. Mrs. Van Hyning wrote me a warm letter and primed me to go deeper into her own brand of politics:

We must go into the primaries with independent candidates, and I'm hoping the soldiers will be the candidates. Enclosed is a copy of *Women's Voice*, outlining our plan more definitely. Votes are won in precincts, and that means house to house work. . . . We are sending under separate cover some literature which we feel will be acceptable to you. Do please write us again. May we interchange helpful information, for there are many boys like yourself who are reaching out as you are.

Women's Voice has advertised a large amount of hate literature, including *Jewish Ritual Murder*, handled in this country by Homer Maertz, and four pamphlets by Henry H. Klein, a New York lawyer of the Jewish faith, who defended Elmhurst and Mertig in the Queens trial. Nationalists point to Klein as a "good Jew" and consider him one of their own. He has spoken and been welcomed at many of their meetings. A passage from Klein's address before the Federal jury hearing the sedition case in 1944, shows that "nationalism" may have little to do with one's religion or birth:

We will show that so-called democracy is synonymous with mobocracy, and that the term democracy has been used and fostered by government propagandists in order to confuse the people and pave the way for Communism. . . . We will prove that Felix Frankfurter, Sidney Hillman, and Harold Laski of London are the chief instruments of Communism in the United States. . . .

So far as the Nazi propaganda in the United States is concerned, it probably amounted to only a very small fraction of the amount of British propaganda and now of Russian propaganda. This country is now in the hands of British and Russian internationalists in spite of all efforts by these defendants and others to keep our national patriotism alive.

Prince Feisal, son of King Ibn Saud of Saudi Arabia, according to Eugene Segal in the Cleveland *Press*, met a nationalist "Mothers" leader during the San Francisco Conference at a breakfast arranged by Salem Bader, a Los Angeles nationalist. Bader spoke at Mrs. Van Hyning's mothers' convention in 1945, and *Women's Voice* has printed his advertisements. Born in Jerusalem of German-British-French parents, Bader came to this country in 1925 but waited till 1942 to become a citizen. The Portland *Oregonian* on October 18, 1941 referred to him as an "ex-British agent." Bader apparently enjoys the friendship of Arabian royalty and he claims to have been "part of the British Colonial Government that ruled" Palestine.

Bader's position among nationalists may be gathered from a frank letter he wrote from Los Angeles to Eugene Flitcraft, which was published in the November, 1945 issue of Flitcraft's anti-Semitic *Gentile News:*

Yesterday while I was sitting across the desk, and talking over various things with Upton Close, he handed me a copy of your Sept. *Gentile News.* I scanned it hurriedly and was so impressed that I brought it home with me. . . . I can tell you truthfully that you are really putting out quite a paper and one that is very much needed in this county [country?].

. . . I am glad you are giving space to Frederick Kister's movement. I know Mr. Kister very well and am quite in harmony with what he is doing.

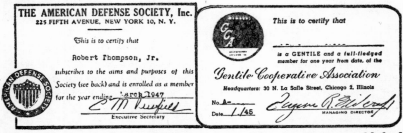

Flitcraft's hate sheet, *Gentile News*, organ of his Association, published Bader's letter; for comment on the American Defense Society, see page 154.

I should have been in Chicago in a week or more, as I was taking a trip with Upton Close on his lecture tour, and perhaps give one or two myself. . . . But my plans were changed suddenly. . . . Enclosed check covering one year's subscription.

Bader is the author of booklets entitled *Is America a Christian or Jewish Civilization? Is the White Race Committing Suicide?* and *Let's Go to War Again!*

Whether or not the nationalists' meeting with Feisal, at which the Prince is reported to have expressed the desire to meet other American nationalists, was responsible, thereafter our home-grown nationalists and the hate presses from coast to coast launched an anti-Zionist crusade, denying Jewry its right to a homeland. For a while the "Communist Jews" were shelved and the Zionist Jew became the epitome of evil. Father Terminiello blared: "Zionism means the inducing of American citizens to leave the United States to form a new SUPER STATE which will directly or indirectly control the destinies, the morals, the liberties, and finances of this nation." He declared: "ZIONISM IS TREASON!" Marilyn Allen—who declared that the Jews in Germany had "reaped what they had sown"— declared: "I am only against the plot and program of the ZIONIST Jews who are intent upon ruling the world under INTERNATIONAL COMMUNISM." And so on, *ad nauseam*.

The Arab Office, operating quietly from an exclusive hotel in Washington, attracted attention by issuing large volumes of expensively printed and craftily written anti-Jewish propaganda. The Arabs have a right to argue in defense of their national interests, but that doesn't condone their feeding the fires of religious hate with anti-Jewish fuel. The nationalist bund immediately fell into line. Homer Maertz reprinted the Arab Office's literature, followed by Carl H. Mote and Charles Hudson, who repeated an Arab official's statement that World War II was a "Jewish war."

The new nationalist flame reached Philadelphia, where Herbert Lawson Smith, Gerald Smith collaborator and a leading nationalist, wrote to the Arab Office on March 22, 1946: "Democracy is nothing but Jewocracy and it is about time that the American public got wise to this fact and got over being a lot of suckers, both for Bloody Joe and Churchill."

Instead of receiving a rebuke, Smith got a courteous response and an offer to speak from Anwar Bey Nashashibi, registered as an

Arab agent with the State Department. Smith then arranged for the Arab leader to speak for Mrs. Brown's Coughlinite mothers, operating as the Current Events Club, on April 12. Nashashibi, Smith and Charles Edwin Wallington, a cohort, were dining that night when an urgent call from Washington recalled the Arab envoy, and the meeting was called off.

It indicated, however, the extent to which the Arab propaganda agency was corrupting Americans with its venomous anti-Jewish propaganda, using American nationalists as transmission belters. Arab Office officials have indicated their wholehearted approval of Haj Amin el Husseini, ex-Grand Mufti of Jerusalem, Hitler's Moslem Quisling, who headed the Arab Axis legions, who spoke on Goebbels' radio, who was received by Hitler personally. The ex-Mufti is now directing anti-Zionist propaganda from Egypt, where he has taken refuge.

The Arab-American Nationalist Axis was aired in Congress by Congressman Adolph J. Sabath, Chairman of the Foreign Affairs Committee of the House on August 12, 1946. This time the trail led to New York, where Mr. Sabath charged Habib I. Katibah and Dr. Fuad I. Shatara, both now associated with the Institute of Arab-American Affairs in New York, with former Bund ties. Sabath charged that the former Arab National League, with which Katibah was linked, was "closely associated with and promoted" by the Bund. The two were familiar figures in the Nazi underworld in which I once moved as George Pagnanelli. I heard Shatara speak with Joe McWilliams and a dozen other fascist leaders in New York in the fall of 1939.

The Arab Office—sponsored by the governments of Egypt, Iraq, Lebanon, Saudi Arabia, Syria, Transjordan and Yemen—is known to be spending enormous amounts in anti-Semitic propaganda. Their lecturers are zig-zagging across the United States. Their propaganda bullets are pelting Americans everywhere. The Motes, Baders and Maertzes are merely the capillaries of this global propaganda network. They are being used merely as tools. In Argentina, Arab agencies are distributing anti-Democracy literature, some of which has been translated directly from former Nazi sources.

Anti-Zionist propaganda in this country is actively embattled by Jewish groups such as the American Jewish Congress, a leading Zionist organization.

In Colorado, Kister's storm troopers are recruited by James Piggott, Denver Chairman of the Christian Veterans of America. I knew Piggott as a worker in the offices of the New York chapter of the America First Committee. His address in Englewood, Col., however, was the same as that of the so-called Colorado Committee for Constitutional Rights, sired by Dewey M. Taft, one of Denver's nationalist Big Four, with Springer, Blessing and Goff. Piggott seemed a mere Charlie McCarthy working under Taft's guidance.

Taft sponsored a meeting for Gerald Smith; his *American Digest* denounced General Eisenhower because Ike allegedly praised "the Communist system while fawning at the feet of Butch Stalin." Taft denounced the "outrageous incarceration" of seditionist William Dudley Pelley and demanded his release. On the other hand he praised Tyler Kent as "America's No. 1 Hero." *

When I wrote Taft he answered on the letterhead of the National Association for Abolition of the Office of Price Administration, Inc. Its objective was "the earliest possible liquidation of OPA." Taft's warped thinking was betrayed in his letter of March 26. Weigh its effect on a veteran just home from overseas and whose mind is politically receptive:

Our biggest job during the next 30 days is to stop OPA. That Russian organization is more responsible for inflation than all the other causes put together. It is the deliberate purpose of the Russia Firsters in our government to cause such a condition of chaos . . . as to bring about the planned revolution. . . . Never in the history of our country has monopoly run riot as it has with the blessing of the un-American Russian system which we have degenerated into. And there is reason for that. It has all been "planned that way."

* Propaganda source for Kent was a booklet, *The Case of Tyler Kent*, published by John Howland Snow, who formerly worked in the New York office of Lawrence Dennis. The booklet became an important nationalist tract and was sold extensively from coast to coast. Associated with Snow is G. S. West, who recommended in a letter to me that I read Rev. McIntyre's book *Rise of the Tyrant*.

Also defending Kent is the American Justice for Tyler Kent Committee whose members include Frank Chodorov, Dr. Maude S. DeLand, Mrs. Edmund C. Evans, Mrs. Hamilton Fish, Norma Lundeen Holman (Mrs. Rufus Holman), Frederick J. Libby, Albert Jay Nock, Gerald P. Nye, Robert E. O'Brian, Charles Parsons, Robert R. Reynolds, Rev. Arthur W. Terminiello, Mrs. Myrtle Walker, Miss Ellen Winsor, Mrs. Margaret H. Worrell.

In Philadelphia, Meinhart's veteran gang had the support of W. Henry MacFarland, Jr., publisher of bi-weekly bulletins which serve as unofficial organs for Philadelphia nationalists. "Our task is to smash democracy," he says frankly. I wrote to him as Thompson, supposedly seeking information on a "nationalist veterans' group." MacFarland wholeheartedly endorsed the Christian Veterans of America as "a splendid anti-Communist group, staunchly nationalistic in program and operation." His ambition was to transform the "City of Brotherly Love" into a community seething with racial and religious discord:

My program here is to build our city above all others in the Nationalist movement; to coordinate the activities of the four Nationalist groups here into one Christian Nationalist Front; to make Philadelphia the leading city in the fight for renewed independence and freedom.

They [democratic groups] might be surprised if they could know our numerical strength and plans. We have a program mapped out for the creation of a Nationalist Youth group, a local unit of the Christian Veterans, an expanded Mothers organization, a general Nationalist association for both men and women, and a special Women's Auxiliary Unit.

Right now, I and my associates are working on the latter, and it is our desire to bring together more of the younger women into this Nationalist fight. This is true, since the Mothers organization, already created, will serve those women who are married and have families. The younger and unmarried ones must also be organized, however, since this struggle requires TOTAL MOBILIZATION. The Youth group will be next in line, and the general organization last. The veterans, of course, are already being recruited.

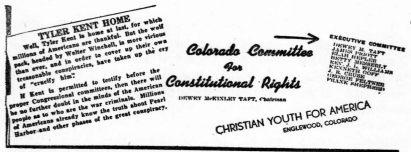

Taft, Goff's "Christian" Youth, Springer, *et al.*, constitute the core of the Denver nationalist cell.

Except for the exposé articles of Philadelphia newspapers, notably the *Record,* democratic opposition to nationalist activity in the city is negligible. A similar situation existed up to 1943 in Boston, which did not "clean house" until its democratic groups adopted a militant policy against the Coughlinites. A policy of hush-hush is useless and merely encourages undercover hate activity, as reflected in the increasingly inflammatory contents of MacFarland's *National Progress.*

In Georgia, Gerald Smith's mobsters are championed by Charles H. Emmons, Secretary of the Commoner Party of the United States of America, with headquarters in Conyers. It's small, but one of the most vicious Jew- and Negro-baiting groups in the South. It claims to have close relations with Father Terminiello, ex-Senator Reynolds, Kister, Mrs. Van Hyning and many others. I wrote Emmons as Thompson, Jr., and received several letters:

March 4, 1946: Just yesterday a young veteran came to our office, bubbling over with a spirit to get into action over present chaotic conditions. We spent most of the day discussing the future outlook for our country. We mapped out a tentative line of action for the near future. We are going to try to start the ball rolling here in Atlanta.

March 14, 1946: We have named the new organization The American Gentile Army, An Organization for Independent Political Action. The Plan calls for the formation of Army Companies of ten or more members to a company. It would be impossible for us to handle the details for the whole country from here, so we are going to limit our efforts to the formation of State Departments. . . . Just yesterday I wrote a similar letter to this to a young man who was anxious to get into action in New Orleans.

In Salt Lake City, that beautiful Mormon community with its inspiring people, a particularly outspoken nationalist has made her appearance. She is Marilyn R. Allen, and her writing is sponsored by the Pro-American Vigilantes. It drips poison although emblazoned with red-white-blue and patriotic clichés. Her 36-page booklet, *America Forever—God Made Me Free,* is a hodgepodge witch's brew of the confused thinking, lies, distortions and prejudices of the nationalist mind poured into one hate kettle. Tyler Kent, who betrayed our national secrets, is praised for keeping "his oath to defend the Constitution." Gerald Smith, John Rankin, Upton Close and Samuel Pettengill are praised, too. An attack on Jews takes up more than ten pages. Miss Allen refers to the late President Roosevelt as Van Rosenfelt and questions the Americanism of Supreme Court Justices Louis B. Brandeis and Felix Frankfurter, and of Henry Morgenthau, Bernard M. Baruch and Albert Einstein.

I do not escape an excoriation. I'm called a Communist and an "America-baiter"—whatever that is! My lectures on "The Enemy Within" for the Army orientation programs are described as the "source-cause of the rebellion among our troops, particularly in the Far East." I'm puzzled about this otherwise unreported rebellion, and to know how I could ever have been behind it without being discovered by Army Intelligence.

After finishing with me, Miss Allen resumes with a staunch defense of Frederick Kister as a super-"Christian." She follows this with a page on the Anglo-Saxon Israel race theory. "Jesus was NOT a Jew, but an Israelite," she tells us. "Abraham and Isaac were Hebrews (not Jews): Jacob, son of Isaac, was the first Israelite, because the Lord changed Jacob's name to ISRAEL: so all the sons of Jacob (Israel) were ISRAELITES, as well as Hebrews (but not Jews)." Later on we learn that "ISRAEL IS THE ENGLISH-SPEAKING PEOPLES (including the Nordic)." Presto! Jacob,

America Forever

PEACE-mongering in America

★ ★

MARILYN R. ALLEN

Sponsored by Pro-American Vigilantes

●●● What a soft, slushy, spineless people we are becoming —all in the name of PEACE! Peace has become a fetish, which we worship.

●●● Most of these peace-mongers, no doubt, call themselves "Christian," (like the Left-wing Bishop Oxnam, of Federated Council of Churches of Christ in America);

●●● GENUINE AMERICANS in this country: AMERICAN Americans: Upton Close, Tyler Kent, and Gerald Smith.

●●● genuine Aryan Americans are no longer allowed free speech in their own country!—NOW I begin to understand the wherefore of the Jewish pogroms in Germany.

●○● Now, it happens that I am an AMERICAN American, a decent law-abiding, free, tax-paying citizen, and my forbears were among the first and oldest settlers in Cincinnati, Ohio: I am NOT a gangster nor a lunatic nor a hoodlum●●●

How AMERICAN is Senator Thomas?

And then the elected representative of the FREE American PEOPLE: upholder (?) of the AMERICAN CONSTITUTION, Elbert D. Thomas, says that the "Russian goals of freedom and of EVERYTHING FOR THE PEOPLE are the same as those of the United States." Fire-tipped words cannot express my scorn and shame that a United States Senator, who claims the advantages of culture, travel and education, should make such a fool of himself!

This is the "party line" of a super-"AMERICAN American" nationalist!

Isaac, Jesus were not Jews, but ANGLO-SAXONS! Amen. Her authority for this mumbo jumbo is a booklet by the British Israel Association of Greater Vancouver, British Columbia. There's more to Miss Allen's profound erudition. "The descendants of Abraham, Isaac and Jacob were Aryan Hebrews," she says, "NOT Jews."

In addition to race and religion, Miss Allen is also an expert on labor. Completely ignoring the legality of strikes, she says: "The organized strike weapon is utterly at variance with the American tradition of fair play and a square deal for ALL. The strike is not an American-born institution," she says. "It was foreign-fomented by foreigners."

Miss Allen exhorts nationalists: "The time is very late. In every community in America PRO-AMERICAN VIGILANTE groups should be organizing to promote good Americanism, to defend, protect and save America and her freedom. . . . Believe me when I say that our FREEDOM HANGS ON THAT SLENDER THREAD."

In a second booklet, *Peace-Mongering in America,* Miss Allen adds to her list of one hundred percent Americans Rev. Terminiello, Rev. Harvey Springer, and Dewey M. Taft. She doesn't like to hear talk about peace because it pulls "the wool over our people's eyes." She is for aggressive "Americanism" of the vigilante brand to fight Communism at home and suggests war to fight it abroad. "No less an authority than God Himself says that war between paganism and Christianity IS INEVITABLE," she says. "I am NOT a gangster nor a lunatic nor a hoodlum, nor was I formerly anti-Semitic," she assures the credulous. "I am an AMERICAN American, decent, law-abiding, free."

I wrote Miss Allen as nationalist Thompson. She answered with a long letter written on legal-sized stationery, confessing that she had been active in "patriotic" work for the past six to seven years and complaining that she had been unable to find a publisher for her books and had had to spend her own money.

I restate my position regarding the Jews [she wrote], since there has been some criticism of my statements. I am NOT against Jews because they are Jews; but because it is the Zionist Jews who are behind Communism; it was U.S. wealthy Jews who supported the Jew-Bolshevik Revolution in Russia; it is the Jews who rule Russia today, as Communists; it was the Jews who were about to overthrow Germany, which is why Hitler overthrew them. It is Jews who are largely in control of our Government today. . . . I have inclosed a copy of Eliz. Dilling's latest bulletin. From her office, you can obtain copy of the Jewish PROTOCOLS OF ZION.

Together with her own material, Miss Allen sent me "patriotic" leaflets: Kenneth Goff's *The Pilgrim Torch;* two issues of Upton Close's *Closer-Ups;* John T. Flynn's distorted article, *"Uncovering" Under Cover;* Charles B. Hudson's *America in Danger;* Mrs. Dilling's *Patriotic Research Bureau Bulletin,* with a notation: "This organization is OK." It carried the tragic story of an elderly woman whose income was $40 per month. She had cashed her $100 war bond, realized $77, and sent $75 of it to Mrs. Dilling. She also told "of a man over 70, a cement laborer, who gave us $100 and brought me his will leaving his entire small estate to my work."

Miss Allen is one of the few nationalists who apologizes for her attitude toward the Jews. Does she defensively explain that she's not anti-Jewish because her conscience bothers her? Miss Allen's latest masterpiece of logic is a leaflet denouncing Elbert D. Thomas, the distinguished Senator from the Mormon State. as a "liberal." Says Miss Allen: "Thomas is one of those pro-labor, pro-Communist LIBERALS: hmff: he's a LIBERAL just like that French Communist stooge, Leon Blum."

Countless others are aiming propaganda bullets at the veteran—and scoring. One of them is Court Asher, whom I met at the Smith-Kister rally at Celina. A World War I veteran, Asher belongs to half a dozen fraternal and veterans' organizations in Muncie, Indiana.

The X-RAY

COURT ASHER, Editor and Publisher

"Entered as Second Class matter June 14, 1945, at the Post Office at Muncie, Indiana, under act of March 3, 1879."

INDIANA'S GREATEST WEEKLY NEWSPAPER

"Democracy" a Deceit Word

The "brand" of democracy as practiced by the Roosevelt New Dealers; Russia and subversive Organized Jewry in this country should never be taught nor "sneaked" upon any nation as it was on the United States.

During the past 10 years we have seen and ex-perienced "democracy" or rather the word, used as a protection; a shield, a mask for subversive, Communistic, dictatorial people and organization. Always, when they pursue their insidious course, carry on their Communistic action and plans, it is under the false banner and disguise of "democracy!"

Democracy! To hell with democracy! The mere word has become a stench; a bomb and deceiving weapon for those subversive, un-American, alien-minded imps of hell who thru organization, deceit and trickery—ever using "democracy" as their slogan—have brought this once free REPUBLIC to chaos, disgraced the Constitution and planted the seeds of civil war and revolution in this country

If we are to teach totalitarian countries lessons in government, we must teach them Americanism—Democracy, never, and may heaven forbid such.

A 100 percent super-patriot isn't worthy of the name until he roundly damns Democracy.

He sent me copies of his weekly *The X-Ray*, that seemed to have been selected to corrupt the veteran reader.

An editorial (November 3, 1945) denounced the purchase of war bonds as "Bonds for Enslavement—Gift Bonds for Bondage in Foreign Nations." The October 27 issue defended the Klan: "Some misinformed people have been told that the Ku Klux Klan was subversive and un-American." They're mistaken, said Asher, who is known to have belonged to the hooded empire after World War I. "The Klan does not advocate overthrow of our Constitution, and the Communists do. Bring on the Klan." Asher's hatred for democracy is almost Goebbelsesque. On October 20, 1945 *The X-Ray* published a long editorial entitled, "Democracy, a Deceit Word."

Democracy! To hell with democracy! The mere word has become a stench; a bomb and deceiving weapon for those subversive, un-American, alien-minded imps of hell who thru organization, deceit and trickery—ever using "democracy" as their slogan—have brought this once free REPUBLIC to chaos, disgraced the Constitution and planted the seeds of civil war and revolution in this country.

American taxpayers helped support Asher's poison-pen publication. The U.S. Army Recruiting Office at Muncie published a large ad in *The X-Ray*, urging veterans to re-enlist. The snafu appeared on December 8, 1945, the day after the first peacetime anniversary of Pearl Harbor!

Another veteran of World War I whose uncontrolled hatred of Communism has led him into the nationalist camp is Edward F. Atwell, of New York. He received his early nationalist training with the America First Committee publicity bureau. He is now freelancing as anti-Communist specialist, and among other nationalist activities he is involved with Christian Front-type groups. In March, 1946 he addressed a meeting of the American Defense Society, Inc., of New York, a super-"patriotic" group of the "Park Avenue" variety. After World War I it went overboard with its professed "Americanism" by distributing as truth the infamous *Protocols of the Learned Elders of Zion*, the anti-Semitic forgery which later became the Bible of the Nazis the world over.

Taking a new tack, the Society is now displaying its "Americanism" by "working through its Speak Up America Committee to arouse the public to assert its opposition to the wave of strikes which is . . . imperiling the rights of the public." Old, retired Army and Navy officers and conservative businessmen of yesterday's generation are prominent among its sponsors. It ran a series of expensive advertisements in New York newspapers, soliciting members.

Those who look upon organized labor as "Communist" flocked to this new haven of respectable nationalism. "I am knee-deep in an anti-Communist publicity campaign," Atwell wrote me. His recommendation was that I join the Regular Veterans Association * post in Buffalo. Atwell, who used to write a veterans' column in Capt. Frank S. Flynn's *Plain Talk*, now publishes the *Passing Caravan*, which screams about the imminent menace of Communism but sees no other enemy on the home front.

An indefatigable booster of Kister's Veterans and the hate cause in general is probably Father Arthur W. Terminiello's greatest admirer in the East. He is F. H. Sattler, who claims to be a veteran of World War I. In Meriden, Conn., Sattler edits a sprawling, yellow-jacketed journal, *The Malist*, "Published by Catholic Laymen—Devoted to St. Jude." Sattler out-Coughlins Coughlin and goes beyond the wildest fulminations of his patron saint, Terminiello.

Readers of *The Malist* are fed an indigestible diet: the infamous *Protocols* are truth; international cooperation is "a time bomb to destroy Christian groups"; Truman "is not the President of the American people nor the defender of our constitutional and Christian way of life." In the magazine's columns appear many of Terminiello's releases. Sattler urges membership in Terminiello's version of the Christian Front, his Christian Crusaders. "The Holy Father asks for Crusaders. If you are a confirmed follower of Christ, join the Crusaders."

Sattler has one overpowering dislike which transcends even his animosity toward Communism and the Jews. It's Communist, anti-God, anti-Christian, cowardly, Satanic, Free Masonry! Sattler didn't answer my Thompson letter for more than two months. I learned why when he finally wrote a seven-page letter, 3,000 words long. It was devoted to one topic: the alleged depredations of Masonry. I'm not a Mason, but I don't believe any legal fraternal order could equal Sattler's conception of Masonry.

* Atwell's recommendation must not be construed as reflecting on the Regular Veterans Association.

I too was a soldier [Sattler wrote "Thompson"] and I couldn't get a trial in a court of law to defend myself against the false claims of a shameless creature because he was a free mason. . . . The free mason is not only anti-Christ but anti-God. Many of them actually believe that Lucifer will conquer over God. A true free Mason, believe me, cannot stomach the teachings of Christ or Christ Himself. . . .

We can speak frankly that communism is the scum of hell and free masons their scab coats. . . . We have been betrayed by both New Deal Presidents. All because free masonry serving the anti-Christ has seduced the people that made our soldiers fight a war in vain for despotism instead of freedom.

If you are sincere to put on an armor of steel and cast your lot in defense of the good, pray God you denounce the works of the free masons. . . . You ask about a GI outfit that is okay to join. I can highly recommend Mr. Frederick Kister, national chairman of Christian VETERANS OF AMERICA. His cause is noble and his principles good. Another who is doing much good is Gerald L. K. Smith. . . . My advice is to organize your group and contact these men.

Sattler, in his January, 1946 *Malist,* advertised the works of one Philip Campbell Argyle-Stuart, a veteran who wants to "execute by firing squad" members of the "Better Business Bureau, Chamber of Commerce, Securities and Exchange Commission . . . who are an effective drag on promoters." Argyle-Stuart also wants to abolish Post Office Department inspectors. This is understandable: on November 24, 1936 Post Office Fraud Order No. 9762 was issued against him, forbidding his sale of stock in the Delaware Light Metal and Marine Corporation.

From Pasco, Wash., and a maildrop in New York, Argyle-Stuart now conducts an astrological business, selling a "Predictive Service," or the art of running a business or bank on the laws of "planetary cycles." Let the stars guide your business. He charges $100 a year.

Argyle-Stuart has a third enterprise in full bloom. As "navigating secretary" of his Whig-Federalist Party, he devotes himself to "Pure Right Wing Politics" and believes in "disfranchising the Negro." In *The X-Ray* Argyle-Stuart called for "trained private detective operatives or Veterans of Army, Navy Intelligence." He also advertised in Flitcraft's *Gentile News* that he wished "to hear from politically ambitious young people." One of his collaborators is Ira Calvin

White, writer of Brookline, Mass., who has assailed Jews and Negroes in print.

Philip Campbell Argyle-Stuart is also known as Philip Frederick Lynnhaven. According to a report by the New York Better Business Bureau, he is also known as Philip Glassel and Gene Miller. Stuart-Lynnhaven-Miller claims to be a "veteran of combat." I posed as a veteran sympathizer and carried on a lengthy correspondence with Argyle-Stuart, etc. He wanted me to become "Intelligence Operative" in Buffalo. After I had procured my information, I dropped the correspondence.

Other super-"patriots" to whom I wrote as Thompson also recommended Kister's Veterans. One was Edward A. Koch, publisher of *The Guildsman,* Germantown, Ill., and propagandist for a Catholic Corporate state. In November, 1945 Koch defended Naziism and denounced anti-Nazi citizens as un-American. The virtues of Naziism, Koch said, had been "studiously concealed from the American public." According to him, the "essence of Nazism" was a laudable "social-reform movement" and not the evil thing "presented in this country. . . . Anti-Nazism is not pro-American; whereas the *Guildsman's* position is such."

Pro-Nazi backers of Kister's Veterans include Milo Blish Pinkerton of Madison, Wis., author of a sensational book, *The Right to Work Versus Slavery,* advertised in *Women's Voice.* Pinkerton believes America should adopt the philosophy of A. Robert Jacques Turgot, eighteenth century philosopher. Turgot's principles, Pinkerton says, "have been adopted almost 100 percent by the Nazi Party.

Is Anti-Nazism Pro-American?

The answer ~~~~~~~~~~~~~~~ must be: No; for Nazism sought to prevent the sequence from Liberalism to Communism by interposing its efforts in behalf of a Corporative structure. The frustration of such interposition—the object and result of anti-Nazism—will leave the field free for Communism—which is not in America's interests. Therefore, *anti*-Nazism is *not* pro-American; whereas the *Guildsman's* position *is* such.

This choice item of patriotic reasoning was published by Edward A. Koch in the November, 1945 issue of *The Guildsman.*

. . . I.e., A centralized form of government . . . religious tolerance and universal education. . . . Most of these principles . . . have been adopted by the Japanese."

Pinkerton's 96-page book, plugged by Mrs. Van Hyning's *Women's Voice* as something which "should be read by everyone," went through four editions between 1941 and 1944. Dedicated to his son, a soldier, it explains that the war was fought "on the one side," by men who understood the "scientific allocation and distribution of natural resources, etc., as set forth in the Nazi platform; and on the other side, by men who are almost wholly ignorant." Pinkerton reprints the entire 25-point Nazi platform adopted by Hitler on January 30, 1933, defending, excusing, justifying, praising and recommending the Nazi arguments. On page 47 he refers to Nazi hoodlum leaders as "patriots of the first World War." Quoting the Nazi oath of allegiance, Pinkerton remarks:

The stimulus which this open, unreserved Oath of Allegiance gave to the Nazi cause cannot be overestimated. It at once marked the men as men who had this supreme purpose at heart. It gave them explicit faith in each other, as no secret pledge could do, and engendered confidence in their honesty by the citizenry. . . . This frank, open Oath of Allegiance stood them in good stead as they went before the people with their cause. . . .

I read on, finding it hard to believe that this book was being circulated in 1946. Who said Naziism in America was dead?

It is sad, but true, that American friends of Naziism include former wearers of their country's uniforms. In San Diego a dishonorably discharged soldier, C. Leon de Aryan, publishes *The Broom,* weekly hodgepodge of superstition, pseudo-science and native-fascist politics. It appeals to the fist-swinging elements of the American Nazi underworld. De Aryan claims to be "patriotic," but he confesses collaboration with Nazi workers Hans Diebel and Herman Max Schwinn. A leading apologist for ex-Nazis, he bewails the alleged "persecution" of "American Germans" and champions Mertig, Elmhurst, Maertz and similar political gangsters. De Aryan followed an intensely anti-war policy and tried desperately to block pre-Pearl Harbor defense measures. In a letter to me he called veterans "war slaves."

On April 8, 1946 De Aryan printed two cartoons, titled "On Their Way," the first showing a herd of cattle boarding freight cars for the slaughterhouse, the second showing a group of soldiers boarding passenger cars. A similar cartoon in 1941 drew the fire of Army recruiting officials and was a contributing factor to De Aryan's indictment for seditious conspiracy by the Department of Justice. De Aryan has admitted in sworn testimony that he attended Bund meetings and was friendly with San Diego Bund führers and used seditionist Pelley's material.

In addition to his campaign of white-washing Germany and trying to absolve it of war guilt, De Aryan's sheet prints kindly sentiments by columnist Washington Adams toward the Japs. Adams decried the slaying of Japanese "young men" and the destruction of "Japan's civilization." "We have reduced to rags, wretchedness and starvation the ablest and most progressive of all the dark race of men," he wailed. "To give Japan as Christian treatment as lies in our power might undo some of the harm we have done." Needless to say, not a word of sympathy appeared for our prisoners of war who were bestially treated by Jap soldiers, or for the sadistic treatment of captured civilians in China and the Philippines.

De Aryan was born Constantin Legenopol, the son of a Polish mother and Greek father, in Rumania in 1886. According to evidence introduced by the Joint Fact-Finding Committee to the Fifty-Fifth California Legislature in 1943, De Aryan at 19 was placed in a mental institution in Austria. After fourteen months he was removed to "another insane asylum located in Vienna," according to the Committee's report. He reached Boston in 1912 after living in Italy, Egypt and India. Enlisting in the Army late in 1912, he was dishonorably discharged on February 10, 1914, at Fort Logan, Colo. When the United States declared war on Germany he withdrew to Mexico City until after the Armistice. He then went to Belgium and re-entered the United States as an immigrant. Later he became an American citizen.

De Aryan has repaid his adopted country by becoming one of its leading merchants of hate and disunity.

At the trial of Mertig, Elmhurst and Maertz late in February, 1946 I saw a tall, gaunt man in his thirties huddled in conversation with a group of hate-scarred nationalists. It was Conrad Grieb, Coast Guard veteran of World War II, a "one hundred percent

American" who was trained in nationalism by Seward Collins, former editor of *The Bookman*. (Collins told me in 1940, "I am a fascist. Of course I am.") Before Pearl Harbor I used to meet Grieb, manager of Collins' bookshop, and buy the latest fascist literature. His ideas haven't changed since the old days.

Grieb has a brush mustache and prematurely gray hair, wears gold-framed glasses and walks with a stiff gait. He lives on East 88th Street in New York's Yorkville district. He uses the name of John Selden to receive mail from the Friends of Democracy and snoop into the work of democratic organizations. He is careful with whom he corresponds, but he wrote "Robert Thompson, Jr.," enclosing a booklet, *The Peace We Lost*.

Shortly before his arrest after the Queens rally, Maertz had published Grieb's open letter to the President, clamoring for "justice" for the "defeated enemy who heroically defended their country against overwhelming numbers." Stressing that Britain and France "declared war on Germany," Grieb urged that we "try America's own war criminals" instead of the Nazis. Ignoring the record of Nazi bestiality and looting in occupied countries, he wrote that the German armies "brought discipline, order and security wherever they went in protecting their homeland against an ever tightening encirclement."

Having whitewashed the Nazis, Grieb applied his brush to the Japs. Quoting the convenient John T. Flynn, he charged that President Roosevelt "and those who influenced him"—such as the former Secretaries of State, War and the Navy, Cordell Hull, Henry L. Stimson and Frank Knox— betrayed "this country into war." Grieb's article sounded like a joint short-wave broadcast by Lord Haw-Haw and Tokyo Rose.

Late in June, 1946 Grieb sent me reprints of the Congressional speeches of Senators Langer, Kenneth S. Wherry and Homer S. Capehart, alleging mass starvation in Germany.* An accompanying booklet by Austin J. App was entitled *Ravishing the Conquered Women of Europe*. App described himself as inducted into the Army in 1942 and currently a professor at Incarnate Word College, San Antonio. His leaflet alleged that the Allied armies were blood-

* Within a day I received the identical material from the Steuben Society, which before Pearl Harbor served as the German-speaking wing of the America First Committee.

thirsty rapists and "the German armies the most decent armies of the war."

Grieb reflects the mentality of the "nationalist" veteran. Such nationalism is the product of no one hate-instilling agency. It is the combined effect of many hate-boosters who since 1932 have been hammering their propaganda into the American mind. The technique is traceable to the plans of Nazi agents after 1932 to organize a mass native-American movement to serve as an operating base for Hitler's psychological warfare and his planned ideological conquest of the United States. William Dudley Pelley wrote to a Nazi agent in 1933 that this movement would be "American in character and personnel," and would "work shoulder to shoulder with German aims and purposes."

We are reaping today the seeds implanted in the heyday of Nazi propaganda. For years these seeds were cultivated by thousands of cunning minds, promoted by hundreds of thousands of pieces of propaganda, backed by millions of Reichsmarks and American dollars. That is a major reason why, in a time of race and class tension, the flames of hate are reaching aloft and clouding the American sky.

It's like fighting a forest fire which has been smouldering over a wide area and suddenly breaks into flame. Some American communities are already ablaze. More fire fighters are badly needed. Feeders of the hate flames are trying desperately to expand their

Vanguard of the N.Y.L. (Nationalist Youth League)

| ★ SPEAKERS: Kenneth Goff Frederick Kister Cecil Tanner Gordon Haines Virginia Kendell Lawrence Reilly Don Lohbeck Gerald L. K. Smith | Independent Young Democrats Independent Young Republicans Christian Veterans Intelligence Bureau The GI Non-Partisans Friends and Relatives of Veterans Young Brothers of GIs N.L.C. (National Lindbergh Club) Canadian Nationalists Latin-American Christian Nationalists | Young Friends of Father Coughlin Pilgrims of the Little Flower Christian Temple Youth Christian Veterans Youth for Christ (Local Unit) Christian Youth for America Western Hemisphere Committee Against Communism United Farmers (Youth Branch) | America First Youth Auxiliary Lutheran Research Society Puerto Rican Junior Nationalists Oriental Nationalists (Chinese Branch) Youth Society to Preserve a Christian Palestine Kingdom Fellowship Youth Group Nationalist Student Union ·Collegiate Branch· Nationalist Student Union ·High School Branch |

We shall give much thought to the formation of a world-wide youth group which emphasizes respect for the national sovereignty of each nation and which recognizes the menace of Communism, world government and international conspirators.   Kenneth Goff

Ex-Communist Goff, now protégé of Gerald Smith, turns his energies to the organization of youth.

forces with war veterans and others. They can do it with little effort and money. They speak and write in the American tongue and sing with American voices. The veteran's hand is Jacob's, but the voice is that of Esau. When Homer Maertz was interviewed by the St. Louis *Post-Dispatch* he divulged his technique: "I harped on one theme. I repeated a key sentence seven or eight times. It was indelibly impressed. The people went into their neighborhoods, spread the message among their friends."

Hitler and his henchmen used the same tactics.

This has been going on in America for thirteen years.

CHAPTER SEVEN

I Was Patricia O'Connell, "Mother"

They say Hitler is a beast—let us finish the sentence—Churchill is a beast. Didn't he confess that his life's aim was accomplished when he got America into this war? Roosevelt is a beast when he gave our substance to England, when he left our boys in Bataan without food or guns. Queen Wilhelmina is a beast. She drained the Dutch people of their earnings. The King of England is a beast.

Women's Voice, April, 1944

A WARTIME INVESTIGATOR, determined to uncover home-front enemies of the war effort, had to undertake many odd assignments. One of the oddest in my case was the role of "mother." I became a "mother" in order to learn what the hatriots were bootlegging to women victims. With some 12,000,000 males away in service, I wanted to know what the mothers, sweethearts and wives of the boys overseas were receiving from organized female nationalist hate-

It's Time For A Showdown!

WE WOMEN WANT THE PLAIN TRUTH ABOUT THIS WAR NOW. WE MOTHERS ARE DETERMINED TO BREAK DOWN THE WALL OF SILENCE BEHIND WHICH OUR BOYS ARE DONE TO DEATH AND OUR COUNTRY BETRAYED.

JUST WHAT ARE WE FIGHTING FOR?

WHEN WILL THE BOYS BE THROUGH?
WILL MILITARY VICTORY BE WORTH THE SACRIFICE?
ARE AMERICA'S YOUNG SONS BEING SACRIFICED TO COVER UP THE BLUNDERS OF DODDERING DIPLOMATS?

National Women's Movement

mongers. I learned the answer by posing as Mrs. Patricia O'Connell, purely imaginary resident of Queens County, N. Y.

As an investigator, I wasn't content to be a prewar or World War I mother. I didn't want to admit I was that old. I felt my letters to the female of the hate species would be more appealing if I posed as the young wife of a serviceman. After I had so introduced myself to correspondents I decided to have a baby. I accomplished this simply by announcing: "Since writing you last I've given birth to the most bouncing little baby boy in the world. He was just this side of seven pounds. He has been doing well, but the same cannot be said of his mother. You see, my husband is away, fighting somewhere in France, and I'm practically alone, except when I can get some of my friends to stay with the baby. You know how it is, you dare not trust your *first* little precious darling to *anyone*. Francis Patrick, Jr. keeps me busy indeed."

This chapter is by no means a condemnation of mothers' organizations in general. The patriotism and sacrifices of the overwhelming majority of American mothers are great and obvious; and genuine democratic mothers' organizations performed heroically on the home front. Every serviceman remembers the canteens, the advisory and entertainment services provided by American mothers. It's my job, however, to dig out anti-democratic elements in the national scene. In this spirit I introduce the nationalist mothers. They are in a class by themselves.

I was a "mother" for about fifteen months, after which I was discovered and had to abandon motherhood. During that period I had a lot of laughs—and unearthed considerable evidence on the way our war effort was being sabotaged on the female front. In several instances I got my "marriage" and "child's birthday" dates mixed up, with the result that an arithmetically inclined nationalist could have declared Francis Patrick an illegitimate "victory baby." Fortunately, there was no such scandal in the O'Connell family, for I caught the error just in time. Francis Patrick, Jr. remained the legitimate son of Francis Patrick O'Connell, Sr., fighting somewhere in Europe. I was never sure where he was.

I was inspired to blessed motherhood through the example of a relative of mine. I saw her infant shortly after birth and watched it grow. I listened patiently to her problems of motherhood, nursing, diapering, etc., particularly noting her diction. I must have absorbed carefully, for my letters proved convincing. Take the reply I received from Mrs. Edward Nelson Dingley of Washington, D. C., in April, 1945:

Your little note was the most refreshing piece of mail I have received in many, many a day in my effort to WAKE UP AMERICA, and AMERICANS. . . . Although your husband is overseas, you have him with you in your little son. . . . How old is your little boy? I can't determine from the wording of your letter. . . . You just continue in the fine spirit your letter evinces, and mind little Francis Patrick, seeing that no harm comes to him. Do your duty to absent husband's little son he has never yet seen.

I couldn't possibly accept your dime, dear young mother—you just put it in Francis Patrick's "piggie bank" if he has one, if not I'll send him the first one I spy.

I shall put your name on my list and you will receive informative literature with every batch I mail out. It will cost you nothing. I invite [others] to follow my example. Obtain the "literature" and mail it to their acquaintances in Church or Club, or Organization. . . . I have a copy of Rev. Terminiello's masterly sermon, "Santa Claus or Christ," but I sped it on its way to *take root in another consciousness and bear fruit.* [Italics mine—J.R.C.]

This is how agents of the "mothers movement" worked as missionaries. Quietly and unobtrusively, they circulated enormous amounts of literature by mail at a time when open sales were banned. It ranged from seditious material to less poisonous tracts and reprints from nationalist papers.

Mrs. Dingley's contribution to my "education" was a selection of reprints carefully excerpted from Westbrook Pegler's columns. In one he called Congress "mean and yellow"; Secretary of State James Byrnes appeared as a mere "political handshaker," while labor "loafed" on its job during the war. Mrs. Dingley added in postscript that she was the daughter-in-law of ex-Governor and Congressman Nelson Dingley, Jr. of Maine. "Mrs. Van Hyning is a fine patriot," she wrote, referring to the Chicago Jew-baiter. "Thank God I know a hundred at least just as firm and splendid patriot women. We all are sisters under the skin, you know." Mrs. Dingley closed with *"Pro Deo, Pro Patria."*

From the other end of our country, Portland, Ore., Miss Grace Wick sent me two loads of hate propaganda. I felt that it was deliberately calculated to lower the morale of an uninitiated reader. Here is the fare Miss Wick intended for the wife of a serviceman who was fighting against Hitlerism:

1. *The Cross of War*, by Rev. Arthur W. Terminiello—thoroughly defeatist.
2. Leaflet entitled "A Jew Battle Royal Fight," depicting "a fight to the finish to decide which clique of Jews are to rule the people of America."
3. Another leaflet which, Miss Wick said, she received "at the Detroit America First Convention" (Gerald Smith's). It advocated: "Set aside islands in the middle of the Pacific Ocean to be occupied by Jews with Roosevelt as their Commander in Chief and Willkie as their Prime Minister. It is a dirty deal for the natives of these islands, but anti-Semitism will disappear as there will be no Jews around."
4. Three copies of William Kullgren's nationalist newspaper, *America Speaks*, one of them containing a resolution of the United Mothers of America denouncing world cooperation as "false and impossible."
5. A copy of the *Protocols of the Learned Elders of Zion*.
6. Reprint of a speech by Senator William Langer, of North Dakota, defending the 30 alleged seditionists as blameless patriots, and denouncing our Department of Justice for the indictments.
7. Three-page leaflet denouncing Governor Thomas E. Dewey as an internationalist because he had repudiated ex-Congressman Ham Fish, who was again running for Congress. "Fish is a loyal American Nationalist. God bless him. I wish he were a whole army."
8. A 48-page booklet by Miss Wick herself, entitled "A Personal Message to Members of the Congress."

This last was an amazing plea for the immediate release from prison of the seditionist and arch pro-Nazi, William Dudley Pelley. Identifying herself as the daughter of a Civil War veteran, Miss Wick called Pelley—who bluntly advocated an American form of Naziism—a "Christian, American refined gentleman" of "honorable intentions." After eulogizing him, she reproduced in its entirety Pelley's booklet, *Dupes of Judah*, in which he addressed himself to the American Legion and called it a "Jew muzzled organization." "The Jews have you right where they want you," Pelley charged. Miss Wick had 1,200 copies of her booklet printed, mailing some to a selected list of Congressmen and officers of the American Legion and Veterans of Foreign Wars. William Kullgren, California astrologer and nationalist publisher, wanted 100 copies. Another 100 went to "patriots" in the State of Washington. "I am hoping to have another 1,200 printed before the type is destroyed," Miss Wick wrote.

Miss Wick was a confirmed Pelley disciple. I suspect that her contacts include the seditionist's henchmen, for she wrote that she had talked like a "dutch uncle to the party" who had a supply of the infamous *Protocols*. "They are willing to let them go at 40¢ a copy," she said. "They are losing 10¢ a copy, but I read them part of your letter and explained about your being the wife of a soldier and that the books would fall into the right hands, so they said OK." In a postscript she urged me to serve as her co-agent in hate, suggesting, "Why don't you sell the *Protocols* for a dollar or even . . . 60¢ and make a little for yourself . . . ?"

Miss Wick liked Mrs. O'Connell's letters. "Heck, I can't call you 'Mrs. O'Connell,' so please pardon my calling you Patricia," she wrote. That was agreeable to me; nationalists have called me less pleasant names. The advice which she gave me in the form of a "must" nationalist reading list was deadly:

April 21st 1945

Dear Patricia:

       You wrote me such a sweet friendly letter, heck, I can't call you "Mrs. O'Connell", so please pardon my calling you Patricia.

       I would surely like to see that baby boy, Francis Patrick, and I do think it is a shame that his Father, like so many other young Fathers, hasn't been able to see him and sort of watch him grow. I can never forgive these jews that have caused these wars and so much sadness and separation and death in so many Christian families. I do hope the good Lord will give them good measure in all they have coming to them, or perhaps that is the devil's job.

       I had intended writing you sooner and telling you about the 25 copies of the PROTOCOLS that you can get. I went and talked like a "dutch uncle" to the party that has them and they are willing to let them go at 40¢ a copy of the 25 copies for $10.00. They are losing 10¢ a copy but said they would do it if you want them. 50¢ has always been the very cheapest but I read them part of your letter and explained about your being wife of a soldier and that the books would fall into the right hands,

Grace Wick.

Grace Wick.

PS. Why don't you sell the PROTOCOLS for a dollar or even 50¢ or 60¢ and make a little for yourself while handling them? That is if you decide you want them.

Miss Wick tries to induce Patricia O'Connell to earn money by peddling the notorious *Protocols of Zion*. Patricia, however, was too busy with "Francis Patrick, Jr.," to accept the offer.

Do you get *Women's Voice?* Mrs. Van Hyning is publisher. I intend to cooperate with them in organizing here with the Gentile Group. . . . I have talked with several mothers who have lost their boys to make the world safe for the Jews. Of course I take Senator Bob Reynolds' *National Record*—just subscribed, also get W. *Lee O'Daniel's News.* Also *America Preferred,* published by Carl Mote—a very excellent magazine, solid MEAT. Of course I always listen to Upton Close every Sunday.

From Seattle, 3,000 miles across country, Miss Charlotte Wettrick rushed her wares to Mrs. O'Connell. Included in her "patriotic" kit were booklets denouncing progressive education, the Carnegie Foundation and the Rockefeller Foundation—all of which allegedly had something to do with "collectivist democracy." I couldn't understand what she was driving at. Most damning of her enclosures was a petition prepared by and returnable to Rev. Terminiello after signatures had been obtained. It demanded an investigation of the "parties guilty" of Pearl Harbor. Any nationalist knew that Terminiello did *not* mean the Japs!

I was surprised to discover the extent to which Father Terminiello's poison had seeped through the mothers' network. This helped confirm reports that Terminiello had not only corresponded with, but fallen heir to sections of Father Coughlin's mailing list.

Father Coughlin's name is inseparable from the mothers' movement. He spawned it late in 1939 as Hitler strutted across Europe's defenseless nations. Coughlin launched a program of isolating America "from European quarrels." His aim was to give Hitler a free hand. The December 11, 1939 issue of *Social Justice* hailed the founding of the first mothers' group in Detroit, the Mothers of America. Coughlin pledged his everlasting support. Pelley and Smith followed with similar pledges. Nazi agent George Sylvester Viereck also promoted the drive. These fascists and their henchmen from coast to coast kept whooping up nationalist sentiment against intervention. They stimulated a constant stream of "mothers" to Washington to high-pressure Congressmen into opposing internal security measures as well as international guarantees like the Lend-Lease Act.

It's a matter of record that many of the so-called "mothers" were either spinsters or unblessed with motherhood. Many of the members were frustrated and neurotic women who spent their energies on hate politics. I'm qualified to make these statements because for four unforgettable days I served as a collateral New York delegate to the Mothers' Congress in Washington, early in 1941. I saw the antics and had opportunity to talk with some hundreds of excited "mothers." Their warped patriotism and perversion of the word "motherhood," as demonstrated by mobs of ill-mannered vixens shrieking and stampeding through Congressional corridors, hanging Congressmen in effigy, scowling and defying Capitol police—all in an attempt to sabotage the passage of Lend-Lease—are a haunting memory of my Pagnanelli days as an investigator.

Throughout the war all-male nationalist groups operated strictly underground. Male attendance at "patriotic" meetings fell off sharply. Men stayed home while women carried on, usually under male instructions. I can testify that the female of the nationalist species is equally as vicious as the male, and in some instances even more so. I would prefer to face a mob of men rather than a smaller mob of nationalist women. They're out of this world. Most of them received their training and guidance under Father Coughlin's evil wings.

I have a definite statement from a reliable source to the effect that throughout the war Coughlin kept in personal touch with Mrs. David Stanley, chairman of the United Mothers of America. When I visited their office in Cleveland late in 1943 I saw a large stack of *Social Justice.* Most of the United Mothers are elderly women. The leadership was vested in Mrs. Stanley, Mrs. Ella Philip Monreal, Mrs. Ida Girard, Mrs. Sue Braun and Mrs. A. H. Berwick. The inner council also included Michael G. Kelly, promoter of Father Coughlin's National Union of Social Justice. Gerald Smith is the hero of the Mothers and has addressed many of their meetings. Martin L. Sweeney, former Congressman reported to be an ardent follower of Coughlin, had the staunch support of the Mothers, as did Gerald Smith when he ran for Governor of Ohio in 1944. Sweeney founded and now heads the Intelligent American Voters League, Inc., of Cleveland. Mrs. Monreal is secretary-treasurer. Mrs. Stanley is an Executive Committee member. John Braun and David Stanley also have executive positions with the League.

The United Mothers' meetings in Cleveland were among the most vicious held throughout the war. At one such meeting Mrs. Stanley suggested that "the hunk of cheese in the White House be impeached because he is a Jew and is receiving orders from Moscow." All our Allies were severely condemned and our war aims ridiculed.

The Rumor Clinic of the Cleveland *Plain Dealer* traced many flagrant lies to Mrs. Stanley's group. These included the lie that British soldiers visiting our country were really here "to get control of the American Army." They stated that the war was "controlled on both sides by the Jews so that whichever side wins the Jews will be the winners." A variation of the "ritual murder" theme was the lie that Jews never served as blood donors; that blood banks were a Jewish invention installed by the Jews to drain blood from, and thus weaken, the Gentiles. Mrs. Stanley's mobsters discouraged the buying of war bonds because "our money system is controlled by the Jews."

But that's not the whole story of their role as destructive agents. Certain "mothers" spread the lie that soldiers who refused to go overseas were shot. Others, according to a Cleveland reporter who investigated them personally, urged that soldiers revolt rather than take ship abroad.

The female hate-mongers invariably had a good word for Representative Clare E. Hoffman, their hero. They distributed his speech dealing with the "Judas-like betrayal of our people"—not by the Japs or Nazis but by the Administration, of course. They distributed Senator Reynolds' nationalist speeches. They distributed enormous quantities of defeatist and hate-inciting literature to parents of dead servicemen. United Mothers' meetings were addressed by "patriots" from outside Cleveland, including Mrs. Catherine Baldwin, New Yorker, President of the Defenders of the Constitution of the U.S.A., and Mrs. Agnes Waters, Washington mother who wanted some of our leaders to "hang for treason."

The Cleveland Mothers collaborated with similar groups throughout the country. Their purpose obviously was to hamstring the war effort. They were expertly advised and kept just this side of committing sedition. Experts in whispering campaigns, they spread the three d's of Hitler's psychological warfare—disunity, distrust and defeatism. They were not registered as Nazi agents, and it is not likely that they received funds they knew to be "hot Nazi money," but their work aided the Nazi cause immeasurably.

Another of their stunts was ganging up in belligerent groups to disrupt wartime unity rallies. They constantly hounded democratic groups. When students of Cleveland's Glenville High School presented a symposium on "Fascism and How to Fight It," anonymous telephone calls and letters began to plague those who participated. One of the girl students was threatened: "Our sons will get you when they get out of the Army."

Often seen at the United Mothers' meetings was John P. Moran of Cleveland, who publishes a labor-baiting bulletin called *Police*, under auspices of his League for Justice. His publication expressed full accord with the Mothers' aims. Its title may derive from Moran's own record: he was arrested on January 8, 1927, on charges of issuing a check to defraud, but was released. On February 24, 1930 he was arrested again for embezzling funds from Collinwood Lodge 584 of the International Association of Machinists, AFL, and sentenced to one year in the Ohio Penitentiary. Moran was disbarred as an attorney for allegedly keeping $2,500 he collected for a client from the Travelers Insurance Company. The disbarment is recorded in Court Journal No. 254, page 354, January 16, 1929. According to the Cleveland Better Business Bureau, Moran has also been evicted from offices for nonpayment of rent.

As publisher, Moran has a new scheme. He calls all labor "Communist" and "racketeer." Progressive candidates for office also receive the Communist smear brush. The labor-baiting racket may be practiced "honorably" and profitably, without risk of imprisonment.

Mrs. Stanley's schooling may be surmised from a letter she wrote on June 5, 1944 to Mrs. Lyrl Clark Van Hyning. I quote: "The *PM* [newspaper] of yesterday Monday had your letter in and all the different groups. Hopeing to seeing you all next Monday." The letter was in reference to the Women's National Peace Convention sponsored annually by Mrs. Van Hyning. Like Smith's "Christian" conventions, these affairs served as a device by which to keep the hate fires blazing.

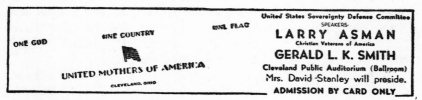

Letterhead (*left*) and announcement used by Coughlinite Mother Mrs. Stanley and some of her friends.

Mrs. Van Hyning is a dynamic Chicago woman. A member of the DAR, she regards that organization, together with the Parent-Teachers Association and the League of Women Voters, as Communist-front groups. She is assisted in her work by Mrs. Grace Billings. Mrs. Van Hyning wrote Patricia O'Connell two letters. With the first, in October, 1944, she enclosed her speech before the Women's National Peace Convention, a tirade against war. In war, Mrs. Van Hyning argued, the "odds are heavy against the investment." "Are we wise to continue this course?" she asked. "Shall we invest our resources in a more sane business?" The speech had the earmarks of having been written by an anti-New Deal "public relations counsel." It referred to the United States as a "great business" and a "great corporation." The convention was termed a "stockholders' meeting." Mrs. Van Hyning ended with an appeal for the impeachment of President Roosevelt. "Ours is the hiring and the firing power. The mismanagement of our business is not the fault of the General Manager, but ours for condoning the incompetency."

National elections were held less than five months after she spoke.

Mrs. Van Hyning's We, the Mothers Mobilize for America, Inc. kept hammering for a "negotiated peace now" throughout the war. An article in *Women's Voice* pleaded: "Poor broken Mothers of America, they are sick and become broken women. They know why they are crying. They know that negotiated peace is the only salvation for civilization."

The piece quoted Representative Jessie Sumner (R.–Ill.), one of their favorites: "American resources and lives are being dissipated all over the world. Today we have left just enough independence to make us believe our republic is still alive."

Another article, entitled "Who Is the Beast," was published in the April 27, 1944 issue:

They say Hitler is a beast—let us finish the sentence—Churchill is a beast. Didn't he confess that his life's aim was accomplished when he got America into this war? Roosevelt is a beast when he gave our substance to England, when he left our boys in Bataan without food or guns. Queen Wilhelmina is a beast. She drained the Dutch people of their earnings. The King of England is a beast.

We, the Mothers claimed more than 1,000 members in Chicago alone and a national circulation of 20,000 for *Women's Voice*. They flooded mothers mourning the deaths of their sons with defeatist tracts. "We believe that further participation in this war is inimical to the welfare of the country," the propaganda screamed.

Mrs. Van Hyning wrote me a second time on March 28, 1945. By that time I had announced the birth of Francis Patrick, Jr. Mrs. Van Hyning said:

We congratulate you on the birth of your little baby and we congratulate ourselves for having among us a young mother who has now such an incentive to go on with the work. We need you young mothers, for you will have to carry on what we have started. We hope, too, that your husband will soon be returning to you. It is a great joy to issue you a membership card and I hope that you can interest many young mothers and you will carry the torch which we have carried thus far.

Mrs. Van Hyning's letter came plastered with a sticker reading "Bring the Boys Back Home." She enclosed a copy of former Representative Jeannette Rankin's speech on December 8, 1941. Miss Rankin was the *only* member of Congress to vote against our declaration of war on Japan and Germany. For her supreme patriotism, she gained undying fame among America's fascists and the esteem of Nazi short-wave commentators. Miss Rankin blamed our "ultimatum" to Japan for Pearl Harbor. The Japs? They weren't mentioned.

Patricia Lochridge, who interviewed Mrs. Van Hyning for a splendid article, "The Mothers Racket," in *Woman's Home Companion,* July, 1944, quoted her as saying: "My women are not intelligent. In fact they are rather stupid. But they are a group of women who will work hard for me and that's what is important. Later perhaps we will be able to attract a higher type woman to the cause."

Mrs. Van Hyning's stalwart Los Angeles supporter is Miss Adelle Cox, large, powerfully built. She runs a defeatist column in *Women's Voice.* In one issue she whitewashed the Japs and Nazis and stated that war was "brewed up by selfish, blind old men without true patriotism." Miss Cox denounced the Federal Council of the Churches of Christ in America because it pleaded for the mobilization of our united resources against the enemy. To nationalists who strove day and night to disrupt American and Allied unity, this was tantamount to treason. The Council, said Miss Cox, was "the most insidious body in America today," and of course, "Jew-inspired."

Miss Cox answered my letter. "It is indeed encouraging to find a Mother with such a young baby interested in our work," she said. "We should like to have many more to work for the protection of their children. . . . I am sending you *The Modern Canaanites.*"

This 56-page, yellow-jacketed book proved to be a treatise by Rev. Jonathan Elsworth Perkins, a member of Gerald Smith's Committee of California Pastors, and a cousin of Rev. Winrod. It was "written in opposition to Communistic and Atheistic Jews." It followed the Anglo-Saxon theory of race superiority, and discussed with a show of learning the mumbo jumbo of that movement's ideology. "Fascism and Communism are merely the Jewish State," Perkins contended. "Both ideas spring from the Jewish brain of Carl Marx." He defended as "courageous" Mrs. Dilling, Col. E. N. Sanctuary and Rev. Winrod—all under indictment for sedition.

An inveterate contributor to *Women's Voice* was Miss Pearl Bussey Phinney, whose pride and joy was the way she *thought* she kept under cover. Miss Phinney doesn't know it, of course, but she has invited me to visit her penthouse on West 110th Street, New York. I have instructions to be sure to phone her first. Her letterhead was topped by a large flag and a quotation from Daniel Webster. The envelope was plastered with a huge American flag.

In one of her *Women's Voice* articles Miss Phinney observed, "The State Department is nothing but Jews, as are the post offices and all other government positions. Let's clean them out one way or another, and out of the country for good." In another article, equally untruthful, she called Terminiello "one of the great patriots in American history." Miss Phinney was visited by Homer Maertz. A close friend of Sanctuary and Mrs. Catherine Baldwin of the Defenders of the Constitution of the U.S.A., she bobs about on New York's nationalist currents.

More temperate in her defeatism, but more comic in her answer to Patricia O'Connell, mother, was Mrs. Martha C. Hubbard of Chicago. She advertised herself as a former high-school mathematics teacher, "representing Mothers of America." Her motherhood was genuine. She had five sons who up to April 7, 1945 had made her a grandmother nine times. Mrs. Hubbard pleaded for a negotiated peace in doggerel verse, song and fable. The one entitled "Paul Revere 1941" (sent to me in April, 1945) began:

leaflet, "The Anti-American Conspiracy," proved to be an hysterical diatribe against international cooperation. "Shall we be EURO-PEANIZED and ORIENTALIZED or remain the one and indivisible country of Washington, Jefferson and Lincoln, REVOLVING ON OUR OWN AXIS?"

Lohle-Madden placed their names on a leaflet defending Tyler Kent. In the form of an open letter to Ambassador Joseph P. Kennedy, they charged that Kent had received an unfair trial and denounced Mr. Kennedy as "un-American, uncharitable and un-Christian." The two peerless patriots justified Kent's action and darkly hinted that "there could be treason in high places"—meaning Washington, of course. A concluding paragraph injected the Jewish issue:

Mr. Kennedy, you have said: "Kent seems to have built up a terrific anti-Semitic complex, and I am certain that this attitude was the driving power for his behavior in London." If such be the case, then what was the Roosevelt pro-Semitic conspiracy in which Winston Churchill and Franklin D. Roosevelt used the American secret code? Were the preliminary arrangements for Lend Lease Semitic in intent rather than American?

Mrs. Patricia O'Connell's mail included several propaganda packets from a tireless worker for the nationalist cause, Mrs. Marguerite Cummings of San Diego. She's elderly, but works indefatigably in a nation-wide hate network. Writing on April 23, 1945, for example, she enclosed bulletins of the Mothers of Sons Forum, whose chairman was Mrs. Lucinda Benge of Cincinnati. These Cincinnati Mothers spread the lie that a Senatorial investigating committee inspecting American bases abroad had found our soldiers cold, hungry, neglected and driven to suicide. Even after the Senators hotly denied the Hitleresque lie and the WAC Mothers Association of Cincinnati attacked them, the Coughlinite Mothers persisted. One of Mrs. Benge's bulletins alleged that the S.S. *Warrington* had sunk because it was "sent to sea without repairs, in the face of hurricane warnings."

Mrs. Cummings enclosed a poem which wouldn't boost morale. One stanza read:

Shattered by shot and shell,
Stark in their gore,
Each by the other slain,
Lie true friends of yore.

Another Cummings enclosure was Terminiello's familiar *The Cross of War*. This was accompanied by a booklet entitled *Smear*, written by John T. Flynn and distributed by the National Economic Council. In it, Flynn, a super-smear artist, replied to the attacks on Merwin K. Hart. Another leaflet, *Federal Aid for Schools*, by Samuel B. Pettengill, denounced government aid to build more schools and promote education in those states (especially in the South) which needed it most. Pettengill's attitude was that our national debt was "increasing." Such aid, he said, would "solidify completely the totalitarian nature of our government."

The extension of popular education is one of the greatest anathemas of nationalist leaders and reactionary business men who dread a change in the status quo. They fear the consequences of education, for one cannot easily frighten or mislead an informed man or keep him "in his place." On the other hand, the ignorant can be easily dominated and led by the nose. The attitude is a carry-over from medieval times, when the educated aristocracy of royalty, landed peerage and clergy controlled and oppressed the illiterate masses! A basic reason for nationalist fear of democracy is that it provides the individual with opportunities for self-education and intellectual development. In the face of these, prejudices normally vanish, depriving the extreme nationalist of his greatest source of strength in the hate racket. Fascism is a regressive philosophy based on ignorance and fanned by hate which in itself is often the result of ignorance and blind fear.

Mrs. Cummings' *pièce de résistance* was a speech by Rankin, entitled "White Americans Betrayed." It flayed Negroes equally with whites whom Rankin didn't like. Mrs. Cummings' liberal hate packet also contained a reprint of a Washington *Times-Herald* article in defense of Tyler Kent. It was written by Arthur Sears Henning, Chicago *Tribune* correspondent who, together with John O'Donnell, Washington columnist for the New York *Daily News* and Washington *Times-Herald*, is a hero to the nationalists. Mrs. Cummings wrote me a cordial letter, but she was defeatist:

It's so hard to have your husband away at such a time. But such is the horrors of war—this cruel, useless war. Do you take *Women's Voice?* If not, I wish you'd subscribe for it. Until people understand how money is manipulated by the international Jew bankers, we will always have poverty and wars. . . .

Mrs. Van Hyning wrote that she was coming to visit me, then go to [the] Frisco [Conference]. The Bretton Woods and the Dumbarton Oaks are equally pernicious for Americanism and freedom for its people. They both doom us to slavery and totalitarianism. I'm glad you can distribute literature among your friends, and I'll send you all I can. I've given so much away, especially for the election.

The poison writings of John T. Flynn were also being distributed by the Peace Now Movement, founded by starry-eyed stay-at-homes who in 1944 attracted national attention with the following sensational demands:

1. The abandonment of that cannibalistic slogan "Unconditional Surrender" which may prolong the war for years.
2. The publication of fair and reasonable peace aims which will appeal to plain people in the Axis nations just as they appeal to us.
3. An Armistice on all fronts and negotiations for peace which can be a permanent peace if it is agreed upon among equals rather than dictated by victors to vanquished.

★   ★   ★   ★   ★   ★   ★   ★   ★   ★   ★   ★

The *Peace* Now *Movement*

HOW MANY TIMES A DAY DO YOU WISH THE WAR WERE OVER?

ARE YOU DOING ANYTHING MORE THAN WISHING TO STOP THE WAR?

Or are you one of the do-nothing group who say "I can't stop it?"

DON'T HAVE IT ON YOUR CONSCIENCE THAT YOU DID NOTHING TO STOP THE SLAUGHTER

"Patriotism"—1943–4–5 version!

Peace Now was engineered by a group of extreme pacifists who seemed to have little understanding of our war aims or of the enemy. Chairman was Prof. George W. Hartmann of Columbia University, Socialist and Vice-Chairman of the War Resisters League. Most of its members seemed to me anaemic, intellectually emasculated escapists from life who believed that peace could live side by side with ruthless, dynamic, ever-expanding Naziism and Jap imperialism. Dr. Dorothy Hutchinson, Francis Behn Briggs and Bessie Simon were Vice-Chairman, Treasurer and Secretary, respectively, of the movement.

Branch units mushroomed overnight throughout the country in 1944. Headquarters were first established in Cambridge, Mass., where Miss Simon and Miss Dorothy A. Hickie, another secretary, carried on. Their letterhead was a gaudy red-white-blue affair sprinkled with a border of thirty-two blue and sixteen large red stars. That made Peace Now very, very patriotic. Both Miss Simon (on April 24, 1944) and Miss Hickie (on June 26, 1944) wrote to Mrs. Van Hyning. Miss Hickie said: "Since we have the same goal we have much in common." Miss Simon asked Mrs. Van Hyning: "Don't you think we should draft Charles Lindbergh?" The dominantly female officers of Peace Now bear out my point that during the war male isolationists handed over the reins to female followers and drove from the back seat.

The myopia under which officials of the Peace Now Movement labored was illustrated in a series of questions and answers prepared by Prof. Hartmann. One of these read: "Can we do business with Hitler?" Here is the answer:

We do business with Stalin, Franco and other dictators, also with Hitler, in treatment and feeding of war prisoners. Most ordinary business transactions in America today take place between suspicious corporations or individuals subject to credit safeguards, inspection of goods, etc. Nations do the same. If we *entice* the German people with a *fair* set of terms, they will force Hitler to accept them whether he likes them or not.

Hartmann did not explain how we were to get our offer and supporting arguments to the mass of the German people. Or, assuming that we performed that considerable feat, how we could "entice" them to fire Hitler and his cutthroats. Nazi concentration camps thronged with Germans who had tried much less. Popular revolt in Germany, on which the well-meaning but visionary Dr. Hartmann pinned his faith, was impossible under the Nazi police machine.

Prompted either by conscience or fear of prosecution for corrupting the morale of the Armed Forces, Peace Now used on its literature a rubber stamp reading, "The Peace Now Movement publications are to be distributed only to civilian citizens."

Several months after Peace Now broke into print, the ideological fervor of its founders was supplanted by the fanatical isolationism of those who wrested control from them. The movement became a repository for the same verminous elements which had flooded the America First Committee. Its branch offices in the East began to distribute Representative Jeannette Rankin's writings, as well as hate-inciting "educational literature" by others greatly admired by the nationalists. Among this was a reprint of an article in the isolationist Washington *Times-Herald,* devoted entirely to "Uncovering 'Under Cover.'" Of all the drivel circulated against me and the book, Flynn's was the most venal and thoroughly distorted.

The New York office of Peace Now carried a good stock of Flynn's output. I visited it during the summer of 1944, this time posing as a pacifist. The office was small, but stacked neatly with piles of literature. I was met by a short, plump lady who said her name was Bette Harris. I told her truthfully that I had been a member of the America First Committee, Manhattan Chapter, and had met John T. Flynn. Her eyes brightened at the name.

"Mr. Flynn is a fine American," she said. "We distribute his material. What can I do for you?"

"I'd like to have some of your literature," I said. "I want to give it out to my friends. I want them to know about your movement."

Miss Harris went over to the stock pile and returned with a thick stack of defeatist literature.

"Here's another by John T. Flynn," she said. "It's *Uncovering 'Under Cover.'* It tells all about the author of the book. Have you read the book?"

"I've heard about it," I answered with a serious face.

"It attacks Americans like Mr. Flynn," Miss Harris explained, spreading out Flynn's article. "And here's a picture of Carlson. Look at that face!"

"Some face!" I said, restraining my laughter. I looked straight at

Miss Harris, giving her an opportunity to recognize me so that I could come back with a few well-chosen words about the Peace Now cult. But Miss Harris merely kept pointing at my photograph. "It's the only picture that has ever been published of Carlson," she said. "He only goes out at night, so people won't see him."

"Let me have some extra copies," I said. "I can use them."

The two rumors apparently were going the rounds, like the fiction that I had a red beard. It was a satisfaction when I later went on a long lecture tour to feel that the trip was at least partly counteracting these colorful tales.

As I looked at Flynn's article a feeling of disgust swept over me. I did not so much mind his pointless distortions aimed against me personally. It was another matter when he smeared Archbishop Leon Tourian, martyred prelate of my church, as a "Communist agent." The Archbishop was slain at a Christmas Sunday procession in 1933 while celebrating Mass at the Armenian Holy Cross Church in New York. The nine assassins—one of whom did the killing with a butcher knife—were all convicted. All were members of the Armenian Revolutionary Federation, also known as Dashnags, who were once branded as Armenian Fascists.

It was this murder which aroused me against the brutality inherent in fascism and impelled me to begin investigation of fascist and other anti-democratic activities. The use of terror and "direct action" against their critics has long been a tenet of the Dashnags. Their leadership is a small, but powerfully organized, highly nationalist, fanatical group ostracized by the overwhelming majority of Armenian-Americans, who are loyally democratic. Before Pearl Harbor the Dashnags' official organ, *Hairenik*, printed articles praising the Nazi regime and philosophy.

After V-E Day, the Armenian-American press revealed that Dashnag chief General Dro had sold out as a Quisling and made a deal with the Nazis through Alfred Rosenberg, Hitler's Minister of Eastern Occupied Areas, whereby Dashnags in exile were to set up a puppet government upon Hitler's conquest of Armenia and the adjacent oil fields in the lower Crimea. Charges that Dashnags served the Nazis as spies in the Soviet Army were also reported by the Armenian-American press, together with the report that Dashnag contingents from France and Germany fought with Hitler's legions.

In his article, however, Flynn called the Dashnags "patriotic Armenians"! According to this reasoning, the only "patriotic Armenians" would be the few thousand Dashnags, while the rest of us, more than 100,000 strong, on whose side was the murdered Archbishop, would become "Communist." Apparently Flynn, the highly touted researcher, got his information from biased sources and used it without checking them. Mrs. Dilling, too, has praised the Dashnags as "nationalist patriots." This can only be regarded as insulting to a democracy-loving, historically Christian people who have happily made their homes in America and contributed of their modest talent and capacity for hard work.

Flynn's charges were without foundation and a mere adaptation of the lies propagated by the Dashnags in a shabby attempt at self-defense. As an "expert" in Armenian political affairs Flynn is a

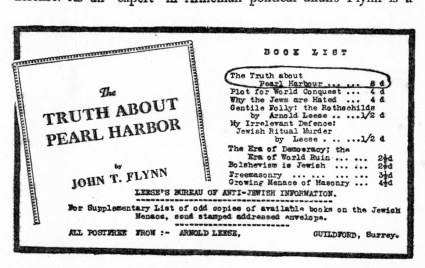

Flynn, super-patriot and reputed super-investigator, proved himself super-wrong about Pearl Harbor. But no one can deny that Flynn *et al.* didn't try hard enough to prove that President Roosevelt and members of his cabinet were responsible for it.

In England the notorious Arnold Leese, former führer of the Imperial Fascist League and now hate-monger at large, thought enough of Flynn's *The Truth About Pearl Harbor* to venture outside his usual field of distributing Jew-baiting and anti-democracy poison and sell the Flynn article to fellow British "patriots."

failure. But as the smearer of an innocent high dignitary of the Armenian Church he is tops.

Archbishop Tourian was a close friend of the Rt. Rev. William T. Manning, Bishop of the Episcopalian Diocese of New York. While living in England, he was a friend of the then Archbishop of Canterbury. Since his brutal assassination I have met with no one who approaches him in devout selflessness and stature as a man and servant of God. At the hands of Flynn, however, a great Christian clergyman becomes a "Communist agent," just as at the hands of other careless or irresponsible writers honorable Catholic prelates become fascists.

Whenever I received literature as Mrs. O'Connell, Flynn's output was almost invariably included. One batch came from the National Blue Star Mothers of America, who later took up Paul Meinhart and his Christian Veterans and whose leader, Mrs. Catharine V. Brown, harangued the Queens Christian Front rally in October, 1945. A copy of Flynn's *The Truth About Pearl Harbor* was inserted between a leaflet opposing the entry of women into the service and seeking to keep prospective WAVES, WACS and SPARS from enlisting, and another which screamed:

"While our boys are away, the slickest gang of racketeers that ever operated are taking over the government. BRING THE BOYS HOME!"

This item was distributed from 1943 on. The trash Mrs. Brown sent me in February, 1945 included a tract reading:

Christian Mothers: is this the price you are paying for Jew revenge? Now, nurses are to be drafted. Next it will be all women between 18 and 45, just as [has] been done in Communist Russia. . . . How much blood, sweat and tears has this JEW holy war cost you Christian Mothers in the United States? Has your son been sacrificed on the altar of this "holy war?" Or do you Christian Mothers feel that $10,000 is a fair price for a dead son and perhaps a dead daughter? DEMAND PEACE NOW.

A reprint of Rep. John E. Rankin's speech in the House on July 1, 1943 was also included. After excoriating the "Communistic Jews and Negroes," Rankin ascribed all Negro-white tensions, and particularly the bloody Detroit rioting, to Communists. Rankin quoted a Detroit serviceman who threatened to clean up the "mess" at home after the job was finished overseas. In view of the fact that Lorence Asman, Gerald Smith's stooge in Detroit, boasted that Rankin used his material in a Congressional speech, Rankin may have been quoting Asman as follows:

There are millions of us who are now training for war against the Jap and Nazi aggressors. In the name of God, in the name of our country, in the name of our Republic let us destroy that horrible beast known as the Communist International. If it is not done now, we will do it when the mess is cleaned up over there.

Mrs. Brown sent me a four-page Jew-baiting leaflet, entitled "Who Started the World War II—Read How You Were Taken Over by a Jew Plot," which readers were asked to "Please reprint and distribute." Its thesis was that "for persecutions suffered by 600,000 Jews in Germany the world was catapulted into a 'sacred war.'" It was so vitriolic that it bore no authorship. Jeannette Rankin's white-wash of the Japs and Nazis supplemented Flynn's smear leaflets. Also included in Mrs. Brown's packet was a tract issued by the National Women's Movement of Chicago. Published just before the 1944 elections, its defeatist intent was obvious:

It's time for a showdown! Just what are we fighting for? Will military victory be worth the sacrifice? Are America's young sons being sacrificed to cover up the blunders of doddering diplomats? We mothers are determined to break the wall of silence behind which our boys are done to death and our country betrayed.

One of my gooniest correspondents as Patricia O'Connell was Mrs. Agnes Waters, "only woman candidate for president of the USA." At one time I was tempted to dismiss her as an ineffectual crackpot, but her enormous energy, her role as spokesman for We, the Mothers Mobilize for America, the National Blue Star Mothers of America, the Mothers of America and the Mothers of the USA enabled her to play a sinister role during the war. Grace Wick described her effectively: "She fights like a fox terrier." She added, "To my way of thinking Agnes Waters is doing a vast amount of good"—as a defeatist, of course.

A sniping pamphleteer, Mrs. Waters cared little where her insults fell. Take this sample of wartime "patriotic" literature:

The final complete collapse (of the USA) is planned after we are enticed into this world revolution with millions of our beloved and brave men to be slaughtered in a suicide brigade for England and Russia. If the Jews and the Communists want a 2nd Front, let the Jews go. Stop the American expeditionary force from going all over the earth. . . .

Why are you so DUMB and so BLIND? Are you [members of Congress] a bunch of jackasses, going to sit up on your haunches on Capitol Hill and let this happen again? What kind of damn fools are you all anyhow? . . . IMPEACH THE PRESENT COMMANDER IN CHIEF, who is a traitor. The only way to win this war is to get these traitors out by IMPEACHMENT at once! Any jackass knows that you can't win a war on thirty different fronts.

Mrs. Agnes Waters says she is descended from "the last Stuart King of England, James II," and from "one of the Bravest of Irish Kings." "When I am President," she cooed, "I shall arrest, try and hang for TREASON any bureaucrat guilty of the crime of conspiracy to get us into the war. I will round up all the enemies of this Republic and take great satisfaction in administering JUSTICE by signing their death warrants."

Mrs. Waters expressed her sentiments at many Mothers' meetings throughout the country. She spoke for Mrs. Stanley and Mrs. Van Hyning and Mrs. Benge. She held her own forums in Washington. She also addressed the Mothers of America at the "Women's White House" in Detroit in 1945. Mistress of the mansion on Detroit's "Gold Coast" is Mrs. Blanche Winters. The house has sixteen rooms and five bathrooms. In 1945 it served as meeting place for a so-called Congress of Monetary Organizations. Announcement of the forthcoming Congress proved to be a clarion call for nationalists to emerge from under cover and meet in an old-fashioned, pre-Pearl Harbor hate fest. Most of those who attended were women. But among the men folk was "General" Jacob S. Coxey, the aged delegate whose "money-reform" notions have made him popular with Mrs. Van Hyning and the nation's screwball economists.

Mrs. Waters kept up her barrage throughout the war. Like Mrs. Dilling and Gerald Smith, she continually begged for money. "I need to raise $300 at once," she wrote me on one occasion, "and I do hope you can help me out with at least a part of it. . . . You

otic fervor, mixed with the sinister threat of "concerted action." On April 10, 1945 he wrote me on his red-white-blue stationery emblazoned with two crosses:

Under separate cover you will receive literature explaining what I believe to be the solution for these evils and outlining a plan of action. . . . We cannot allow irresponsible rabble-rousers at home to be successful in their plans for revolution and chaos.

Three weeks later Patricia O'Connell received another letter from Terminiello:

Our list is growing beyond all expectation. When the number is sufficiently large to make concerted action by legal means effective you will be informed either by air mail or through the meduim of the newsletter. . . . Let us pride ourselves that some would put us on their so-called "LUNATIC FRINGE," for the enemies of God and our country are not found in this fringe. May the Almighty God bless our efforts, may He reward you for your share in His Crusade for freedom and justice and charity. Wishing you God's choicest blessings, Yours for Christ and country.

Several months after I received Mrs. Waters' letter of May 22, Mrs. Patricia O'Connell's mail dropped sharply. Mysterious men and women called to see Mrs. O'Connell at the stationery store where her mail was received. The proprietor told them that he knew of no such person. It was the truth, since my arrangements there were with an employee.

On August 5, 1945 the storm broke. I was exposed as a mother "who did not meet the standards of the Christian Crusader." The exposé came in Terminiello's *Crusade Bulletin*. Neither Terminiello nor anyone else since then, however, so far as I know, has identified Patricia O'Connell as Carlson. They were suspicious of Mrs. O'Con-

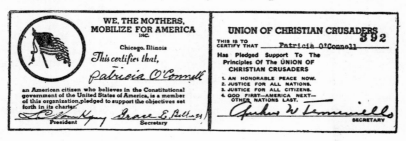

nell, but beyond that they knew nothing. I believe they took her for a living mother who, in their opinion, had "sold out to the enemy."

It would have been easy to carry on under another female name. Fifteen months of "motherhood," however, was enough. It was hard work, for I had sweated over the processing of my letters.

For my part, I do not know *how* Patricia was discovered as unworthy of nationalist support. I have some theories. As Mrs. Waters wrote, she had stopped at my address and found it a store instead of an apartment house. There is the possibility, also, that the investigation may have been the work of an undercover investigating group. I have irrefutable evidence showing that one ostensible "educational" organization, incorporated and with headquarters in Queens, has quietly carried on investigations of various people. All of its officers except one lived in the vicinity of the stationery store where Patricia received her mail.

The story of Patricia O'Connell had a sad denouement. Early in the fall of 1945 tragedy overtook the stationery store. Fire of undiscovered origin swept its premises and gutted it thoroughly.

Had some nationalist vendetta group, I wondered, taken revenge on the innocent owner, who was eking out a living for his elderly wife and family?

Thus mothers of men who went overseas to preserve the Four Freedoms sabotaged the principles for which their own sons fought.

I indict these mothers—and the many spinsters and childless married women who worked with them—on two counts. First, for their failure to share the responsibility of prosecuting the war as a united American people. Second, for developing a brand of nationalism which, when carried to its unalterable conclusion, spells an American fascist form of government that would sweep away our liberties and make a mockery of our Constitution.

Mrs. Dilling's veteran son, Kirkpatrick, appeared with Kister at Gerald Smith's St. Louis convention in May, 1946. Mrs. Van Hyning's son, Thomas Clark Van Hyning, threw his hat into the political ring after his release from the Air Corps by running unsuccessfully for Congressman in the Illinois Republican primaries. His candidacy was advertised on a full page of the March 28, 1946 issue of *Women's Voice*.

In the meanwhile, nationalist mothers are sabotaging the postwar peace program even more vigorously than they sought to sabotage the winning of the war. With emergency restraints relaxed, their shrill cries of false patriotism can now be heard more loudly and farther away than their wartime semi-undercover whispering campaigns and "patriotic" activity. The female of the species is as deadly as the male, and in most cases even harder to counteract effectively because of America's sense of chivalry toward womanhood. I was often shocked by the stealthy approach of some "Mother" correspondent who played upon the emotions of a stranger whom she believed to be a young mother, cultivating her goodwill by pulling her heartstrings with the sentiments that every woman knows, as she prepared to inject their defeatist poison.

The Mothers' patron saint, Coughlin, and their lesser saints, Rev. Gerald L. K. Smith and Rev. Arthur W. Terminiello, use Christianity to cloak their divisive program. In much the same way, female merchants of hate try to make themselves look simultaneously as much like Whistler's Mother and the Goddess of Liberty as possible. Behind the camouflage, home-grown fascist nationalism is poised to strike.

Offices of Chicago's We, the Mothers Mobilize for America, Inc., are a clearing house for a vast amount of un-motherly hate literature, of which this is only a small sample.

CHAPTER EIGHT

Orphans of World War II

> We want to help the needy merchant marine veteran. The Veterans Administration doesn't want to help him. The social organizations don't help him. The Army and Navy won't help him. The Government says he's a civilian and won't do anything about him. There are thousands of these veteran seamen. They're the orphans of this war.
>
> *Paul L. Specht*

THE ADDRESS is fancy, but the building at No. 296 is one of the shabbiest structures on Fifth Avenue. I walked up rickety stairs, past a synagogue, to the third floor and entered the office of the Merchant Marine Veterans Foundation, Inc. It was bare except for several chairs, some empty desks, a washstand, a calendar and an American flag. It was floored with rough, uneven boards. In one corner a man with a high domed forehead, and a henna-haired woman were talking in low voices.

"Who signs the letters now?" I heard the woman ask.

"Lambert signs them."

They meant, I knew, Lambert Fairchild, Chairman of the Advisory Board of the Merchant Marine Veterans Foundation, who had written to me. When the woman had left I introduced myself to her associate, Paul L. Specht. The Foundation was organized, Specht explained, to raise funds for disabled seamen.

"We want to help the needy merchant marine veteran," he said. "The Veterans Administration doesn't want to help him. The social organizations don't help him. The Army and Navy won't help him. The Government says he's a civilian and won't do anything about him. There are thousands of these veteran seamen. They're the orphans of this war."

I agreed with him genuinely. Members of the American Merchant Marine have received shabby treatment at the hands of the Congress, the Army and the Navy. All have disclaimed responsibility for those "civilians" who were engaged in the hazardous job of transporting munitions, food, clothing and the vital armaments of war. Many ineligible to join the Navy served their country by joining the Merchant Marine. Admiral Chester W. Nimitz said of their work: "The sea lanes of the Pacific, extended westward more than 4,000 miles, are crowded with merchant ships. . . . Without these ships, wholly devoted to winning the war, our substantial progress would not have been possible—a tribute to the ability and patriotism of the American Merchant Marine."

I did not doubt the sincerity of the founders nor of Specht. But their judgment in selecting Lambert Fairchild as Chairman and one of the incorporators of the Foundation is questionable. Didn't they know his record? Didn't they know that when Fairchild came East from St. Paul, Minn., twenty-five years ago, he left a string of unpaid debts? I have photostatic copies of court records showing that the following unsatisfied judgments are pending in the Minneapolis District Court:

File No. 178699   Wenzel Eitter vs. Lambert F. Fairchild, $828.31
File No. 97611   Winslow Furniture & Carpet Co. vs. Lambert F. Fairchild, $108.62
File No. 99050   Kate Marvin Harris vs. Lambert F. Fairchild, $244

MERCHANT MARINE VETERANS FOUNDATION INC

FIFTH AVENUE
NEW YORK   N. Y.

January 29th, 1946.

Dear Mr. Thompson:

       This is a duly constituted organization consisting of members whose personal beliefs do not enter into the administration of its objectives.   We believe in Americanism, and our principles are not dictated by any outside pressure groups.

       Thank you for your inquiry.

       Sincerely yours,

       Lambert Fairchild

Lambert Fairchild, Chairman,
Advisory Board.

File No. 127819   Kahos & Bielenberg vs. Lambert F. Fairchild, $86.20
File No. 137892   John Polumbo vs. Lambert F. Fairchild, $23.75
File No. 138040   Julius A. Haussner vs. Lambert F. Fairchild,
                  $391.47

These facts were exposed in 1941 while Fairchild was Chairman of The National Committee for Religious Recovery and associated with one Howard Kiroack. His job was "to stimulate regular church attendance and support" and combat "Godless ideologies." According to *Newsweek*, the Committee was organized by "a few Wall Streeters" who "decided that what the country needed was a religious revival and that businessmen could promote it better than the clergy." Fairchild, who traces his ancestry to Pilgrim John Alden, spoke over the radio, damned the New Deal and whooped up Wall Street's sudden religious fervor which came on just prior to national elections.

So zealously did Fairchild, Kiroack and Wall Street propagate the gospel that Willkie, Frank Kingdon, Frank Knox, Herbert Lehman and industrial concerns endorsed the drive. "Can Corporations Be Religious?" was the topic of one of Fairchild's radio talks. "For God and Country," promised Fairchild, "you're going to see religion and business formed into a solid phalanx. Let no rabble-rousing Communist tell you anything else, you security-holders who want security for your holdings." When the facts about his past were exposed, Fairchild silently resigned from the Committee. Kiroack merely renamed it The Laymen's National Committee, Inc., and carried on from where Fairchild left off.

Fairchild is a stylish figure. He's usually dressed in a checkered or striped gray suit. He wears a black Homburg, bow tie and white carnation. His spectacles dangle from a black ribbon worn around his neck, which swings jauntily over his white vest. Fairchild's teaser mustache is stiffly waxed and the points stick out briskly. He wears gray spats and carries a black cane. Fairchild is the *bon vivant* of yesterday.

Fairchild was a familiar figure in the nationalist political underworld. I met him many times while investigating for *Under Cover*. He was known to the public at large as a former New York Alderman and past Commander of the American Legion. (He's now chaplain of a Legion post.) Fairchild joined the Army late in September, 1918 and was out in a few weeks, he told me.

His undercover politics have received less publicity.

Fairchild was among those who served on the "Committee of Honor" at the testimonial dinner given to General George Van Horn Moseley in New York in December, 1938. The following September 23 he spoke for Coughlinite Allen Zoll's so-called American Patriots, Inc. That same year he met with Mrs. Dilling in New York. Fairchild, Father Curran and John Eoghan Kelly, the convicted Franco agent, served on the advisory board of *The Patriot Digest*, one article in which urged that those on relief be denied the right to vote. Another article, by Canadian Nazi leader Adrian Arcand, spoke of the blessings of the "corporate state." In 1940 Fairchild and Christian Fronter George U. Harvey of Queens joined hands to defeat liberal Republican candidates for Congress.

On November 19, 1940 Fairchild spoke at the "Brown House," the Bronx hangout of the German-American Bund. The telephone book listed Henry von Holt, Bundist, at that address. The bulletin board was lined with Germanic notices, including a picture of the Hitler Youth showing a swastika banner. In an inner room were thirty-six black-lacquered shovels, the kind Hitler's labor battalions used in parades. The meeting was sponsored by the Committee for the Preservation of America, of which a Mrs. Gloss Edwards was President. Covering the meeting with me was Roy Tozier, then research director of Friends of Democracy, who during World War II served as a lieutenant in Army Intelligence.

About forty of New York's choicest Bundists, Christian Fronters and Christian Mobilizers were present. I have their names listed in a carefully prepared report. Von Holt and another Bundist, Willy Yockl, were both there. Waiting for the meeting to start, I counted twenty-eight American flags of all sizes. I couldn't translate the Germanic inscriptions which lined the walls. The meeting finally started with singing led by Charles Albert McLain, song leader at America First Committee meetings, and a correspondent of Father Terminiello.

Fairchild was the first speaker. "Let us begin with a prayer," he announced. Closing his eyes, sticking out his jaw as if squaring off for a fight, he gave an unconvincing invocation and then a speech. Used to the rabble-rousing of Kuhn and McWilliams, the audience did not appreciate Fairchild's references to "Marxists." Every time he mentioned "Marxists," members of the mob called out:

"You mean Jews."

"Under Roosevelt we are living under a national-socialist dictatorship," Fairchild opined.

"Jewish dictatorship," one of the mobsters yelled.

Fairchild derided democracy as a sham. "What is this thing called democracy anyway? We don't have it in this country! Maybe we'll have it a thousand years from now!"

The hooligan mob liked this better and applauded. With a final reference to "Marxists," which brought the instantaneous comeback, "Jewish," Fairchild closed in a flurry of religious phrases. It brought down the house. Willy Yockl leaned over to me and said:

"He ain't educated enough on the Jews, and he don't know nuthin' about national-socialism, but he ain't bad! He'll learn!"

With this background, Lambert F. Fairchild was appointed Chairman of the Board of the Merchant Marine Veterans Foundation, Inc. I've made a careful check of its other promoters and officers. Their preponderantly non-seaman status seemed unusual. Specht, for instance, was never a merchant seaman. He is described as an "organizer of many 'name' band units" which played on American merchant ships. He is well known and well liked in the entertainment world as an honest, well-meaning fellow. The twenty-two listed officers of the Foundation included shipping and business executives, actors, publicists and others. I found one listed as belonging to the maritime service. One of its officers was Rudy Vallee. I wrote Vallee for information. He answered on February 22, 1946:

I cannot tell you much about the Merchant Marine Veterans Foundation because I do not know too much about it. I think Paul Specht, former orchestra leader, whom I knew for many years happily, is a reliable person. However, it's quite possible, having turned promoter, that he might consider this a promotion as well as a very fine and worthy cause.

Membership in the Foundation ranges from $5 to a life membership at $1,000 for individuals and a suggested $5,000 for firms and corporations. It started out with high hopes. Its budget for 1945 was $800,000. It opened a drive for $1,000,000 but took in less than $2,000. Fairchild's presence is a kiss of death. The non-seaman character of its backing is also partly responsible.

When I called on Specht again in May, 1946, he was on his way to see James A. Farley. Farley appeared at a "benefit" show and dance on May 21 in New York. Together with Farley and Representative Frank Boykin of Alabama, Fairchild spoke on a nation-wide hookup. Paul Whiteman and his band played. The stage show included well-known Broadway stars. The "National Honorary Committee" included Orson Welles, Eddie Cantor, Drew Pearson and others to whom doubtless the work of the Foundation had not recalled the un-American past associations of Fairchild and his professions of scorn for democracy.

There has been some speculation as to whether "union-busting" elements may be trying to control the Foundation with an eye on the 1948 elections. The merchant seaman has a right to ask: Why aren't the promoters merchant seamen? Who is really behind the Foundation? What are its real purposes? Why is a former associate of Christian Fronters and other nationalists given a major role in its policies? Will Fairchild participate in the administration of publicly sponsored funds for the relief of merchant seamen?

A want ad in the October 28, 1945 issue of the Philadelphia *Inquirer* read:

MERCHANT SEAMEN—Unusual opportunity in organization work. Weekly income possible, $125. For further information write Walter Wheeler, 922 Avenue O., Brooklyn, N.Y.

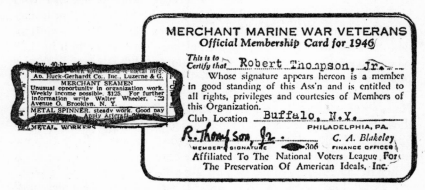

The advertisement was for the Merchant Marine War Veterans, which mushroomed in the fall of 1945. Its loud promises for reform of merchant seamen problems have dwindled to a whisper.

I interviewed Wheeler at his home, posing as a Merchant Marine seaman. As district organizer for the Merchant Marine War Veterans, Wheeler claimed that he averaged $125 a week by hustling for members. He kept $1 out of every $2. He tried to induce me to become a hustler-organizer. "Every member of the MMWV," he said, "has gotta get members so that in November, 1946 we can have a convention and elect officers." For the present he and Lieut. George W. Blakeley were in charge.

"We're just a young organization trying to give the GI Bill of Rights to the merchant seaman and get him in on the benefits," Wheeler said. The literature he gave me was studded with stars and drawings of Lincoln. It stated that the Merchant Marine War Veterans were "Affiliated to the National Voters League for the Preservation of American Ideals, Inc.—The Organization That's 'TRUE AMERICAN.'" Another leaflet—of which 150,000 copies had been printed "in the interests of 'AMERICANISM'"—was sponsored by the League itself. It was on "Preserving Self Government" and written by "National President" Lieut. George W. Blakeley.

The display of stars and repetitious emphasis on "Americanism" urged me to interview Blakeley. I located him at his tiny two-room apartment in New York's Yorkville section. I posed as Robert Thompson, Jr., merchant seaman, who had come from Buffalo on a visit. I stated at the outset that I was not a member of the National Maritime Union, whose organ, *The Pilot*, had described the Merchant Marine War Veterans as "greedy" and "dangerous" and had warned readers against joining it. *The Pilot* asserted that Blakeley, while a member of the Marine Engineers Beneficial Association, had opposed "the American Radio Telegraphers Association in 1938 when they went on strike," and "made anti-labor appeals to the public against the ARTA."

Blakeley was wearing a lieutenant's uniform and service ribbons. He seemed a cautious and an unwilling talker on topics other than those concerned with solicitation. I asked why the MMWV had affiliated with the National Voters League. "It was mainly to save money. The League is a Philadelphia corporation, and it costs us only $10 to affiliate with it. In New York it's $42 plus lawyer's fees."

I asked him about the League. "It's a patriotic organization," Blakeley answered. "A couple of years ago we put out a leaflet demanding that Earl Browder be jailed." I suggested joining it. "Membership is limited," he objected, "and it costs $300 to join."

Instead of joining the League, I paid Blakeley $2 to become member number 52 of the Merchant Marine War Veterans and, *ipso facto*, an organizer. I was loaded down with literature.

Before leaving, I called Blakeley's attention to his leaflet which claimed the endorsement of the American Legion and the Veterans of Foreign Wars. Blakeley produced photostatic copies of letters, one of which was dated May 6, 1938, signed by H. L. Chaillaux, Director, National Americanism Commission of the Legion; the other, by R. B. Handy, Jr., National Adjutant of the VFW, was dated May 6, 1938. Both letters approved the program of the League in a general way. Neither writer committed himself on the *execution* of that program nor, of course, did he discuss the various interpretations which the words "Americanism" and "patriotism" may be given by various users. Blakeley's use of the letters seemed a device to exploit their innocuous contents to promote the Merchant Marine War Veterans.

Blakeley had referred to a Philadelphia lawyer who was acting as "Trustee" to the MMWV. I found John T. Doughten in Room 908 of the Schaff Building. He was a large, jovial man and he was talking on the telephone. A hearing device was placed against the receiver while he talked directly into the mouthpiece. After fifteen minutes Doughten came up for air and apologized for the delay.

"I've advised them to keep track of every cent that comes in and goes out," he said. "I'm doing this as a personal favor to Blakeley. I have nothing to do with the Merchant Marine War Veterans. I don't want a cent out of it." Doughten showed me a stack of letters dangling with checks, money orders and dollar bills. "I'm holding these for Blakeley. He or Wheeler come down every two weeks to pick it up."

I decided to investigate further. The incorporation papers of the Voters League for the Preservation of American Ideals, Inc. listed its "purposes":

To foster and promote such legislation as shall be for the good of the people of the United States. To be a non-partisan, *political* body and to promote the election of officials who will act for the good of the people. To be a social, fraternal and educational group to discuss current events. To form a national group and set up branch organizations and affiliates which will further the above purposes.

The charter listed ten incorporators, headed by Blakeley. I wrote letters to all except Blakeley; eight were returned marked "Not Found."

The literature of the Voters League revealed that it was a super-patriotic setup. "Smash Hitlerism, Fascism, Communism [in red ink] and all other 'Isms' except Americanism," one of its leaflets screamed. "ACT NOW! SAVE AMERICA!" Another was worded hysterically: "S.O.S. Save Our System of Democracy. Do You Prefer G.P.U. [Russian Secret Police] to American G-Men???" Other League leaflets urged members "to continue the Dies Investigation Committee." They charged, with irresponsible "patriotism," that

The Communists in the Government want a Bolshevik G.P.U., a political Secret Bureau with which dishonest politicians can persecute their enemies, oppress the public and take another step toward Russian despotism. . . . Defeat any move on the part of any administration to reorganize the U.S. Government to a particle [partial?] or direct dictatorship.

Unlike those of the Foundation, however, the Merchant Marine War Veterans' officers all seemed to be legitimate merchant seamen. Blakeley claims that it is not a "ship-owners' organization, or a union-busting proposition." What assurance has the joining seaman that as soon as the Merchant Marine War Veterans has grown Blakeley and others like him will not attempt to swing it in the direction of the National Voters League policies? What guarantee has the merchant seaman that it will not be perverted to serve narrow political ends?

A trend toward this was shown in releases bearing the address of Doughten's office, by one George W. Strimmel and "Brother Albert Hokins." These two named "certain influences, generally believed to be communist-directed" as the cause of legislation which excluded the merchant seamen. They followed the nationalist line by denouncing credit loans to Great Britain and Russia, alleging, "This money will seep down to the British World War Veterans directly. . . . The same thing will happen to Russian War Veterans of World War II. . . . We want more than just an organization. We want results that will mean cash to all of us."

It's my conclusion that the deserving cause of the merchant seaman—of whom 5,500 died or are missing in the line of duty, with thousands more injured—will hardly be served well by the Merchant Marine War Veterans. One reason why seamen are denied benefits on a par with Armed Forces veterans is because their cause is not championed by groups which command universal respect and can therefore promote their interests vigorously.

One such group refused to answer my queries on its history, membership, the way it obtained thousands of dollars and what it did with the funds. It's the Merchant Marine Veterans Association of the United States. Headquarters are on Boylston Street, Boston. Boston merchants have filed many complaints on its methods of solicitation. I've pieced together the story of the Association after six months of investigation.

It began with my correspondence with its Adjutant, Henry B. Burridge, and his invitation to "merchant seaman" Thompson to attend the Association's convention in New York at the Capitol Hotel, on January 20, 1946. I posed as a cook's assistant who had shipped to the West Indies on a fruit liner. About thirty delegates were present from Massachusetts, New Jersey, New York, Maryland and Florida. The Merchant Marine Veterans Association had fourteen chapters in ten states. Membership figures were not stated. I queried chapter leaders individually and learned that New York had 145 members; Baltimore, 150; Jersey City, 40. I estimated the total membership at about 750.

Burridge proved to be a short fellow in his forties, who timidly said that he could no longer devote his full time as adjutant unless he was paid for the job. His complaints were eased by Commander John J. Coughlin, a large, extrovert type with thick black hair and a slight brogue, who said he would talk to Burridge later. The convention established a Ladies' Auxiliary and Junior Merchant Marine Auxiliary, and boosted the membership and initiation fees. The endless discussions, arguments on the drawing up of the constitution and by-laws, and the election of officers by secret ballot made it a dreary afternoon for me. Lewis M. Doyle, auditor of the MMVA, was elected National Commander.

I kept pretty well to myself because I was so ignorant of seagoing terminology that I knew I'd give myself away if I engaged in lengthy conversation. My strategy was to make my queries, then tactfully withdraw in order to avoid answering questions. If I had known that the MMVA accepted Army men I could easily have posed as Robert Thompson, Jr., the veteran, instead of a nervous and unsocial merchant seaman.

I saw no indication of prejudice except on the part of one delegate who arrived late. "We gotta do somethin' about these Jews. They ganged up on me in the elevator so I wouldn't get here on time." His case seemed isolated.

Merchant Marine Veterans Association is a misnomer. It accepts Army and Navy veterans. Minimum dues have been set at $5; individual posts could charge as much as they liked. The only considerable item of regular expenditure reported was $100 monthly to the Washington representative for "expenses," but a balance of only $175 was reported. This left a sum of about $3,000 which, it was explained, had been given to the "promoter" of a "yearbook" which the Association published in 1945.

After the convention was over I looked further into the Association. I learned that twenty-four questions had been asked of it by the National Maritime Union. The NMU wanted to know, among other things, what the stand of the Association was on discrimination, on the right of organized labor to take political action, United Nations cooperation. Were the founders seamen? What was the meaning of the term "true, 100 percent Americanism," as used in the Association's program, from the standpoint of the foreign born? When John J. Coughlin, former Commander, refused to answer these questions, *The Pilot* investigated and charged the MMVA with being a "Goldbrick" group whose real aim was to take the veterans' "money or use them for suspect political ambition."

All this prompted me to investigate further. I was well aware that magazine promoters are notorious for their rake-offs and often charge more than fifty percent of income, plus expenses. In three trips to Boston, early in 1946, I followed many blind leads. Finally I learned that on October 19, 1945 Coughlin's Greater Boston Post had sponsored a dance at the Bradford Hotel and solicited by mail the sale of tickets at $2.50. In April it had solicited by phone and through the mails funds for the yearbook at the rate of $100 a page, $50 a half page, $30 a quarter page, $15 for one eighth of a page. The appeal used was the typical tear-jerking letter used by professional promoters:

We are publishing an Official Year Book giving the History of the Merchant Marine, also advertising from prominent business houses. We would appreciate your kind co-operation in subscribing to an ad in this Book. The proceeds are being used for the welfare of the Merchant Seamen, such as Hospitalization, Rehabilitation, Child Welfare and a Bill now pending in Congress, asking for compensations and benefits for the men of the Merchant Service who have done such outstanding and courageous work on the high seas, and in foreign ports under enemy shell fire. . . . The casualties to date have been heavy, therefore these activities are urgent.

Our Honorary Board numbers such gentlemen as the Hon. Charles F. Adams, Hon. Joseph P. Kennedy, Dr. Leonard Carmichael—Pres. of Tufts College, and others of like character.

W. L. Drew
Association Adjutant

My next task was to discover the promoter and obtain a copy of the yearbook. Oddly enough, instead of being made public, the book seemed to be kept strictly under cover. It seemed strange. After considerable research I located the offices of the MMVA at 755 Boylston Street. But my attempts to meet "John H. Kimball, Merchant Marine Veterans Association, Room 602," as listed on the directory, proved fruitless. Who was Kimball? On my third trip, on March 30, 1946, I finally found someone in Room 602. He was a pale-faced, nervous, suspicious person, wearing a slouchy hat which came down to his eyes. I identified myself as "Thompson from the Buffalo post."

"I have nothing to do with running the organization," he protested. "The man you want to see is Burridge. He lives in Marblehead. Here is his address and phone. Call him up." He talked with machine-gun speed.

"But isn't this the office of the Merchant Marine Veterans Association? It says so on the directory. I send all my letters here from Buffalo," I said.

"I have nothing to do with the organization," he insisted. "Go see Burridge."

"You must be Mr. John Kimball," I said. "How are you connected with the Association?"

"Yes, I'm Kimball. I raised money for 'em last year on a dance.

Gave 'em $1,500 from advance sales. We sold 900 tickets at $2.50 each."

"How about the yearbook?" I asked. "We want to put one out in Buffalo. How about a copy?"

Kimball went to a desk and brought out a large 144-page book. "Who put it together?" I asked.

"I did. Did all the work myself, got the ads and all. We printed four or five thousand. It was a war baby. Went over good. Can't do it as good this year."

"How much did you make on it?" I asked Kimball.

"Don't know. Nobody lost money on it. All expenses were paid," Kimball said in a clipped way. Then he cut me short. "I gotta go now."

Later in the day I phoned Kimball. Posing as the chairman of a veterans' organization which wanted to issue a yearbook, I asked if he had had experience.

"Sure, sure," Kimball said. "I put out a yearbook for the Merchant Marine Veterans Association."

"How did it turn out? Make any money?" I asked. "We want to be sure we're going to make something."

I jotted down his answers as he talked.

"That yearbook took in $15,000 and I gave them $8,000. That's over half."

On the train I analyzed the copy of the yearbook. It contained 32 pages of copy matter. The 112 pages of advertising brought in an estimated revenue of $12,500. With the yearbook and the advertising rates in my possession I knew why those who wanted to keep the revenue secret kept the book under cover. A report from my confidential source is to the effect that Kimball and two associates kept an unusually high percentage of the income and turned over the balance to the Association.

My next step was to find out Kimball's associates. It was logical to assume that the enormous amount of solicitation could not have been handled by Kimball alone. By a peculiar turn of good fortune which we loosely call "luck," but which is also the result of hard work, I found a highly trustworthy Boston group which had investigated this phase of the Association. A trained member of that group had actually interviewed Kimball and his *two assistants*. I quote verbatim from the report he filed to his research organization, the name of which I have been asked not to use:

. . . We both went personally to the office of the Merchant Marine Veterans Association and there interviewed a man who said he was Henry B. Ginsberg, solicitor; Sidney S. Pollak, solicitor and John H. Kimball. It was very difficult to get anything very tangible from any of these men and during the course of the interview, Kimball said he was a big banker and was contributing his time to this organization. Upon being questioned, it developed he was employed by Hayden & Stone Company in Boston about 30 years ago. . . . He denied he was a fund raiser. . . .

Merchant Marine Veterans Association

ASSOCIATION OFFICERS
JOHN J. COUGHLIN, Commander

W. L. DREW, Adjutant

MICHAEL J. RUANE, Finance Officer

LEWIS M. DOYLE, Auditor

DONALD W. McKONE, Judge Advocate

of the

United States

We are enclosing information about our Merchant Marine Veterans Association in order that you may know the aims and purposes of our organization, which is non-union, non-sectarian and non-profit.

An Official Year Book is being published by our Organization, giving the History of the Merchant Marine, also containing advertising from prominent Manufacturing Plants and Business Houses. We would appreciate your kind co-operation in subscribing to an ad in this Book. The proceeds are being used for the welfare of the Merchant Seamen, through a program of Hospitalization, rehabilitation, child welfare, and for a Bill now pending in Congress asking for compensations and benefits for the men of the Merchant Marine who have done such outstanding and courageous work on the high seas, in foreign ports and under enemy shell fire.

If we can give you further information regarding our Association, or our Year Book, please do not hesitate to contact our headquarters, or me personally. Our rates for ads are $100 full page, $50 half page, $30 quarter page, and $15 for one-eighth page.

Our casualties to date have been heavy, therefore these activities are urgent, and we believe its worthiness is attested by the character and prominence of the companies who have to date reserved space in this Book. For your convenience in replying, we enclose a self addressed, stamped envelope. May we hear from you by return mail?

April
2
1945.

Very sincerely yours,

Merchant Marine Veterans Association
of the United States.
W.L.Drew, adjutant.

Sample of a tear-jerking letter used to solicit advertisements.

. . . He became very much annoyed as a result of my questioning and said it was none of the business of anybody as to what the Merchant Marine Association did with the money it collected. I accordingly asked him if it was all right with him if I advised inquirers accordingly, and he said it certainly was. I, therefore, informed Mr. Kimball, Mr. Drew, Mr. Pollak and Mr. Ginsberg we would advise inquirers that we had been authorized by John H. Kimball to tell them that if they wanted to know what the Merchant Marine Veterans Association of the U.S. did with the *money they are soliciting from the public,* that John H. Kimball refused to give them this information, feeling it was none of their business.

Mr. Pollak admitted he had previously been a securities stock saleman although he was reluctant to state with what companies he had been connected. Also, Mr. Kimball said that he had at one time been active in the securities line of business in the vicinity of New York. . . . The Messrs. Kimball and Ginsberg maintained that they were contributing their time as voluntary workers and reimbursed only for expenses. They said expenses ran about 20%.

Further investigations disclosed that neither Kimball, Pollak nor Ginsberg had ever served in the Merchant Marine. All three were "honorary members" of the Association. Article IV of the constitution permitted honorary membership to those "civic-minded persons who have, by their efforts, enhanced the welfare of the Merchant Marine and Maritime Industry of the United States." Kimball, Pollak and Ginsberg could hardly be called "civic-minded," inasmuch as they received a certain percentage of the take.

Despite these glaring facts, Merchant Marine Veterans Association officials insisted that solicitation was not done by professional promoters or professional salesmen. They insisted that it was done by "voluntary workers" who received a small percentage for expenses. Annoyed by the tactics of an MMVA official, Charles F. Mills, Chairman of the United Seamen's Service for the Boston Port Area, wrote them:

We are not willing to have the seamen who use our facilities solicited for membership in any organization or annoyed in any way by any particular group. It has come to my attention that you have recently been again active on our premises, and this letter is written to you to say that we must now deny admission to officers or representatives of your organization and affiliated organizations.

When I wrote Mr. Mills to make sure I had quoted him correctly, he phoned me from Boston and confirmed the quotation. Mr. Mills added, however, that he had made no charge against the MMVA as a whole because he knew nothing about it beyond W. L. Drew and his wife who, Mills alleged, had insisted on soliciting jointly for memberships.

My continuing suspicions led me to inquire whether Dr. Leonard Carmichael, President of Tufts College; Charles F. Adams, Boston banker; and Joseph P. Kennedy, former Ambassador to England, had given permission to have their names used in the solicitation of funds. Mr. Kennedy, who had previously received similar inquiries, wrote: "I think I will look into the matter myself." Mr. Carmichael said: "I made a memorial address for this association during the war, and I felt disturbed at the fact that a group of men who were doing a good job were somewhat neglected. I therefore agreed to allow my name to be used in connection with the organization."

Mr. Adams wrote: "I have no recollection of ever consenting to the use of my name in connection with the Merchant Marine Veterans Association. I certainly have no record of having done so and in view of the enclosed correspondence * it seems wholly improbable that I did so. There is a difference in the title between the Merchant Marine Veterans Association and the Merchant Marine Veterans Foundation, but if I refused one I would not have been likely to accept the other."

As I reviewed my investigation, a number of questions remained unanswered. What was the disposition of the funds? How were they expended? Were they spent for "the welfare of the merchant seaman, such as Hospitalization, Rehabilitation, Child Welfare," as claimed in the letter of solicitation? Were Boston merchants aware that the money was raised by professional fund-raisers who received a large percentage? Kimball's reported attitude that the affairs of the MMVA were "none of the business of anybody," and the secretiveness of the MMVA leadership, can hardly inspire confidence. My repeated registered letters to Coughlin, seeking information, went unanswered. He refused to cooperate as he had refused to answer other legitimate queries. *The business tactics of any organization which solicits funds from the public in the name of patriotism and*

---

* Mr. Adams wrote Paul Specht of the Merchant Marine Veterans Foundation: "I really ought not to serve on your Advisory Board."

charity are the vital concern of the public. A public-be-damned attitude is autocratic and leads to suspicions.

In contrast to this treatment was the wholehearted cooperation I received from the World War Veterans of the American Merchant Marine, with headquarters in Newton, Mass. It was founded in 1936 and chartered by the state. George Walsh is Adjutant. From Walsh I received copies of their constitution, sample membership cards and several explanatory letters. Only members of the maritime services or the U.S. Transport Service of World War I or II are eligible to join.

As a result of Mr. Walsh's cooperation I'm able to explain that the World War Veterans of the American Merchant Marine have pioneered a number of bills intended for the benefit of the merchant seaman. Mr. Walsh claims the loyal friendship of many Congressmen. On April 4, 1946 he wrote me that Representative John W. McCormack, House Majority Leader, had introduced Bill H.R. 9485 as early as 1940. Later, Representative Thomas H. Lane filed Bill H.R. 1858. Representative J. Hardin Petersen filed Bill H.R. 4846. In addition, Bills H.R. 2346 and 2449 are now being considered by the Merchant Marine and Fisheries Committee. All bills are to help the merchant seaman with hospitalization, Seeing-Eye dog service, burial expenses, provisions for needy dependents, and other urgent benefits for those who manned our ships during the war.

Mr. Walsh told me that there are no paid officers or paid legislative representatives. Sole income is through membership dues, which are $5. Albert Lyons is National Commander; LeRoy Booth is finance officer.

Attempts to "help" merchant seamen continue to mushroom. In Chicago "a group of public-spirited business men" have started the Merchant Marine League of the United States. Founder is Harry A. Ackerburg. In March, 1946 he wrote me on the stationery of Shillinglaw, Bolger & Company, investment brokers, as follows:

Quite frankly, we haven't got the organization functioning the way we hope to have it some of these days, but the enclosed will give you a line on some of the objectives. Rest assured we have no patience with communism, and having served as an officer in World War I, I am all out for 100% Americanism.

Ackerburg's program for the Merchant Marine seaman included a plea for benefits, the combating of inaccurate accounts of the role played by seamen, the fostering of a more cordial relationship between the U.S. Maritime Service and the U.S. Navy. Another plank was to "help develop the best possible employer-employee relationship, standing ready to impartially arbitrate misunderstandings." As Ackerburg's organization was just starting, it could be of no immediate help to seamen.

Seamen are not completely neglected. The Seafarers International and the Masters, Mates and Pilots are AFL unions. The National Maritime Union is a large CIO affiliate. The United Seamen's Service, Sailor's Snug Harbor, the Seamen's Church Institute and other institutes assist various categories of seamen. But these are unions and charitable societies. Merchant Marine veterans have no militant group of their own to champion just legislation and demand benefits.

They deserve adequate insurance and provisions for unemployment. Widows and dependents of seamen who were killed or incapacitated in war service deserve lifetime benefits. Injuries received while manning the life lines to our fighting men should be cared for on a parity with other veterans of World War II. The merchant seamen who worked the munitions and food ships deserve equality with those who fired the munitions. They deserve a GI Bill of Rights. It's elementary justice.

The cause of the merchant seaman awaits a national, well-financed and well-directed organization worthy to serve it.

CHAPTER NINE

The American Communist Party

> Our Party [under Earl Browder] was weakened, the fighting
> calibre was undermined. What we are doing now is to teach the
> Party to fight once more, to stand up on its feet and take an
> active part in these great struggles that are now developing all
> over the country. You veterans will be particularly valuable in
> this respect.
>
> *William Z. Foster,*
> in a speech before New York veterans, Dec. 2, 1945

IN ALMOST every issue of the *Daily Worker,* the American Communist Party flaunted with unbounded egomania the claim that 15,000 Party members fought in World War II, not one of whom, it is claimed, received a dishonorable discharge. Few other groups exploit the war records of their veterans, for political purposes, as loudly as the Communists.

"If there was one organization in America that went down the line to win this war," Communist Chairman William Z. Foster modestly declared at their New York State Veterans' Conference in December, 1945, "it was the Communist Party. We gave this war a support that no other organization in the country gave it, and we must see to it that the veterans understand this fact." This line is carried through in the May 26, 1946 issue of the *Sunday Worker.* "Captain Alexander Seur got himself a fistful of medals," says the *Worker,* "including the Distinguished Service Cross (twice). How come?" it asks. "Why did he fight so brilliantly? The answer can be summed up in one short word—COMMUNIST."

With convenient disregard for the Party's embarrassing record of anti-war agitation and sabotage of American preparedness—a policy suddenly dropped upon the invasion of Russia in 1941—the American Communists since V-J Day have gone all out to make hay among the veterans by screaming of their "patriotic wartime service." In April and May, 1946 they waged an intensive drive for 20,000 new members, emphasizing the recruiting of "2,500 returned veterans." By May 5, six hundred veterans had joined in New York alone. A directive of the Party's National Veterans' Committee on March 17 urged:

Veterans hardly out of uniform are alarmed by the big business drive to imperialist war. Let us recruit these vets into the Communist Party and strengthen the fight for peace. . . . These veterans can be won for the Communist Party. Just as when they were in the service they are ready to get into a "bull session" to bat the breeze about the problems they face today. Let us organize such sessions and let's tell them about the Communist Party.

Having banished with appropriate publicity their wartime chief, Earl Browder, on whom devolved the delicate task of keeping the comrades' minds on the capitalist war effort while the Comintern was dismantled for the duration, the Party is getting back to fighting trim. Browder later flew to secret conferences in Moscow, where press dispatches reported that he was not only received with due respect, but also rewarded with a five-year contract as representative of Soviet publishing firms in the United States. Over here, meanwhile, the Party's dynamic reconversion for peacetime has proceeded apace. Defense of Negro rights is one of the major wares stressed by the new leadership, but the Communists' darling remains the veteran.

The Party has no distinct veterans' division. The National Veterans' Committee acts as a recruiting agency and formulates policy. On March 12, 1946 I interviewed three of its leaders. Short, intense, grim-lipped John Gates, 32, fought with the Abraham Lincoln Brigade in Spain, enlisted in our Army after Pearl Harbor and served as sergeant overseas. Volatile Irving Goff, 34, also fought in Spain. In World War II he served on an OSS "cloak-and-dagger" team, reached lieutenant's rank and was decorated with the Legion of Merit. Saul Wellman, 32, with large brown eyes and cropped hair, was a major in the Spanish Republican forces. Wounded twice in World War II, he has a hundred percent disability rating and wears the Purple Heart with cluster. He was a paratrooper.

I met the three men as Carlson. It would have been impossible to see them any other way; Communist screening is too thorough. When the *Daily Worker* published application blanks for membership I filled one out, using a pseudonym, and sent it in. Here's what happened. Within a few weeks I heard from Miss Betty Gannett, National Organization Department, on the stationery of the American Communist Party, USA. Her letter read:

We have forwarded your name to our State Organization in your area, asking them to have someone visit you and give you the information personally. If you do not hear from them within a short period of time, please write or call:
  Wm. Norman
  35 E. 12th St. Room 500
  New York 3, N. Y. ALgonquin 4-5705

Within a week two Party workers—a young man and woman—called to see me. Of course I wasn't in and they were told so. They left word for me to get in touch with them and bring credentials along. That was the end of the episode.

Without forging identification papers I couldn't get away with posing as someone else. The American Communists, I can assure the reader, are under even closer scrutiny from multiple private and official sources than was the Bund. One government agency in New York alone has subscribed to six copies of the *Daily Worker*, which is catalogued and read with microscopic care. The Communist Party's schools, summer camps and "front" organizations are thoroughly infiltrated by government undercover agents, some of whom are recruited from anti-Communist political organizations. They keep important Communists under constant surveillance and use an amazing variety of devices to gather evidence. Communists couldn't operate secretly even if they wanted to. In the face of this professional investigation, what new evidence could I, as a lone investigator, unearth?

Gates, Goff and Wellman looked like average Americans, with certain exceptions: each of the trio was uncommonly serious, sharp as a razor at repartee, and thoroughly indoctrinated with Communist dogma, which they regarded as both scientific and infallible. They impressed me as being more efficient than the nationalist dopes of their age I had met. These boys knew their business. They had been trained for it and they had the guts to practice it regardless of the consequences.

I interviewed the three in the dingy *Daily Worker* building on East 13th Street, New York. A creaky elevator took me up six floors. I walked into a large reception room, its walls papered in a simulated wood pattern and hung with portraits of Marx, Lenin, Engels, Stalin, Lincoln and Washington. A receptionist ushered me into a tiny, cramped office overlooking New York's drab tenement and factory-loft skyline. The air was stuffy. A narrow window rationed a small amount of light and downtown New York air. What a contrast this little, roach-infested, semi-dark room was to the palatial Radio City offices of the National Association of Manufacturers, which I had visited the day before!

The trio received me with apparent curiosity. I had hardly sat down, facing Gates across the plain desk, when they charged me with "Red-baiting" in *Under Cover*.

"The Communist Party welcomes criticism, but we don't like Red-baiting," Gates said. I replied that my remarks constituted justifi-

Communist Party, U.S.A.

NATIONAL OFFICE

35 EAST 12th STREET • NEW YORK 3, N. Y •

Chairman
WILLIAM Z. FOSTER

Executive Board
BENJAMIN J. DAVIS, JR.
EUGENE DENNIS
ELIZABETH GURLEY FLYNN
WILLIAM Z. FOSTER
JOSH LAWRENCE
STEVE NELSON
IRVING POTASH
JACK STACHEL
ROBERT THOMPSON
LOUIS WEINSTOCK
JOHN WILLIAMSON

Treasurer
CHARLES KRUMBEIN

Dear Friend:

Thank you for sending in the form printed in the Daily Worker, asking information on how to join the Communist Party.

We have forwarded your name to our State Organization in your area, asking them to have someone visit you and give you the information personally. If you do not hear from them within a short period of time, please write or call: Wm. Norman
35 E. 12th St. Room 500
New York 3, N.Y. ALgonquin 4-5705

Enclosed is a copy of our Constitution

Sincerely yours,

B. Gannett
National Organization Dept.

The American Communists recruit for members through direct, personal methods.

able criticism of the Communist Party and explained that it was my serious purpose to interpret truth as I saw it.

"What is the purpose of your National Veterans' Committee?" I asked Gates.

"To educate the veterans in socialism. We Communists believe that monopoly capital is trying to establish a military *coup d'état*. When that time comes, we want the masses—and veterans in particular—to be ready for the final struggle between socialism and fascism."

"Don't you put any faith in reform?" I asked.

"History has proved that reform doesn't work," Goff said. "The fascists will shoot the trade unionists—if the unionists succeed in getting their rights."

"The logic of monopoly capital leads to events as they took place in Germany," Gates interpolated. "The lesson we've learned from World War II is that fascism can be defeated, wherever it comes up."

"Even in this country?" I asked.

"Yes. Fascism is the same everywhere. It can be defeated if the people are trained to fight it."

"By bloody means?"

"The course of monopoly capital is inevitably leading us to revolution," Gates answered grimly.

I asked him, as the chief spokesman of the three, why the Communist Party didn't work with middle-of-the-road democrats who believed in a workable capitalist order provided necessary social, political and economic reforms were carried out.

"We don't believe in middle-ground capitalism because it won't work," Gates said. "Socialism is the only answer. But we're willing to work with the middle-of-the-roaders. We Communists are in every organization. We're people. We're Americans. We have the right to join and take part in the work of all groups. When we get in, we try to influence those around us with the work of the Communist Party."

Goff handed me a copy of the Party constitution. On page three was: "The Communist Party upholds the achievements of American democracy and defends the United States Constitution and its Bill of Rights against reactionary enemies who would destroy democracy and popular liberties."

"Defends the United States Constitution"—how often I had found almost the same words in the programs of nationalist groups of the far right! The Communist revolutionary intent, however, appeared in the sentence in the Party constitution stating that the "final abolition of exploitation and oppression . . . will be achieved only by the socialist reorganization of society—by the common ownership and operation of the national economy under a government of the people led by the working class."

"Which veterans' group are you urging men to join?" I asked.

"We don't advocate any union or veterans' group," Gates answered.

"Then why has the *Daily Worker* been more partial to the American Legion than any other veterans' organization?" I asked.

Gates evaded the question.

"Our party stand toward the national policy of the Legion is well known," he said. "Fascist groups have found a happy hunting ground in the Legion."

In making this statement Gates may have been expressing a higher-level Communist viewpoint. But to the rank and file, *Daily Worker* directive writers were putting it differently. They were busily urging Communist veterans to join the Legion and, once inside, to make their influence felt in its councils. And in his address to the Communist veterans of New York State, Foster instructed them: "There must be no stand-off attitude toward these [conservative and reactionary veterans'] organizations, as there was after the last war."

In a *Daily Worker* column published in June, 1946, Max Gordon explains the principle of transitory cooperation and boring from within:

It is necessary for the Communist Party and the working class to have an independent policy and program, and to fight for that program. But it is also necessary for the Party and the working class to form alliances, even though they may be temporary and conditional, as it advances toward its final Socialist goal. Otherwise it will be crushed by the superior power of a united bourgeoisie.

To support his thesis, Gordon quotes a well-known passage from Lenin's *Left Wing Communism:*

To carry on a war with the international bourgeoisie, which is a hundred times more difficult, prolonged and complicated than the most stubborn of ordinary wars between states, and to refuse beforehand to maneuver, to utilize the conflict of interests (even though temporary) among one's enemies; to refuse to temporize and compromise with possible (even though transient, unstable, vacillating and conditional) allies—is not this ridiculous in the extreme?

Meanwhile, the Communists are aping the nationalists in one piece of strategy: they are taking on a consciously native coloration. The *Daily Worker* on March 30, 1946 made this abundantly clear:

Communist parties are rooted in the soil of their native lands. They arise and grow wherever there are capitalist employers using living labor as the source of unearned profit. They grow wherever the majority of the people who do the country's work do not own the machines with which they work, and where their product is appropriated by the minority owners.

A *Daily Worker* editorial in May, 1946 sounded a similar note as it hailed the impressive results of the membership drive:

It is good for the whole country that more than 7,000 Americans have joined the Communist Party in the past few weeks. That is 7,000 new recruits to the movement for a better America. Be a true American by becoming a Communist. . . .

Communists loudly deny that they are dominated by a "foreign interest," claiming that they are organized to "defend the welfare of the working class" and nothing else. I presume a survey would indicate that most Party members are American-born. The bearded "bolshevik" of yesterday has disappeared; the accented, foreign-born revolutionists are being replaced by youthful Americans who are even more determined and militant than yesterday's pioneer generation. Despite their protestation of no "foreign ties," Arthur M. Schlesinger, Jr., eminent historian and author of *The Age of Jackson*, stated in his article on the Communist Party in *Life* on July 29, 1946: "The party, for a long time billed as the American section of the Communist International, has always received directives and in the past some funds from the U.S.S.R. via courier. Probably Moscow's most effective control has been through Comintern representatives—the famous 'CIreps.'"

Veterans becoming members of the Communist Party are offered special Marxist training in a series of courses given at the Party's Jefferson School in New York. Additional lecture meetings are held to enable "Communist vets to catch up and get oriented." In the *Daily Worker*, Veterans Editor Joseph Clark conducts a regular column. He writes of "rent-free homes" in the USSR and paints a rosy picture of "how a Socialist land takes care of its vets." To supplement the *Daily Worker*, the Party pours forth voluminous, inexpensive, well-written propaganda literature on subjects ranging from *Our Country Needs a Strong Communist Party* to *The Path of a Renegade*.

The latter booklet is calculated to aid and indirectly explain Party reconversion from wartime cooperativeness in support of the Allied military machine to new militancy in the class struggle. Having done his bit, Comrade Browder, former Chairman, is now cast in the role of renegade for the benefit of the rank and file. There is an elaborate program of meetings, lectures and discussions for the indoctrination of all Party members. In *Our Country Needs a Strong Communist Party*, Foster exhorted his comrades:

It would, of course, be stupid to think that in the United States, the richest and most powerful imperialist country and one least damaged by the war, the conditions are propitious for building the Communist Party as they are, say, in France, Italy, China, or Brazil. Nevertheless the conditions for the Party here are very favorable, provided only that we know how to utilize them. . . . We need a new militancy in our Party, a rejuvenated and burning enthusiasm, as befits our great cause and which would enormously increase our Party's efficiency.

At the same time that it has unrolled the crimson carpet for the returning veteran, the Communist Party is pushing another all-out drive for new members in the South. Alabama was the first state to fill its assigned quota. On this happy occasion the *Daily Worker* boasted optimistically: "The Bilbo-Rankin reactionaries will have the battle of their careers, as the progressive South bids to oust reactionary control of Congress and to smash the semi-feudal system." One significant result of the invasion may be the appearance of an organized and fanatical opposition to the Klan. In the event of a head-on clash, the cowardly nightshirters will find themselves up against a tougher proposition than their past exploits have accustomed them to. They may well lose to the harder-headed Communists if the latter use their best *white* members. The use of Negroes in anti-Klan work might easily result in the slaughter of innocent Negroes.

The *Daily Worker* quotes a Negro veteran who had come home to Alabama:

I spent 30 months overseas. I didn't expect to find this when I came home—hate, fear and the terror imposed upon my people. The South will always stay this way if we let it. Nothing for the Negro vets, no hospitals, no loans, no jobs, no houses. You'd think we didn't fight a war for freedom.

Under such conditions, the drowning man will clutch at any life line. The Communists' promise of a heaven on earth is an attractive mirage to the poor Southern white or Negro sharecropper veteran with his brood of ill-fed, ill-clothed, ill-housed children. If we neglect our veterans, it's clear why many of them turn to a revolutionary party which promises a decent home and jobs.

Communist success in recruiting in the South is one more proof that genuine American democracy, with all its promises of security and freedom, is at a low ebb there. The cure is not a witch-hunt or rash of anti-Communist propaganda. Only the extension of democracy in the South will stall the Communist invasion.

Meanwhile, in New York's Harlem section Party membership doubled during the membership drive, according to the *Daily Worker*. "Fifty-five percent of the recruits are Negro veterans. Many came straight from the armed services looking straight for the CP." Discrimination against the Negro was the major propaganda weapon exploited by the Communists. Equally effective were incidents of lynch law and other cruelties perpetrated against such Negroes as Isaac Woodward, Jr. A 27-year-old veteran of the New Guinea and Philippine campaigns, Woodward actually had his eyes gouged out by a pair of South Carolina policemen, one of whom used the end of his billy to render Woodward permanently blind. The tragic incident followed an altercation with a bus driver. Walter White, Secretary of the National Association for the Advancement of Colored People, called it "sheer brutality and fascist terror" and a "terrible story without parallel in all my experience."

Isaac Woodward is now living in the Bronx. The only advice the Veterans Administration could give him was to recommend that he join a blind school. The ravages of "white supremacy" are driving some frustrated and persecuted Negroes into the arms of a revolutionary party which promises relief.

American Communists make claims as lavishly as they make promises. Readers of the *Daily Worker* soon get the impression that the Communists are the backbone of the labor movement in America. The reason for this obvious distortion is apparent. All revolutionary organizations boast of their prowess, their influence, their strength. It boosts morale. William Z. Foster himself explained this in *Our Country Needs a Strong Communist Party:*

One of the most important things necessary in the building of the Communist Party is to raise our Party's morale. We must infuse our membership with a glowing pride in being part of the world-wide Communist movement, with its glorious record of struggle and accomplishment. We must also make our members prouder of the many achievements and splendid record of our own Party.

One-Fifth of New CP Members Are Veterans

By MAX GORDON

More than a fifth of the 3,000 members who joined the New York state during the current

VETS' **O**ICE

Communists Fight for Vets Needs— Is That Subversive?

Need Communists

Communist parties are rooted in the soil of their native lands. They arise and grow wherever there are capitalist employers using living labor as the source of unearned profit. They grow wherever the majority of the people who do the country's work do not own the machines with which they work, and where their product is appropriated by the minority owners.

The 'Foreign Interest' Lie

The *Times*, as do all other papers in our country controlled by big capital and devoted to its interests, systematically propagates this falsehood. When the American Communists, for example, fought against the Munich pact, it was the Times which could find no other retort to the logic of our position than to charge us with acting for a foreign interest... Communists defend the welfare of the working class of which they are a part, the exploiters of labor fall back on the same stale accusation that it is a "foreign interest"

Communists Are Needed

It is good for the whole country that more than 7,000 Americans have joined the Communist Party in the past few weeks. That is 7,000 new recruits to the movement for a better America.

Thousands more are needed to join the fight against the profiteers, against the war-makers and for a future America where the people not Wall Street will own the industries.

How about you? Be a true American by becoming a Communist.

"Subversive?"

JUST thought the War Department would like to know. Of the 15,000 Communists who served in the armed forces not one received a dishonorable discharge.

Subversive? Directed from abroad? Not us, protest the American Communists.

The same strategy of boastfulness is being applied to their alleged strength in the labor movement. America had its labor movement for nearly four decades before Communism was achieved in Russia. The AFL, for example, was founded in 1881. While it is true that the Communists control certain unions, the idea that "labor is Communist" is a fiction. This vain Communist boast of control over labor provides good ammunition for the demagogues and anti-union employers, who themselves are generally inclined to overstate the matter. It is a damaging thing for the labor movement.

Another incorrect notion entertained—or at least stressed in propaganda—by the Communist Party is that capitalism is already on the verge of collapse. Michael Gold, for example, writing on June 27, 1946, would have his readers believe that "Capitalism is on its last mile, a blind hog ready to run over the cliff chasing its illusion of super-profits, of another inflation and another world war. Capitalism could fall tomorrow, if the people were united." Gold wrote his piece to refute the observation of Samuel Grafton, liberal columnist, who had observed on his return from a nation-wide trip that the country was apathetic to politics. That started Mr. Gold on his prophecy. I select Mr. Grafton for his veracity and not the visionary Mr. Gold.

What is the Communist Party strength today? According to a letter I received from Betty Gannett in July, the Party musters 75,000 members and has about 2,000 clubs throughout the country, each ranging from five to seventy-five members. Some of them have more. This includes some 15,000 new members (the Party failed to reach the quota of 20,000). "It is perhaps important to emphasize," Miss Gannett wrote, "that we laid little stress in this campaign on numbers, but placed the major emphasis on quality and selective recruiting." She estimated that, of the total recruited, "from 15 to 20 percent were veterans." Communists collected $150,000 to carry on the publication of the *Daily* and *Sunday Worker*.

In July the National Board of the American Communist Party dispelled all doubts as to its future course. Going back to its pre-Pearl Harbor revolutionary ardor, the Party pledged to wage a "counter-offensive" against "Wall Street trusts" and defeat their "criminal goal." This is old-fashioned fighting talk, denuded of all Browderite camouflage. The Party required a one-year period of reconversion to get back into its old fighting trim. Eugene Dennis was elected General Secretary, to replace Browder's deserted post. Its immediate objectives include thumping for the election of "progressive" Congressmen, launching a circulation drive for the *Daily Worker,* and fighting against inflation and for severing relations with Franco.

That Communists may again "invade the streets" was presaged in an article by Elizabeth Gurley Flynn in the July 20 issue of the *Daily Worker,* wherein she urged: "It is high time for revival of this art of the street-corner agitator which was so effective in reaching the people of other years." Herself an outdoor speaker of note, according to the Comrades, Miss Flynn said: "It is on the streets that we reach the people." Her views were buttressed by William Weinstone, New York State Educational Director, who offered helpful hints to prospective street corner spokesmen.

The Party will continue its policy of "boring" within democratic groups, and at the strategic moment using disruptive methods to break up the democratic solidarity of an organization if the Communist members fail in their efforts to become dominant within it. No organization today is safe from Communist infiltration. Democratic groups must be on guard more than ever before.

A determined effort to impose its influence upon Congressional, state and municipal candidates for office constitutes another major objective of the National Board of the Communist Party from now to the 1948 elections. The ballot is another—and perhaps the most democratic—of the many methods used by the Communists to make their influence felt.

Considerable emphasis is also being placed on the role of "art as a propaganda weapon." William Z. Foster gave the green light to the fusion of "art" and Communist propaganda in an article in *The New Masses* (April 23, 1946): "The special task of the Communists in the development of the new "democratic" [quotation marks are mine—JRC] trends in our national culture is to enrich them with Marxist understanding and to carry them to the people." While Mr. Foster may consider politics and art compatible, I'm inclined to view the injection of cold-blooded political propaganda into art as the prostitution of art.

Vulnerable, of course, are the major veterans' groups. At a conference of the Communist Veterans of Michigan in June, 1946 "resolutions" were passed as directives to party workers "to find ways and means of carrying out the indicated program, particularly with regard to your work in established veterans' organizations and labor unions." The American Legion, Veterans of Foreign Wars, Disabled American Veterans and Jewish War Veterans, among the older, established groups, were aimed at as particular targets for infiltration. In addition, Party Clubs were instructed "to designate at least one person to be responsible for veterans' work" and "to be responsible for planned recruiting of veterans into the Party."

On July 1 the *Daily Worker* carried a news dispatch from Detroit stating that Hugo Beiswenger, an aerial gunner and winner of the Distinguished Flying Cross, was chosen by 150 delegates of the Michigan Communist Party to run against Senator Arthur Vandenberg. Abner W. Berry, identified as "a nationally known Negro Communist," was nominated to run for Michigan Secretary of State.

I saw some of the Communist veterans—several thousand grim, two-fisted soldiers—walk in the 1946 May Day Parade. They were bedecked with ribbons and medals, and paraded in open defiance of regulations making it unlawful to wear the uniform for political demonstrations.

"Weren't you afraid of being arrested by the MPs?" I asked a group of veterans, each husky and towering.

"What? Us afraid of the MPs? Take a look at us again, buddy. There would be a war right in these streets if an MP tried to lay his hands on us. Us guys are sticking together."

This defiance seemed symbolic to me. The American Communists today are a cocky and strutting crew. Hasn't Comrade Foster told them they won the war almost singlehanded? Aren't they supposed to dominate the labor movement? The Communists remind me of the cocksure prizefighter who was floored. Overconfidence is a bad trait for any political minority.

Michael Gold, leading *Daily Worker* columnist, once charged me with Red-baiting because I allegedly called the Communists "subversive." Although I had never used that specific term before, I am doing so now. If a political party dedicated to the overthrow of the established order is not subversive, what *is* the meaning of the word?

A good way to lose friends and make enemies in both left and right camps is to write candidly on Communism. Nationalists will renew their attacks and brand me a Communist for not demanding the outlawing of the Party or "fighting Communism" by Hitleresque, Red-baiting methods. I cannot hope to satisfy hysterical persons who regarded the New Deal first as "Stalin's step-child" and later as "National Socialist." No doubt the Communists will renew their charges of "Red-baiting" and call me a fascist tool. In reply, I can only submit that my opinions are entirely my own, and based on my own observations and investigations. I have fought fascism and bigotry continuously since 1938, without taking time out between August, 1939 and June, 1941 to determine whether Hitler was really a bad man.

At the same time, let me state for the record that I'm not in any way affiliated with the Socialist Party, the Social-Democratic Party, or the so-called "Trotskyites." Neither am I a member of the Democratic or Republican Party. On the other hand, I do consider myself a voting, fighting, thinking, forward-looking, middle-road American. I consider that the American capitalist way, having worked eminently well in past decades, has been abused by the selfishness and greed of certain Americans and now needs economic, social and political refurbishing to make it last as a capitalistic institution. Unless this is done I believe that our ultimate end will be war followed by utter chaos.

It was because of Party intolerance of criticism that I wrote Michael Gold, leading columnist for the *Daily Worker,* for information. Gold replied in his column of June 15, 1946:

Mr. Carlson asks: "I would like to get your forthright definition of a 'Red-baiter'. . . . I want to know, if one has the freedom to criticize the Republican and Democratic parties, the Protestant and Catholic churches, our President and other public officials, whether one also has the right of 'fair criticism and comment' on the tactics of the American Communist Party."

The answer is a loud Yes—of course. I defy him to produce a single statement by a Communist in which anyone is denied the right to debate against Communism. Leading Communists have participated in many such debates. . . . Red-baiting is the systematic spreading of slander, hatred and big and little lies about Communism and Communists. Red-baiting is a fascist tactic, it can only help the fascists.

Gold mentioned Dies and Rankin as Red-baiters. They are obvious tools of native fascism. I had asked Gold for a more precise definition, but Mr. Gold merely said: "I will not attempt some academic definition of Red-baiting, then get into a long-winded, sterile argumentation." It's not a satisfactory answer because Mr. Gold ignored my distinctions between the USSR and American Communists.

I have never been to Russia and the only Russian word I know is "tovarich." But I believe I can more easily understand, and therefore respect, the Russian people and Communism in the USSR than its loud imitators here. My attitude toward the splendid role played by the Soviet Union in the defeat of Hitler is expressed with admirable clarity in War Department Pamphlet No. 20-3:

It is not necessary or desirable to defend communism in order to enlist the sympathetic interest of the American soldier in the defense of the USSR. We hold for ourselves the right to determine our own form of government and cannot consistently maintain that any other people has a lesser right. . . .

Though we do not agree with their political ideas (and they do not believe in ours) we believe utterly in the defense of the principle for which they are fighting. Likewise, it is in the defense of this self-same principle that we stand guard against the infiltrating of Communist ideas into the realm of democracy.

It is my belief, as I have previously stated in *Under Cover* and am merely explaining in my second book, that Communist propaganda is as undesirable as Nazi propaganda. I am opposed to the idea of a Communist America, just as I am opposed to the idea of the union of church and state, as in Spain; of army and state, as in Hitler's Germany; or of army, church and state as in Mussolini's Italy. Under any of those systems the *dominant* factions can possibly be happy *for a time,* but even that only at the sacrifice of the liberty of their fellow countrymen. I believe in the ideal of the American democratic capitalist order which, all factors considered, including its failings, I still regard as the method which best provides the basic needs of most of its people. I have been conditioned in this belief by my experiences as an American. It was by free and capitalist America that I was welcomed on being brought here as a child from war-ravaged southeastern Europe in 1921. My parents and I have made a completely happy adjustment as American citizens. It is in the friendly atmosphere of our democracy that I have found infinitely the greatest measure of happiness and self-expression.

But this democratic order of ours, to the ideals of which I personally owe everything, can continue to flourish only if we make democracy a living reality—not a sham—to millions of underprivileged Americans. A government, like an individual concern, may go sterile if it is not constantly improved. Neither can it thrive long if it remains rigid and insulated against influences of growth, and smugly recites its accomplishments of the past without an eye to adapting itself to a constantly changing world. Sensing the need, even a conservative thinker like Attorney General Tom C. Clark stated in May, 1946:

We shall and must have in America a distinct change in some of our ideas. . . . Inasmuch as we have come of age in world affairs, we must put away childish things. We have some habits which are too expensive and too juvenile for vast, rich and powerful America.

To dwell on the viciousness of the Nazi-Fascist philosophy would be superfluous. As to Communism, the idea of a one-party, one-voice, one-labor-union commissariat of party members is not my conception of democracy. It's the Russian idea. As President Roosevelt said on February 10, 1940: "The Soviet Union, as everybody who has the courage to face the facts knows, is run by a dictatorship as absolute as any other dictatorship in the world."

Perhaps the dictatorship of the proletariat—a government by and for the benefit of the Communist-believing masses *only*, under conditions where no political liberty exists—suits a majority of the Russian people. But we Americans thrive on political liberty and cannot get along without it. That is the basic distinction between our democracy and the Russian brand. For anyone to accept as superior to our way a brand of popular dictatorship—unseen and untested and largely on the say-so of ideological fanatics, most of whom have never been there—is not only foolhardy but dangerous to the integrity of our own institutions.

It would be tragic indeed for the Russian concept of limited "democracy" ever to triumph in the United States under the hot-headed, short-sighted, bellicose leadership of the American Communist Party. We must be on our guard lest as we listen to the Communists' highly vocal promises of social advances, we forget what they keep hidden in the background—that the price to be paid is a one-party, one-voice control if and when they achieve full power. Our agents, if we had any such, would not be allowed the same courtesy of revolutionizing Russia. As long as the American Communists remain a legal party, however, name-calling or emotional arguments will not be adequate to check their activity.

To be objective in my brief analysis, I regard the Russians today as less subject than we to racial prejudice, even though our Constitution guarantees equal rights to all. Perhaps we can learn something from the Russians in that one respect, just as some of us finally learned from Hitler that hate does not pay. Only an ignoramus or a die-hard nationalist will deny that we can learn something useful from a people who remained so heroically united in the face of such an unprecedented assault.

On the other hand, Russians should learn that the historic concept of democracy is one whose benefits are intended for all of the nation's citizens, and which makes no provisions for liquidating those in disagreement. Democracy is real only when there is freedom of speech, press, and assembly; when labor unions are controlled democratically, not under autocratic state rule; when freedom to own and develop private property is extended to all citizens; when the cultural arts are given complete freedom for development and are not subservient to state interest. I agree with foreign correspondent Alexander H. Uhl:

The Russians, of course, can say to American Liberals: "If you are not with us all along the line, then you are against us." They will be damn fools if they do!

Least effective and most futile of all ways of checking the spread of Communism in America is the fight against it on a religious basis. Communism is an *economic* philosophy. It appeals to the bread-and-butter instincts of a people—and these are more primary urges than religion. A hungry man wants bread first; God and church are luxuries. To him a loaf is worth more than a place in Heaven. In their zeal to preserve our Christian institutions most anti-Communist

American church leaders, both Protestant and Catholic, depend far too much upon appeals to emotion and tradition; it would be more effective to give greater attention to the improvement of conditions which permit Communism to flourish.

Another unsound and ineffective approach to the Communist problem is to "smear" progressive trends and legislation with the Communist paint brush. Red-baiting was the Hitler way of "fighting Communism," and if it's kept up in this country—continuing to obtain the support of certain industrial and clerical interests—it will inevitably lead to similar consequences here. When done systematically, as it is today, Red-baiting is a propaganda device used to camouflage fascist ends and purposes. This method not only befogs the fight against Communism, but in the long run plays directly into Communist hands.

The threat which American Communists present to our democracy is obscured from view when nationalists like Merwin K. Hart denounce the Child Labor Act as an "inspiration from Russia . . . a Russian law for American youth"; when the National Association of Manufacturers fights the Wages and Hours Law as a "Communist" measure; when Hearst papers assail the Social Security Act as Moscow-inspired. Similarly, price control and Federal subsidies for veteran housing were also damned as "Communist" because the Communists supported the measures. The nationalists were stumped at President Truman's recommendation of a law to draft into the Army those who refused to abide by a Government settlement of a strike. The *Wall Street Journal* and Senator Robert A. Taft opposed such a measure, together with the *Daily Worker*.

When rabble-rousing Red-baiters who also attack Jews, Catholics and other minorities, attack Communism they dignify it. I doubt if decent Americans will be influenced by Jew-baiters and Catholic-baiters. When nationalists, religious leaders, and so-called committees to investigate un-Americanism lump progressive and liberal Americans with Communist Party members they automatically plead for the cause of Communism through its identification with respectable members of the community. That is just what the Communists want. They take refuge behind the sweeping charges and pose as martyrs.

The hyper-hysterical treatment publicizes the Communists' cause. It makes them feel important, enables them to show off their strength in noise, bombast and paeans of self-praise. Worst of all, the staccato screeching renders ineffective the practical antidotes to American Communism. Instead of hacking at the roots of Communism we are flinging ourselves against its branches. Many wealthy Americans have become the victims of racketeers "fighting Communism." This is especially true of our businessmen, many of whom have been "taken" for millions of dollars. Billions of words and great volumes of hot air have been expended against the "Communist menace, the hydra-headed monster, the Red, atheistic enemy," etc., etc. All of which has proven fruitless. This in itself should be conclusive proof to a reasonable mind that the popular method of "fighting Communism" via Red-baiting and indiscriminate labeling is increasingly proving itself a gross failure.

When will our moneyed classes and some religious leaders learn that you can't stop Communism by hissing at it and calling it bad names? When will they cease their flailing at windmills? When will they stop pouring their money into the hands of racketeers allegedly "fighting Communism"?

To be fought effectively, Communism must be fought by what I call the "Deflation Method"—that of deflating Communist arguments and proving that *our* brand of democracy can perform the job of making democracy work. Communism must be fought head on, on an economic basis. Its challenge must be met in terms of employment, security, homes, happiness! Feed a man well. Give him a job and the means to raise a family properly and build a decent home. Give him self-respect and hope for his own and his family's future, and you have produced an American who will frown on Communism and banish it from his system. We can permanently get rid of Communism—and refrain from walking into it by the Hitler route—by accomplishing the following:

1. To all Americans, regardless of race or creed, give the security of a permanent job at a fair, living wage, provisions for vacations, bonuses for faithful service, provisions for dependents, for death or accident while at work—full welfare benefits to all who produce our economic wealth.

2. Eliminate slums, deathtraps and ratholes which pass for "homes" for our underprivileged. Increase the number of schools and vocational and recreational facilities throughout the country. Elevate an American to

the dignity of an American—or let's stop being hypocritical about the "blessings" of democracy!

3. Establish an interchange of ideas and greater intercourse between so-called Anglo-Saxons and the newer European immigrants, and between workers and employers, to demonstrate their common basis as Americans. Help level sharp anti-social distinctions and reduce prejudice and discrimination by the democratic process of mutual respect and understanding of mutual problems.

4. End continued hostility of die-hard employers against labor unions; cultivate a greater consciousness on their part of the social obligations of business to the community. Above all, let us establish that America was not founded for the benefit of the few, or to be controlled by private government, but as an institution to house *all* of us.

5. Determine a fair, and not an exorbitant profit, on all business enterprise. Turn excess profits into a national welfare fund devoted to clearance of slums, extension of education, sanitation and hospitalization and, in general, to be used for the benefit of the ill-clothed, ill-fed, ill-housed.

6. Stop, for the present, the cry of "social-equality" propaganda. The battle cry is like throwing sand in the machinery of inter-racial relations. The urgent need and salvation of the Southern Negro lie primarily in the ending of discriminatory measures against millions of Negroes in the South, and against the extension of democracy in the South in terms of job, educational, recreational and political opportunities. So-called "social equality," an empty phrase which means little and does much to retard the entire Negro program in the South, should come last on the agenda. First things come first. For the present, it's more important for the Southern Negro and underprivileged white Americans to eat three well-balanced meals a day than to eat in a "white" restaurant.

7. Abolish the poll tax and extend the full voting franchise to Southern Negroes to help eliminate such political goons as Rankin and Bilbo. To anxious white Southerners who fear another "carpet-bagging" invasion, let me suggest that once the Negro's economic plight is improved and he is given full educational and other advantages, his status as a community asset will increase far more than his present deplorable plight permits it to. The South *can* lift itself up by its own bootstraps, and the Negro can help. The Negro is a friend of the white man.

8. Decentralize financial power from the hands of the few to permit the extension of genuinely free enterprise to more "small" businessmen. The threat of private government by concentrated "big business" screaming

"free enterprise" is no less inimical to democracy than the "Communist threat."

9. Promote a national fighting faith in democracy. All too few among the moneyed classes have any conception of real democracy. If among many in that group the spark cannot be reignited, it *can* be revived in the humble masses of the people. If many of these are abused and denied the privileges of democracy, can they be expected to fight for something which they have not tasted?

10. Establish under private auspices a national educational youth movement to further the cause of democracy and counter Communist youth movements. Big business is sponsoring "Junior Achievement, Inc." It merely seeks recruits for private government and to perpetuate the idea of corporation management. There is little democracy in that. In the meanwhile, American youth is without organized democratic guidance.

While Communists may advance some of these measures, they are also recommended by social and religious agencies, particularly in the famous encyclical of Pope Pius XI called *Quadragesimo Anno*. American Communists advance some of them because they seek for themselves the credit for their accomplishment. We—America's democratic people—should promote these democratic measures. If we can make democracy work at home we can deflate Communist arguments and force the American Communist Party into bankruptcy. This is the gist of the deflation method of fighting Communism.

I consider our democracy, with its maturing sense of responsibility, national and international, a workable theory of government, in contrast to the Communist idea that it's outworn and must be replaced by the "only scientific, democratic, workable system in the world." The Communists use the either/or line of argument: either accept Communism or its alternative, chaos. It is unconvincing to those of us who have been reasonably happy under our own system and refuse to accept anything unless we personally investigate it first. Communists, however, have succeeded in selling an alarmingly large number of Americans on the either/or theory that America must either accept Communism or perish.

As I have already stated elsewhere, I personally hold to the middle road. Following it has been a major factor in making the nation incomparable in its actual and potential might. But consistent with this fighting faith is the realization that no machine is permanent. Worn-out parts have to be replaced. Joints have to be oiled. We can't run the machine and say that, just because it has worked so far, it will continue to work indefinitely without replacements or improvements. No engineer will disagree with me on that. Is it illogical to suggest certain needed basic reforms for our capitalist system in order to preserve it and expand its growth?

A year before he died Wendell Willkie said: "The best answer to Communism is a living, vibrant, fearless democracy—economic, social and political. All we need to do is to stand up and perform according to our professed ideals."

Wendell Willkie was one of America's first great businessmen to foresee the urgent need. He happened to be a Republican. Certain die-hard business and newspaper men crucified Willkie on a cross of ignorance and greed. Indications are that Eric Johnston is another such great Republican. His words are prophetic and, unfortunately, far beyond the grasp of elements who live in the yesterday of politics, economics and social science. On May 2, 1946, at the 34th annual convention of the U.S. Chamber of Commerce, Eric Johnston spoke as its retiring President. He pleaded for an "enlightened"

onstitution

of the

ommunist

Party

OF THE UNITED STATES
OF AMERICA

PREAMBLE

The Communist Party upholds the achievements of American democracy and defends the United States Constitution and its Bill of Rights against its reactionary enemies who would destroy democracy and popular liberties.

The Communist Party recognizes that the final abolition of exploitation and oppression, of economic crises and unemployment, of reaction and war, will be achieved only by the socialist reorganization of society—by the common ownership and operation of the national economy under a government of the people led by the working class.

The American Communists' Constitution comes out 100 percent for the U. S. Constitution. The joker is contained in the lower paragraph—where the right for "the socialist reorganization of society" is reserved.

capitalism. He warned against "petrified prejudices against organized labor, government activity and community planning":

We must never forget that we live in a democracy and the majority rules. The majority must feel that they share in the profits of the profit system. . . . There is nothing eternal, nothing sacrosanct about it [capitalism]. Unless it justifies itself by works instead of words, it must go with the wind of change. . . .

Under progressive capitalism, the individual is a free agent, but not a freebooter. He has the right to choose, the right to make his own decisions, but he does not have the right to ride roughshod over the rights of others. . . . The new view, which I earnestly recommend, holds that capitalism is a human institution, vibrant and evolutionary, capable of adjusting itself to the new conditions.

We in business must liberalize or face the threat of economic liquidation. The law of life applies: Adapt or die. . . . Up to now, we've put all the emphasis on the known and measurable past and present achievements. From now on, let's put the accent on the immeasurable possibilities of the future under a new brand of capitalism.

Unless this is done, John Gates' grim predictions may become reality. Should that happen, I should not blame the John Gateses alone. Communism prescribes a borrowed "remedy"—revolution and the enthronement of a dictatorship of the proletariat. It crystallizes the undeniable truth that "something is wrong with our economy." If American democracy does not meet the challenge, America will turn fascist within our lifetime.

Unless America meets the challenge of democracy through a program of regenerating capitalism, "they," says Eric Johnston—meaning the majority—"may decide some day that they want another system." If and when that conflict comes, it will not be confined to America alone, for we are living in one world. That human explosion will instantly spread around the globe and will be fought with weapons deadlier than the atom bomb. There may be no more Communism after it's all over, or capitalism, or a United States. Utter chaos will follow the folly of utter madness. We can "settle" our arguments that way—gangster fashion, "winner" lose all—or make democracy work at home. There is no third alternative.

Fascism and Communism are like twin vultures hoping to feed on the corpse of our democracy. Communist and nationalist advances are symptoms of an ailing society. A healthy economic organism may carry these political bacteria in its blood stream, but they can attack successfully only when the organism is weak. Their success is an exact measure of the state of America's health. Name calling may afford temporary relief for some. The cool, far-sighted American will adopt measures to strengthen America in order to resist the twin plagues. Only a healthy nation can survive them.

CHAPTER TEN

Fingers in the Veteran Pie: Left Wing

We came equals into this world, and equals we shall go out of it. All men are by nature born equally free and independent. To protect the weaker from the injuries and insults of the stronger were societies first formed. . . . Let us never lose sight of this fundamental maxim—that all power was originally lodged in, and consequently is derived from, the people.

George Mason,
Delegate to the Constitutional Convention, 1775

IN THIS CHAPTER my purpose is to report, as fairly and objectively as my ability permits, on major labor and other left-wing elements and how they are seeking to recruit veterans to their ranks. The next chapter will deal with corresponding efforts by moderates and extremists on the right wing, including anti-union elements. Both wings—those to the right and the left of democratic center—are legitimate; the moderates in each take part smoothly in the democratic process, the extremists of each are a threat to the American system. Both want the veterans on their respective sides. Whoever captures the mind of the veteran may rule the destinies of our country.

In civilian life nearly one third of the members of our Armed Forces in World War II held union cards, according to best available estimates. Brig. Gen. Frank T. Hines calculated that, of the total of more than thirteen million men and women in service, about three million belonged to unions affiliated with the American Federation of Labor or the Congress of Industrial Organizations. Memberships in other unions added to the impressive total. Eighty-five percent of America's war matériel was union made. In the nation as a whole, a growing total of some fifteen million Americans belong to unions. These formidable facts cannot be ignored. Those who think they can "abolish unions" and "rid" America of organized

234

labor by branding it "Communist" have to contend with more than one ninth of America's increasingly vocal masses.

On the other hand, military service tended to create a lessening of sympathy for labor on the part of the serviceman. Inevitably he compared his own lot with that of the man who stayed at home with his family, earning more money than in peacetime, while the fighting man faced death, boredom, separation from loved ones and loss of personal liberty, for small pay.

Naturally, too, the few serious strikes which did occur in wartime shocked the GI to his boots. When boss John L. Lewis led his United Mine Workers out on strike in the crucial spring of 1943, crippling the nation's coal and steel production, he performed a disservice to his country that is remembered as a blot on the labor cause by countless veterans who have forgotten, or have never heard, that the national union leadership disapproved of the coal strike and that on the whole the no-strike pledge in wartime was well kept.

There were other, smaller things. The soldier bound overseas in a transport or Liberty ship, living in a hold tiered with bunks four high and obliged to spend hours each day in the mess line, compared his Army fare with the better meals served to the Merchant Marine crew. It got under his skin and, being human, he may remember it longer than the United States Bureau of Labor's more important statistics showing that, between December, 1941 and June, 1944, only one tenth of one percent of total working time was lost because of strikes.

Probably few veterans remember, either, that Father Coughlin endorsed John L. Lewis in *Social Justice* for November 24, 1941. During the 1944 elections Lewis delivered speeches which in spots somehow suggested the views of the National Association of Manufacturers. Finally, on May 21, 1946, NAM President Robert R. Wason praised Lewis above any other labor leader, saying, "The loyalties of John L. Lewis are to America, first and foremost."

On August 15, 1946 James A. Wechsler, correspondent for the New York *Post*, reported an interview with O. John Rogge, special assistant to the Attorney General who had just returned from a lengthy trip from Germany, gathering evidence on the links between Nazis and their American dupes. Wechsler made the following disclosures:

Rogge has unfolded evidence revealing Charles E. Coughlin sent an emissary to Germany early in 1939 urging the Nazis to proclaim their "friendship" for Christianity and to disavow any anti-religious bias. Coughlin wrote a letter embodying this plea for transmission to the highest Nazi authorities. There is no indication as to what answer he received.

Rogge reported finding verbal testimony and documentary evidence showing that John L. Lewis, celebrated leader of the United Mine Workers, was unwittingly "used" as a front by pro-Nazi elements to push for a negotiated peace in 1939. William Rhodes Davis, deceased oil magnate, was the sparkplug behind these moves in which Lewis appealed directly to President Roosevelt to play ball with Goering, it was learned.

James C. Petrillo, dictator of the American Federation of Musicians, and Joseph P. Ryan, boss of the International Longshoremen's Union (both AFL), provide two other examples of autocratic union leadership. Boss Joe Ryan, known as King Ryan, runs his political bailiwick, New York's Chelsea slum area, with the paternalistic hand of the Tammany machine. Through the Joseph P. Ryan Association, picnics, boat rides and Christmas baskets are handed out. Ryan had himself elected lifetime President of the ILU at a salary of $20,000 a year.

In addition, a few unions are temporarily controlled by thugs and cold-blooded racketeers. These men, whose doings unfortunately attract more than their share of publicity, have given the labor movement a black eye. Columnists like Westbrook Pegler and George Sokolsky have helped to build up the one-sided impression. As Leo Huberman writes in his book, *The Truth About Unions* *:

The presence of some racketeers in the labor movement has been seized upon by union-haters as the perfect weapon with which to discredit the whole trade union movement. They have cited the crimes of the few who were guilty to damage the reputation of the many who were innocent. They have tried to make it appear as though unionism and racketeering were one and the same. . . . This is far from the truth.

That there are some racketeers in labor is not surprising, since practically every profession and walk of life has them. Labor's ranks are being cleaned out, and there are grounds for hoping that labor rackets are on the way to complete eradication. Meanwhile, the age

* Pamphlet Press. Copyright 1945 by Leo Huberman.

of skulduggery and strikebreakers is fading out. Despite the excesses of a few leaders, union growth is inevitable as long as unions serve the needs of American workers, as long as they sufficiently resist the temptation to make unreasonable demands, and as long as discrimination, insufficient wages and periodic unemployment continue. Suppression, in the long run, could only intensify the struggle for greater social, economic and political concessions. Organized labor is here to stay, demanding to be treated on a basis of equality with employers. Unless extremists on both sides can be controlled and labor-management differences settled amicably and fairly, the result may be a drastic dislocation of our economy.

That labor organization is democratic and thoroughly American in principle has, of course, been repeatedly ruled by the highest courts and panels of the nation. As early as 1902 the United States Industrial Commission said, "By the organization of labor, and by no other means, is it possible to introduce an element of democracy into the government of industry." In 1937 the United States Supreme Court pointed out:

Long ago we stated the reason for labor organizations. We said that they were organized out of the necessities of the situation; that a single employee was helpless in dealing with an employer . . . that union was essential to give laborers opportunity to deal on an equality with their employer.

Labor points out that employers, representing a comparatively small fraction of the population, have set up associations, publicized and unpublicized, which provide machinery for united action. Why, then, shouldn't labor organize on its own behalf? Those who fought for America have a stake in America. Those who manned its factories and worked its mines have a moral share in the future.

The democratic method is the legislative method. Labor says that employers are adequately represented in Congress and the state governments. If the moneyed portion of our population has a political voice, labor asks an equal right of self-expression. If the right to "fight labor" is management's inherent American right, the Constitution accords labor the same right of "fighting" by democratic means in its own behalf. There's nothing "Communist" or "alien" in that. The courts have ruled it as American as the Bill of Rights.

We must abide by the democratic decision. This—not strikebreaking, violence or other extremist tactics—seems to me the essence of the American way.

In all this, both sides regard the veteran as a prize. The bulletin of the Veterans League of America asserts:

The future of America is locked in the minds of the veterans. The combination of what they think and what they do will make history. The conflict between what they think and what they will do may make that history violent. It could hardly be otherwise when there are so many of them, with varied interests, diverse personalities, individual demands on society.

The founders of the Veterans League are a group of Socialist, union-minded veterans and merchant seamen. Leo Johnson is Chairman and E. Muravchek, Executive Director. Brig. Gen. Herbert C. Holdridge, West Point graduate and former Assistant Professor of History there, is its Legislative Chairman. League headquarters are in New York. Membership dues are $3.00. The League has an articulate program for the veteran. It demands a 65-cent minimum wage law, the raising of the pension rate for 100 percent disability, the immediate release of conscientious objectors, and a permanent Fair Employment Practices Committee. The League opposes compulsory military training. It is also pushing a program for "democratizing the Army to eliminate class cleavages and the caste system." Testifying before the House Military Affairs Committee on February 20, 1946, Holdridge excoriated the Army as follows:

The Army's most prominent characteristic is its medieval caste system, which sets up unsurmountable barriers between the officer aristocracy and the enlisted man. This is not an aristocracy by birth, but by act of Congress. It teaches blind obedience to orders of an aristocratic ruling class. It promotes class consciousness and class distinctions. It creates bitterness from one end of the Army to the other. It is undemocratic and un-American. . . . Our Navy is in about the same situation.

The ouster of Chairman Rankin (also of the House Committee to Investigate Un-American Activities) from the Veterans Legislation Committee was demanded by the League. "By virtue of his 'lynch-law' psychology," the League said, "[Rankin] is unfitted to deal with the problems of 400,000 Negro war veterans. . . . He cannot legislate fairly with regard to veterans of the Jewish faith." The League is firmly opposed to Communism:

> The VLA is opposed to all manifestations of fascism, native or foreign. We shall oppose any philosophy, whatever it may be called, that seeks to destroy democracy in America or abroad. We regard the philosophy of the Communist Party as anti-democratic, in that it seeks to impose its own brand of totalitarianism upon the American people.

The League has the endorsement of the Socialist Party, which has no veterans' division of its own, and the New School for Social Research in New York. William Becker of the Socialist Party has described it as "the organization in which most of the people we know have chosen to function." The League is the catch-all for anti-Stalinist Marxists. Its membership is about 2,500.

An extreme revolutionist group, the Socialist Workers Party, is even more hostile to Stalinism. Better known as the Trotskyists, named after their assassinated leader, Leon Trotsky, they believe militantly in the literal interpretation of the teachings of Marx, Engels and Lenin. They hold uncompromising fealty to the cause of world revolution. Their fanatical political fervor may be compared to the religious fervor of Winrod's Fundamentalists. The Trotskyists are a small group who spend a great deal of their time in attacking the Stalinists.

Unlike the more opportunistic Stalinists who overnight made a "people's war" of World War II when Hitler attacked Russia, the Trotskyists claimed from the outset that it was an "imperialist war." Eighteen of its leaders were convicted of sedition in December, 1941, under the Smith Act. Just before going to jail, seditionist Farrell Dobbs said: "We are a party of professional revolutionaries who put service to the party before all other considerations. We are a party of one-hundred percenters."

I interviewed Alvin Royce, Secretary of the Veterans Committee and himself a veteran of World War II, at Trotskyist headquarters on Union Square, New York. Royce said there was no veterans' division within the Party and that members were not urged to join particular veterans' groups. Instead they were urged to strengthen the trade-union movement. Trotskyists regard the American Legion as the tool of the "reactionary capitalist class." They denounced the kindly sentiments of the *Daily Worker* toward the Legion. Their organ, *The Militant*, subheaded "Workers of the World, Unite!" wrote:

Resentment is mounting among World War II veterans as a result of incidents such as these [a run-around received by some ex-servicemen] which thoroughly expose the glib promises made by Wall Street propagandists as nothing but a vicious hoax.

Royce started on a favorite topic. "The Stalinists have betrayed the workers," he said. "They aren't revolutionary at all. . . . Lenin said there were two kinds of revolutionists: those in speech and those in deeds. We're the militant, old-line, Bolshevik revolutionists." The Trotskyists believe in world revolution on a simultaneous world front.

Meanwhile, the Congress of Industrial Organizations, through a neighborhood network of union locals and special veterans committees, is making a determined effort to help the new civilian with his readjustment problems. Far more than the American Federation of Labor, the CIO has printed a wide range of reading matter for the veteran. Another inducement is the waiving of initiation fees—ranging from $2 to $5—for new veteran members.

The CIO is also out to get the merchant seamen into its union ranks. "The GI Bill of Rights does not cover merchant seamen—a serious injustice," one of its bulletins reads. "The percentage of merchant seamen killed in the war is several times greater than the percentage for all the armed forces." Legislative units of the CIO are working for the liberalization of the GI Bill of Rights.

The American Federation of Labor seems less veteran conscious and less ambitious in promoting its work among veterans. Both unions have fought the super-seniority ruling (Board Memorandum No. 190-A), advocated by former Selective Service Director Gen. Lewis B. Hershey, as detrimental to the rights of union members. Hershey ruled that on his return the veteran "is entitled to reinstatement even though such reinstatement necessitates the discharge of a non-veteran with greater seniority." The rigidity of this ruling has caused many injustices. Take, for instance, the case of an AFL veteran who had been drafted after working for the U.S.

Rubber Company for only four months. Upon his release from the Army he got his old job back on the basis of Hershey's super-seniority clause. In so doing he displaced a veteran of World War I who had worked for twelve years.

Neither the AFL nor CIO recommends any particular veterans' groups. Meyer Bernstein, representative of the CIO Veterans Committee, said to me: "The veteran is a civilian now. He can use his own judgment and join anything he wants. We only warn him against fascists who parade as 100 percent Americans and who play no constructive role." The attitude of the AFL is similar.

In the Southern states both the CIO, with perhaps 750,000 members in the South, and the AFL, claiming 1,750,000, of whom some 300,000 are Negroes,* are instituting drives for a million new members each. One reason back of this is the fact that the majority of the more than a million Negroes, about half of them from the South, who served in the armed forces, are unorganized. Although the peonage of yesterday, when twelve hours of work daily for a week brought a white man $5.00, is over, a vast majority of unorganized Southern poor whites and Negroes still work at starvation wages.†

FREE THE SLAVES OF 1946

The United States has more slaves today than 90 years ago.

Millions of our best citizens are not permitted to work where they want to, or with whom they want to, as long as they want to, or what wage they want   If they try to, they get beaten up by the pickets!

Many years ago the slaves were only mistreated if they did not want to work. Now they are beaten if they wish to work.

The slaves of 1946 pay high fees to become slaves, for they cannot work without a card.   Then they get bossed around by the walking delegates.

Let every American Citizen urge our government to emancipate these slaves by abolishing labor unions.

Union-made goods cost more.

The consumer is the one who always pays.

The great mass of the common people are always the ones who suffer.

Help Free the Slaves!   **Abolish Labor Unions!**

Let Us Set Our Own House In Order!

Sample of anti-union leaflet distributed by the Ku Klux Klan.

* The figures are approximations as of May, 1946. Exact statistics are not available.

† A minimum wage of $12 under the NRA and a subsequent minimum of 40¢ an hour under the Minimum Wage Law have brought up living standards in some sections.

The AFL and CIO will extend democracy in sections of the South where it is now reserved for a small number of whites.

With unions moving boldly into Southern territory dominated by advocates of white supremacy, deep-smouldering animosities may be expected to flame up with unprecedented violence. Race and class warfare is likely to be instigated by anti-labor interests rooted largely in Northern corporations and supported by ultra-conservative Southern businessmen. They will use the Klan to fan the fires of racial hate and as a source of vigilante squadrons. Already the Klan has distributed thousands of inflammatory anti-union leaflets headed "FREE THE SLAVES OF 1946"—slavery, of course, being what the Klan has always hated above all else!

Gerald Smith stated on June 21, 1946: "A new organization is being formed in the South to fight the CIO 'carpetbaggers.' Opposition will be the bitterest since post-civil war days."

Ku Klux outrages are but one indication of the brewing storm. The recently established Veterans' Industrial Association, James Karam, President, of Little Rock, Ark., announced late in May, 1946, according to the Associated Press, that it had formed a "vigilance committee," which was ready to "handle" any so-called "labor goon squads" and "labor-agitators," who "caused trouble" in the South. The VIA plans to extend its activities into all Southern states in opposition to the CIO and AFL organizing drives.

At the same time, within the larger fight to extend labor organizations in the South, there looms a short-sighted intra-labor war waged by the AFL against the CIO. To meet the competitive, aggressive tactics of the CIO, AFL leaders have decided to renew their application of the "Communist" smear brush. William Green, AFL President, declared at the 1946 convention of United Textile Workers that prospective members must be told that they had a choice between "a foreign controlled organization and an American organization. That is the issue that will be drawn in the South."

Van A. Bittner, director of the CIO campaign, has countered: "No crowd, whether Communists, Socialists or anybody else, is going to mix up in this organizing drive. That goes for any organization living off the CIO."

Many of Van Bittner's organizers will be veterans. "Employers and their stooges will have an awful time convincing the people that these boys are here to destroy the government," he said. He has challenged the Klan: "If the CIO can't lick the Ku Klux Klan then we ought to be put out of business."

The rivalry between the AFL and CIO goes back to 1935, when a number of dissatisfied AFL unions split to form the Committee for Industrial Organization (now the Congress of Industrial Organizations). The AFL, with its 7,000,000 members, looks upon its younger, more militant and heady rival, with 6,250,000 members, as an interloper. To some extent this resentment is understandable in view of the fact that the AFL has carried the brunt of the organization of labor since its founding in 1881 by its beloved leader, Samuel Gompers. The heads of many AFL organizers were split open during the years when a Commodore Vanderbilt could safely shout: "The public be damned!" The groundwork for CIO victories was partially laid by idealistic men who belonged to the AFL.

Continued AFL attacks on the CIO as "Communist" persuaded me to interview Frank F. Fenton, AFL Director of Organizations, in Washington. I found him to be a tanned, thin-faced, outspoken man, with an injured right arm. He has helped greatly in the adjustment of handicapped veterans. Fenton said he had enjoyed *Under Cover.*

"You should have come to me for information on Cathrine Curtis," * he said. "She was doing all the publicity and writing for the Remington Rand people. She was getting a lot of money for it. We organized the Remington plant, but it sure was a tough fight."

I led off by asking Fenton if damning the entire CIO as "Communist" might not eventually reflect on the AFL and labor as a whole. I stated that once the anti-union employer settled scores with the CIO he would next assault the AFL unions.

Fenton didn't think so. "We just think that the CIO is influenced by prominent Communist leaders," he said. He named Harry Bridges, Michael A. Quill and Joseph Curran,† three among many CIO leaders.

---

* Miss Curtis headed The Women Investors in America, Inc., up to 1943. She now operates in Washington a reactionary service for businessmen, called the Women's Investors Research Institute, Inc. On its incorporation in 1939 one of its directors was Michael Ahearne, a former associate of George Deatherage and James True, both currently under indictment on sedition charges.

† Since this was written the N. Y. *World-Telegram* has reported that Curran, anti-Communist official of the National Maritime Union, has had a fight with American Communists within the NMU.

"Is Philip Murray a Communist?" I asked.

"There's no doubt of Phil's being anti-Communist," Fenton replied heartily, "but he's a prisoner of the Communists."

"How about Van Bittner?"

"Van is not a Communist. We're not going to predicate our Southern campaign on our charge of Communism alone," Fenton added. "We're out to organize the South, and that's only one of our methods."

"John L. Lewis," I said, "is dictatorial and arbitrary and harder to get along with than the Communists. He belongs to your AFL."

"You've got to give Lewis credit," Fenton answered. "He gets what he goes after."

I didn't bother to ask about James C. Petrillo and Joseph P. Ryan, both of whom head AFL unions, who "get" what they "go after" and run their unions with an iron hand. Petrillo's high-handed tactics finally compelled Congress to pass the Lea Law, which denies a labor czar the right to dictate to radio broadcasters the hiring of more employees than are needed "to perform actual service." As to "King" Ryan, he is the ruling autocrat of his union.

"Are Walter Reuther [President of the United Automobile Workers] and James B. Carey [National CIO Secretary-Treasurer], Communist?" I asked Fenton.

"I know Walter from way back," Fenton said. "Oh my, no! Reuther is no Communist and neither is Carey. They're strongly anti-Communist, but all they do is talk against them. We never let them get in."

Reaching for a copy of the AFL constitution, Fenton read: " 'No organization, or any persons espousing Communism or advocating the violent overthrow of our institutions, shall be allowed representation or recognition by any Central Body or State Federation of Labor.' " *

"The best friend of the Communists," said Fenton, "is the greedy anti-union employer. He denies the basic needs a man and his family must have. He leaves the way open for the Communists to come around and promise the millennium to the Negro and the

---

* In April, 1946 the Utility Workers Union of America, CIO, with a membership of 50,000, inserted a similar clause in its constitution, barring Communists. Alan S. Haywood attended as Murray's personal representative.

poor whites. Many fall for it. The real solution is to lift the economic standards of the South."

This statement of Fenton's impressed me as highly sensible.

After interviewing Fenton, I asked Meyer Bernstein of the CIO Veterans' Committee to comment on the AFL's charges of Communism. Bernstein wrote: "This has been their strategy for a long time. It hasn't worked in the past, and I don't think it will work this time."

Van A. Bittner countered AFL charges by saying that George Googe of the AFL had "no more right to call the CIO a Communist organization because it has some Communists in it than I have to call the AFL a racketeering organization because some of its union presidents are in the penitentiary for stealing money."

I am not an expert in labor policies, but it's my impression that blanket charges of "Communist" will play into the hands of those who once paid Southern workers starvation wages. To divide labor has always been their strategy. Common sense suggests that, unless labor leaders stick together in a spirit of "competitive free enterprise," both their houses will suffer. The South has enough unorganized workers to satisfy the hungriest unionist.

Among these alleged CIO "Communists" is one of the finest women I've ever met. A gray-haired, genteel Southern lady, Miss Lucy Randolph Mason, a descendant of the famous Mason family of Virginia who have produced so many statesmen and legislators

CIO POLITICAL ACTION COMMITTEE

NEW YORK 17, N Y

Dear Mr. Carlson: July 17, 1946

The officers and members of CIO PAC are listed on this stationery with two exceptions. Mr. Philip Murray is ex-officio a member, by reason of his being President of the CIO. Mr. L. C. Buckmaster is also a member having been appointed to fill a vacancy which existed at the time this stationery was printed. As you can see, the leaders of CIO PAC are all loyal Americans working conscientiously for the progress of our country. We are not dominated by either Communists or anti-Communists. We believe that we are making a great contribution toward the welfare of our country and our citizens and I think that all progressive Americans join in the program which we espouse.

Very sincerely yours,

Tilford E. Dudley
Assistant to the Chairman

The roster of the PAC officials appears on page 248.

through the generations, is CIO's Southern Public Relations representative in Atlanta. Her ancestry is more American than Washington's, I believe.

"I do not belong to any 'patriotic organization,'" Miss Mason wrote me, "but I could get into the Colonial Dames on seven different lines and the DAR on a much greater number." Thomas Jefferson described George Mason, her great-great-grandfather, as "one of our really great men, and of the first order of greatness." Mason was a delegate to the Constitutional Convention and helped in the drafting of the Constitution. When the document was finally drafted, however, he refused to sign it because "it lacked a Bill of Rights and because the importation of slaves was to be continued for twenty years." A large landowner with many slaves, George Mason wrote in 1775:

We came equals into this world, and equals we shall go out of it. All men are by nature born equally free and independent. To protect the weaker from the injuries and insults of the stronger were societies first formed. . . . Let us never lose sight of this fundamental maxim—that all power was originally lodged in, and consequently is derived from, the people.

Were George Mason living, he would have been branded a "Communist agitator" by the Talmadges, Rankins, Bilbos and others of their pattern. Miss Mason is also related to Gen. Robert E. Lee. There isn't a drop of "Yankee" blood in her. She is an Episcopalian. In an article, "Why I Joined Labor," she explained in *The Witness*:

The answer is simple. My father and mother taught me that religion includes one's relationship both to God and to man. They made their own cause the cause of the oppressed and the destitute. Father was an Episcopal minister, as was Mother's father. I grew up in a deeply religious atmosphere permeated with positive acts not only to help individuals, but to work at correcting causes. With that heritage, I could not keep religion and social action in separate compartments. In that long past, and while I was still in my teens, the sixty-four hour week for girls in Richmond's tobacco factories, and the seven-day week for young men in steel plants bit deep into my conscience.

For being a practicing Christian, Miss Mason is called a "Communist."

The much-criticized and (by the anti-laborites) roundly hated Political Action Committee, a unit of the Congress of Industrial Organizations, is the sinew of the labor movement. Without a political wing, labor would fight a losing battle; anti-labor laws could ride roughshod over temporary labor gains. The AFL has participated in politics before, but its participation has been piecemeal. The program of the PAC is concerted, planned and led by a central leadership which gives autonomy of action to local unions and affiliated groups. Although the PAC is a CIO brain child, a victory for it may be a victory for the AFL, the Railroad Brotherhoods and organized labor everywhere.

The PAC disclaims being a "Third" or a "labor" party, or even a political party. It will support candidates of either major party "in accord with the PAC objectives." Holding the balance of power, it proved itself an effective instrument in the 1944 elections. The PAC declares it is not for labor alone, but for the "common man" everywhere. Philip Murray, President of the CIO, declared: "For the first time in American history, the forces of labor are now setting up a nationwide organization to protect the political rights of the working man, as well as the rights of the returning soldier, the farmer, the small businessman, and the so-called 'common man.'" The social program of the PAC is listed as follows:

1. All-out aid for the returned servicemen.
2. Full employment at fair wages.
3. All-out planning for a lasting peace.
4. Good housing, medical care, and schooling for all our people.
5. Equality of opportunity for all, regardless of race or religion.
6. A just and adequate Social Security System for the aged, the sick, the unemployed, the crippled, the orphaned and the widowed.
7. Fight inflation and keep prices down.

This is Lucy Randolph Mason's program. It's "Communist" only to those who want a monopoly on democracy. In Georgia the thought of more schooling has been anathema to such socially illiterate governors as Eugene Talmadge. In other states the plight of thousands of the destitute, the mentally ill and the crippled—both whites and Negroes—is little better than it would have been centuries ago. Gen. George Van Horn Moseley, long the white hope of the nationalist advocates of a fascist America, admitted to me that he advocated the sterilization of such people. It is reliably estimated that the number of "ill-clothed, ill-fed, ill-housed" American citizens reaches the staggering total of twenty millions. The PAC is the political spearhead of a social-reform movement aimed at doing the most good to those who have least enjoyed the benefits of democracy. It is battling for the equal extension of those benefits to all our population. Its opponents, through ignorance or malice, prefer to keep them for themselves and their own fortunate class.

The PAC is financed by CIO union contributions and through voluntary donations. Cries of "buying out" the 1944 elections with a slush fund of $15,000,000 (through $1 contributions) vanished into thin air as the PAC and NCPAC collected a total of $1,405,169, and spent $1,327,774 for salaries, travel, primary, state and presidential elections. On the other hand, expenditures of the National Republican Committee in 1944 were $13,195,375. The DuPont family alone contributed $109,832.83; while the Pew family of rock-ribbed Republicans contributed $96,995.76. A thorough Congressional investigation of PAC disclosed its full compliance with the law.

Since Hillman's death PAC has undergone a reorganization. No longer under his personal leadership, nor subject to his rare ability in keeping differing factions working harmoniously toward a common democratic goal, the degree of harmony in the new leadership is, at this writing, an unknown quality. Jack Kroll, who came up from union ranks with Hillman and was his assistant, has replaced the deceased leader.

Under him is a five-man executive board which includes David J. McDonald, William Pollock, George F. Addes, Julius Emspak. In addition, a PAC National Committee includes: R. J. Thomas, Frank Rosenblum, Albert J. Fitzgerald, Van A. Bittner, John Green, Joseph Curran, Reid Robinson, L. C. Buckmaster, Emil Rieve, Alan S. Haywood, James B. Carey, Philip Murray. Of these Addes, Emspak and Thomas are recognized as "left-wingers"—which is not the same thing as Communism. To charges of "Communism" Tilford E. Dudley, assistant to Kroll, said to me: "We're like the proverbial goldfish in the glass bowl. We're constantly under scrutiny. We *have* to keep our house clean, and keep our leadership clear of Communists. We can't afford the luxury of relaxing our vigilance, nor violate the law in any way at all."

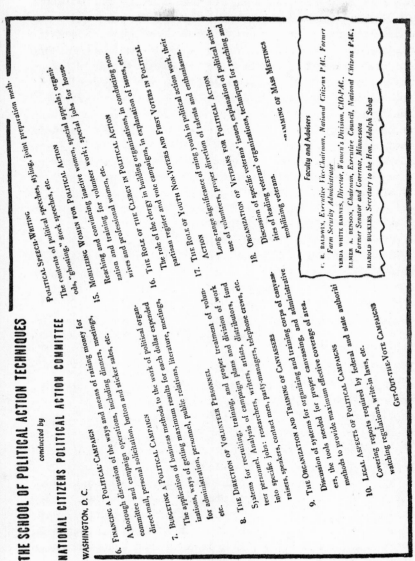

THE SCHOOL OF POLITICAL ACTION TECHNIQUES

conducted by

NATIONAL CITIZENS POLITICAL ACTION COMMITTEE

WASHINGTON, D. C.

6. FINANCING A POLITICAL CAMPAIGN
A thorough discussion of the ways and means of raising money for political organizations, button and sticker sales, etc. A thorough discussion of the ways and means of raising money for committee and campaign operations, button and sticker sales, etc. direct-mail, personal solicitation, button and sticker sales, etc.

7. BUDGETING A POLITICAL CAMPAIGN
The application of business methods to the work of political organizations, ways of getting maximum results for each dollar expended for administration, personnel, public relations, literature, meetings, etc.

8. THE DIRECTION OF VOLUNTEER PERSONNEL
Systems for recruiting, training, and proper treatment of volunteer personnel. Analysis of campaign plans and division of work into specific jobs: researchers, writers, artists, telephone crews, etc. raisers, speakers, contact men, party-managers, telephone crews, etc.

9. THE ORGANIZATION AND TRAINING OF CANVASSERS
Discussion of systems for organizing and training corps of canvassers, speakers, contact men, party-managers, and administrative methods to provide maximum effective coverage of area.

10. LEGAL ASPECTS OF POLITICAL CAMPAIGNS
Covering reports required by federal and state authorities, the tools needed for proper canvassing, and administrative watching regulations, write-in laws, etc.

GET-OUT-THE-VOTE CAMPAIGNS

POLITICAL SPEECH-WRITING
The contents of political speeches, styling, joint preparation methods, "ghosting," stock speeches, etc.

15. MOBILIZING WOMEN FOR POLITICAL ACTION
Reaching and convincing inactive women, special appeals; organization and training for women, etc. The contents of political speeches, styling, joint preparation meth-

16. THE ROLE OF THE CLERGY IN POLITICAL ACTION
The role of the clergy in building organizations, in explanation of issues, etc. wives and professional women, etc.

THE ROLE OF NON-VOTERS AND FIRST VOTERS IN POLITICAL ACTION
The role of the clergy in building organizations, in explanation of political action work, their partisan register and vote campaigns, in explanation of issues, etc.

17. THE ROLE OF YOUTH NON-VOTERS AND FIRST VOTERS IN POLITICAL ACTION
Long-range significance of using youth in political action work, their partisan register and vote campaigns, literature, meetings, enthusiasms. Long-range significance of using youth in political action work, their use of volunteers, proper direction of talents and enthusiasms.

18. ORGANIZATION OF VETERANS FOR POLITICAL ACTION
Long-range significance of using youth in political activities, explanation of political action work, use of volunteers, proper direction of political activities, explanation of political and use of volunteers, proper direction of political activ-
Discussion of specific veterans' organizations, techniques for reaching and mobilizing veterans.

....MMING OF MASS MEETINGS

Faculty and Advisers

C. B. BALDWIN, *Executive Vice-Chairman, National Citizens PAC, Former Farm Security Administrator*

VERDA WHITE BARNES, *Director, Women's Division, CIO-PAC.*

ELMER A. BENSON, *Chairman, Executive Council, National Citizens PAC, Former Senator and Governor, Minnesota*

HAROLD BUCKLES, *Secretary to the Hon. Adolph Sabat*

In anticipation of the 1948 elections, the NC-PAC is training organizers, speakers and political strategists.

The charge that some CIO unions have been penetrated by Communists seems to be true in specific instances. The Transport Workers, the American Communications Association and the Fur and Leather Workers are among those unions whose leadership has followed the Party line. Charges of "Communist" against the National Maritime Union are offset by the violent anti-Communist attitude of Joseph Curran, its president, who was re-elected to office in July, 1946 by an overwhelming majority. In August, 1946, ten thousand members of the United Furniture Workers of America in Philadelphia were reported quitting their posts in protest against alleged Communist control. Also in August, five locals of the United Electrical and Radio Workers passed resolutions against their national leadership, charging Communist control. On the other hand, neither is the AFL clear of Communist infiltration. A case in point (at this writing) is the Hotel and Club Employees' Union of New York, notwithstanding the AFL constitution which bars Communists.

The role of Communists in CIO affairs seems, on the whole, to be minor—comprising only a small proportion among numerous CIO unions. To call the CIO "Communist" on this basis is tantamount to playing a dangerous game of labor-baiting and Red-baiting. It is worthy only of the Westbrook Peglers and others who feed on blackening the entire trade union movement because of some culprits. Given time and patient treatment, labor will adjust its difficulties.

Those who intemperately maintain that the PAC is Communist are blind to certain undeniable truths. The President of the CIO, which maintains the PAC, is a practicing Christian of the Roman Catholic faith. The late Sidney Hillman, PAC Chairman, was President of the Amalgamated Clothing Workers of America, which is far from being Communist. Hillman was Chairman of the Board of Directors of the Amalgamated Bank in New York, and a director of the Amalgamated Bank and Trust Company of Chicago. These aren't positions that go to Communists. But more than that, in 1940 Hillman, an American of the Jewish faith, was appointed to the Commission on American Citizenship of the Catholic University of America. In the October 20, 1944 issue of *The Commonweal*, a learned, liberal Catholic journal, John C. Cort wrote:

Is Hillman a Communist? The evidence against this claim is strong. Actually, no labor Czar in the AFL ever hunted down Stalinists with more relentless zest than Hillman in his own Union. . . .

Sidney Hillman is today as good an example as you could find in America of the labor leader who preaches, and practices, the theory of capital-labor cooperation for mutual interest, the theory of let's-reform-capitalism-and-make-it-work. Actually a typical speech of Hillman's on the function of labor in industry sounds far more like a papal encyclical than a Marxist tract, and it would be an encouraging thing indeed if a few more Catholic labor leaders in this country knew as much of Catholic social doctrine as Hillman regularly preaches. It is also an interesting fact that the PAC program not only plunks for "free enterprise" but contains a plan for economic self-government. . . .

America magazine, organ of the American Jesuit order, and staunchly anti-Communist, said of the PAC in its November 4, 1944 issue: "Those who know labor, in fact, agree that Hillman's union . . . has persistently and successfully resisted attempts at Communist control. The Dies Report further shows that no one in the national leadership is a Communist. Such testimony, from an unimpeachable source, must force revision of a judgment formed upon the current press campaign. . . ."

The PAC refused to open its books to the Dies Committee, but it cheerfully opened them to the Department of Justice. The findings of the FBI cleared the PAC of any charges of alien domination as well as of any political or financial irregularity.

An offshoot of the PAC is the National Citizens Political Action Committee, reserved for non-labor Americans who contribute to the PAC's fighting fund.

Working ahead to the 1948 presidential campaign, the NCPAC held in Washington, in June, 1946, the first of a series of four-day "Schools of Political Action Technique" designed to stimulate political activity. About 500 students from all parts of the country paid $12 each for the classes. The complete series will comprise 39 courses. The "faculty" included Congressmen, prominent teachers of political science and representatives of democratic groups. Among them was Senator Wayne B. Morse, Oregon Republican, supporter of progressive legislation. The NCPAC feels that by the time the presidential elections roll around students will have organized voting districts to endorse PAC candidates. The National Association of Manufacturers apparently plans counter action; three of its delegates were present as "observers."

Under Sidney Hillman's personal guidance the PAC in 1944 was unimpeachably democratic. Since the beginning of the extended illness which preceded his death, reports have been circulated of successful Communist infiltration within the PAC in certain localities. I have tried to trace these down to "names and figures." My demands for proof of Communist domination so far have been evaded by those who most loudly made the charges. After exhaustive investigation—including a request to a Federal agency for information on the alleged Communism of the PAC or NCPAC—I am convinced that at this writing the leadership of both CIO groups is free from the taint.

President Philip Murray has stated "this union will not tolerate efforts by outsiders—individuals, organizations or groups—whether they be Communist, Socialist or any other group, to infiltrate, dictate or meddle in our affairs. . . . As a democratic organization, we engage in no purges, witch-hunts." Nor, Murray said, would he give ear to "false prophets and hypocritical advisers from without who mean us no good."

Just as the South's anti-union crust is being cracked by organized labor, by the same token the anti-union armor of the American Legion has been punctured by the National Conference of Union Labor Legionnaires, Inc. The Conference is composed of 138 trade-union Legion posts, with a growing membership of 30,000 recruited from the AFL, the CIO, the Railroad Brotherhoods and other unions. The moving spirits behind it are two veterans of World War I, Charles Vencill, President, and George C. Danfield, Secretary; Maurice A. Frank, Chicago attorney and World War II veteran, has charge of public relations.

The liberalizing influence of the Conference has been resisted by the Legion. Former National Commander Edward S. Scheiberling, a man with a union background, pledged "sympathetic and understanding treatment." Since his retirement, however, the ingrained policy of the old Legion has made it difficult for the Conference to obtain new charters. The Conference is comparatively small in numbers, but articulate:

We plan to continue along the road we have been travelling. We plan to increase our influence and prestige within the Legion by greater membership. We want to build our strength up to the point where we will no longer merely safeguard the interests of labor in the Legion, but where we will affirmatively use the power of the Legion to promote the —welfare and security of the working man. We will continue to be the voice of the conscience of the Legion. . . .

The Conference claims that a million ex-GIs won't join the Legion because of its many "anti-labor acts and speeches." It has needled the leadership of the Legion with much carping criticism. In its May, 1946 convention in New York the Conference issued a bill of particulars, citing specific charges ranging from strikebreaking to fascism. The complaint reminds us:

The record of Legion anti-labor activities is one of the most violent chapters in American history. No less than fifty illegal acts of violence were committed in 1920. Farmers' Non-Partisan League speakers were tarred and feathered, many of Eugene V. Debs' meetings were broken up, as was a concert by Fritz Kreisler. From 1919 to 1937 the Legion was one of the main anti-labor strikebreaking forces in the nation.

Very few wage earners have ever held an important office in the Legion, despite the fact that about 90 per cent of the men who went to war were wage earners.

Pearl Harbor did not cause the Legion to change its fascist spots. After Roane Waring, Memphis utility executive, was chosen commander in

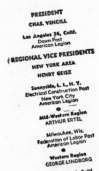

PRESIDENT
CHAS. VENCILL

Los Angeles 36, Calif.
Dawn Post
American Legion

REGIONAL VICE PRESIDENTS
NEW YORK AREA
HENRY GEISZ

Sunnyside, L. I., N. Y.
Electrical Construction Post
New York City
American Legion

Mid-Western Region
ARTHUR ERTEL

Milwaukee, Wis.
Federation of Labor Post
American Legion

Western Region
GEORGE LINDBORG

Los Angeles 3, Calif.
Milton Konode Post
American Legion

Southern Region
WALTER ROGERS

National Conference
of Union Labor Legionnaires

TREASURER
EDW. DeKEYSER
Detroit 14, Mich.
Detroit Union Labor Post
American Legion

NATIONAL HEADQUARTERS
SUITE 1006-160 N. LA SALLE ST.
CHICAGO 1, ILL.

SECRETARY
GEO. C. DANFIELD
Chicago Union Labor Post
American Legion

March 26th, 1946.

Dear Mr. Carlson:

Please excuse the delay in replying to your letter of March 5th. I believe that I can best and most honestly answer the first question contained in your letter in the follow'ng manner: We are not a political organization. We have absolutely no connection or contact with the American Communist Party or with any other political party. We do not engage in "Red-baiting", or in any other kind of baiting.

Sincerely yours,

Maurice A. Frank

1942, he toured the country denouncing unions and threatening to shoot strikers. He delivered a vicious anti-labor, anti-democratic diatribe to the soldiers at Fort Bragg in May, 1943.

Meeting in Indianapolis, the Legion Executive Committee approved the proposal to accept $20,000,000 from the corporations for an Americanism program, and agreed to campaign for laws to prohibit the closed or union shop. . . . The 1943 national commander, Warren Atherton, publicly suggested electrocuting of striking union leaders.

The Conference denounced the Wall Street Post for awarding the Americanism Medal to Cecil B. DeMille, who since his suspension as a member of the American Federation of Radio Artists, AFL, has become highly critical of organized labor.

I investigated the inevitable rumors of "Communist" leveled against the Conference. Frederick Woltman, Scripps-Howard reporter who has specialized in anti-Communist articles, told me, "I don't think the Conference is Communist at all." Alvin Royce, Secretary of the Trotskyist Veterans Committee, said to me: "No, the Conference is not Communist."

I asked my friend Mort Levy, active Buffalo, N. Y., Legionnaire, who has no more love for the Communists than for the fascists. After a month's inquiry, Mort cleared the Conference. William Green endorsed the Conference, hoping "that all members of the AFL" would form union labor posts "and in this way promote and advance the common interests of both the American Federation of Labor and the American Legion." Finally I asked Maurice Frank to answer the charge, and he wrote me:

I can best and most honestly answer the first question in the following manner: We are not a political organization. We have absolutely no connection nor contact with the American Communist Party or with any other political party. We do not engage in "Red-baiting," or in any other kind of baiting.

I also put the question to Donald G. Glascoff, National Adjutant of the Legion. He did not answer it, but did not hesitate to say that the Legion had no use for the Conference. Glascoff wrote me on March 13:

The so-called "National Conference of Union Labor Legionnaires" has no official connections with the American Legion. The Legion does not recognize subsidiary or special interest groups of this nature. . . . A special sub-committee of the National Executive Committee has been engaged to investigate un-authorized groups, such as the Conference.

In denying charters to new Conference posts, the Legion leadership based its decision on the New Orleans mandate of 1922 which decided to "revoke the charter of a Legion Post which takes public and official action in direct conflict with the policies established by the national convention." The Conference has opposed Legion policy by approving a 65-cent minimum wage bill, endorsing Henry Wallace for Secretary of Commerce, and opposing General Hershey's discriminatory super-seniority Board Memorandum 190-A.

When the Legion revoked the charter of the Willard Straight Post of New York for disagreeing with Legion policy, however, the State Appellate Court held that the Legion's mandate was wrong. Quoting the Constitutional guarantee of freedom of speech, the Court held that the New Orleans mandate "unreasonably prohibits this fundamental right." It declared the Legion's mandate to be "contrary to the law, unsound in principle." The post's charter was restored.

The National Conference of Union Labor Legionnaires "intends to see that labor is properly represented in any and all veterans organizations of the present or future and to avoid the mistakes that were made when the American Legion was created at the close of World War I." Despite the official opposition, it is determined to avert the danger of millions of "servicemen returning to civilian life and being enrolled into a veterans organization unfavorable to labor."

When the veterans editor of the Communist organ, the *Daily Worker*, queried the Legion as to whether it would bar Communists from membership, the Adjutant "replied by reading the induction ceremony statement which specifically pledges that no one will be barred because of political affiliation." It's a far cry from World War I, when Commander Franklin D'Olier, shortly after the first Legion Convention in 1919, threatened: "The battle is on and the Legion shall not relent until America is purged hide and hair, of every member of the IWW and Bolshevik breed."

In many respects the Legion has been a tool of "reactionary" business. Today labor has gained a fighting toehold. The change within the Legion is symbolic of the change in our nation. Democracy is on the march. Its mass base can no longer be whipped into control by the willful handful of private government tycoons who once controlled power, wages, economy and politics. During the "free-booting era"—which ended with the 1929 crash—they ruled America and rationed its benefits to a handful of favorites. The mass American base is fast growing into counter-organized power. In the showdown battle between General Motors and the United Automobile Workers in the winter of 1945–6, labor stood its ground. It would no longer be bullied into a corner, brass-knuckled into submission or smeared as "Communist, alien, un-American." The tactics followed after World War I failed after World War II.

America is undergoing a social and political revolution, so far bloodless. Throughout the world the mass mind is awakening to its rightful share of the wealth it produces through labor. Those who have had the lion's share of everything are defensively trying to retain the *status quo*. Eric Johnston says it won't work. Speaking before the U.S. Chamber of Commerce, he looked back at the "free-booting era" and urged the immediate need for a revised concept of capitalism. Said Johnston:

Four years ago, I thought we needed a new creed for capitalism. . . . I think so more now than I did then. The definition of capitalism in the books is as dead as the dinosaurs. It ought to be. Let me recite the standard dictionary definition: "Capitalism. The concentration of capital. The power or influence of capital as when in the hands of a few." . . . It fits only the free-booting era, . . . the days of the wasters and the plunderers, the spoilers and the monopolists. . . . We need a new definition of capitalism just as much as we need a new dimension in our thinking and in our advocacy of a progressive economic system.

Suppose we try this: "Capitalism is a competitive economic system designed for the enrichment of the many and not to make a few men rich." We ought to be able to go hell-bent for that kind of capitalism. In fact, what I propose to prove to you is that we've got to go hell-bent for it if we don't want the good things we've got to go to hell.

If capitalism should fail—I hope it will not—the unpredictable aftermaths may be ascribed largely to economic nationalists and totalitarian-minded advocates of private government who, having ignored Willkie and Johnston, will have germinated the ground through continued neglect of their social responsibilities. Greed and the resultant disaster of mass unemployment can doom our capitalist order. In that case, those who failed to allow for the needs of America must share in the blame.

CHAPTER ELEVEN

Fingers in the Veteran Pie: Right Wing

The American ideal is a . . . brotherhood of free men . . . There remains an internal threat, which . . . assumes sinister and formidable proportions. It consists simply of individuals who . . . belong to economic groups which possess the greatest measure of security. . . . Blinded by fear of changes they cannot understand or control, they desperately defend their special interests. . . . They seek to restrict democracy . . . and, if they are allowed to continue, they will destroy it completely.

Bernard J. Sheil, Auxiliary Bishop of Chicago

INDUSTRY FOR VETERANS, INC. maintained impressive offices in Chicago. A beauteous receptionist inquired the nature of your business and presented you with a series of booklets. You read: "Both labor and the government have exploited opportunities to cement relationships with service personnel, but industry to date has not." Industry for Veterans was the answer. Founded by Captain James Simpson, who served in the Marine Corps, it urged firms "to give preference to veterans in all new employment until at least 25 percent of their payrolls are veterans." By December, 1945 more than 3,000 concerns had signed the pledge.

General Robert E. Wood, former Chairman of the America First Committee, was on the Board of Directors, together with former isolationist General Charles G. Dawes. But their political views received no encouragement. "We will not attempt to influence legislation," the organization promised. "Our purpose is to do a public relations job for industry among veterans."

It *was* good public relations, and a laudable purpose. Other good public relations jobs, interpreting industry's problems to returned veterans and aiding veterans financially or otherwise, are being done today. A minority of politically, socially and economically regressive businessmen, however, are seeking to exploit the veteran for their own political and economic purposes. Some of them are trying to build up a mass nationalist following in order to take America back to the "days of the wasters, spoilers and monopolists," to use Eric Johnston's phrase. They want to take us back to the days when certain Congressmen, justices and even Presidents bent to the will of their private government. Today they talk smoothly in terms of "private enterprise," of preserving "initiative" and "the profit incentive," and thereby keeping "America American"—phrases as glib as the nationalist's "patriotism" and "Christianity."

A fine example of genuinely good public relations has been set by Cudahy Brothers Company, Milwaukee meat packers. Cudahy's have a plan of awarding $100 U.S. Savings Bonds to employees on leave of absence with the Armed Forces who return to work within ninety days after honorable discharge and continue with the Company at least sixty days. In addition, $1,000 is granted to the dependents of each such employee who died in service unmarried; and $2,000, plus $500 for each child, to the dependents of married employees who fell. The Company awarded an employee who lost both legs in the war $1,000 for a specially fitted automobile.

Certainly this is more effective than the program of the Society of Sentinels, Detroit, self-styled "educational, patriotic organization of American citizens." In January, 1946 the Society fired the opening gun of a campaign to turn the clock back to yesterday. In an amazing advertisement, published nationally, they urged the President to ask Congress to:

INDUSTRY *for* VETERANS, INC.

This is a list of 3,026 firms who have signed the Industry for Veterans Pledge to give preference to veterans in all new employment until at least 25 per cent of their payroll are veterans.

Genuinely excellent "public relations" for industry.

Repeal the Social Security Act because the Constitution does not authorize Congress "to care for destitute citizens, or to establish compulsory and discriminatory systems of insurance, or to pay money to citizens because they are not working."

Repeal the Fair Labor Standards Act and the Wages and Hours Law "because the Constitution gives Congress no authority to determine the hours a citizen shall labor or the wages he shall receive. . . . This law which tends to restrict the hours of labor, necessarily restricts production and lowers the standard of living of our citizens."

To pass "no appropriations . . . for federal housing. It is not the function of the federal government to build houses for the people to live in. . . ."

Immediately repeal the National Labor Relations Act, "because the . . . Constitution does not authorize Congress to legislate on matters pertaining to employer-employee relations," etc., etc.

Except for the organization's name and the location, "Detroit," the advertisement was anonymous. No officers were listed, no address appeared. Through undercover means, I learned who the men were behind the society of economic vigilantes. Its original promoter was John W. Scoville, who solicited my membership in the fall of 1945 and later sent me a notice announcing that he had opened a new office as a consulting economist and statistician in the Penobscot Building, Detroit. Vice-Chairman was Stephen DeBrul, chief economist of the General Motors Corporation. Another General Motors official from whom I received propaganda was Henry Grady Weaver, associated with the customer research department. The National Labor Relations Board questioned Weaver for allegedly flooding the mails with booklets paralleling the Sentinels' advertisement, according to a newspaper report.

Posing as Robert Thompson, Jr., disillusioned veteran, I wrote the Sentinels. One L. C. Allman, Chairman, answered on stationery printed in blue ink with "SOS" in red, enclosing two membership applications, one for myself and the other "for a friend or business associate." Allman flooded me with reprints of the advertisement and hoped I would "distribute these to people who need to be awakened to the necessity for quick action to save America." My membership card was signed by Wayne Stillbacher, Secretary. Enclosed with it was a booklet, *Collective Bargaining,* by Scoville, and a leaflet by Dr. George W. Crane, newspaper columnist, denouncing "government interference" and plugging the free-booting philosophy. "Uncle Sam has acted solely as business referee in free enterprise since this nation was formed," Crane said. He did not add that a referee has the right to penalize those who break the rules of fair play.

In June, 1946 the Society renewed its drive for members. I received a kit of blazing red-white-blue literature. One 12-page booklet was crammed with an outline of the United States map, the flag, shield, star-decked streamers, the Statue of Liberty, the Liberty Bell, the Capitol, drummers depicting the "Spirit of 1776" and the flag-raising at Iwo Jima. In the testimonials section was Robert Thompson's letter entitled: "Discharged GI Disgusted Over Strikes." The Society claimed to be speaking on behalf of "the laborers," and the "white collar class." It was also out to save those who "love America."

In Little Rock, Ark., the Veterans Industrial Association, Inc. helps give industry a black eye. It started business in February, 1946 with a series of full-page ads (a mark of big-money backing) headlined, "Wake Up, America!" They began provocatively: "We boys just returning from the Armed Services find our country in greater danger from WITHIN than it ever was from the enemies

SOCIETY OF SENTINELS ━━━━━━━━━

Dear Mr. President:

As stockholders in the great corporation of which you are President, we desire to help in whatever way we can to promote the successful operation of that great enterprise known as the United States of America. We understand that you will soon advise our Board of Directors, the Congress, on the condition of our enterprise.

3. I ask for the repeal of the Fair Labor Standards Act, because the Constitution gives Congress no authority to determine the hours a citizen shall labor or the wages he shall receive. The number of hours that a citizen works is a personal matter which depends on his age, health, ambition and circumstances. This law which tends to restrict the hours of labor, necessarily restricts production and lowers the standard of living of our citizens. I suggest the repeal of The Wages and Hours law.

8. I ask for the repeal of the Social Security Act as of June 30, 1947. Legislation should be enacted to distribute to the States on that date any funds which have been accumulated as the result of this Act, on an equitable basis. I fail to find in the United States Constitution any article which authorizes Congress to care for destitute citizens, or to establish compulsory and discriminatory systems of insurance, or to pay money to citizens because they are not working.

Poor "public relations" for industry! The Society's social theories are 66 years behind the times—at least!

we were fighting ABROAD. Great numbers of us have come home—eager to get back to work, and to enjoy the benefits of peacetime civilian life—ONLY TO DISCOVER THAT THE FREEDOM WE THOUGHT WE WERE FIGHTING FOR IS NOT HERE." The advertisement continued in that vein for a full page, denouncing labor leaders as "dictators" whose "slave-driver tactics" persecuted "the great majority of American workers." The Association urged sending back "foreigners with foreign ideas to the place they came from," and ended on the note:

If We MUST FIGHT, We Will

The time has come to put an end to appeasement as far as this dictatorship by labor bosses is concerned—to quit compromises and the babying of radical leaders and foreign born agitators. We are not hunting for trouble, any more than we did with Germany, Italy or Japan. But we don't believe in appeasement, either. . . . We also had a hard time abroad. We won that—AND WE WILL WIN THIS ONE. . . . WE ARE PREPARED AND READY TO FIGHT IF WE HAVE TO.

The sabre-rattling, union-hating Veterans Industrial Association, Inc. claims to be a "trade union," but promotes the views of self-seeking businessmen. A few veteran officers serve as fronts. Despite the fact that membership is open to "everybody," the Association claims to be a "veterans" group! "We veterans of World War II are offering to the American people a union that is ALL American—a union which assures to EVERYBODY, a union member or non-union member, protection against gangsterism and dictatorship!" Unlike the charters of legitimate labor unions, the Association's charter forbids members to negotiate labor-management contracts and advocates the open shop. The constitution states that "no member of this Association, shall ever negotiate, sign or adhere to any contract or agreement governing wages, hours of labor, and working conditions of the members hereof, with any employer." It places the white and Negro worker at the complete mercy of the employer.

James T. Karam (described as "Jimmy Flash," an "all-American football player") is "National President and Chairman of the Board." Karam responded readily to my letters written under the name of Thompson, unemployed and disgruntled veteran. "We are veterans like yourself," he replied, "who are sick and tired at the way our country is being taken over by a bunch of racketeers." As I had surmised, the Association had the ultimate aim of exploiting veterans for political objectives. Karam answered me as Thompson as well as to another name I used. In April, 1946 he wrote:

The CIO here in Arkansas gives us the most trouble but we are getting ready to open up State offices in Shreveport for Louisiana, and the AFL are the roughest there. We expect real trouble but we feel like we are able to handle them. . . .

Veterans Industrial Association

Join because:

An Incorporated, Independent Trade Union for ALL Americans!

v 22, 1946   LITTLE ROCK, ARK.

Everything is going along fine and we have opened up headquarters in Louisiana for that state and intend to open up in Texas and Florida within the next thirty or sixty days. 95% of our membership comes from veterans, whom we are particularly interested in.

We veterans must take the lead in things like this because we are the ones who primarily earned the right to take this lead. We intend to take a very active part in all political questions where the freedom of our country is involved.

Sincerely yours

James T. Karam
JAMES T. KARAM
National President and Chairman of the Board

You pay nothing to join VIA!

Your VIA cooperates with your employer because you know the more money he makes, the more he can pay you!

The Communist-dominated labor unions cause y o u nothing but trouble, all t h e y want is your money and the power to tell you WHEN to work, HOW to work and for how MUCH!

You were smart enough to find the job you have, so the VIA knows you are smart enough to figure out what is best for you!

You will be your own boss and do your own thinking!

You do not need a lot of "foreign" labor bosses you don't know or who don't know you to do your thinking for you—all they want is your money and a fat-paying easy job for themselves!

This is supposed to be a union!

*We intend to set up a political organization to go along with our VIA but
we feel it should come after we grow stronger.* [Italics mine.]

About six weeks later he reported:

Everything is going along fine and we have opened up headquarters in
Louisiana . . . and intend to open up in Texas and Florida within the
next thirty or sixty days. 95% of our membership comes from veterans,
whom we are particularly interested in.

We veterans must take the lead in things like this because we are the
ones who primarily earned the right to take this lead. We intend to
take a very active part in all political questions where the freedom of
our country is involved. . . .

The VIA "handled" a Little Rock strike by old-fashioned strikebreaking tactics. In a letter written to a worker whom they apparently tried to inveigle as a strikebreaker, Karam wrote: "The
Wrape Stave Mill will start work Monday, March 18. The Veterans
Industrial Association has men there now to guarantee you protection against anyone or anything." One of Karam's leaflets denounces
"Communist-dominated labor unions," and pleads: "You do not
need a lot of foreign labor bosses. In the VIA you are your own
Union Boss—you run it yourself." Through such divide-and-conquer
tactics a minority of unscrupulous employers have made the average
Southern worker the worst paid in the country.

Thomas L. Stokes, Southern-born political columnist, threw more
light on Karam's tactics in the New York *World-Telegram* on August
7, 1946:

It does not seem to be generally known, but Jimmy Karam was a strong-
arm leader several years ago in one of the squads in Cadsden, Ala. Those
squads were composed, I was told, of former college athletes and tough
boys from the hills. Jimmy Karam himself was a football star at Auburn.
He leans to athletes today for his assistants. His organization, he said,
is to take care of labor and racial agitators. The testimony of newspapermen is that the atmosphere about his Little Rock headquarters is quite
alarming because of the gangster touch.

In an interview with Harold B. Hinton in the New York *Times*
on August 26, 1946, Karam said that VIA had 11,000 members.

Striking a new note, he expressed disillusionment with regard to employers as a class, and was quoted: "We . . . started out under the illusion that all employers were fair and honest and would do the right thing if given a fair chance to help their employees. We were bitterly disappointed and have found out in the six months we have been organized that a great majority of employers are as big racketeers as certain unions and union officials."

Karam resented the fact that the VIA had been called a strike-breaking outfit. He claimed that the group supported strikes "if the workers are on strike to obtain benefits for themselves," but not strikes called by others than the workers themselves. Nor did he approve the closed shop, maintenance of dues, or check-off.

The Association has the backing of Dr. George S. Benson, President of Harding College, in Searcy, Ark. Dr. Benson is a radio speaker and writes a "free enterprise" column for small-town weeklies. He harps constantly on the "persecution" of industry by the "government," the purity of large corporations and the evils of the New Deal, labor and radical propaganda. When I wrote as Thompson, Dr. Benson voluntarily boosted the VIA on the stationery of Harding College:

A group of Veterans here in Arkansas have formed a new labor union which guarantees the open-shop and prohibits the check-off and which allows an individual to work whether he wishes to belong to a union or not and which protects him from penalty in event he decides to quit a union. . . . I think you will relish knowing what is being done. . . . I believe this is a good organization and one that will make a contribution to the industrial field in America.

He enclosed the VIA handouts, one of which was a reprint of a radio talk in which Dr. Benson himself claimed to be "a long time friend of labor." Dr. Benson also presented me with a four-page leaflet written around "men of industry," "private management" and taxpayers who "shuddered" at high taxes and "regimentation." The propaganda he sent was printed on the stationery of Harding College and released by "C. D. Brown, Business Manager." Benson's purpose seemed to be to belittle organized labor and boost monopoly interests in the name of "free enterprise."

Why is propagandist Benson permitted to exploit a college for political ends? Is it the function of a college president to recom-

mend union-busting organizations to veterans? These are questions
which the student who intends to matriculate should ask. The Veterans Administration, which pays the college tuition of ex-GIs with
public funds, should also know the answer.

Another self-styled "union" in the South was the Veterans and
Patriots Federation of Labor, Inc., of Chattanooga, Tenn. To join
you didn't have to be a veteran or a working man, as long as you
were a "patriot" and opposed "foreigners" and unions. The Federation began business by publishing the following ad in Chattanooga
newspapers:

50 EX-SERVICEMEN

Preferable [*sic*] experienced in office work. Starting salary, $157 per
month, sick and retirement benefit. Must have reference and honorable
discharge. Apply Replacement Bureau. Veterans and Patriots Federation
of Labor.

Veterans who responded were merely told they were to "replace"
workers at Chattanooga steel mills. In many instances they didn't
know they were being used as strikebreakers until they arrived at
the plant. In another instance, the Federation sent white veterans
of World War II to break a Negro picket line at the Mascot Stove
Works. The Negroes were replaced at the last minute by whites,
and only this quick action by the CIO union averted a race riot.
As soon as I learned that the moving spirit behind this "union" was
Ulis Keith, I wrote him. He answered on March 4, 1946:

It cannot be said by the AFL, CIO, or any other unions that we are
not favorable to organized labor, [are] strikebreakers, scabs, etc. We are
not radicals but we do not believe in these many strikes that are wrecking
our nation. . . . Needless to say we are all veterans of World War II and
have all fought overseas.

"Is this a union or a 'racket'?" asked L. A. Lea, Secretary of the
International Association of Machinists Success Lodge 56. J. C.
Stafford of the Chattanooga Industrial Council called the Federation "a subservient company union and a union-busting propaganda
and lobbying concern." This Chattanooga prototype of the VIA was
short-lived. An exposé in the *News-Free Press* caused the phony

"veterans union" to fade out of the picture. It was, among other things, a sample of unfortunate public relations for industry.

Chattanooga's other super-patriot who's out to "save America" by knocking labor out of the American scene is Sherman A. Patterson, publisher of *The Militant Truth*. Patterson hates *all* organized labor, from Lewis up, but aims particular invective at the "alien-Communist-controlled CIO." Patterson has a new wrinkle—religion. The masthead of his monthly eight-page dope-sheet carries an open Bible super-imposed on a Cross and the legend "The Word of God," on one side. Splashed on the other side is an American flag and the legend, "Constitutional Americanism." It's devoted to "Interpreting Current Events from a Fundamental Christian and Constitutional American Viewpoint!"

A combination of Winrod, Bible-Belt Fundamentalism, flag-waving, and Red-and-labor-baiting make *Militant Truth* an irresistible potion for impressionable Southerners. Patterson "wows" them when he says: "We urge every person in America who LOVES THE LORD and who LOVES AMERICA to STAND UP and be counted ON THE FIRING LINE for CHRIST AND COUNTRY." It's made to order for anti-labor employers who want an open shop.

Patterson's favorite seems to be Samuel B. Pettengill. The June, 1946 issue of *Militant Truth* carried *three* articles by him. "Loyal Americans are rejoicing that Upton Close has again returned to the air waves," Patterson wrote and reprinted a column by Close. He rejoiced so much at Kenneth Goff's "Americanism" that articles of his were reprinted, too. Patterson could not overlook Harvey Springer's writings, nor Senator "Pappy" O'Daniel's articles hinting darkly at "Moscow-inspired" strikes. As might be expected, the Federal Council of the Churches of Christ is regarded as Communist.

Walter Steele, editor of the *National Republic*, and his friend Dr. Dan W. Gilbert, together with George A. Blasser, Steele's New York

representative, are perennial favorites with Patterson. One of the three appears in nearly every issue. Also reprinted are the outpourings of ex-Senator Reynolds and Gerald Smith. *Militant Truth* carries advertisements of Rev. Carl McIntire's anti-Catholic books, *The Rise of the Tyrant* and *Twentieth Century Reformation*. It also runs ads of the Constitutional Educational League, whose director, Joseph P. Kamp, was once associated with fascist Lawrence Dennis. Patterson sent me Kamp's booklets when I wrote, posing as a veteran. The Department of Justice is denounced as sympathizing with a "fifth column."

Patterson is a trouble-shooter. Whenever a Southern plant is threatened with a strike, he will rush batches of *Militant Truth* to the scene. On the eve of a National Labor Relations Board election his sheet appears mysteriously in the mailboxes of workers. The subscription is 35¢ a year in group lots. Spasmodically, his normal circulation of about 50,000 copies doubles.

Patterson spends most of his time travelling through the South's industrial areas hustling for business and group subscriptions. Some employers give him checks and the addresses of their workers. When an investigator suggested that the owner of a plant was having "union trouble," Patterson answered, "All he has to do is to send in the mailing list [and check] and I'll take care of the rest."

Out in San Francisco, the organization formerly styled the Veterans Union of America has changed its name to Society of World War II. This group once occupied a small office on Montgomery Street. Now that it has been refurbished as the Society of World War II, its headquarters are a twenty-room mansion on Jackson Street. Before Pearl Harbor the house was occupied by the Japanese Consul. The Society was said to be started by "four veterans recently returned from the South Pacific." Spark plug of the enterprise is Folsom Hayward, former Army Air Corps major. A sprinkling of veterans operate as fronts; the promoters actually seem to be bankers, advertising managers, business executives, a Hearst employee. All went well with them until Eric Webber exposed the Society in the San Francisco *Daily World* as a labor-baiting project.

An advertisement also served to launch the Veterans Union of America on its career:

146 Rooms to Let—Furnished

VETERANS UNION OF AMERICA

has furn. rooms in priv. homes available for servicemen, discharged veterans or their wives; registration fee $1. Apply 617 Montgomery. Rm. 408.

The bait brought veterans in droves. For a dollar you first were signed up as a member of the "union." More than 1,200 joined in four months. Membership campaign letters demanded: "Are you satisfied with the housing available to returning veterans? . . . Shall a veteran be compelled to join a labor union?" Out of every 100 so queried, Hayward claims, 95 answered No on the latter point. The letters also asked whether the GI Bill of Rights was "anything but a political hoax." Those who agreed were invited to "get aboard and help. . . . There is no greater force for good in America than the veterans of World War II, if only they get together. . . . IT IS LATER THAN YOU THINK."

One objective of the Society of World War II is "to espouse the maintenance of the Profit Motive and Free Enterprise in the American economic system." The Society opposed the FEPC and loans to Europe's devastated democracies. "World War II was fought to make America safe for the Union Racket," W. H. Brewer, Society official, says. When the extreme labor-baiting of the Society's radio program led to the banning of the broadcast from Station KGO, Hayward threatened to obtain a million signatures to a petition of protest. He failed. In his wrath, Hayward followed the usual nationalist line and denounced the American Veterans Committee, which had joined in a mass protest against the program, as "sponsored by a labor group dominated by Communists taking orders from the Kremlin." In spite of this, Hayward insists that the Society "has no axes to grind."

According to Eric Webber, the undercover organizer and coordinator of West Coast groups striving for the open shop is S. P. Bennett, a lieutenant of Merwin K. Hart's National Economic Council. Bennett was given the West Coast assignment in the summer of 1945, when Hart and a select number of America's leading anti-unionists and Roosevelt-is-worse-than-Hitler-and-Tojo fans met to plan a postwar strategy against organized labor. The Hart group is known as American Action, Inc.

Texas harbors two super-promoters who for a cash fee promise to save America from the Reds, the Federal Council of the Churches of Christ, the CIO, PAC and whatnot. Their main stock in trade is to sponsor in Southern states anti-union legislation advocating the closed shop. The prize characters are Lewis Valentine Ulrey and Vance Muse of Houston. Muse, the more aggressive, who is well over six feet tall, is dubbed Jumping Jumbo by labor circles. The two have been in business since 1936 playing rich industrialists as suckers and operating under the trade name Christian American Association, Inc. Like that of Patterson, their preachment is that it's against church principles to belong to a labor union. It's an old artifice but it has always worked among the gullible. It exploits fear psychology among the backwoods folk.

Ulrey is an old-time Winrod Fundamentalist who used to write regularly for *The Defender* such high-class patriotism as the following:

Human nature being what it is, it is not strange that the Germans decided against the Jews and in favor of Hitler. . . . Hitler put it up to the Germans to decide between Jewish ownership and domination of the country or domination and ownership by the ninety-nine percent German population.

Ulrey's other writings for the Christian American Association were equally acceptable to the Nazis, with the result that the March 1, 1938 issue of *World Service,* Goebbels' overseas organ, recommended the Ulrey-Muse project as 100 percent American. To make the record complete, I should add that back in 1936 Ulrey wrote an article in the *National Republic* in which the Federal Council of the Churches of Christ was described as "a screen from behind which to 'snipe' at Christian orthodoxy."

Ulrey claims to have been a former Democratic State Senator of Indiana, also a "geologist, engineer and oil producer." He struck it rich in greenbacks when he went to work for Maco Stewart, wealthy Galveston oil man, and took charge of his "anti-radical activities." In 1945 Texas newspapers exposed how Maco Stewart, chairman of the State Board of Education (also a foe of Homer Rainey, former president of the University of Texas who was ousted for his liberal views), employed Ulrey as secretary and assigned

to him the task of censoring books for State schools. Ulrey did his
job along "Christian, Fundamentalist" lines.

As for Vance Muse, his angel proved to be a wealthy Texas lum-
berman, now deceased, named John Henry Kirby. Muse's job in the
twenties and early thirties was in various capacities as "public relations counsel" and general crier for tax, tariff and managers' associations—all devoted to tax reduction, resistance to liberal movements, the stricturing of democracy, and of course, opposition to
organized labor. Kirby, according to Muse, "revered the Constitution as second in sacredness only to the Holy Bible" and contributed heavily to organizations which furthered the free-booting era.

Muse went after "big money" and got it. The 1936 Senate Lobby
Investigating Committee disclosed that his "sucker list"—as the
Committee called it—brought in $41,000. Many of his contributors
were members of the old Liberty League; John J. Raskob gave
$5,000 and the Du Pont family $10,000. Earlier, the 1930 Senate
Lobby Investigating Committee unanimously described Muse's
work with the American Taxpayers' League, Inc., and the Southern
Tariff League as "highly reprehensible." Over a period of four
years these two groups shook down the gullible for $860,754. Muse
claims he only got $24,434; his sister, $24,898 and her husband $14,-
958 for services rendered.

In recent years Muse has set out to "Americanize the Supreme
Court" by limiting membership in it to native-born citizens. A
lot of his money now comes in from rural, non-industrial farming
folk who shudder at the words "union" and "Communist." The
claim to fame of Ulrey and Muse is based on their sponsorship of
what they call Anti-Violence-in-Strikes and God-Given-Right-to-
Work legislation. The measures they advance oppose union organization and outlaw the closed shop. Through persistent, crafty public
promotion propaganda, and backed by anti-labor funds, the Texan
pair have succeeded in getting restrictive legislation passed in Mississippi, Arkansas, Florida and Alabama.

Extremely friendly to them has been Senator O'Daniel. Returning the compliment, Muse called O'Daniel "a Christian businessman who neither fears the financial buccaneer, the labor racketeer
nor the professional politician. When O'Daniel introduced an anti-
labor bill in Congress, it got just one vote—his own!

Following the Stewart-Ulrey publicity, the twin saviors from Texas went under cover for a while. Since the gubernatorial elections and the renewed labor drives in the South, however, they have resumed their activity and are riding high, cussing the CIO, the PAC and democracy with considerable relish and profit.

When I wrote to Muse, he not only made me a member of his Right-to-Work Club, but he sent me a stack of literature. Neatly clipped together and marked—"These 2 patriots expose the 'Smear Brigade,'"—were a leaflet by Upton Close and a reprint of an article by George Sokolsky, who was described as a "Splendid Jewish Gentleman." Sokolsky is one of several "good Jews" whom more than one fascist keeps up his sleeve and rolls out to show his "Christianity" and "tolerance."

When Walter Davenport interviewed Ulrey-Muse, Inc., for *Collier's* magazine and hinted that the Christian Americans were a modern version of the Ku Klux Klan, Muse replied:

Why, I helped drive the Klan out of Texas. However, the original Klan Reconstruction days did a lot of good. Maybe we need something like that now. I'm against it but it might be a good thing. . . . Christian American is the workingman's friend. . . . Don't let the atheistic Communists tell you different. They call me anti-Jew and anti-nigger. Listen. We like the nigger—in his place. . . . Good niggers, not these Communist niggers. Jews? Why, some of my best friends are Jews. Good Jews. . . .

A conspicuous attempt to shackle labor to the open shop is being made on a national scale by Cecil B. DeMille, Hollywood film director, and his DeMille Foundation for Political Freedom, of Los Angeles. The story of the inception of the Foundation is unusual. In the November, 1944 elections, California voters were to cast ballots for or against a proposed amendment to the State Constitution, which would have outlawed the closed shop. So drastic was the measure that it was opposed by Governor Earl Warren and church and business groups, as well as by labor.

A meeting of the Los Angeles Branch of the American Federation of Radio Artists (AFL affiliate union), of which DeMille was a member, also voted to oppose the proposition, and agreed unanimously to tax members $1 each for a fighting fund. DeMille refused to pay the assessment, protesting that he, a good "union man" (he hadn't attended a meeting in six years), was being ordered "to oppose a political proposition which I favored." His political liberty, he declared, was being infringed upon. Suspended from membership, according to the regular rules of the union, he went to court, where Judge Emmett H. Wilson ruled that AFRA "had in no way interfered with his political liberty . . . that he had been quite free to vote against Proposition 12 if he so desired." The Superior Court Judge upheld the union's right to levy assessments by due democratic process when convinced that a prospective law "was a threat to a union's existence." DeMille is appealing to a higher court.

DeMille retaliated with his Foundation. He and a group of like-minded lovers of unions have gone on a rampage to preserve America from "the overlords of political freedom." They scream that unions have denied DeMille his Constitutional liberties and trampled on his rights as an American. Which is, of course, an un-American distortion of the facts, but they are still pushing their program.

The stationery of the Foundation displays a cut of the Liberty Bell topped by the slogan, "Not one cent for tribute" (to labor unions). DeMille's backing is seemingly "big business." His self-perpetuating board of directors includes William M. Jeffers, President of the Union Pacific Railroad; Victor Rossetti, President of the Farmers' and Merchants' Bank; Y. Frank Freeman, motion picture executive; Willard W. Keith, director of a steamship company and four hotel corporations; Samuel M. Haskins, insurance company director; and Neil S. McCarthy, vice-president of a tool company. Brig. Gen. Amos Thomas is Executive Director. I wrote him and asked whether the group welcomed veterans. Thomas assured me: "As a veteran of both world wars, I am tremendously interested in securing as many veteran members as possible. . . . It is the

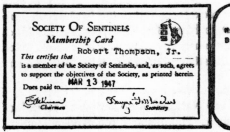

veteran groups we must look to if individual freedom is to be preserved in our land."

W. H. Zelinsky, Public Relations Director, wrote me that the program of the DeMille Foundation "is intended to be a militant one and no one probably is better fitted for it than returning servicemen." In May, 1946 General Thomas wrote me as Thompson, Jr.:

Our program [is] one of education. . . . When a former . . . Senator was here recently . . . at least one-third of his speech was taken from our material. The Senator explained he had heard . . . some of the dozen recordings which we have distributed to small groups. . . . We have distributed approximately 150,000 pieces of literature and had over 125 broadcasts from stations throughout the country, besides many addresses given by Mr. DeMille.

We are now preparing a rather extensive program, including a plan to interest high school seniors, and likewise their parents. . . . We expect to inaugurate very shortly a direct mail campaign which will reach thousands of citizens, and also to substantially augment our radio broadcasting. . . . These features require thousands of dollars, which we are in the process of raising.

But according to Mrs. Louise Roberts, sister of Upton Close, things haven't been going so well with the Foundation. She wrote me in May, 1946, in Close's absence, that he had "heard some good reports" on the Society of World War II. As for the DeMille Foundation, they had "known [it] ever since it was started. We had great hopes for this movement when it first started, but now we are not so sure." She blamed "subversive elements" which had "infiltrated."

Both the Foundation and Upton Close, however, have received high praise from the "very tolerant, kind and charitable" Dr. Jon A. Lovell of Los Angeles: "Let's keep our eye on Cecil B. DeMille, who is doing a great work throughout the country—giving people the 'lowdown' on certain labor racketeers and union leaders who are exploiting labor. My hat is off to him. May God increase his kind. . . . Upton Close is another gentleman you may watch . . . Let's back up such fearless, patriotic Christian gentlemen with our prayers and influence."

A smoother job is done by the National Association of Manufacturers. When I wrote to them as Thompson I received a lengthy letter from A. E. Whitehill, "Supervisor of Veteran Activities." It was a masterpiece of innocuous writing which said absolutely nothing. Nonetheless, it would flatter any ex-GI to receive a long personal letter from an official of the NAM.

Accepting Mr. Whitehill's invitation "to stop in at our New York office," I visited him at the sumptuous Rockefeller Center headquarters. Running a gauntlet of glamorous "Miss America" type employees, I found Mr. Whitehill to be a tall, blue-eyed, soft-spoken veteran of World War I and a member of the American Legion. He was very nice, very sympathetic, very cautious, and as innocuous as his letter. I got nothing out of our interview. I went back to the NAM literature to learn what the NAM fed the veteran.

An expensively printed booklet, *Competitive Enterprise Versus Planned Economy*, observed that industry "cannot be combined with government control and still function as competitive enterprise." It said that "planned economy" was "very alluring" and was all right for insurance, old age security and education, but that industry could thrive best without it. "Government control" was a very dangerous "ism." The booklet drew a picture of tyrannical "government interference." It said nothing about the enormous increase in profits, which in 1944 averaged 217.7 percent over 1936–39 for 1,743 major industrial firms. Major transport equipment manufacturers alone made a profit (before taxes) amounting to 1,469 percent of 1936–39; producers of lumber goods increased their profits by 1,110 percent over the same period.

Competitive Enterprise Versus Planned Economy was by H. W. Prentis, Jr., former Chairman of the Board of the NAM. Prentis has been a warm friend of John B. Snow, the "gentleman fascist," who in 1940 headed the labor-baiting, nationalistic League for Constitutional Government and sold the "educational" booklets of Japanese agent Ralph Townsend. Through Snow, Prentis met Merwin K. Hart, a kindred spirit. "Hope for the future of our Republic does not lie in more and more Democracy," Prentis once observed.

Prentis' booklet overlooked the continued abuses of a certain "big business" minority within the NAM, and its exploitation of human resources. It overlooked the well-known fact that those who have abused the privileges of capitalism are responsible for government regulation and are thus a main cause of so-called "bureaucracy" and the increased number of government employees. Such agencies as the Securities and Exchange Commission (SEC) would not exist if Wall Street speculators had not swindled the public with watered stock. The function of government is to protect the public.

Except for Prentis' pamphlet, which in effect pleaded for the resurrection of the "free-booting era" and private government, the NAM literature was good public relations. It showed how industry was helping the veteran readjust himself; it illustrated the work of the NAM veterans neighborhood committees and their methods of aiding handicapped veterans. Of course it said nothing about the NAM's policy of lifting all price controls and jacking up the price of veterans' homes, clothes, food and all-around living costs.

Principle I of the NAM policies, under "Labor Relations," stated:

Management and labor must deal with each other in a spirit of mutual respect, with full realization of their common interest, and these dealings should take place at the plant level where both parties have a first-hand knowledge of the issues involved.

If some NAM members actually followed this advice by leaving their mahogany desks for a tour of our slums, coal towns and textile-mill villages to see how millions of underprivileged Americans live, the experience would help them understand the social forces which make for a successful and dynamic labor movement. The extension of democracy to the humblest American worker would do more to restore post-war harmony than any other single factor.

From Chicago, the National Small Business Men's Association bombards the public with Prentis-type literature. I wrote them as Thompson and got a letter from President DeWitt Emery, with a series of booklets. *The Post-War Outlook for Young Business Men* was a reprint of a speech of Emery's before the Chicago Junior Chamber of Commerce. It began with a diatribe against the New Deal and ended with flag-waving. Another leaflet blamed "the financial plight of Britain" on the "New Deal's policy of deficit spending." Emery and his associates made a gloomy forecast for postwar America.

In Lincoln, Neb., L. L. Coryell, Sr. manages a group of small corporations. Every day "in a very personal way" he sees "five to ten of these dear boys"—servicemen. What does L. L. Coryell tell them?

Probably pretty much what he publishes in his weekly house organ, the *Morning Messenger*. In one issue he blamed "stolen records" for the fizzle of the Pearl Harbor political witchhunt which tried to whitewash Tojo, Inc. In another issue Coryell denounced the OPA as a tyrannical measure designed to stifle "free enterprise."

I wrote Mr. Coryell a short note. His answer filled more than two closely written pages. "Our government took you boys without any apology and then just dumped you back here without provisions for housing, etc." (He said nothing about the sabotaging by the NAM and real-estate profiteers and inflationists, of Federal attempts to build low-cost housing and keep prices within the veteran's income.) The rest was in the same vein. "So much of the advice the young men get about going to school is nothing," Coryell said, and complained: "Everyone has yelled for high wages. If you want 65 hours of work done now you have to pay for 100." Whatever the motive back of Coryell's advice to veterans, it probably doesn't help morale. With an almost self-conscious admission that he might be wrong, Coryell ended by saying, "My convictions are probably stronger than my reasoning."

Immediately after getting this letter I heard from Herbert U. Nelson, Vice-President of the National Association of Real Estate Boards, Washington, D. C. I had written Nelson as Thompson, stating that I hated "Communist labor racketeers." Nelson replied, "I have two sons who served, . . . and they feel the way you do. Your letter was most encouraging."

The propaganda of the National Association of Real Estate Boards was patterned after that of H. W. Prentis. It attacked government subsidies to assure low-cost housing for veterans. "We are fighting for the preservation of small business and freedom of opportunity," Nelson wrote. "I do not believe all of our veterans want the government to get into the housing business." Veterans want decent homes to live in, at prices they can afford to pay. That is imperative! When private industry insisted on charging exorbitant power rates, TVA competition forced prices down and made a paradise of arid land. If private industry and housing interests insist on profiteering, the alternative is for the Government to step in and keep its promise to the GI.

As the defeatist, anti-Administration barrage poured in, it seemed increasingly clear that it was part of a plan thoroughly to disillusion the veteran, a plan which exceeded normal political criticism and was aimed to reach a climax in the 1948 elections. The plans now in operation could influence more than 12,000,000 veterans. When the number of their parents, wives and other relatives is added to this, the figure reaches a formidable total.

In my search for those who give industry a black eye, I repeatedly crossed the trail of one of the most extreme. His organization was twice named as a "factor" in the mass indictments for seditious conspiracy. He himself acted as co-sponsor of Christian Front rallies. The Nazi *World Service* endorsed his writings. He was associated with the influential American fascist, Lawrence Dennis, and collaborated with an array of other native fascists. Nonetheless, Joseph P. Kamp, Chairman of the Constitutional Educational League, which has headquarters in New York City, continues to receive active support from "big business" elements who are too rock-ribbed to see the impending collapse of narrow, self-seeking economics.

Kamp is a short, squat, fleshy man, his squarish face pale, his expression cold and resentful. He talks from between his teeth in a grating voice. Kamp carries a cane for protection.

Super-patriot Joseph P. Kamp tries to win the ex-GI by quoting Senator O'Daniel's hysterical warnings.

Curious to know what Kamp was feeding veteran readers, I wrote him briefly as an ex-serviceman. He responded with eleven booklets (worth about $2.50), weighing two pounds, four ounces. It was the biggest collection of lie-packed trash I had received in a long time. One booklet, printed on cheap, yellowing paper, was an abusive tirade against Walter Winchell. It made the fantastic charge that Earl Browder (!) was an author of *Under Cover*.

The other booklets were no more accurate. According to one of them, Dr. Frank Graham, distinguished President of the University of North Carolina, was "Communist." So was the YMCA! Another booklet, *The Hell with G.I. Joe,* was prefaced with an excerpt from Senator W. Lee O'Daniel, alleging that New Dealers and others "in both the Democratic and Republican parties" were making our government a dictatorship. The paper-covered bullet went on for 16 pages, denouncing every phase of our economic, political and social life. The booklet was calculated to embitter the veteran and stir him to discontent. His natural reaction to it would be, "This country is going to the dogs."

One of Kamp's collaborators, a more important figure and politically on a par, is Merwin K. Hart, New York lawyer and President of the National Economic Council. Hart is a beloved figure to the nationalist political underworld. He started on his nationalist career with an article in Father Coughlin's *Social Justice* bearing his name, then appeared as the chairman of a rally sponsored by Christian Front elements. He visited Spain, where he spoke over the Falange radio. With that experience, Hart graduated to the role of an apologist in this country for Franco. On his return he wrote a book praising Franco's Falange and denouncing democracy as nothing more than Communism. As for fascism, he dismissed it as a "bogey." One phase of his "patriotic" activity before Pearl Harbor was that he recommended a friend of his, Jane Anderson, to acquaintances in Spain. She broadcast for the Spanish propaganda agency and was then picked up by Goebbels. GIs who fought in Germany cursed or laughed at her broadcasts as they lay in their dugouts and foxholes. Jane is now under indictment for treason.

Major George Fielding Eliot has termed the National Economic Council "one of the most dangerous influences in the United States."

Fostering hatred for democracy is a paying proposition. From a series of dingy offices, Hart has moved to a skyscraper suite in the

Empire State Building. Eyeing the veteran like a hawk, Hart called on subscribers to his *Economic Council Letter*, barely two months after V-J Day:

Will each of you send us the name and address of some veteran of your acquaintance, of World War II, whom you think would be interested in learning something about what is going on in the world today? We will send this man our publication for a number of months.

What happens when an ex-GI writes in saying that a "business friend" has asked him to write, as I did? Hart is a suspicious man. He asks questions, then sends around someone to investigate you personally. Here is his reply to my letter:

We will make it a point to get in touch with you the next time one of our people is in Buffalo. Enclosed are two or three Council letters that may interest you. What are you doing yourself? What is your occupation? What is your Congressional district, and who is your Congressman?

What has Hart fed his veteran readers? For one thing, he has blamed the New Deal for Pearl Harbor, with not a word against Tojo or Hitler. "Pearl Harbor," Hart wrote, "is likely to become the greatest scandal in the nation's history—a scandal that will throw the Teapot Dome incident completely into the shade."

Hart and his fellow brain-truster John T. Flynn, former New York Chairman of the America First Committee and a prolific writer for the magazines, tried hard to make this stick. They published booklets, releases, bulletins—hundreds of thousands of copies. Behind Flynn has been the machine of Hart's National Economic Council, which has sponsored the publication of booklets by Flynn, with its enormous mailing lists and extensive contacts among America's most economically totalitarian and politically backward-looking circles.

Hart, who was one of the founders of the America First Committee, stated at a Senate hearing a few months before Pearl Harbor that "an unfriendly attitude on the part of the United States drove Japan into the arms of the Axis."

Both Hart and Flynn opposed national preparedness for an inevitable war. While they shouted "war-monger" at men like Willkie, Roosevelt and William Allen White, who foresaw the danger, the armies of Hitler and the Japanese were already under way on the road of world conquest. While I do not accuse these men of being agents of any foreign power, their work tied in with one of the main strategic plans behind Goebbels' propaganda, with which he had a large measure of success. America Firsters like Flynn and Hart lulled many Americans into feelings of false security. They shared and taught an ostrich-like attitude which contributed largely to our being surprised at Pearl Harbor. Hart sees Communism everywhere and writes as if there were no other danger:

There is Communist propaganda in much of our daily press. There is Communism in the armed services. . . . There is Communism on the radio. There is Communism in the Protestant churches, largely under the direc-

GENERAL COMMITTEE
MASS MEETING FOR AMERICANISM AND NEUTRALITY
WAR FILM "SPAIN IN ARMS"

PROMINENT SPEAKERS

SEVENTH REGIMENT ARMORY
PARK AVENUE AT 66TH STREET
NEW YORK

—

FEBRUARY 19. 1939 AT 4:00 P. M.

MERWIN K. HART
CHAIRMAN
HILDRETH MEIERE
TREASURER
JOHN EOGHAN KELLY
SECRETARY

PARTIAL LIST OF MEMBERS
ANNE MORGAN
FRANCIS X. TALBOT. SJ
DR EDWARD LODGE CURRAN
REV CHARLES J. MULLALLY
LESTER M. GRAY
HOFFMAN NICKERSON
PATRICK SCANLON
DR. FRANCIS X. CONNOLLY
CHARLOTTE C. STARR
THEODORE STARR. JR
MARGARET H. BACHE
MARCELINO GARCIA RUBIERA
WILLIAM R. WHITE
ARTHUR T. O'LEARY
ROSS HOFFMAN
REV. COBMAB SHAUGHNESSY
WARD CLARKE
GEORGE A. TIMONE
A. D. SIMPSON
THOMAS J. HIGGINS. SJ
KNOWLTON DURHAM
WALTER M. WALTERS
PHILIP M. ALLEN
THOMAS R. HODGE
JOSEPH P. KAMP
JAMES E. BROOKS
REV THOMAS F. HOLDEN
DR. JOSEPH F THORNING
H. L. SMITH
REV. THEOPHANE MacGUIRE
ROBERT C. PATTON
REV. EDWARD L. HUGHES
CATHERINE P. BALDWIN
DR. H. MacALLISTER GRIFFITHS

COMMITTEE OFFICE
ROOM 417
17 EAST 42ND STREET
NEW YORK CITY
—

To All Distributors of
Social Justice Magazine.

As chief distributor of Social Justice Magazine I am assisting the Committee to make a big success of the Mass Meeting described above.

There are being sent you herewith - under separate cover - some copies of the bulletin about the meeting. If it is possible for you to put one of them in each copy of your magazine this week, it will be very helpful to the Cause, and the Committee will greatly appreciate it.

Yours very truly,

Bernard T. D'Arcy

Bernard T. D'Arcy.

In 1939 Hart was chairman of a pro-Franco rally sponsored largely by Christian-Front type elements. Some of the members got on the list innocently, but among those who must have known what the meeting was all about were John Eoghan Kelly, convicted Franco agent; Rev. Edward Lodge Curran, Joseph Kamp and Robert Caldwell Patton, former editor of *The Patriot Digest.* Bernard T. D'Arcy was a leading henchman of Father Coughlin.

tion of the Federal Council of the Churches of Christ in America. It is cunningly and craftily handled. . . . Gentlemen of the Congress, you probably have little time to save this Republic and the liberties of its citizens. For God's sake, act!

In keeping with his "Park Avenue" nationalist tradition, Hart engages high-tone literary figures to write book reviews. When his offices were small and dingy Hart used to do the writing himself. Later Albert Jay Nock served him. After Nock's death Rose Wilder Lane took over. She's a novelist, formerly a Communist "at heart," she said, though "not a member of the Communist Party." For a while she lived in the Soviet Republic of Georgia, Stalin's birthplace. Her political leanings have now turned in the extreme opposite direction and she now dispenses her peculiar wisdom on books which fit into Hart's nationalist scheme.

I wrote Miss Lane as Robert Thompson, Jr. Her lengthy letters made little sense. Her extreme individualism and extreme *laissez faire* attitude have seemingly alienated her from events in this world. "I can tell you," she wrote in March, 1946, "that when Americans were ordered to apply for ration cards, I did not do it. . . . What I did was to live on this little piece of land, and raise my own food from it." Could millions in New York, Chicago, Los Angeles have done the same?

She describes her philosophy as the "restrained anarchy of capitalism." Her booklets plead for the banishment of all regulations by government. She's even got it in for the Danbury, Conn., Public Service Commission, which regulates the number of taxicabs in town. "It is tyranny," she says, "it gives Jones the authority over you; it reduces you to the status of a child or a slave."

When I wrote to her under another pseudonym, Miss Lane in a letter recommended the outlandish Society of Sentinels, and sent me John W. Scoville's booklet, "The Theory of Collective Bargaining." She sent "Thompson" "Thought Starters Regarding Free Enterprise & Why," by the Consumer Research Staff of General Motors. In turn, Henry Grady Weaver of that staff issues a brochure on Miss Lane entitled "Portrait of a Fighting Lady" and sends gift copies of her booklet, *Give Me Liberty*.

Hart, together with Upton Close, has championed jailbird Tyler Kent. Readers of the *Economic Council Letter* were fed another fantastic story: "There is strong suspicion that the messages intercepted by Tyler Kent would disclose that Roosevelt had conspired to get the United States into the European war, just as John Flynn says he did to get us into the Pacific war."

John T. Flynn made this irresponsible charge in his booklet, *The Final Secret of Pearl Harbor,* in which he wrote: "It was Roosevelt who personally managed the whole crisis. It was Roosevelt who bottled the fleet in Pearl Harbor. It was Roosevelt who stripped the base of its defenses. . . . Roosevelt, . . . who was now assured of the attack which would bring him safely into the war, went off to Warm Springs to enjoy the Thanksgiving Holiday."

In *The Truth about Pearl Harbor,* Flynn charged that Kimmel and Short had been "crucified in order to shield the guilt of the President." The isolationist and nationalist press from coast to coast ate up these totally unsupported statements by a man who was reputed to be a reliable investigator. In July, 1946 the report of the full-scale Congressional Pearl Harbor Investigating Committee refuted Flynn's findings. The majority report found:

Beginning in 1931 Japan embarked on a career of conquest no less ambitious nor avowed than that of the Nazis. . . . The story of our negotiations with the Empire of Japan during the year 1941 epitomizes the traditional purpose of the United States to seek peace where compatible with national honor. . . . [Tojo's] Government launched the infamous attack on Pearl Harbor while instructing her ambassadors in characteristic duplicity to maintain the pretense of continuing negotiations. It is [therefore] concluded that the diplomatic actions of the United States provided no provocation whatever for the attack by Japan. [Pp. 47–9]

Both Admiral Kimmel and General Short have insisted they received no information that Hawaii was to be attacked. Yet commanders in the field cannot presume to expect that they will be advised of the exact time and place an enemy will attack or indeed that their particular post will be attacked. As outpost commanders it was their responsibility to be prepared against surprise and the worst possible contingency. . . . That Admiral Kimmel and General Short were supplied enough information as reasonably to justify the expectation that Hawaiian defenses would be alerted to any military contingency is irrefutable. [Pp. 155–6]

In Flynn's writings one finds little criticism of the Japs and their lengthy preparations for Pearl Harbor, of Hitler's aggressions, or of the Hitler-Tojo pact. His virtual whitewash of the Axis and his relentless attacks on the Administration endeared him to the nationalist political underworld from coast to coast. Flynn's fame spread overseas. His defeatist pamphlet, *The Truth about Pearl Harbor*, was published by the Strickland Press in Glasgow. Arnold Leese, who headed the Imperial Fascist League, so admired Flynn's effort that he became one of its leading distributors, selling it for 8d together with such Leese specialties as *Jewish Ritual Murder, Bolshevism Is Jewish* and the *Protocols*. Leese sent books freely to American nationalists, and I have authenticated instances in which Flynn's pamphlet arrived in a bundle of Imperial Fascist League literature on which the swastika was prominently displayed.

Since he first became New York chairman of the America Firsters, Flynn has been admired by nationalists. His stock rose still higher when in 1941 he demanded the impeachment of the President, which the Bund had been urging for some time. *Social Justice* cited his views as those of a "noted economist," Rev. Winrod printed an abridged version of *The Truth about Pearl Harbor*. When Flynn denounced Dumbarton Oaks and called the UNO an "international monstrosity," when he attacked the Bretton Woods agreement for international currency stabilization as a "boon-doggling" experiment by "collectivists," the nationalist vermin press quoted him widely. On January 18, 1946, Gerald Smith issued a manifesto to "a group of leading nationalists":

You are among those who enjoy the respect and confidence of millions of Nationalists in America. I challenge you to join with such men as John T. Flynn, Upton Close, Colonel Robert McCormick, General Robert Wood [former national chairman of the America First Committee], Merwin K. Hart and Sam Pettengill in the formation of a new dynamic crusading Nationalistic political committee. If you will accept this challenge such a committee will sweep the nation. . . . Yours for the saving of America before it is too late.

It is interesting to note the name of Colonel Robert McCormick, publisher of the Chicago *Tribune*, given high rank by Smith as he surveyed the field. Far more powerful than the strange nationalist bulletins, papers and magazines which flourish so amazingly in postwar America, the *Tribune*, like the other two papers which form the so-called McCormick-Medill-Patterson newspaper axis—the

New York *Daily News* and Washington *Times-Herald*—have readily brought certain parallel views into millions of American homes together with the sports news, household hints and circulation-building comics. Though Colonel McCormick of the *Tribune* interests himself in military matters,* his newspaper went all out before Pearl Harbor in the America First appeasement movement, opposing the passage of Lend-Lease, the Conscription Act, and other defense measures.

It was an American newspaper's democratic right, of course, to oppose defense measures even at a time when Hitler and Hirohito were arming to the teeth and American troops, on maneuvers, were using dummy tanks and antique rifles. But events proved that it was mistaken policy. On August 21, 1942, the Nazi short-wave radio praised the *Tribune, Daily News* and *Times-Herald* as "true American papers." It wasn't the first such experience for the *Tribune,* which was recommended by Goebbels' bulletin, *World Service,* as early as 1935, together with the strictly Bundist *Chicagoer Weckruf.*

It would seem that the science of protecting military secrets has continued to advance, but that the *Tribune* had to learn the hard way. A few days before Pearl Harbor it published confidential figures and plans prepared by the War Department in order to cope with possible national emergencies. Secretary of War Stimson denounced the paper's use of the material as showing "lack of loyalty and patriotism." Six months after Pearl Harbor the *Tribune* published a "dope story" on the Battle of Midway which outraged the Navy Department. The Japs could deduce from it that we had ways of getting advance information on their naval strength and dispositions—a priceless advantage. They changed their codes and scrapped their plans.

* On February 20, 1942, Colonel McCormick wrote to a correspondent: "You do not know it, but the fact is that I introduced the R.O.T.C. into the schools; that I introduced machine guns into the army; that I introduced mechanization; I introduced automatic rifles; I was the first ground officer to go up in the air and observe artillery fire. Now I have succeeded in making that the regular practice in the army. I was the first to advocate an alliance with Canada. I forced the acquiring of the bases in the Atlantic Ocean.

"On the other hand I was unsuccessful in obtaining the fortification of Guam; in preventing the division of the navy into two oceans. . . . I did get the marines out of Shanghai, but was unsuccessful in trying to get the army out of the Philippines."

Referring to the mass sedition trials in a speech before the annual convention of Rotary International at Reading, Pa., on April 18, 1944, Colonel McCormick himself declared, "I regret that a trial is being carried on in Washington of people of no political consequence, that outrages every American conscience. We should petition Congress to correct this national disgrace."

Instead, twenty-four Berks County, Pa., veterans' organizations, including units of the Legion, Marine Corps League and Jewish War Veterans, and the Combined Veterans Council, passed a joint resolution which said in forthright terms:

Though we accord to Mr. McCormick his right of free speech, we reserve to ourselves the right to point out that we believe his utterances are inimical to the basic American principle for which our organizations were founded. There is no criticism of our enemies anywhere in his talk, and we consider his speech a reflection on the integrity of constituted authority, especially our Courts, and tends to create disunity and lessening of morale, and therefore, likely to interfere with the successful prosecution of the war.

John O'Donnell, Washington columnist for the New York *Daily News* and Washington *Times-Herald,* sometimes comes up with conclusions strongly reminiscent of the nationalist line. O'Donnell's pen, which so staunchly defended Tyler Kent, ridiculed the San Francisco Conference as being "as phony as a seven dollar bill." O'Donnell reached a low in vilification when on November 21, 1945 he wrote in the *Daily News:*

As it now stands, the evidence builds up to the simple brutal fact that F.D.R., the Big Brain, through blind stupidity and an obsession that Father knows best, was directly and personally responsible for the blood and disaster of Pearl Harbor. . . .

And this writer looks forward to the day when he can hitch up his chair, sharpen his reportorial pencil and sit down in the press row of the criminal court weighing the guilt or innocence of the U.S. war-mongers. We think it can happen here—and will!

In a broadcast a few days later Mayor LaGuardia of New York attacked the *News* for this article, calling it "an insult to every American." The final majority report of the Congressional Pearl Harbor Investigating Committee imputed no blame whatsoever to President Roosevelt for Pearl Harbor. In another column, O'Donnell blamed Jews for the removal of General Patton. He had to retract that one. "On the evidence," he said in apology, "our statements were untrue."

Merwin K. Hart was a founder of the America First Committee. He is also a founder of the super-secret, super-patriotic body known as American Action, Inc., "a militant movement to defeat the PAC." This organization is so unpublicized that some officials of Hart's National Economic Council know little about it. Inquiries at Hart's office are received with a blank stare. But sitting in an inner office is a Col. Edward D. Gray, reserve Army Air Force officer and a resident of Bellport, N. Y. The Eastern management of American

---

O'Donnell "Regrets"

By JOHN O'DONNELL

Washington, D. C., Oct. 18.—On Oct. 3 this column attributed the removal of Gen. George S. Patton Jr. from his command of the U. S. 3d Army and as military administrator of Bavaria to pressure applied by influential members whose racial background was Jewish. Their antagonism to Patton, it was stated, came from the slapping by Patton of a soldier hospitalized in Sicily during the Summer campaign of 1943.

The slapping was described as accompanied by derogatory references to the victim's Jewish origin.

After careful investigation we have determined that the one identified soldier whom Patton slapped is Charles H. Kuhl of Mishawaka, Ind. He is not a Jew, but of German extraction. He is a member of the Nazarene Church, akin to the Methodist.

On the evidence, our statements were untrue.

We regret having made them.

By JOHN O'DONNELL

Washington, D. C., July 2.—President Truman has asked for the resignations of four members of the Supreme Court—an action never before taken in the history of the republic.

The four members—all appointed by the late Franklin Delano Roosevelt are:

Associate Justice Hugo L. Black
Associate Justice Robert H. Jackson
Associate Justice Felix Frankfurter
Associate Justice Frank Murphy

White House Says No

Washington, D. C., July 2 (U.P).—Charles G. Ross, White House press secretary, was asked tonight to comment on published reports that President Truman had requested verbally the resignations of Supreme Court Justices Hugo L. Black, Robert H. Jackson, Frank Murphy and Felix Frankfurter.

Ross called the reports "fantastically untrue" and "absolutely, unqualifiedly false."

Ross said Truman had not seen or talked to Frankfurter since becoming President.

Readers of the July 2, 1946 issue of the New York *Daily News* were amazed to read—on the same page as the story itself—a denial of O'Donnell's unfounded charges against the Justices of the Supreme Court. The White House nipped the phony story immediately after it was hatched.

As for O'Donnell's story attributing General Patton's removal to the General's having slapped a Jew, it was just an incident that he had to pass off with "regret." Most newspapers would immediately censure or fire a bad reporter who had twice committed such glaring errors in fact. But John "Regret" O'Donnell's position with the isolationist *Daily News* seems quite secure.

Action, Inc., is under his direct charge; national offices are listed as being located on South LaSalle Street, Chicago.

A "declaration of principles" was adopted in a quietly organized convention of American Action, Inc., held July 30 and 31, 1945, in Chicago. Long-range strategy was laid to defeat labor and curb America's progressive forces. Plans extended to the 1948 elections. This new economic vigilante bund issued a twelve-page booklet, outlining its purposes, of which I have a rare original copy. "Sustaining" membership is $100, but "any amount up to $5,000" will be accepted. "Security," the group explains, "means enslavement," because "organized minorities promised 'security' to the 'common man' in Russia, Italy and Germany." The hysterical declamation winds up with: "If you are willing to lose your liberty, and become a ward of a totalitarian state, 'don't stick your neck out.' Just be 'passive.' Await 'liquidation.'"

The national council of American Action, Inc., includes Harold N. Moore, merchandising executive, Los Angeles; Malcolm McDermott, Professor of Law, Duke University, Durham, N. C.; James E. McDonald, Commissioner of Agriculture, Austin, Texas; James H. Gipson, President, Caxton Printers, Ltd., Caldwell, Idaho. W. Homer Hartz, of Chicago, is treasurer of American Action.

According to Eugene Segal of the Cleveland *Press*, who wrote a series of articles on the group, the meeting at Chicago's Palmer House at which American Action was organized was attended by about 40 persons, including Merwin K. Hart, acting as chairman, and Upton Close, who the following February went on the air over a big network as commentator for Hart's National Economic Council. Smaller conferences were held at the Drake Hotel. The meeting was arranged, Segal states, by Salem Bader, an associate of Close:

Bader also had an opportunity while in Chicago to appear as principal speaker at the June 1 session of the convention of "We, the Mothers," at the LaSalle Hotel. Presiding was Mrs. Lyrl Clark Van Hyning, head of these "mothers" and one of the most vocal hate propagandists.

Bader told the women that our war with Germany was started by antiGerman films made in Hollywood with President Roosevelt's approval.

Among the men who attended the Chicago meeting, besides Hart and Close, Segal reported, were John T. Flynn; DeWitt Emery,

Akron printer and head of the National Small Business Men's Association; Sam Pettengill of the Committee for Constitutional Government; William H. Regnery, Chicago industrialist, former America Firster and former treasurer of Earl Southard's nationalist Citizens U.S.A. Committee; Col. Charles Vincent of Chicago, whose American Foundation, a nationalist fund-raising project, advertised in *We, the Mothers'* anti-Semitic sheet, *Women's Voice; A.* Dwight Nims of Los Angeles, former executive secretary of the National League of Mothers and Women of America; and Thomas N. Creigh, Chicago corporation lawyer and head of the Chicago branch of Hart's National Economic Council *; William A. Larner, Jr.; R. E. Minnis; and Maurice F. Franks. Pledges totalling $300,000 were made, and more promised "as needed."

AMERICAN ACTION

* * * is a militant movement, local and national in scope, carefully planned by Democrats, Republicans and Independents.

Its Program

1. To organize the great *majorities* of the Right more effectively than alien-minded radicals have organized the vociferous *minorities* of the Left;

2. To meet head-on the CIO-PAC and its anti-American collaborationists by openly challenging and exposing their terroristic tactics, their smears and their deceits;

3. To purge both major parties of opportunist leadership that sells out American principles for minorities' votes;

4. To protect from smear and political reprisal party leaders and public officials who uphold American principles, and drive out those who compromise American principles.

Economic Council Sponsors
UPTON CLOSE
on Mutual Network

1. Will each of you send us the name and address of some veteran of your acquaintance, of World War II. whom you think would be interested in learning something about what is going on in the world today? We will send this man our publications for a number of months.

These excerpts (except for the two at bottom) are from Hart's super-secret booklet on American Action, Inc. *Extreme lower left:* Slip attached to literature of the National Economic Council. *Extreme lower right:* In a form letter, the Council announces a network program.

* Creigh has moved in the hierarchial core of Chicago's nationalist circles. Although he belongs to the "Park Avenue" set he, like Hart, on occasion descends to a "democratic" level within the nationalist orbit. On August 21, 1943 Creigh spoke for Earl Southard's Citizens U.S.A. Committee and he attended its meetings, notably the one on October 27, 1943, rubbing elbows with Chicago's confirmed hate-mongers.

Certain members of American Action, Inc. were formerly associated with the American National Democratic Committee, founded in February, 1944 to support "Republican nominees." Among the founders were William J. Goodwin, treasurer, associated with the Coughlinite American Rock Party in Queens County, N. Y., and Robert M. Harriss, long recognized as an ardent supporter of Father Coughlin.

According to the findings of the Special Committee to Investigate Presidential, Vice-Presidential, and Senatorial Campaign Expenditures in 1944, the American National Democratic Committee held a convention in June, 1944, in Chicago. Among the speakers were Eugene Talmadge, Senator Wilbert Lee O'Daniel, former Congressman Martin L. Sweeney of Cleveland, and John O'Connor (a political friend of Sam Pettengill), who later became an official of the Democrats-Vote-Republican crowd. Pettengill praised O'Connor and his "flint-like courage" in a lengthy letter published in *Social Justice* on September 5, 1938.

It's bad news for the veteran who thought he fought for a democratic world.

One of Hart's warmest friends is Rev. Carl McIntire, the Collingswood Fundamentalist preacher. Hart recommends McIntire's book, *The Rise of the Tyrant*, as "must reading." In it McIntire reaches into the Bible to justify the "basis of our private enterprise system and the validity of the profit motive." He damns the Federal Council of the Churches of Christ in America as "Communist." The phrase "common man," he tells us, "is an innocent-sounding term, but it is filled with all the tyranny of State control." The word "brotherhood" is in the same category. And behind "liberty" and "democracy" is the sinister shadow of a "planned society," says McIntire.

In another spiritual work, *Twentieth Century Reformation,* McIntire defamed the Roman Church as "this false religion" (page 92); and inquired, "Is the Mass Christian? Surely we could not call the Inventions of Rome Christian. Men who believe these teachings of the Roman Church are without saving faith."

I saw a copy of this book on the desk of Howard Kiroack, once a friend of Lambert Fairchild, with whom he severed relations, and now Executive Director of the Laymen's National Committee, Inc. (formerly the National Committee for Religious Recovery). The Committee announces that its purpose is to "promote religious recovery," and encourage "attendance at Sunday Schools." Actually, it serves as a religious front to advance the viewpoints of "big business" interests. Incorporation papers in New York show that one of the Committee's directors was George U. Harvey, former Borough President of Queens, who was affiliated with Coughlinite Christian Front circles. Another was Lambert Fairchild.

My first interview with Kiroack was in 1941. At that time John T. Flynn was being attacked for his isolationist views. Kiroack told me that Flynn had asked him to investigate the "smears." Why Flynn should have gone to Kiroack was not clear, but Kiroack said that he had recommended Joseph P. Kamp.

"Do you know Kamp?" I asked.

"I know Joe very well," Kiroack answered. "He's a darn swell fellow." This interview took place on August 7, 1941, at Kiroack's office in the Murray Hill Hotel. My detailed report, made from notes which I made immediately after an earlier interview with him, on April 1, read:

Suddenly [Kiroack] asked me to leave the room with him. His secretary had come in and we were talking within earshot. So we went out and sat in the lobby. Kiroack grew confidential. He said he had once headed the Guardsmen of America, a secret fraternal order. "When?" I asked. "Back in 1931," he answered. . . .

He then told me of his plans for reviving the Guardsmen of America.

"We intend to wrap the American flag around the ritual," he said, "make it emotional, actually squeeze the American flag so it'll squeak." Kiroack said that he and I would go to some hotel and write out the new ritual. He said that with an organization of 100,000 we could all tell Roosevelt to "go to hell."

Late in October, 1945 my interest in Kiroack was revived through a statement by Danton Walker, New York *Daily News* columnist, who said that a new, patriotic veterans' organization with an open-shop program would soon make its appearance. I wrote Walker and he answered: "The American Federation of Independent Citizens is located in the Vanderbilt Hotel, 34th Street and Park Avenue. Address your communication to the attention of Howard Kiroack."

I wrote Kiroack as Robert Thompson, Jr., saying I was "coming" from Buffalo and would like to meet him. My appearance had changed since *Under Cover* days. Would he recognize me? I decided to cross that bridge if and when I came to it.

On November 15, 1945 I took the subway downtown and interviewed Kiroack at the swanky Vanderbilt Hotel. Kiroack received me alone. As he talked on the telephone, I took out some folded notepaper and a pencil, which I used throughout our interview (unnoticed by him because his desk was between us) to jot down notes as he spoke. I asked Kiroack about the American Federation of Independent Citizens.

"The idea came while I was lunching with some businessmen," he began. "I told 'em that the white-collar office workers and the professional men were not organized. They have no one to look out for them. They are paying tribute to labor unions. So these businessmen asked me to go to work and organize the unorganized whitecollar men."

I asked Kiroack how veterans figured in on the scheme.

"The Federation of Independent Citizens will be headed by veterans of World War II," he explained. "The officers will be veterans. We'll have to pick them carefully. When they speak, these men will be listened to with respect because they are veterans."

"How about finances?" I asked.

"Oh, the industrialists will have to put up the money. It's their show. If they want labor to run the country, it's their business. I have my job here. I'm doing all right." (Kiroack's salary during 1945 was $8,040.) "But it's the industrialists who had better do something or they'll lose their business." Kiroack's plan was to insert an advertisement in 2,200 newspapers and start chapters all over the country. "It'll take $250,000 to get it going," he said. "Unless we do something on a big scale, this country is going to go national socialist."

Kiroack voluntarily changed the subject and said he was seeking a "high-pressure evangelist. He doesn't have to be well-known as long as he's got the stuff. We'll build him up. We can do that. We'd want this speaker to go into a community and take it over, stir the bowels out of them."

As Kiroack warmed up and began indiscriminately to call loyal Americans "Communist," à la Merwin Hart, I asked what he thought of Bishop George Bromley Oxnam, President of the Federal Council of the Churches of Christ in America. "He's a rank Communist," Kiroack said with feeling.

I learned that Kiroack worked closely with Merwin K. Hart. I discovered this by writing Kiroack from another city, this time posing as a "veteran" with a Germanic name. I received no answer. But on February 13 Merwin K. Hart wrote me on his "undercover" stationery. It was marked "Room 7501" and bore only the Council's address and telephone number. Hart wrote cautiously: "Answering your letter of January 28th addressed to the Laymen's National Committee and referred to us, I wish to say that in the near future we will be able to make a constructive suggestion to you." This was my first indication that Kiroack was apparently sharing with Merwin K. Hart the task of "organizing the unorganized white-collar men." Later I gathered that Kiroack had given up his veterans' project and was sticking close to his less explosive religious work.

In 1945 the Laymen's National Committee gave its Annual Award of Merit to William Randolph Hearst, on the ground that Hearst had "stimulated religious thinking." Rear Admiral Reginald R. Belknap,* U.S.N., retired, is Chairman of Kiroack's Committee, which "neither solicits nor accepts contributions from any church or church organization." It doesn't have to. My notes show that Kiroack said ninety percent of his contributions "came from corporations."

My letters written as Thompson, anti-Communist, "free-enterprise" veteran, received the most lavish response and the most solicitous letters from one of the country's most powerful groups engaged in the dissemination of super-conservative literature. I wrote four letters to Frank Gannett's Committee for Constitutional Government and received an answer from Gannett, two from Pettengill, and three from Sumner Gerard, Treasurer. I also received 51 assorted pieces of literature, weighing nearly three pounds and ranging from a two-page leaflet to a 320-page book. Apparently all veterans who write in get about the same dosage.

The consignment included Samuel B. Pettengill's book, *Smoke*

---

* The Admiral has a fine military and patriotic record, but the sad fact is that he also served on the "Board of Governors" of Coughlinite Allan Zoll's American Patriots, Inc., together with Mrs. Elizabeth Dilling and A. Cloyd Gill, former associate of Joseph P. Kamp.

Screen, which on its fiist page lays down the irresponsible thesis: "This book is written to demonstrate that we are moving *toward* National Socialism. . . . The New Deal is fundamentally fascist." By Pettengill and one Paul C. Bartholomew was another book called *For Americans Only,* which "picks up from where *Smoke Screen* left off." It reiterated, "This book shows how the New Deal is taking America into national-socialism." In a final petulant blast, it charged, "The New Deal Party is European." Pettengill based the charge on emergency relief projects such as the Civilian Conservation Corps, which during the depression years helped keep depression victims from starving. He denounces TVA, the miracle project which is helping rebuild the South. He denounces the Banking Acts of 1933 and 1935. The 1933 act reorganized insolvent banks, which had robbed countless Americans of their savings. The second compelled banks to join the Federal Reserve System, which guaranteed the savings of depositors up to $5,000. Both measures were answers to abuses by an unscrupulous minority who placed the dollar before human welfare. Does Pettengill condone them?

Pettengill's syndicated column, "Inside Your Congress," goes to 8,000 "principal business executives" and "daily papers from coast to coast." The Committee for Constitutional Government boasts that it reaches 4,000,000 readers weekly. During the prolonged automobile strike, the National Committee to Aid Families of General Motors Strikers, Inc. was organized to meet the urgent need of feeding the large families of strikers during the winter months. The Treasury Department ruled that contributions were deductible from income tax. A nonpartisan board, including Republican ex-Governor Harold Stassen and Democrat Harold Ickes, were among its directors. Pettengill ridiculed the misery of strikers whose limited savings were dwindling, whose children needed or would need the necessities of life. With biting sarcasm, Pettengill wrote:

But why stop with strikers? . . . Treat all Americans alike, I say. Don't limit this bonanza to strikers. Humanitarianism Unlimited! Let that be our motto. And think of all the lawyers' fees organizing "Committees of Loving Children to Aid Mrs. Fanny Thinpurse, Widow, Incorporated."

The Constitution of the United States, which I also received from Pettengill's office, was a 320-page tome by Thomas J. Norton, printed on cheap paper for mass distribution to servicemen. It went on in the usual vein, but this time the New Deal was portrayed as unconstitutional. Pettengill had written a special introduction slanted at servicemen. "In the hands of the 13,000,000 veterans . . . who served in World War II rests in large part the future destinies of our country," he said. It seems to me doubtful that the political judgment of a man who orders 100 copies of Rev. Terminiello's hate-mongering leaflet and encloses his check for it should be relied on by the open-minded veteran.

The Committee's literature is used in turn, for example, by Claude Buchanan Smith, director of the Christocrats, a Detroit "patriot" group which advertised its wares in *Women's Voice*. As Thompson, Jr., I wrote Smith my usual nationalist-veteran letter and on May 27 received a bulky package. Atop the pile of "patriotic" literature was the May 15, 1946 release of the Committee for Constitutional Government bearing, in stencil, Smith's name and address. It urged the reader to help Pettengill's column "reach this year's goal of 100,000," pleading,

If you have not yet contributed personally, and/or bought literature, DO SO NOW. We must have the help of tens of thousands of new supporters. Have companies in which you are interested buy and distribute to stockholders, workers, suppliers, Norton books on the Constitution, Pettengill of "The Man on the Street" [another Pettengill propaganda leaflet], who can be converted to the friend of private enterprise.

In addition to the Committee literature, Smith sent me:

1. The March, 1946 issue of Homer Maertz' Jew-baiting bulletin, *Dispatch*.

2. The March 23, 1946 issue of Court Asher's *The X-Ray*, alleging that Jews were "herding us," and carrying Gerald Smith's weekly column.

3. The May 17, 1946 issue of Rev. William L. Blessing's *Showers of Blessing*, alleging that "the Jews are Communists."

4. Two Christocrat leaflets, one of which, on "Monkey Business," was "published to promote clear thinking by Republicans so no BIG APE will be able to make monkeys of them."

Claude Smith also inclosed his 24-page booklet entitled *Political Christianity for the Republican Party*. Its gist seemed to be the recommendation that the Jews be smeared as a campaign policy. Smith's letter to me left no doubt of his feelings. One particularly genteel paragraph read as follows:

I had a argument with a damn fool last night. He has been living in New York and those sheenies over there got him all filled up to the neck with their crap. He said it ought to be impossible for one man [John L. Lewis] to tie up the country. He was too stupid to see that one man did not tie up the country. But some 400,000 men were. . . . It was all right while a bunch of kikes were tying up General Motors, and the others. . . . Soon we will be organizing Christian Political Action Units to combat the Communistic damage being done by Jew Sidney Hillman's Political Action Committee.

Smith closed on the note: "We are also sending you some other material. If you have seen it please pass it on to others. . . . As soon as our booklet on rearranging the election is ready copies will be sent you, if you indicate that you want them. We will be glad to hear from you anytime."

Among the fifty-one pieces of literature which I received from the Committee for Constitutional Government, not one directly attacked monopoly, cartels, fascism, Naziism or trusts. An order blank listed thirty titles which could be obtained free by any veteran. The list was devoted almost totally to attacks on the New Deal and Communism and a screeching defense of the Constitution, "free enterprise," etc. Nationalist hate-mongers and the ravages of extreme nationalism were nowhere listed as equally undesirable to the "American way."

The Committee for Constitutional Government has reached into schools, churches and colleges for its spokesmen. I received another leaflet which carried an article by Pettengill on one side and, on the reverse, one by Rev. Norman Vincent Peale, pastor of the Marble Collegiate Church in New York and former "acting chairman" of the Committee. Peale's article followed Pettengill's political pattern.

Rev. Peale was offended when I listed him in *Under Cover* as a joint speaker with Father Curran and Mrs. Dilling. He wrote me a long, moving letter, explaining that he had given only the invocation and not his blessings to the "patriotic" meeting held in New York in 1938. His experience (with Mrs. Dilling) "for me was not satisfactory," he said. I believe him. I do not suggest that Rev.

Peale curb the expression of his political views. But I do consider it against the public interest for a minister to allow his church to be used by a high-powered group for political ends. Rev. Peale's name dignified its work with apparent religious sanction.

Rev. Peale also stated in his letter: "I have never found anything but uprightness, honor and decency in Dr. Rumely." I made no reflection on the personal qualities of Dr. Edward Aloysius Rumely, Secretary of the Committee for Constitutional Government. I simply stated that he was convicted and had served thirty days in jail in 1920–21 for his failure to report to the Alien Property Custodian funds he obtained from Germanic interests serving the Kaiser's cause. With the funds Rumely bought the New York *Evening Mail* and used it as an instrument for German propaganda. Dr. Rumely's self-indicting testimony appears in Part 7 of the Hearings of the Special Senate Committee to Investigate Lobbying Activities, in March and April, 1938.

Dr. Rumely is still an integral part of the Committee for Constitutional Government, although his name does not appear on the letterhead. I'm surprised that a man with his background should still be associated with a group which lays claim to such grandiose patriotism. As for Rev. Peale, his latest association is a quasi-religious group called Guideposts whose object is "newly" to "interpret the relationship between Christianity and Democracy and American enterprise." He has seemingly quit his role with the Committee.

Included in the weight of Committee for Constitutional Government propaganda was a beautifully printed 250-page book on the life of Frank Gannett, wealthy Rochester, N. Y., owner of a string of newspapers and founder of the Committee. Gannett is undoubtedly sincere and has good intentions. When I lectured recently in Rochester my impression was that my audience was about equally divided between those in general agreement with the editorial policies of the local Gannett newspaper and those who didn't agree with them.

I do not consider Gannett a jingoist. My impression is, however, that he has been victimized by political friends who have sought to use him to their advantage. Gannett's political thinking, as expressed, for example, in a long, friendly letter I received as Thompson, completely lacks the foresight, ingenuity and boldness of his business ventures. Had he not applied more vision to his business

than in the formation of his political philosophy I doubt that he
would have built so important a publishing institution. Here, in
part, is Gannett's advice to a serviceman:

For a long time I have been contending that our free enterprise system
and American way of life were in grave danger. That peril increases
every day. You ask what you can do about it. It is difficult for me to
lay out any definite program. I'll see that you are put on the mailing
list to receive literature from our Committee for Constitutional Government. This will keep you informed on current questions. . . .

Unless the country wakes up, we will find [extreme socialists] some day
in complete control of our government and all that you and your buddies
fought for in the war will be lost. I hope you and your friends take active
interest in politics. Get busy in your election district and see if you cannot in that way render a real service in the fight against these people
who would overthrow our form of government.

The letter reflected an essential lack of any program. And the
Committee for Constitutional Government likewise offers little
which is constructive. They hold out no hope, no encouragement,
no objective enlightenment. They lead the citizen into the blind
alleys of yesterday. In a sense, Gannett and his Committee are symbols of an era which made America strong and great. But we cannot
stop there, as Eric Johnston says in a well-reasoned passage:

There'll have to be some changes made to meet new conditions, new
concepts, new thinking. The old capitalism, despite its sins, built a great
United States. The new capitalism can build a great *united* people. The
American economic system galvanized into superb unity to win the war,
but once the tensions of a common danger were relaxed, the divisive
pressures of fear and greed and appetite for special privilege took command. . . .

Life goes forward, always forward. The trouble is that some people are
moving forward all right, but they're looking backward. . . . Under the
old or standpat conception of capitalism, people seem merely the inert
tools of the system. Under the new, or progressive conception, the system is a tool in the hands of the people. It is to be used, but not abused,
for the general welfare and the good of all. . . . A decisive decade lies
ahead. . . .

The Gannett Newspapers

Executive Offices
Rochester, N.Y.

March 13, 1946

Dear Mr. Thompson:

I have your letter of March 6 signed also by Corliss H. Wayne, your buddy,

It was interesting to me to see your reaction to conditions that you found on your return from service. They are shocking and disturbing. For a long time I have been contending that our free enterprise system and American way of life were in grave danger. That peril increases every day. It is encouraging to me to see you young men fully realizing the situation.

You ask what you can do about it. It is difficult for me to lay out any definite program. I'll see that you are put on the mailing list to receive literature from our Committee For Constitutional Government. This will keep you informed on current questions. I am sending you copy of a talk I made on the Constitution which has been in great demand all over the country. I think in this talk I hit at the fundamentals.

I hope you and your friends take an interest in politics. Get busy in your election district and see if you cannot in that way render a real service in the fight against these people who would overthrow our form of government.

With all good wishes, I am

Cordially yours,

Frank Gannett

PETTENGILL

"The Gentleman from Indiana"

INSIDE YOUR CONGRESS

June 27, 1946

Dear Mr. Thompson:

Thank you for your letter.

We must all do what we can, along the line of the old saying that "If everyone swept in front of his own door the road to Rome would be clean."

You have contacts which I do not have and you are the best judge of what you can do. When you see one of our pieces which you think your former buddies would like, let us know and we will send you copies and you can pass them around.

I have a friend in Milwaukee who makes it his business to distribute our stuff to policemen. He finds that policemen are so gratified to be complimented with the idea that they could read something serious. Of course, the best thing of all is personal conversation. There is an old saying in politics that if an office-holder would spend half an hour on the front porch of every home in his district he would never be defeated. His constituents would be pleased with the attention he paid them, and on the other hand he would pick up an immense amount of down-to-earth wisdom.

Another thing is to occasionally write a letter to the Voice of the People Column, especially in answer to some other letter written by some "pink" or "red".

Best regards.

Sincerely yours,

SAMUEL B. PETTENGILL

Free advice from two men who look to yesterday for their—and America's—future. One letter refers to the flattering of policemen with "something serious" for them to read.

Today a body of interests, various in many respects, some open and sincere, others more or less clandestine and cynical, have in common the determination to restrict the fruits of our capitalist democracy to some of the people only. "The old capitalism was monopolistic," Johnston writes. "It stifled competition and thereby throttled opportunity for the little fellow. The new capitalism must encourage competition and thereby open up opportunity."

"Conditions are shocking and disturbing at home," Frank Gannett wrote me. But I submit that to support a Committee which stands stolidly for yesterday's *status quo* is to aggravate the condition. A deep Catholic thinker who has reached much the same conclusion is Bernard J. Sheil, Auxiliary Bishop of Chicago, who certainly cannot be accused of being a "Communist." Bishop Sheil takes a detached view of our future. He wants to preserve the workable and human aspects of capitalism and discard the millstones around its neck. His clerical tradition is a conservative one. Those who seriously want to strengthen our "American system" will gravely take to heart the Bishop's analysis:

"The American ideal is a . . . brotherhood of free men. . . . There remains an internal threat which . . . assumes sinister and formidable proportions. . . . It consists simply of individuals who . . . belong to economic groups which possess the greatest measure of security and which—up to now—have had the greatest influence upon American affairs. Blinded by fear of changes they cannot understand or control, they . . . desperately defend their special interests. . . . They distrust the common people. Distrusting the people, they seek to restrict democracy; restricting democracy, they emasculate it; and if they are allowed to continue, they will destroy it completely. Obviously, there is no lack of faith in democracy among the masses of people throughout the world. They believe, and rightly so, that the answer to any threat of fascism is not less democracy but more democracy.

"If you doubt this, read the record of the resistance movements in Europe. . . . They hungered and thirsted and died because they believed above all in freedom: freedom from every oppression; freedom to work as dignified human beings; freedom to live in the way God intended His own children should live.

"Let us have no illusions about the real issue of this struggle. . . . Are the common people to be considered capable of *real* freedom?

Are they to be granted their rightful participation in the political and social institutions which they have helped to create, which they support, and under which they live? Above all, are the people, the workers of the world, to be given an equitable share of the wealth of the world? These are questions which ruthlessly cut across all lines of race, of political beliefs, of national differences. . . . And they are questions upon the answers to which the existence of democracy depends. To these questions we must give clear and fearless answers."

America can create a new capitalism. The word "new" has never frightened us. America has always been the home of the new. But it is frightening the die-hards, the exponents of private economy and private government. For guidance they are looking not forward, but backward. Fascism, too, never looks forward, but always backward.

*

CHAPTER TWELVE

The Big Five

I feel that we have a different Army, a different spirit, different
aims. I don't think that many of the men in the Army today
want to see their efforts deteriorate into . . . plugging for benefits. We constitute an important political factor and I'm sure
that each one of us is fighting today to mould that factor into
an instrument for not only making over our country into a better
one, but for promoting genuine lasting peace. We're doing the
fighting. We certainly should have a voice afterward.

Lieut. Keith D. Skelton,
in a letter to Yank *magazine*

WE ARE the greatest nation of joiners in the world. Even if we
can't pay our dues, we join up anyway. Upon his discharge the returning GI wants to be let alone, for a while, but sooner or later he
usually joins up. He ought to. Comradeship, more than isolation,
helps him get back into the swing of civilian life, and eases him
over the rough spots of readjustment. Then, too, when he wants to
throw off steam nothing helps like a bull session with his ex-buddies.
On the practical side, the veteran can assure himself of a square
deal only by adding his voice to the volume of a major, democratically led veterans' group.

Of a potential membership of some twenty millions from all
wars, about 6,000,000 have already joined veterans' organizations.
Awaiting the others are more than 450 groups, running the gamut
from extreme revolutionaries to cold-blooded money-making rackets. Which one should the veteran join? Should it be an established
World War I organization or a World War II group aflame with the
zeal to do a better job for the ex-GI and the country than the older
outfits? President Truman stated his choice when he said: "Were
I a veteran of this war, I would prefer to have a veteran of World

War II looking after my affairs than a veteran of some other war."

The older groups have the advantage of established headquarters, larger funds for promotion, the stability born of experience. Most World War II groups are still feeling their way; they are handicapped by lack of funds and apt to be led astray by untested leadership.

At this writing three veterans' groups emerge as the dominant service organizations. They are the American Legion and the Veterans of Foreign Wars—these two have a combined, frequently overlapping membership of more than five millions—and the Disabled American Veterans, which fights for the battle-scarred group. In addition, there is the American Veterans Committee, a World War II group that claims about 85,000 members. American Veterans of World War II, or AMVETS, have undergone a turbulent history of organization and at this writing are not established dominantly, in membership or influence, as are the Legion, VFW, DAV and AVC. The Catholic War Veterans and Jewish War Veterans serve those who want to join on a religious basis.

In earlier chapters I have written mainly of the hate-mongering veterans' organizations and those which exploit the veteran for selfish ends—thereby hurting the whole country. The veteran and the rest of us are in the same boat. Anything which helps the veteran, helps America. If he lets himself be inoculated with the hate virus, it eventually injures everyone. In joining a veterans' group, the ex-serviceman assumes the moral responsibility of helping to shape the destiny of our country. It might make a lot of difference if—the Lord forbid!—100,000 fanatics should join Kister's storm troopers or some similar group yet unborn.

Most, though not all, of the many groups named in this and the next chapter are legitimate and worth joining. I do not wish, however, to advise the veteran as to which he should join. Let him judge, on the basis of the facts, which organizations best meet his needs and personality, and through which he can continue to serve his country best.

The American Legion, with headquarters in Indianapolis, is the best organized, best publicized, most criticized, most aggressive veterans' group, with a membership of more than three millions. Dues are about $5 a year, depending on the local post. John C.

Stelle is National Commander. The Legion has been both praised to the heavens and damned as "fascist and unpatriotic" by such a responsible educator as Dr. David Gellerman in his documented book, *The American Legion as Educator*. Dr. Gellerman refers to the labor-baiting, strike-breaking, book-banning political hierarchy within the Legion which heretofore flouted democratic methods and fronted for business interests which financed it originally. He cites the round-robin letter on Swift Company stationery sent on December 26, 1919 to solicit $100,000 from Illinois big businessmen alone. The founders made no bones about it. The Legion was, originally, largely promoted by "big money" to fight "Bolshevism" and later, organized labor. It often reflected NAM policy. With exceptions, its leadership remained faithful to its masters up to the time of Pearl Harbor.

The Legion membership, on the other hand, is a true cross section of America. Democratic and sincere, it has helped advance community welfare even while its hierarchy long leaned toward servile duty to economically autocratic elements.

A symbol of the old Legion was Homer L. Chaillaux, Director of its National Americanism Commission. A fanatical Soviet hater, he went so far as to distribute Joseph Kamp's booklets within the Legion. Chaillaux was also friendly with Rev. Winrod. His violent Red-baiting tactics alienated many friends of the Legion. In 1937 Chaillaux was authorized to compile a 287-page book called *Isms*. Some 265 pages were devoted to exposing the "Communists." With Nazi agents and Bunds crawling all over the nation, Chaillaux dismissed Nazi activity in 15 pages! Less than three pages were spent on other fascist operatives. The book was not precisely accurate in alleging that "fascist" was a term of opprobrium applied only to "those who oppose Communism." That's how Goebbels used to draw a red herring across his trail and portray his gang as the champions of freedom!

The inexcusable propaganda statement is understandable in view of those who helped Chaillaux compose *Isms*. The list included Elizabeth Dilling; Walter Steele; ex-Representative Hamilton Fish, America Firster and idol of the Christian Front; the American Coalition, a Washington super-patriotic society mentioned as a factor in the Federal indictments for sedition; and the Associated Farmers of California, vigilante fighters of labor. *Isms* was a symbol of yesterday's Legion. At least, let's hope so.

The Legion turned a new leaf when in 1942 it began accepting World War II members. These new vets expressed themselves against Chaillaux' policies. Coincidental with his death in February, 1946, after his resignation from the national office, the Legion's World War II membership passed the oldsters, who were dying at the rate of about 15,000 a year, and this change may have marked the beginning of a new era. Much has been rumored about War II veterans taking over the leadership. So far, however, the old guard remains at the helm. Of this, the 1945 award of the Legion's Distinguished Service Medal to William Randolph Hearst was proof. National Commander Stelle's attack on General Omar N. Bradley as "inefficient"—after the Legion had tolerated the scandal of the Veterans Administration for years—was perhaps another indication of the old Legion influence. The recognition that the organization no longer had the field to itself was a sobering experience.

On the other side of the ledger, many Legion posts have contributed splendidly to the cause of genuine Americanism. The clear-thinking Americanism Committee of the 17th District of California published magnificent exposés of the America First Committee and a roster of California Nazis. It initiated a resolution condemning Representative Hamilton Fish. Buffalo, N. Y., posts have done excellent work against un-American activity. With some blots—such as treatment of Nisei veterans in California and Oregon and the refusal of a single Atlanta post to denounce the Klan—the Legion membership has fulfilled its democratic obligations well, though a broader interpretation of the enemy within to include nationalist hate-mongers would render its work doubly valuable. The work in schools, among Boy Scouts and in child welfare, too, has in the main been excellent.

The National Conference of Union Labor Legionnaires (see Chapter Ten) has charged that a small group of "King-makers" and "brass hats" continue to select national commanders. It suggested that nominations be made from the floor and commanders selected by complete referendum—not voted on automatically. This, of course, is the democratic process. Less than fifty officials and behind-the-scenes advisers in the past are said to have run the Legion.

They prepared the important resolutions, which were passed with lightning speed at conventions and with fine disregard for discussion.

The *Daily Worker* claims that Communists are not barred from the Legion. National Adjutant Donald G. Glascoff, however, wrote me on March 14, 1946 to the effect that posts generally would not knowingly accept "individuals of leftist affiliation," and might not renew the membership of those who slipped in. As indicated in Chapter Nine, the Communist Party is especially interested in penetrating the Legion. Joseph Clark, *Daily Worker* Veterans Editor, wrote me in March, 1946, representing the progressive American Veterans Committee as among service groups "dominated for the most part by big business interests." His first choice was the Legion. It's doubtful, however, that the Communists can bore from within successfully. Federal agents are on the job like watchdogs.

The Legion is "big business." Together with those of its three auxiliaries, the Forty and Eight Society, the Eight and Forty Society and the Ladies' Auxiliary, its assets amount to over $100,-000,000. It has thousands of clubhouses (with bars) and a proven record of pressure in Washington. Equipment of its 100 drum and bugle corps alone is worth $3,000,000. Its 1946 budget for "routine Americanism activities" is $15,000,000. The Legion today has 15,000 posts. Its membership at the end of 1941 was 1,107,075, which means World War II vets already outnumber their elders about two to one.

Will the younger men continue to make themselves heard? Will they clamor for a democratic deal? Or, once their zeal has worn off, will they backslide and become puppets of the entrenched hierarchy and be pacified with the annual convention hysterics? Backsliding will be far easier than a determined struggle to make the Legion increasingly democratic. Paternalism has strong root, and the bureaucracy of officers may be unwilling to surrender comfortable berths to newcomers. Unless World War II veterans continue to assert themselves, the old Legion may eventually knock out the promising new spirit within its ranks, just as old guard Republicans came back to squelch a progressive spokesman like Willkie.

The *Veterans of Foreign Wars of the United States* (headquarters, Kansas City, Mo.; Louis E. Starr, Commander-in-Chief), is second to the Legion with an expanding membership of nearly two millions. To belong costs about $5 a year. The VFW jumped the gun on the Legion by signing up members overseas, but the Legion countered by recruiting in camps here.

Established in 1899 by Spanish-American War Veterans, the VFW by the end of 1941 had a few thousand posts and a mere 225,000 members. It now has 8,800 posts. Merchant seamen and women cannot join, but a flourishing Ladies' Auxiliary has 4,000 posts of its own. Despite its old guard leadership, the VFW may almost be regarded as a World War II organization.

VFW members may tend to be less nationalist, more open to the concept of world cooperation, since service "on foreign soil or in hostile waters" is necessary for membership. The ranks are more varied than those of the Legion, including veterans of the Boxer Rebellion, the Philippine Insurrection, the Haitian, Yangtze River and Nicaraguan campaigns.

Unlike the Legion, which temporarily at least has turned its back on the bonus, the VFW is the most bonus conscious of the major

IDAILY WORKER—

March 12, 1946

Dear Mr. Thompson,

I want to apologize for the delay in answering your letter.

My recommendation is that you join one of the national established veterans organizations. The majority of World War II veterans are joining the American Legion, Veterans of Foreign Wars, Disabled American Veterans, etc.

The old line, as well as the new American Veterans Committee and Amvets, are dominated for the most part by big business interests. But members of the organizations can be influenced along progressive pro-labor lines by the participation of such people in those organizations.

Fraternally yours,

Joseph Clark
Veterans Editor

veterans' groups. It's proposing a bonus of $4 per day for overseas duty, with a maximum of $4,500, plus an extra $500 for those with combat wounds.

The VFW has favored service unification. It asks equality for Indian veterans and the divorcing of their affairs from the Office of Indian Affairs, reduction of Social Security retirement age from 65 to 55, and the franking privilege for patients in Veterans Administration facilities. The VFW also advocates complete cessation of immigration for ten years, adding that this involves "no religious or racial intolerance" but is "purely economic" and based on housing and employment limitations. The Legion makes a similar recommendation but sets no time limit. The VFW asks secrecy on atomic processes and equipment and urges that control rest with "representatives of the American people" rather than an Army-industry group.

The contrast between the Legion and the VFW is symbolized by the Legion plank of fighting "against Federal control." The Legion plugs for "free enterprise"; in publicity it emphasized its help to the Dies Committee. The VFW makes no such issue of its patriotism; it expresses itself quietly, nor does it take it on itself to censor textbooks. It urges "cooperation between government, management and labor toward full employment." The Legion has made no such public declaration. An editorial in the VFW *News* warned against "rowdyism at encampments" because it "can do irreparable harm to any organization."

In community service work and a program of Americanism the VFW is seeking to compete with the Legion. The Legion has a head start, though the VFW could get the jump in the Americanism field by declaring itself against nationalist hate-mongers, mentioning some by name. It is extremely conscious of its obligations to needy VFW families and dependents of disabled and deceased members. At Eaton Rapids, Mich., it maintains a home for servicemen's orphans—not an "orphan home" in the usual sense, but a 640-acre farm with orchards, dairy, playgrounds and hospital.

The VFW claims more World War II veterans than the Legion. It's off to a fresh start and has no reason for lending itself to control by any interests. It will be revealing to see whether it can maintain its present independent course and not let sudden success deviate it from its purpose of serving veteran and country. Indications are that veterans ambitious for leadership have a better chance of climbing than with the more strongly entrenched leadership of the Legion. But at this writing the old guard is still dominant in the VFW.

At the New York State convention in June, 1946, former Commander Joseph M. Stack launched an anti-Communist attack unequalled for its acid quality by any recent statement from a major veterans' group. He advocated that "native-born Communists should be subject to prison, to the firing squad and to deprivation of their rights as citizens. Naturalized Communists," he said, "should get the same treament, and upon completion of their prison terms they should be deported to the country of their birth." This outburst struck me as needlessly vitriolic, in view of the fact that Commander Stack was not reported making any remarks against nationalist hatemongers and others feeding the fires of bigotry.

The *Disabled American Veterans* (headquarters, Cincinnati, Ohio; Vivian D. Corbly, National Adjutant) is the most important veterans' organization serving the disabled soldiers of World Wars I and II. Founded in 1929, it has 1,300 chapters throughout the country and lists its membership as 120,000. Dues range from $4 a year to a $50 wallop in a few chapters. Membership is open to anyone who was "wounded, gassed, injured or disabled in line of duty"; persons who have ever received compensation from the Veterans Administration; persons drawing statutory award for arrested or cured tuberculosis; persons with an SCD (Surgeon's Certificate of Disability, Army, World War I), CDD (Certificate of Disability Discharge, Army, World War II) or BMS (Bureau of Medical Survey, Navy, World War II) medical discharge.

The DAV is a "one-purpose" organization, designed to aid in the physical, mental, social and economic rehabilitation of the disabled veteran. Barred by its Congressional charter from taking part in politics, it works among the disabled without regard to race, color or creed. It has 50 all-Negro chapters and several hundred composed of both white and Negro members. DAV has cared for more than a million veterans for whom it has procured more than $10,-000,000 in benefits. One of its most vital services is properly preparing and presenting veterans' claims for government benefits, actually serving as an attorney for the veteran in this connection. The DAV enables the veteran to get anything to which the law entitles him. Many psychoneurotic cases have come to the DAV for help in presenting their claims, which have been settled satisfactorily for the veterans. All service is free, regardless of whether the applicant belongs to the DAV or not.

The DAV helps veterans' widows and other dependents obtain benefits due them. Another function is its placement service for the handicapped. The DAV is expanding its work to care for a potential 2,500,000 disabled veterans of the recent war. Properly rehabilitated, these handicapped ex-service men and women can be salvaged to carry on as citizens. General Bradley has called the work of the DAV "splendid and purposeful."

The American Veterans Committee (headquarters, New York City) is the most vocal World War II organization, with some 950 posts and nearly 85,000 members. Charles G. Bolte, 26, is National Chairman; Gilbert Harrison, 26, is Vice-Chairman. Membership at $5 a year is open to women and merchant seamen.

The AVC is unlike any other veterans' organization. It is totally new in concept and outlook. It comes nearest to reflecting Willkie's "One World" vision. Thoroughly democratic, it is ruled strictly from the bottom, with no hidden hierarchy. Scripps-Howard political writer Thomas L. Stokes attended its 1946 convention and found the AVC composed of "ruggedly individualistic, independent thinking men and women, and deadly in earnest that this worst of all wars shall not have been fought in vain." Stokes wrote:

An inspiring miracle is perhaps a good description of the performance of the AVC. . . . This convention was something such as was never seen before by this writer in 25 years of covering national and state political and other conventions. It was a fine antidote for the cynicism beginning to spread again through America and the world. There was no high jinks, no drunkenness or disorderliness—nothing but business.

The seed for the AVC was planted in 1943 when Harrison, Bolte and other servicemen exchanged letters on the kind of veterans' group they'd like to have. Bolte, who lost a leg at El Alamein (he joined the British after graduating from college before Pearl Harbor), served as temporary Chairman of the AVC upon his discharge and gained considerable publicity for it. He won prominence by his *Harper's* magazine exposé of intolerable conditions in Veterans Administration hospitals, starting the ball rolling toward the appointment of General Bradley as Administrator to clean up the VA.

Whereas older groups had served the veteran mainly by securing benefits, the AVC took an unorthodox view. It is strictly opposed to bonus handouts, feeling that the bonus is a special privilege which injures non-veteran Americans. The AVC demand is for permanent jobs at decent wages "under a system of private enterprise in which business, labor, agriculture and government work together to provide full employment and full production for the nation." Bonus-begging is defeatist, the AVC says. "We are citizens first, veterans second." While the veteran's heroic role should not be forgotten, he should stand on his own feet. From the outset the AVC has followed a broad social and political program. It sent the only official veterans' delegation to the UNO conference at San Francisco, stood alone among veterans' groups for the Full Employment Bill, plugged for a permanent FEPC. It secured equal rights for Nisei in the Navy and Marines and won increases in grants to veterans returning to school.

AVC policies have attracted as members Col. Evans F. Carlson of Carlson's Raiders; Bill Mauldin; Harold Stassen; Oren Root, Jr., Chairman of the Associated Willkie Clubs in 1940; Tyrone Power; Franklin D. Roosevelt, Jr. The most noticeable quality of AVC members is the dynamic urge to help shape their country's future. They are articulate and deeply conscious of social, national and world issues. The AVC has taken the lead among veterans groups in demanding housing facilities, fighting price increases, picketing against discrimination to veterans and supporting political candidates whom it believes will best serve the cause of veteran and nation.

The AVC has been attacked, of course. The nationalists froth at the mouth at mention of its name. Edward James Smythe has called its members "dirty, stinking Communists." But the *Daily Worker* has expressed its dislike a number of times and has urged members to "renounce" Bolte, who has no love for the Communists. Many democratic organizations today have to cope with Communist infiltration. Some sidestep the issue. The AVC met it directly. Communists tried to wrest control of the 1946 convention at Des Moines, but were defeated at every turn. They tried to inject the party line into resolutions, but got nowhere. An attempt to affiliate

the Communist-led Abraham Lincoln Brigade was crushed by a
vote of 29,469 to 792.

The group's powers and its fearless handling of such sensitive
issues as Negro-white relationships were illustrated when two convention delegates, Oren Root, Jr., and Franklin Williams, a Negro,
were refused service in a café. The AVC suspended its convention
and picketed the restaurant. Its proprietor was later arrested under
the state's Civil Rights Law. Bolte declared, "I hope this will call
dramatic attention to the intent of the AVC . . . to oppose Jim
Crow, anti-Nisei restrictions and all other forms of racial discrimination."

After laying the groundwork for a United Nations Veterans
League, some 840 delegates adopted the following platform, which
places the AVC far in the lead in terms of sharing responsibility for
national and world security:

National Affairs: Backed development of Wyatt housing program, channeling of building materials into low-cost housing. Favored guaranteed
annual minimum wage with full employment, extension of Federal unemployment compensation and social security. Supported widespread
and strong collective bargaining while opposing compulsory arbitration,
use of armed forces in labor disputes, and anti-strike measures. Urged
low-cost mortgages and loans, soil conservation and rural electrification.
Backed strong price and credit control policy. Recommended liberal
credit system for small business, while urging enforcement of anti-trust
laws against big business. Demanded comprehensive national health and
education programs. Backed procedural reform in Congress and regulation of lobby groups.

Veterans' Affairs: Favored unified armed force sufficient for national defense and fulfilling international commitments. Urged enforcement of
veteran seniority job rights, extension of on-the-job training programs,
liberalization of terms for GI loans, and immediate grant of retroactive
terminal leave pay. Voted against a veterans' bonus.

International Affairs: Backed United Nations control of atomic energy;
upheld Lilienthal and Baruch reports. Favored loans to war-damaged
Allied countries, elimination of cartels, and immediate tariff reduction.
Demanded the severance of relations with Spain and expulsion of Argentina from the United Nations. Upheld entry into Palestine for displaced
Jews and backed universal lowering of immigration barriers for all displaced persons.

In addition to Harold Stassen and Henry Wallace, the speakers at the convention included Walter Reuther, anti-Communist President of the United Automobile Workers, and Bishop Bernard J. Sheil who, in a speech agreeing with Eric Johnston's views, said in part:

The "normalcy" our tycoons speak of is a perverted thing, when few are on the top of the economic heap and the rest of us are groveling on the bottom. Normalcy is impossible as long as profit alone remains the guide, the God, the despot of our economy. . . . We want another chance . . . to make our world a place worth living in.

American Veterans of World War II (AMVETS; headquarters, Washington, D. C.) has about 725 posts and 70,000 members and costs $4 a year to join. Women, but not merchant seamen, are admitted. National Commander is Jack W. Hardy, former Lieutenant Commander in the Navy. For those ex-servicemen who want a conservative World War II veterans' group patterned on the elder models, with little "social consciousness" or probing into world issues, this is it.

AMVETS' growing pains were protracted. It was established in Kansas City in December, 1944, with Elmo W. Keel as Commander and Brig. Gen. H. C. Holdridge* as Secretary. AMVETS got considerable publicity but made no bid for vigorous leadership. It also got a temporary black eye in 1945 through its Dallas, Texas post. Lamar Bailey, National Vice-Commander, a protégé of Senator O'Daniel, ran for Congress in 1944 and gained notoriety by launching on an anti-union crusade. He was denounced and expelled by the national office.

Bailey's tactics, however, were continued by his immediate successors in Texas. Issues of *The Texas AMVET* screamed with labor-baiting articles and ran advertisements warning that "the Tentacles of Moscow are many and long AND WILL SOON REACH INTO EVERY VILLAGE AND HOME." Suspecting that the veterans were being used as a "front" for anti-labor activity, L. V. Todd, Second State Vice-Commander, finally called for a showdown. In a stormy hearing the Publications Committee Chairman admitted that the Dallas AMVETS had been receiving $400 a month from a

---

*Now Legislative Chairman of the Veterans League of America.

Texas theatre magnate, Karl Hoblitzelle. Todd thereupon resigned, unwilling, as he wrote me, to stay with an organization that permitted the policies of the paper to be "dictated by non-veteran outsiders."

At a convention in Chicago in October, 1945 Hardy was elected Commander. A Los Angeles attorney, Hardy impresses me as honest, conscientious, independent, conservative. The country-owes-us-a-living attitude was completely absent from the convention, which did not go bonus-begging. "We shall not discriminate," the platform read in part, "between veterans because of rank, service, sex, race, creed or political party affiliations. . . . We shall not permit our organization to be used as a 'front' for any individual, group, party, movement or 'ism.'" The delegates demanded that "both industry and labor 'clean house' and establish responsible leadership and labor-management policies." The convention denounced Bilbo by name and condemned an open-shop resolution introduced by a Dallas delegate. It also went on record for adequate housing and a number of inoffensive nonpolitical planks.

AMVETS' platform was commendable. The organization did not buckle down, however, to specific issues. They failed to declare themselves either for or against the FEPC or full-employment program, and said nothing about foreign policy. The present role of AMVETS seems to be strictly noncommittal and neutral. Perhaps it fears to touch controversial issues lest it lose prospective members. On the other hand, the AVC thrives on them.

AMVETS has arranged with a national restaurant chain for a 26-week, on-the-job training course for veterans who want to open restaurants. In Washington it has organized the Veterans Cooperative Housing Association, whereby, if arrangements are completed, members may purchase homes cooperatively in a new development. For June, 1946 AMVETS inaugurated a campaign to help prevent juvenile delinquency and prepare a community recreational program for young people. For July the program was to find a job for a veteran. Hardy released a statement calling upon Russia to "confine her political ideology to her own borders and abandon her present and continuing program to Sovietize the rest of the world."

When rumors persisted that the 1945 Chicago convention had been "bought" by one Joseph W. Pritchard, I decided to ask Mr. Hardy the truth point-blank. Hardy, a tall, blunt, ruggedly outspoken man, received me warmly and answered my questions without hesitation. The story which he told me illustrates how a reputable veterans' group can be exploited by profit-seeking promoters. Later I double-checked on Mr. Hardy by writing him under another name. In a reply, February 27, 1946, he explained the background of the rumors. Hardy, who had no connection with the earlier AMVETS, explained that on arriving for the convention he learned that Pritchard, a non-veteran Chicago "businessman," had taken an unusual interest in AMVETS. He had "advanced travel expenses, hotel expenses, meals, etc., to a number . . . of the then executive committee"; in April, 1945 Pritchard "had entered into an agreement with the then officials . . . wherein he was given the right . . . to raise funds for AMVETS" for five years "in any manner he chose." For this service, Hardy wrote me, Pritchard was to receive forty percent of all sums collected by AMVETS, except dues, "and was given 'for his own profit' the exclusive right to publish a newspaper, magazine or any other periodical in the name of AMVETS, leaving AMVETS nothing to say about policy, profits, management. It was apparent to many of us that Pritchard had, in fact, been running AMVETS from behind the scenes, and had well dictated its policies and activities through his financial aid and influence upon the then executive committee." At the convention Hardy, who took a dim view of this, was drafted as Commander. Pritchard supporters, he stated, were "still trying to get AMVETS to enter into a fundraising contract with Pritchard." Hardy expressed his intention of resigning immediately if any contract were entered into with Pritchard, "as I am morally convinced that it will result in complete destruction of the things for which AMVETS stands at present."

Hardy has cleared up a number of somewhat similar deals the organization had been induced to accept. AMVETS at present seems clear of contracts with promoters and other behind-the-scenes manipulators. AMVETS, however, hasn't yet matured as a solid, affirmative World War II group. Faced with the competition of the Legion, VFW and AVC, it needs to prosecute its aims with equal vigor in order to emerge as a permanent socially useful veterans' organization.

Some Americans feel that veterans' organizations based on religion or national background are needed to supplement the non-sectarian groups such as the "Big Five." Others disagree. There are no such distinctions in the Army. As one ex-GI told me: "We fought not as Catholics or Jews, but as Americans." Most important groups in this sectarian category are the Jewish and Catholic War Veterans. Their attitude is summed up in the statement of the Jewish War Veterans: "The best way to meet Jewish problems is through a Jewish group. The best answer to accusations that the Jew is not a patriot is the Jewish patriot himself." These two sectarian groups together have a growing membership in excess of 275,000.

The *Jewish War Veterans of the United States* (headquarters, New York City; Maxwell Cohen, Commander) was organized in 1896 to refute false charges that no Jews fought in the Civil War. It has 350 posts and about 75,000 members. Annual dues are about $4. It has a Women's Auxiliary and also admits women veterans.

The JWV have taken a militant stand against Communism and Fascism. Their program includes "promoting American ideals, combating subversive movements, and building inter-faith good will and understanding." Their information service gives excellent statistics on Jewish participation in American wars. Of nearly five million Jews in the United States, for example, about 600,000 served in World War II and 250,000 in World War I.

The JWV urge their members to join other veterans' groups and ninety-five percent have done so. The JWV and Catholic War Veterans collaborate closely, each feeling that the problems faced are common. The groups point out that such organizations as the Legion prohibit bringing up any racial or religious questions on the floor, and take the view that problems of anti-Semitism and anti-Catholicism can be handled effectively by Jewish and Catholic veterans. On their fiftieth anniversary, President Truman wrote the Jewish War Veterans:

As a symbol of patriotic service rendered by our citizens of Jewish faith, your organization is the living answer to those who would confuse our people with the evil doctrines of bigotry and hatred.

The *Catholic War Veterans* (headquarters are in New York City; Max H. Sorensen, National Commander) has more than 1,100 active chapters and a growing membership of some 200,000. Annual dues are $3. The CWV is a lay organization and is led by laymen, although Catholic clergymen appear at installations and conventions and the CWV works closely with the program of the Church. The order was founded in 1935 by Rev. Edward J. Higgins, a chaplain in World War I. Like the JWV, the CWV maintains warm relations with other veterans' groups. It estimates that there are about 6,-000,000 Catholic veterans.

The CWV regards Communism as the dominant danger to democracy. Its Americanism Committee, according to the *Holy Name Journal*, "has been active in widely presenting the attitude of the Catholic Church on current events and answering those persons who have been attempting to smear Catholics as Fascists, anti-Semites and the like." The anti-Communist zeal of the CWV, however, sometimes carries it to excesses. Although Bishop Sheil has addressed both CIO and American Veterans Committee conventions, CWV speakers have denounced both organizations as "Communist." According to the New York *Times,* May 11, 1946, the convention delegates of the New York State section heard Paul L. Murphy, Judge Advocate, charge that "the CIO is dominated and absolutely controlled by alien-minded people."

I have not found in CWV literature any denunciation of Father Coughlin or the Christian Front during their worst years. Indications are that the CWV will intensify its anti-Communist crusade and will become a militant and aggressive spokesman of the Church. It could be wished that the CWV would take an equally watchful attitude toward the other danger threatening Catholicism, Christianity and democracy: it would doubly serve by also denouncing nationalist hate-mongers.

Of the resolutions passed by the CWV convention in June, 1946, many were for veterans' benefits. Delegates came out strongly for measures "to curb and destroy forever . . . the Ku Klux Klan." On the international front, they urged that we be permanently represented at the Vatican by an envoy, opposed Russian occupation of European territory, and urged the President to "refrain from participation in the world conference" involving the Teheran and Yalta agreements. They went to bat for Franco and called the censure of the Spanish dictator by our State Department "ill-advised, unwarranted and prejudicial." On the other hand the CWV delegates elected John C. James, a Negro teacher from Louisiana, as National

Trustee—an example of democracy which might be followed by other veterans' groups, including the Legion and VFW. More than 1,000,000 Negroes participated in World War II. Thousands are members of those groups but have no representation in the national leadership.

As an American of Armenian descent, I am familiar with the instinct of minorities to organize as such. A group of Armenian American veterans in San Francisco solved this problem admirably well. Instead of founding an "Armenian American Veterans Association," they organized their own Ararat Post and affiliated with the American Legion. The post, which has 150 members, is composed largely of business and professional men. As Legionnaires, these young Americans carry on functions like those the Jewish and Catholic War Veterans perform independently. The arrangement has the advantage of drawing on the strength and prestige of the Legion. Thus the group's minority needs are met, and at the same time it becomes a more integral part of the American bloodstream, instead of floating within it as a national or sectarian island. The example of the Armenian American veterans is an example of assimilation, showing the spiritual fusion of a minority group with the democratic whole.

CHAPTER THIRTEEN

Veterans Round-Up

THE SMALLER VETERANS' organizations are multitudinous. An attempt at classification was made by the American Veterans Committee until they were swamped and gave up the project. The Veterans' Organizations Information Service in New York has compiled a large list and plans to publish a comprehensive directory. Founded by three prewar friends, Kenneth M. Birkhead, Richard A. Brown and Jerome Schwartz, who decided upon their discharge to help fellow veterans, the VOIS issues a bulletin which gives veterans news not generally found in the public press. It also operates as a coordinating agency to advise service groups as to common ground on which they can meet to carry out joint programs of democratic action.

I have included in the following miscellaneous roster such large groups as the Army and Navy Union, which claims a membership of 100,000, and the Regular Veterans Association, with nearly 85,000 members. This has been done for the sake of convenience and in the hope that readers seeking a particular organization other than the Big Five and sectarian veterans' groups will find it more quickly through alphabetical arrangement.

The organizations selected for brief treatment in this chapter, out of the hundreds of national and local groups throughout the country, have impressed me personally as being of greatest general interest, for one reason or another. It is not my desire, however, to recommend any particular group to the ex-service man or woman. Let the veteran decide on the basis of as thorough a survey as possible which group suits him the best. Space limitations prevent giving here all the information available, nor have I by any means listed all the interesting groups studied in months of research.

Inasmuch as all the groups mentioned profess their loyalty to

God, Country, Constitution, and are pledged to a defense of all three, in addition to serving the veteran's cause through information, legislation benefits, and camaraderie, I have eliminated these obvious details in most instances. In some cases complete information could not be secured from a group when queried. This is sometimes attributable to inadequate help or to vacillation. The dues mentioned are on an annual basis.

Air Force Association, Washington, D. C. Open to all former military personnel, men and women, who have been commissioned, enlisted, attached or assigned to the Army Air Forces since their inception as the Aviation Section of the Signal Corps. Army air personnel on active duty are eligible for non-voting associate membership. Dues are $3.

Gen. James H. Doolittle is President and Col. Willis S. Fitch, Executive Director. The present officers and Board of Directors, who include both officers and enlisted men, are acting temporarily until a representative group can be democratically elected by the membership at the first national convention. The rapidly growing membership now numbers about 45,000.

The Association was formed in 1946 to preserve and foster the spirit of fellowship among former, present and future members of the Army Air Forces, to commemorate fittingly the memory of former comrades, and to perpetuate the tradition of the Air Forces. The Association seeks to educate its members and the public at large in the proper development of air power and to keep them abreast of new developments. It backs air forces adequate in power for the defense of the country and "appropriately related in status to the Army and Navy." It is planned that local units, to be known as Squadrons, will be organized. These will be affiliated with state organizations, or Wings, which in turn will be affiliated with National Headquarters.

The organization does not attempt to carry on or compete with the legislative and financial programs which are offered by various veterans' groups, and takes an independent position politically. A non-profit organization, it plans to turn over any funds left after meeting expenses, to charity, normally the Air Forces Aid Society. Dues cover a subscription to the Association's official magazine, *Air Force*.

Air Legion, Inc., Marietta, Ga., was founded in 1943 by Johnnie Coleman. Membership, at present small, is open to veterans of the flying forces of all branches of the service. Women are admitted. When I wrote for the attitude of the Air Legion toward Negroes, Coleman replied on April 12, 1946: "As yet we do NOT have a single Negro. . . . If Squadrons up North want Negroes in their Squadrons we of the South will let the North live as they please. As for the South, sooner or later we may have to give Negroes the right to have their own Squadrons." Membership is $5.

Air Service Veterans Association, Denver, Col., was organized in 1925 by World War I airmen. Membership is open to air veterans of World War II. C. M. Tichenor is Commander. Tichenor has expressed the fear that after winning the war militarily, we are losing the peace. The Association does not disclose figures on membership, but I estimate it at less than 1,500. Dues are $3.

The American Veterans Party, New York City, is now dormant, but may be revived at election time. It represented an early but abortive attempt to exploit the veteran politically. Organized in 1945 prior to New York's mayoralty elections, it was ruled off the ballot because of insufficient legitimate signatures on its nominating petitions. Among the backers of the American Veterans Party were former State Senator John J. McNaboe, who acted as Chairman of the anti-Communist Friends of Frank Fay rally at Madison Square Garden, New York City (see Chapter Fourteen) and Robert H. Harriss, Father Coughlin's broker and ardent supporter.

Army and Navy Legion of Valor of the United States of America, Inc., Pittsburgh, Pa. This is an "exclusive" and yet highly democratic organization, open to those who have received the Congressional Medal of Honor, Distinguished Service Cross or Navy Cross. More than 1,500 have joined. National Commander is Leon A. Dombrowski, DSC. Membership is $2.

Army and Navy Union, United States of America, Atlantic City, N. J., is open to all members and ex-members of the Armed Forces; it also has a Ladies' Auxiliary. Founded in 1886, it claims to be "the second oldest veterans' organization in the U.S.A." It's a quiet, clubby group with a claimed membership of about 100,000 and "close to 500" units throughout the country. The Union assumes a quiet role in national affairs; its program is similar to those of other conservative groups. The Union favors the merger of the Army and Navy Departments under a unified command. Henry W. Gerber is Commander. Dues are about $5.

Fleet Reserve Association, Washington, D. C. Membership is open to certain classifications of officers and enlisted men of the U.S. Navy or Marine Corps who have served six years or more, and those honorably retired. The organization advocates adequate naval defense, promotes legislation for the betterment of Navy personnel, and opposes the merging of the Armed Forces under a central leadership. The Association has more than 80 posts and claims about 30,000 members, in addition to a Ladies' Auxiliary. Robert F. Bonamarte is President. Membership is $6.

Global War Veterans, Columbia, Tenn., founded in 1943, has about 1,200 World War II members and an unspecified number of national, including many Negro, posts. A fairly progressive group, it has its main strength in the South and Midwest and in various colleges. It admits women. The Global War Veterans seek "to avoid participation in party politics, but to promote interest in civic affairs and the ideal of service in personal and community life." The preamble to their constitution emphasizes "helping our neighbor, regardless of Race, Creed, Color or Religion."

The Global War Veterans have held two conventions, in Memphis and St. Louis, which were addressed by high officials of the Army, Navy and Veterans Administration. They are not a high-pressure, ballyhooing group, but work quietly for veterans' needs. Thomas H. Chunn is their active National Secretary. Membership is $3.

The Gold Eagle Legion, New York City. This group, when organized in 1945, gave promise of becoming an important veterans' group. It shares offices with Citizens, Inc., headed by one Warren Hunter. Repeated visits to the offices failed to locate Lt. Col. George E. Fahys, Executive Secretary. I interviewed Hunter in February, 1946. He disclaimed any connection with the Gold Eagle

Legion, but admitted that he had suggested the title and was promoting a song for the organization's benefit. "We want the support of both capital and labor," he said, referring to the Gold Eagle Legion. "Yes, we have taken money from business firms. They have promised to support and work with us financially." No labor group, however, had participated financially. The Legion has a large roster of advisory board members, including a number of manufacturers and businessmen.

Organizer of the Legion but no longer active in it, is Dennis Wiegand, Duluth radio commentator. I joined the Gold Eagle Legion under a pseudonym. Membership was only $2, but except for a membership card, I heard nothing from it in six months. Hunter said he expected to stage a number of large public affairs, but up to July, 1946 none of them had materialized.

League of Enlisted Veterans, Inc., Washington, D. C. Membership is open to all veterans with enlisted status, regardless of race, creed or color. The program calls for "terminal pay, equal disability pension benefits, equal job opportunities with those of the commissioned officer, remodeling of the caste and special privilege system." The group, still small at this writing, was organized in 1946. Donald Marr, Chairman, wrote me two letters, the contents of which I abridge:

Our Constitution states in part: "We shall respect the dignity and promote the equality of man." We attempt to overcome all prejudice against race, creed or color. Some of our charter members are Negroes, and one . . . was among the seven elected to the National Board of Directors.

We believe that there is less racial prejudice existing between white and Negro veterans than exists among those citizens who did not fight as comrades in arms. It is our hope to take full advantage of this close understanding among veterans of different creeds and colors and to promote and increase that mutual respect to the fullest extent.

Racial prejudice in America is so deep-seated and of such long standing that it will require the combined efforts of all to make progress toward its eradication. But we believe that because of the large number of veterans in our country, through proper organization and education racial discrimination can be dealt a mighty blow within the next 25 years.

. . . All of our meetings here in Washington have been interracial and our colored and white members have proven to each other that we can meet and work together harmoniously.

Membership in this eminently long-visioned group is $5.

League of Women Veterans, Inc., New York City. Membership is open to ex-service women and those still in uniform in all branches of the armed forces. Objectives are to "achieve economic, political and social equality for women veterans; oppose discrimination of every kind on account of sex, race, creed or color; shield from neglect the graves of the honored dead"; and "oppose subversive groups seeking to overthrow the Government." It claims more than 1,000 members nationally. Patricia M. Deuse, National Commander, wrote: "LWV is nonpartisan and, if humanly possible, we will see that it remains that way." Dues are $5.

Military Order of the Purple Heart, Washington, D. C. Membership is open to the combat-wounded who have been awarded the Purple Heart. The Order has 225 posts and about 12,500 members. It claims to have been founded by George Washington, who suggested on August 7, 1782, that "singularly meritorious action" be rewarded with a decoration bearing "the figure of a heart in purple cloth." The present organization, established in 1932, maintains an active Ladies' Auxiliary. Ray Doris is National Commander. Dues are $3.

National Action Conference on Minority Veterans' Problems, Chicago, Ill. While this is not a veterans' organization, its work is to assure minority veterans—Jews, Catholics, Negroes, Nisei and others—of fair treatment by veterans' agencies. The Conference is an offshoot of the American Council on Race Relations, a Chicago group dedicated to inter-racial goodwill. The Conference was the result of a national survey which disclosed gross discrimination against minority veterans in employment, education, training program and counseling service in some USES and local community agencies.

At a meeting held in New York in July, 1946, the Conference determined to present President Truman with a program to remedy the situation. "Minority group veterans were called upon to make equal sacrifices in war," the resolution stated; they do not deserve "unequal treatment." Favoring the resolution were the American Veterans Committee, Catholic War Veterans, Jewish War Veterans, Veterans League of America and United Negro and Allied Veterans of America.

National Council of Negro Veterans, Inc., Kansas City, Mo. The Council was organized in 1940 to meet the need for a national Negro veterans' organization and to fight discrimination against Negro veterans, particularly in the South. According to the Council, 17,000 World War I Negroes in Georgia and Florida lost their bonus money because they could not belong to a national veterans' group and had none of their own to inform them of the routine for filing claims. According to a leaflet issued by the organization, Robert Springfield of Birmingham, Ala., and a group of Negroes, spent five years and $597.50 in legal fees to get a charter from the American Legion. They failed. Springfield finally joined the Council.

Organized in 1940, the Council has fought for full Negro representation in all departments of the Armed Forces, admittance to OCS, representation in industry without discrimination during peacetime as well as wartime, and Federal legislation to protect Negroes against mob violence. Although organized primarily to help the Negro veteran obtain full benefits to which he is entitled under the law, no veteran is denied membership "because of race, creed or color . . . and all members are granted full participation in every part of the organization." The Council is strictly non-political and no officer may be elected to a public post. It has a Ladies' Auxiliary. B. H. Muldrew is National Commander. Membership is $2.

National Veterans Collegiate Association, Temple University, Philadelphia, Pa. Founded in 1945, the Association seeks to keep student veterans studying under the GI Bill of Rights and in touch with developments on the veterans' front. Its program calls for the formation of a "strong, progressive national student-veterans' organization." At its convention in July, 1945 the Association adopted a program designed to impress upon educators that the veteran "is an adult and not an adolescent," and to bring about closer liaison between education and industry. Membership is about 2,000, and it costs $2 to join. James J. Lynch is President.

National Veterans Committee, Inc., New York City. This organization maintained desk space in Washington, but headquarters are in the one-room office of Wide World Press, Inc., in New York. Dennis Quinn is Director of the press agency and also organizer of the Veterans Committee. In addition, Quinn directs the United States Patriotic Society, Inc., a super-patriotic setup located in the same office.

I interviewed Quinn as Thompson and he immediately made me a member of the Patriotic Society. His Veterans Committee is dormant at present, but it will come to life "at the right time," Quinn said. He read lengthily from its charter. "There's everything in that charter but the kitchen sink," Quinn said. "We leave the door open for politics." The statement of its objectives pledged the organization to "safeguard the rights of Capital and Private Property . . . combat subversive forces by Americanism Educational Programs." I asked Quinn whether his Veterans Committee was opposed to strikes. "Yes, we're opposed to everything un-American," he said. "We've got to have unions, but most unions today are in the hands of racketeers."

Even though he was Director of the Patriotic Society and the Veterans Committee seemed to be its veterans wing, Quinn denied any link.

"I make my living out of the Patriotic Society," he said. "The Veterans Committee is something I've started on the side."

Acting on a hunch, I asked what he thought of the Constitutional Educational League.

"He is doing very good work," he said.

"You mean Joseph Kamp?" I asked.

"Yes," Quinn replied. "There's a man for you who is against the Communists. He's all right. He's doing good work."

My query about Frank Gannett's Committee for Constitutional Government brought the response, "They're all right. They do good work."

I asked Quinn whether he opposed Communism. He laughed and said, "And how!"

Quinn's Patriotic Society has already launched a "five-year-program of fighting un-Americanism." This is confined to the usual name calling and hysterical ranting against Communists and labor unions. Nothing, as usual, is said against nationalist hate-mongers.

Navy Club of the United States of America, Rockford, Ill. Incorporated by an act of Congress in 1940. Membership is open to those who have served in any branch of the Navy or Coast Guard. The Club advocates a powerful Navy so "that there be no more Pearl Harbors." It is strictly non-political, non-partisan, non-sectarian. It pushes legislation for Navy veterans' benefits and is opposed to the merger of the Army and Navy Departments. The main strength of the Navy Club is in the Great Lakes region. It has 60 chapters and about 22,000 members. John L. Zimmerman is Commandant. Membership is $2.

Regular Veterans Association, Washington, D. C. In 1935 the United States Maimed Soldiers League and the Regular and Disabled Service Association were merged to form the RVA. Membership is open to veterans of regular active service in any branch of the Armed Forces. The Association has 416 posts and a membership of 85,000, of whom 70 percent are World War II veterans. Its platform of veterans' benefits is similar to that of other groups, but the RVA is also highly bonus-conscious. Its bill, H.R. 127, demands $4 per day for overseas service, with a maximum of $4,500. The RVA is active in legislative work and claims to have sponsored more benefit legislation "than all other organizations combined."

There is an indication of a nativist attitude in the statement of the RVA that it is "composed of Americans and stands for American principles in America, only." In joining, veterans must indicate whether they are "white" or "colored." The RVA is emphatically anti-Communist, and in August, 1945, its official bulletin demanded "immediate action against ringleaders of Communism." It has opposed Russian territorial expansion and American loans to Allied countries. William Floyd is National Commander. Membership costs $4.

United Negro and Allied Veterans of America, Chicago, Ill. This represents an attempt to achieve inter-racial solidarity between Negro and non-Negro veterans. Membership is open to all veterans "regardless of race, creed, color, political thought or sex," including Merchant Marine seamen, as well as to members of the Abraham Lincoln Brigade, a Communist-dominated volunteer group who fought against Franco.

Joe Louis is Honorary National Commander and charter member. Kenneth Kennedy, Negro holder of the Bronze Star, is actual Commander. The group was founded in Chicago in April, 1946 at a convention attended by 300 Negro and white delegates. They asked bonus privileges, adequate hospitalization and medical care for all veterans, job opportunities and equal political rights regardless of race, and the elimination of Jim Crow. Demands were also made for an end to colonial imperialism, the self-determination of small nations, and the pooling of atomic information among the Big Three powers. The organization has a growing membership of almost 1,200 and about 25 posts. The Charles Ferguson Chapter in New York, named after the veteran killed by a Freeport, L. I., policeman, at this writing has 180 members.

The souvenir booklet of the New York State Organizers' Conference carried advertisements of the Veterans Commission of the Communist Party, the Harlem Section of the Communist Party (full page), and a full-page ad by the Abraham Lincoln Brigade. Membership is $3.

United States Disabled War Veterans, World War II, Inc., Muncie, Ind. Vernon E. Lay is Commander, but the moving spirit and main supporter is Elmer C. Gentry, Adjutant. While in Muncie, I interviewed Gentry, an earnest fellow who lost his eyesight in service. His ambition was to emulate the success of the Disabled American Veterans. "It took the DAV fifteen years to get to the top," he said. "I'm meeting all the expenses now, hoping that some day we can do some good for the World War II veteran." The group files a yearly financial report with the Secretary of State of Indiana. Membership is $5.

The Vanguard, Inc., Tucson, Ariz. Membership is restricted to Americans who served in the Armed and Auxiliary Forces of Great Britain. The organization is non-sectarian and non-political. Its main purpose is to maintain comradeship among its members, "assist the American citizen who is a veteran of British Service" and maintain "amicable relationships with the sister democracies" of the United States and with the British Auxiliary Forces. Major J. Winchcombe-Taylor is President. Membership is $5.

Veterans Committee Against Communism, New York City. My letters to the Rev. Edward Lodge Curran as to which veterans' group to join finally evoked a response, in which he recommended the Veterans Committee Against Communism and urged me to

---

International Catholic Truth Society

Brooklyn, N. Y.

May 13, 1946

Dear Mr. Thompson:

        I am happy to know that you and your associates are determined to preserve our common Americanism against the threat of atheistic Communism. Under separate cover, I am sending you three copies of my own "Facts About Communism." I am also sending you some other material on the same subject.

        The first thing necessary is to study this material so that you may know all the facts. One of the important tasks before every real American is the necessity of acquainting our fellow-Americans with the nature and threat of Communism. As veterans, who defended our beloved country, you are in a particularly good position to do this work.

        You will be pleased to know that a state-wide veterans organization has been established in Queens County on Long Island. This organization, composed of veterans, is formulating a program against Communism in which, I believe, your group will be deeply interested. In order to participate in this program, I suggest that you write a letter to Mr. Vincent Rottkamp, ――――――――― Jamaica, New York. Tell him that I suggested that you write him.

Sincerely yours in Christ,

Rev. Edward Lodge Curran

President

Father Curran advises "Robert Thompson, Jr.," on politics, patriotism and a veterans' group.

write Vincent Rottkamp of Jamaica, Long Island, N. Y., for particulars. An advertisement in *The Tablet,* Brooklyn diocesan organ,
invited "veterans of all creeds" to join the Committee "in this crusade to save our Country from Red Fascist-Communism" and "oppose Communism, Red Fascism or any other alien forces that are
stirring up class, religious and racial hatreds." The Committee's
officers were John H. Galbraith, chairman; Louis Glantzlin, Kenneth
G. Judson. It has units in Brooklyn and Queens and hopes to get a
national following. There are only about 500 members.

Investigation disclosed that Vincent Rottkamp was a former officer of the Catholic War Veterans and an intense "anti-Communist."
In 1943 he was listed as a candidate for Councilman of the American Rock Party, a Coughlinite-type political group endorsed by
Father Coughlin and backed also by the Christian Front variety of
"patriots." A small hotel in Jamaica has usually served as Rottkamp's
office. The address of the Committee was at the same hotel. Rottkamp's name, however, has not been publicly associated with the
organization.

On July 6, the Committee passed a resolution against the United
Nations settling in Queens, claiming that the UN would bring
"many undesirable residents from foreign lands, who are opposed
to our form of government, and at the expense of our taxpayers.
Furthermore," the weird resolution alleged, "many of those connected with the UNO do not believe in God and will not permit
God's name to be used, or His blessings asked in any way in connection with the UNO program."

The Committee has circulated among Congressmen letters and an
article from *The Tablet* excoriating "Red Fascists." The literature
Father Curran sent me included three copies of his book *Facts
About Communism* (a 208-page harangue) and a large packet of
other anti-Communist literature written with the same hysterical,
clerical approach. A bibliography in *Facts About Communism* rec-
ommends Curran's own work, *Spain in Arms,* in which he sided with
Franco. A final plea urges the reader to communicate with the
"American Committee Against Communism of the International
Catholic Truth Society." What a pity that Rev. Curran and many
others of his influential calling seemingly fail to see the danger to
Catholicism equally implicit in the work of nationalist hate-mongers!

Veterans Independent Political League, New York City, was organized to press for the passage of a bonus in 1946. Its Chairman, Thomas F. Burke, stated, "There is plenty of money in the Treasury for England, Russia and other countries, and the veterans are going after their share, too." It has units in New York's five boroughs. This outfit uses the bonus appeal to attract veterans, and seems to have a political axe to grind into the bargain.

Veterans Political Committee of the United States, Inc., New York City. A puzzling World War II group of which Jerry A. Freeman is executive secretary and, apparently, moving spirit. Its objectives are to promote intelligent world cooperation, unmask unscrupulous politicians and promote compulsory peacetime military training. It also advocates "intelligent elimination of racial and religious discrimination" and opposes "Nazi, Fascist or Communist" groups—"all this to be accomplished," its red-white-blue prospectus reads, "by study, investigation, discovery, publicity, political and legal action." The Committee has a membership of about 800. Dues are $2.

"We are so serious," Freeman wrote me, "that our enthusiasm may be interpreted by some as belligerency." I interviewed Freeman and he told me, "Every union leader is a no good racketeer and crook." He later qualified, "I don't mean all labor leaders, but 98 percent of them are racketeers."

Veterans Protective and Welfare Association, Phoenix, Ariz. "Some people call me the one-man vigilante committee and most everybody in the state knows me as a sort of crusader," wrote W. B. Williamson, Executive Secretary. He has opposed slackers, Communism, red tape in the Veterans Administration, and "crooked politicians." "If I know a candidate is a crook, I get up on the platform and tell the public," Williamson says, "and am very handy with my fists whenever it is necessary to use them." A crusader for veterans' rights, Williamson served seventeen and a half years in the Army. His Association has 1,750 members and membership is $5.

Veterans Sounding Post, New York City. A subdivision of the New York League for the Hard of Hearing, a social agency which aids all veterans, including Merchant Marine seamen and women,

free of charge. The Post was organized by the many veterans who
came for the service. Made possible by the Lieut. Lester N. Hof-
heimer Foundation, it has its own headquarters, a combined class-
room, recreation, club and reading room adjacent to the League's
offices. The veteran with impaired hearing feels more at home, when
learning to lip-read or undergoing voice and speech training, in the
company of fellow veterans. Howard S. Ezekiel is President; membership is $5.

War Two Veterans International, Birmingham, Ala. The other
veterans' activities of this group are eclipsed by its official organ,
The War Two Veteran, which had a circulation of about 9,000 in
July, 1946, and is well edited by Eric Smith, Jr. Edward C. Lee is
the publisher. Editorial policy seems progressive; an editorial on
April 20, 1946 advocated the abolition of the poll tax, charging that
the tax "disenfranchises seven white men for every three Negroes."
The War Two Veteran carries considerable advertising, much of
which, about the time of the primaries, was political. The constitution is innocuous and takes no stand on national or international
issues beyond seeking "to promote friendship and good will among
the peoples of all nations." "Even though we carry the name 'International,'" Mr. Lee wrote to me in April, 1946, "we are only organized within the State of Alabama, but are anticipating a nation-
wide organization in the very near future."

War Veterans Bar Association, New York City. Organized in
1945, this organization of lawyer veterans has for its objectives "to
render legal aid to veterans, veteran associations, and members of
the armed forces, improve veterans legislation, and help veterans to
re-establish themselves in the practice of the law." The Association
has made arrangements whereby veterans in need of legal assistance are referred to members of the Association, who have promised to charge reasonable fees. Myron Sulzberger, Jr. is President.
It costs $2 to join this well-intentioned group.

War Veterans Political Action Committee, New York City, is no
longer active, but may crop up again at election times. Founded in
1944, it was one of the first groups to exploit the veteran politically.
The group was established by Robert Paterson, a former County

Commander of the American Legion, and Michael J. Caslin. Strongly anti-New Deal, it urged the end of "bureaucracy" and the limiting of the tenure of Presidential office to two years. It also urged "the acquisition of Lower California and of one, more, or all of the Guianas as United States territory."

Yank Legion, Los Angeles, Cal., is another veterans' group whose publication, *Yank News*, overshadows the rest of its activities. Under the new direction of Charles R. MacFarland and Stan Blumenthal, the magazine has a democratic editorial policy. Included in the membership dues of $7.50 is a special accident insurance policy issued by the Great Northern Life Insurance Company.

On November 29, 1945, under other editorial direction, *Yank News* defended Tyler Kent in an article which followed the nationalist line. Since then the magazine has undergone a welcome change for the better. The credo of the new Yank Legion is expressed by its remark, "The veterans have learned the hard way that all blood is red, that all plasma is colorless."

CHAPTER FOURTEEN

How It Could "Happen Here"

Discharged veterans of this war will be carefully selected for toughness and peculiar abilities, and set to work organizing "Americanism Protective Committees" in ALL towns of the area. These Committees to be organized on the basis of observing, reporting and opposing CIO activities, and to become political campaign organizations. . . . The program includes the erection of a series of permanent billboards at strategic points in the area, each carrying periodically changed vitriolic attacks on the CIO. . . . In this connection certain peace officers will enter into an understanding with "The Organization" whereby the CIO hoodlums will be trapped in attempts to destroy these billboards, with resultant adverse publicity for the CIO.

William Walker, Chairman, Fight for Free Enterprise, Inc.

I'VE BEGUN WRITING this chapter on June 6, the anniversary of our landing in Normandy. Just two years ago the Allied armies began the final drive for victory. The Allies were an unbeatable team then, driving in a powerful, two-pronged offensive against a common enemy. Today much of their energy seems dedicated to mauling each other.

Over here, with President Roosevelt's leadership gone, anti-union forces hope to use this long-awaited opportunity to smash the position of organized labor. After World War I similar tactics met with considerable success. To prevent a repetition, and to consolidate its gains of the past decade, labor is fighting back desperately. The result is a wild scramble for favored position, with an eye on the elections.

In 1929, in Washington, I watched the Bonus Marchers and visited their shack villages on the banks of the Potomac. In 1933 I saw bread lines and soup kitchens while hitchhiking from New York to New Mexico. There was plenty of food then, but many people couldn't buy all they needed. Americans today (except for most veterans) have much more money, but prices are bursting their ceilings and housing for new families is almost nonexistent.

My concern is with the effect of this confusion on the mind of the veteran. How does all this affect *him?* I've been talking with veterans, brushing away superficialities and getting down to brass tacks. I've found most of them good-natured until I begin to talk about current problems. They become serious then. Some show their cynicism. "Look at these battle wounds," one of them said. "They got me two Purple Hearts. What else did they get me? Nothing! All I get is the run-around and a good chiseling when I spend my dough."

The veteran who belongs to a union and has a job isn't so vague about his future. I find that he usually has some notion of the issues underlying our economic distress, and is fortified with greater faith. I am thinking of the vast army of politically and socially unconscious veterans. I mean the fellow who grew up in a Coughlinite home, or whose father was anti-Catholic, or whose mother worked as a volunteer in the America First Committee office and injected prejudice and nationalist poison into the child's blood stream. I mean the unschooled fellow who can be so easily moved by prejudice and persuaded by the demagogue. A survey conducted by the Adult Education Council showed that 455,000 World War II veterans in New York City lack high-school diplomas; and of this number 161,000 range from illiterates to graduates of the eighth grade.

So far we have avoided the excesses to which some veterans were led after World War I. On Armistice Day in 1919, unemployed Legionnaires in Centralia, Wash., were egged on to rush the hall of the International Workers of the World. The rioters emasculated an IWW organizer, then they hanged him. Tremendous advances in social thinking since then will undoubtedly prevent such outrages, but the incident helps illustrate what an infuriated mob of angry ex-servicemen, when coerced by self-seeking interests, is capable of doing.

I estimate the World War I and World War II veteran army of unorganized, politically impressionable, socially semi-literate at roughly 5,000,000, or about one fourth the total of all veterans. Add to this the nationalist mob of at least 15,000,000 and you have the frightful potential prospect of one seventh of our nation contaminated with the virus of hate and ripe for a Huey Long-type nationalist. The role of the demagogues is to keep the nationalist pot boiling, pending the arrival of their messiah. They are confident he will emerge—"when chaos comes."

Our veteran population needs to be watched most carefully. What are the ex-GI's reactions as a $30-a-week salary dwindles three days after payday? Whom is he going to blame? Who will be the scapegoat? Whom is he going to listen to for the cure-all? In wanting to "do something about it," how far is he going to fall for the unscrupulous demagogues' plea for the need of a "strong man" to "save America"? Finally, what are the throes of his own personal reconversion doing to him mentally? Dr. Karl M. Bowman made a startling statement at the convention of the American Psychiatric Association in May, 1946:

A considerable number of returning servicemen who might otherwise have made a good adjustment to civilian life are being thrown into a neurotic state, and this is particularly true of those with wives and children to care for. They become embittered, distrustful, irritated and they develop the feeling that they've been wasting their time defending such a country.

That's the state of mind which the American nationalist bund is trying to nurture. Later, "at the right time," they hope to organize the veteran more completely, promise relief and vengeance, promise more of everything than anyone else. In return, they will demand the postwar era's most precious prize: the veteran's mind. Once they have it, they have enslaved the veteran. Through him they can capture the leadership of the dominant veterans' groups, drive a wedge into the ranks of labor, elect nationalists to Congress, inflame a mob to a white heat of racial and religious hate, organize veterans as vigilante storm troopers and use them as a private army to terrorize the majority. After this, throwing the Constitution out of the window might become a mere formality.

All of this, of course, may be done in the name of white supremacy, anti-Communism and anti-fascism. Once again Huey Long's prophecy rings true; for our native, fascistically inclined "nationalists" have adopted a new phrase—"Red Fascism." The holy crusade is not against Communism alone, but "Red Fascism." Nationalists desperate to discredit the appeal which the New Deal had for the underprivileged, started the fad by branding the New Deal National-Socialist. I expect to see myself denounced any day now as a "fascist."

By citing some examples of how these forces work it may be possible to help forestall the possible American tragedy toward which we have taken the initial steps.

One of these warning episodes took place on January 10, 1946, in New York's huge Madison Square Garden. Twenty thousand howling men and women participated. An array of prominent speakers who were innocently dragged into the meeting gave it a halo of respectability. They included Common Pleas Court Judge Clare G. Finerty of Philadelphia, who has been decorated by the Pope, and Joseph Scott, Los Angeles attorney, who is a recipient of the Catholic Laetare Medal. Many World War veterans in uniform were on the stage and thickly dotted the audience.

The meeting was ostensibly called "to defend Catholic rights." The issue arose as the result of a talk radioed by Prof. Harold J. Laski, British Labor Party leader, to a Spanish Refugee Aid rally in New York. Prof. Laski claimed that the Vatican had indulged in politics, particularly in supporting Franco. Because of Laski's remarks, Frank Fay, a Catholic actor and member of Actors' Equity,

Communists attack Patton ! Communists attack MacArthur ! Communists attack Truman !
LASKI ATTACKS CATHOLIC CHURCH AT COMMUNIST MEETING IN GARDEN !

Of course, You're against Communism But, are you doing anything about it ?

Well, here's a chance to Stand up and be Counted

Participate in the great mass rally . . .

AMERICA'S ANSWER TO COMMUNISM
MADISON SQUARE GARDEN
auspices FRIENDS OF FRANK FAY

They fought Communism the loud, futile way!

although not present, complained against five other actors who had appeared as entertainers. Fay charged that his religion had been slurred by Prof. Laski and demanded an investigation of the five actors (one of whom, a Catholic, was later reported married in St. Patrick's Cathedral).

Equity officials rejected Fay's complaint and by a vote of 470 to 72 censured him for making public his rebuke of his fellow actors. The fight was on. Quick to exploit the issue, nationalists raised the phony cry that an attack on Franco and the Vatican was an attack on the Catholic religion. It was a flimsy pretext. Criticizing the chief of an organization, be it clerical or political, by no means implies censure of its purposes or traditions. Is criticism of our President an act of disloyalty toward our country, the Constitution, or even the Democratic Party?

Prof. Laski denied the charge by saying: "Nothing could be more fantastic and untrue than the tale that I assailed and criticized the Roman Catholic religion." *Commonweal*, a Catholic journal, observed soberly: "We must ever be watchful not to allow our faith to serve as a cloak under which we strive to smother political discussion." Quentin Reynolds, himself a Catholic, stated that Frank Fay was being used as an "unsuspecting tool" and that "members of the Catholic clergy are sincere and honest, and also completely fooled."

As for socialist Prof. Laski, his actual attitude toward Communists is summed up by his statement against them. No Communist nor fellow traveller would excoriate them as did Laski:

The Communist parties outside Russia act without moral scruples, intrigue without any sense of shame, are utterly careless of truth, sacrifice, without any hesitation, the means they use to the ends they serve. The result is a corruption, both of the mind and of the heart, which is alike contemptuous of reason and careless of truth.

The nationalist hotheads prevailed. They organized, then jumped on the "Friends of Frank Fay" bandwagon. Publicity was in charge of Edward Atwell, former official of the America First Committee. Joe Kamp rushed out a 34-page booklet. The anti-Jewish *Gentile News* took its hat off to "Frank Fay—a real American, a true Christian." Father Curran whooped it up in his column in the *Gaelic*

American. Nationalists from coast to coast went wild at the meeting, adopting the slogan, "We still believe in God!"

Came the night of the rally and the politically faithful flocked. Admission was free. When I arrived at Madison Square Garden I found it festooned with flags. It was like a reunion for me. Not since the publication of *Under Cover* had I seen so many of my "friends" under one roof.

They were largely a mixture of Christian Fronters, Coughlinites, America First Committee nationalists of the better-dressed class, and Americans who, I'm convinced, were completely innocent of such ties. They came because they thought it was a patriotic, anti-Communist meeting called to combat bigotry and Communism and nothing else.

I took a quick walk around the huge arena. Joe Kamp was sitting next to Lambert Fairchild. John Henihan, Jr., former Bronx Christian Front leader just out of the Army, shared a box with Father Curran, Christian Front defender. Christian Front speakers John Geis and Daniel Kurts were there. Hamilton Fish sat across the aisle from William T. Leonard, both America First Committeemen. Also present were two American Indians in full costume. For some strange reason a nationalist meeting is never complete without dressed-up Indians. The large America First Committee rallies had them. They were present at Bund rallies, their regalia decorated with reversed swastikas. I have never understood the reason.

To my amazement, I saw Dr. George S. Benson of Harding College on the platform. With him were Rev. Carl McIntire, the anti-Catholic minister, and Joseph P. Ryan, President-for-life of the International Longshoremen's Association. It seemed strange to see this labor leader in the same crowd with labor-baiters. His presence on the platform was no stranger than that of Emmanuel Josephson, M.D., a member of the Jewish faith, who delivered a scathing anti-labor speech and received a hot ovation from the many Jew-baiters present.

Chairman of the evening was former New York State Senator and Army Major John J. McNaboe. I had heard him speak in 1939, together with Joe McWilliams, to a mob rallied under Christian Front auspices. On November 16, 1945 I interviewed McNaboe, posing as Robert Thompson, Jr. "The only thing we can do," he told me grimly, "is to wait for two years till the veterans are kicked around more. Then you'll see a revolution like you never saw one before." In Madison Square Garden I sat under McNaboe in the press box and stared into his beady little eyes and reddish, surly face. Near the end of the platform I saw Edward Atwell bustling about and engaging frequently in whispered conversation with Howard Rushmore, former movie critic for the *Daily Worker*, now turned anti-Communist reporter for Hearst's New York *Journal-American*.

The tenor of the meeting may be gathered by McNaboe's opening remarks: "I say 'Nuts' to Quentin Reynolds, who tried to label this meeting anti-Semitic. To the keyhole peeker [Winchell] I say 'Double nuts'; to all others who tried to smear this meeting I say, 'Triple nuts!'"

After this distinguished display of barroom English the meeting settled down to rabble-rousing of a dignified order and a wholesale excoriation of Communism as the sole enemy of the United States. Speaker after speaker doted on the theme hour after hour. The meeting required five weary hours and didn't end till about 1:30 A.M. It was "patriotism" with a vengeance!

As I have repeatedly stated, I hold no brief for American Communism, but I doubt if this brand of hysterical Red-baiting can ward it off. The orgy was comparable with the dancing of jungle medicine men who try to frighten away "evil spirits" by screaming to the beat of tom-toms. I visualized our capitalist order as the patient; Communism was the unavoidable evil spirit which enters sick society everywhere. I knew that you couldn't erase Communism by howling at it. You can't shoo it away or cuss it out of the country. Those who say you can do it that way alone are quacks.

Communism is the symptom of a sick society. It's rooted deep in the substrata of the economic and social failings of democracy. It's not a superficial growth, but is made of sterner stuff. The speakers didn't know this—they went on their merry-go-round, taking the easy way out by screaming against and taking pot shots at Communism! Little wonder that under such ineffectual opposition, American Communism is growing. We are not fighting the roots or clearing the soil, but merely flailing our arms at the poison ivy vine! You can't fight for democracy by resorting to wild ranting and Red-baiting. That's the way Hitler "fought" Communism. If we insist on doing the same thing here, the same results could conceivably happen here.

Immediately after the meeting started, the sixth sense which most investigators develop warned me. And what I expected finally happened.

As McNaboe continued his attack against "Reynolds-Winchell-Laski-Carlson," he singled me out to such an extent that one newspaper wrote: "It appeared more of a rally to smear Carlson than to defend Frank Fay." At each mention of my name the hotheads became more emotionalized against me. A nationalist and a reporter for a Hearst paper, who recognized me, became finger men and pointed me out to a number of vicious-looking thugs, the kind of Christian Front goons who used to attack defenseless New York Jews when they safely outnumbered them. Four of these characters planted themselves on each side of the press table at which I sat. From several scouts I had sent out, the word came that the goons were out to "get" me as soon as I left the hall.

I decided to test these reports and sense the mood of the hoodlum gang. I got up and walked briskly into their midst. Two of the four followed me. Others came out from corners and began to converge toward me. A well-known nationalist came up to me. "You're Carlson, ain't ya?" he snarled. "G'wan, sit down, or we'll throw ya out!" I stared at him and the other goons and recognized several from the old days. I knew, however, that nothing would happen *in* Madison Square Garden. After all, it was a high-class "Christian" meeting. McNaboe had said so. I went back to my seat. The two goons followed me and took their positions as before, watching my every move, quick to follow if I left.

When two *PM* reporters left at 10 P.M., they urged me to go along.

"I've never been afraid of bums before," I said, "and I'm not going to start now. Look at that gang. There are at least fifteen. Individually they're all cowards. Collectively they're a wolf pack of bullies—a bully is a coward first."

As the speakers droned on endlessly (Joseph Scott was mesmerizing the crowd) I decided to call home. It was nearly midnight and I had promised to phone home at 11 P.M. I gathered my notes and buried them in an inside pocket. I filled my pockets with discarded photographer's bulbs. In my left fist I clutched a certain defensive object. In my right hand I had something else. I could have asked for protection from one of the many police or detectives. Within elbow's reach, I could have tapped expert, trained help. But I felt that I could handle the ruffians alone.

With a silent prayer, I walked straight toward the collection of goons, turned swiftly to the left to give them just time enough to begin following me. The ruse worked; they began following in a pack. Suddenly I wheeled around and reversed my steps, catching the goons off guard. I walked straight through their split ranks and kept walking. While they watched for another surprise move, I strode swiftly from the auditorium toward the Eighth Avenue exit where I could lose myself in a crowd—*if* I got there first.

I had already arranged with writer-photographer Walter K. Lewis to serve as my "distracting" agent. "When they begin to gain on me," I said, "distract them any way you can. Slow them up!" Walter performed his job beautifully. He made believe he'd snap their pictures. The half dozen "Christian patriots" who had taken after me didn't like the idea of being mugged. No coward who is planning to commit mayhem likes to be photographed. By the time they reached the exit I had slipped into a subway kiosk.

Finding me gone, the ruffians cornered Walter against a wall. But even hotheaded nationalists fear to injure a newspaperman when they're identified. It's bad publicity for such "Christian" goons.

"Which way did that Carlson go?" they asked Walter.

"That way," he answered, pointing toward the Hudson River.

By that time I was emerging from a subway exit a block away. I made my phone call and, without losing time, walked back to the balcony entrance of Madison Square Garden, my pockets still filled with flashbulbs. I turned in my balcony ticket (I also had an extra orchestra seat in case of another emergency) and walked in. I took my seat amid the crowd of Coughlinites. The whole operation had required less than ten minutes, and Scott was still talking.

After Scott had finally finished, McNaboe began to denounce me. The crowd began to boo Carlson. Cupping my hands, I booed more loudly than the rest. After the booing, I asked the man next to me: "Who *is* this guy Carlson?"

"The son-of-a-bitch is a radio commentator or something," he said. "Anyway, he ain't no good. I saw him walking outta the hall. The —— had a dozen bodyguards with 'im. We Christians had 'im scairt to death."

"Where's Carlson now?" I asked.

"Runnin' away! It ain't healthy for 'im around here. No, sir!"

I was in time to hear Dr. Benson, the next orator on the program, pounce on Communism, and to hear Rev. McIntire say: "I'm a Protestant, but I'm proud to know men like Father Urban Nagel, the brains behind this meeting. We are going to call on Congress to outlaw the General Motors strike. It's the collectivist closed shop which gives these unions their strength. We must fight Communism step by step, bit by bit."

Frank Fay walked in at 12:20 A.M. He spoke wearily for an hour. I stayed to the very end. Lambert Fairchild and Joe Kamp were among the last to leave. I saw them shake hands with some of the speakers, but they were too far away to be identified.

A few days later I sent a release, documented with photostats, to Cardinal Spellman and New York newspapers. I exposed Rev. McIntire as a Catholic-baiter. The spectacle of an anti-Catholic speaking at a meeting called in protest against anti-Catholicism was news. The New York *Post* used the story. Frederick Woltman of the New York *World-Telegram* ran a column and added something I hadn't known: on September 9, 1935 McIntire was ousted from the ministry of the Presbyterian Church because of "violation of his ordi-

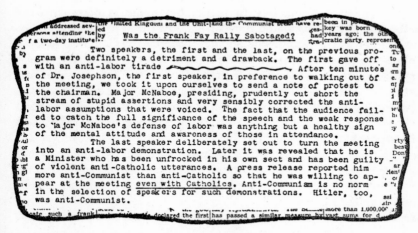

Was the Frank Fay Rally Sabotaged?

Two speakers, the first and the last, on the previous program were definitely a detriment and a drawback. The first gave off with an anti-labor tirade. After ten minutes of Dr. Josephson, the first speaker, in preference to walking out of the meeting, we took it upon ourselves to send a note of protest to the chairman. Major McNaboe, presiding, prudently cut short the stream of stupid assertions and very sensibly corrected the anti-labor assumptions that were voiced. The fact that the audience failed to catch the full significance of the speech and the weak response to Major McNaboe's defense of labor was anything but a healthy sign of the mental attitude and awareness of those in attendance.

The last speaker deliberately set out to turn the meeting into an anti-labor demonstration. Later it was revealed that he is a Minister who has been unfrocked in his own sect and has been guilty of violent anti-Catholic utterances. A press release reported him more anti-Communist than anti-Catholic so that he was willing to appear at the meeting even with Catholics. Anti-Communism is no norm in the selection of speakers for such demonstrations. Hitler, too, was anti-Communist.

Father William J. Smith's *Crown Heights Comment* makes some very pungent comments on the Frank Fay rally—and particularly on those who fight Communism the way Hitler did: by violent Red-baiting and labor-baiting!

nation vows." McIntire then set up an independent church and launched his vicious attacks against the Catholics.

Had Cardinal Spellman, and some of those who attended, known anything of the *sub rosa* aspects of the meeting or of Rev. McIntire's record, I believe the orgy might have been called off. There were a lot of undercover facts which the respectable American Catholics present didn't know. I pieced the story together after an exhaustive investigation. It has never been disclosed in print before that Merwin K. Hart of the National Economic Council was a main instigator of the so-called "Friends of Frank Fay" rally. It was through Hart that Rev. McIntire was invited. The meeting was financed in part through Hart, but Hart wanted his role to remain under cover.

After my news release, storm clouds gathered against the sponsors. Father William J. Smith, S.J., Director of the Crown Heights School of Catholic Workmen, who had previously praised the spirit of the meeting, took exception to Dr. Josephson's labor-baiting. In his *Crown Heights Comment*, Father Smith called Rev. McIntire's speech "a perfect imitation of a fellow-traveler of the National Association of Manufacturers." Father Smith objected to denunciations by various speakers of "the OPA, Closed Shop, Strikes, trade unions, the rabble-rousing subject of the Roosevelt family." He cautioned the Friends of Frank Fay to "avoid the blunders of other well-intentioned but misguided movements."

Neither Father Smith nor other respectable Catholics know how close the meeting came to harming the Church. Only at the last minute did certain members of the Catholic War Veterans who had attended as individuals, and not officially, sense that something was wrong. They withdrew their support promptly. From what seemed an innocent "anti-Communist" meeting the rally degenerated into an instrument for the revival of Christian Front spirit. This was not discovered till a few days before the rally, so carefully had Hart and others covered their tracks through front operatives.

I learned, for instance, that Merwin K. Hart had called a luncheon to initiate the rally. Rev. McIntire was present, together with a representative of the Catholic War Veterans attending unofficially. So was the doctor with the French name and the Whitehall telephone number in New York. Expenses were estimated at $6,000. I know that Frank Mc——, who works intimately with Joe Kamp, accounted for $1,500. I also know that Frank Fay was advised by a certain friendly attorney to get out of it all, but the attorney finally gave up trying when Fay decided to join the Hart crowd. "They wanted to charge admission so they could keep certain people out," one of those who attended the luncheon and subsequent meetings told me. "We didn't like that, and we didn't like it when they wouldn't tell us who was financing the affair."

Facts are stubborn. Truth cannot long be suppressed. I have the roster of other important backers. If I were convinced they were malicious men, I would expose them. I feel they were innocent— duped by the "anti-Communist" publicity cry. The list includes the treasurer of a Long Island savings bank; a professor at Queens College, L. I.; an official of the Knights of Columbus, and others. If educated men can fall for such "patriotism," how much more gullible must be the less literate masses!

It was my job as reporter to uncover these facts. No point is served by publishing the names of innocently beguiled men. I hope they have learned by now that anti-Communism, in order to prove effective, must go deeper than name calling and hysteria provoked in a mob. Emotionalize the mob, inflame its passions, frighten its members out of their wits, exhort them to a holy war against Communism, blind their reason and dull their intellect through fear and hate, and you have enslaved the minds of the people. You have taken a major step toward fascism. If some people want to "fight Communism" that way, let them take to heart Father Smith's profound remark:

"Anti-Communism is no norm in the selection of speakers for such demonstrations; Hitler, too, was anti-Communist!"

And, one may add, so was Major Vidkun Quisling!

The meeting exploited veterans to the full. Rev. (Major) John Curran gave the invocation. Ten medal-winning servicemen were introduced. A tableau was presented in support of Patton and MacArthur. Patrick Boarman, World War II veteran, gave a passionate harangue in keeping with the theme of the evening. I'm certain the veterans present were ignorant of the Christian Front backing of the rally.

In historic San Antonio, Texas, William Walker illustrates the pattern which the die-hard forces of labor will use. Walker is Chairman of the so-called Fight for Free Enterprise, Inc. He shifted from one job to another before hitting on his present "save America" program.

According to a San Antonio Better Business Bureau report, Walker was a mining-stock salesman. The venture blew up. He organized a "victory" publication—a book to be known as a *Who's Who in Home Defense*. The Chief Air-Raid Warden refused to give him the names he needed, and Walker went looking for greener pastures. Recently he set out to save Texas from Communism * and the CIO.

"It's time to get tough," reads one of Walker's bulletins. "We are right out in the open, bare-knuckling these sinister forces with everything we've got." Issues of his *Freedom News* ran notices inviting veterans "opposed to paying tribute" to unions to write for information on forming "a militant veterans union." These veterans were to be recruited for one of the most insidious schemes it has been my good fortune to uncover.

On June 8, 1945 Walker wrote a secret letter to a select list, using stationery blazoned with the American flag and the Statue of Liberty. He enclosed a "Confidential Memorandum" which outlined his plans for spending $52,000. The plans were to be executed by a group he identified only as "The Organization," which he admitted would become "the front for attacking the CIO vigorously and relentlessly, on behalf of those who, for obvious reasons, cannot now make themselves the target for reprisals." Walker outlined eight "Basic Measures." I cite two:

Discharged veterans of this war will be carefully selected for toughness and peculiar abilities, and set to work organizing "Americanism Protective Committees" in ALL towns of the area. These Committees to be organized on the basis of observing, reporting and opposing CIO activities, and to become political campaign organizations in the spring of 1946. They will also become direct action committees. . . .

The program includes the erection of a series of permanent billboards at strategic points in the area, each carrying periodically changed vitriolic attacks on the CIO and its leadership. In this connection certain peace officers will enter into an understanding with "The Organization" whereby the CIO hoodlums will be trapped in attempts to destroy these billboards, with resultant adverse publicity for the CIO.

* Betty Gannett, Communist Party official, admits that there are only about 485 Communists in all of Texas.

As a recruiting agent, Walker formed the Veterans Union for Action, USA—"a militant organization to keep America American." It invited members on a "no fees, no dues, no cost to any veteran" basis. Walker urged vets: "It's our turn to do any pushing around that's needed. . . . This can only be done by political action, by winning and holding actual power."

Walker admires Pettengill, and the latter's column appears regularly in *Freedom News*. A full-page advertisement signed by Benjamin F. Fairless, President of the U.S. Steel Corporation, appeared in February, 1946. Among Walker's writers is George B. Merrill, who spent four years in the Army and now writes on "free enterprise." One of Walker's methods of fighting for "free enterprise" is to write editorials calling unionism such things as: "Robbery, gangrenous pollution of Italy and Germany; the dispenser of serfdom being spawned by Russian agents and pathological, grievance-ridden leaders and men."

Another Walker stunt is the incorporation of the name "Congress for Industrial Organizations," in order to prevent the CIO from using its own name in Texas. Walker claims that the CIO has not registered its name and ought to get out of the state. He lost the first round, when a Texas court ruled in favor of the CIO, but Walker has renewed his efforts to "release the wage earner from the clutches of labor racketeers." Walker is equally hostile to Dr. Homer P. Rainey, distinguished Texas educator and gubernatorial candidate whom he accuses as a "tool of the CIO." At regular intervals Walker requests money from wealthy persons, exploiting his suit against the CIO, the final outcome of which is still pending.

William Walker's plans included the recruiting of veterans for anti-union work.

I corresponded with Walker's executive secretary, Raymonda Turken. "Perhaps you can form an anti-Communist veteran organization yourself," she urged. "I feel that most veterans would join such an organization," she wrote on March 19, 1946.

No less enterprising is Governor Eugene Talmadge of Georgia, who at this writing has won the Democratic primaries for re-nomination for his old job, on a pure-white-supremacy ticket. The victory virtually cinches the governorship for Talmadge. A friend of Grand Dragon Green, M.D., and an idol of Georgia's backwoods "wool hat" elements who stormed Stone Mountain in the cross-burning demonstration in May, Talmadge predicated his campaign appeals to a large extent upon race prejudice.

In his campaign Talmadge appealed to the veteran for all he was worth. His son, Herman, organized GI-Talmadge Clubs in Georgia towns. "My father has pledged that fifty percent of all the appointments to office that he makes will be from the veterans of all wars," Herman Talmadge told an audience of ex-servicemen. In addition, Talmadge, Sr. promised "to give all veterans free business licenses, a 5-year state ad valorem tax exemption and an honorary driver's license for life" . . . free of charge. Herman told the "wool hat" boys: "The Georgia farmer has three friends: Sears Roebuck, God Almighty, and Gene Talmadge."

Talmadge projected himself as the friend of the veteran and his guardian against "Gestapo" justice. Addressing an audience which included many ex-GIs, Talmadge, in shirtsleeves and red suspenders, bellowed that all they could get was "unemployment pay!" He would do right by them. He would install more psychiatrists in Georgia's mental hospitals to treat afflicted GIs, so that those arrested for crimes would not receive "Gestapo trials."

To promise more education, more housing, more of everything—provided the public agrees to take, also, more of intolerance—was the Hitler formula. Whether a religious or a racial minority is the immediate victim, the principle is the same. Hitler, too, appealed to veterans. Hitler, too, promised everything to everybody—except the "enemy." Hitler, too, had his "white supremacy" slogan. This American "Aryan" slogan does not pertain to Negroes alone. In many parts of the country Jews are not considered "white people."

Neither are our citizens from the Philippines and Puerto Rico Islands or other dark-skinned Americans. "White supremacy" also excludes Chinese Americans and Nisei. "White supremacy" when mouthed by a bigot is tantamount to a Nazi's "Aryan German."

To every working man Talmadge promises "a job, a home and the security of livelihood, with opportunity to advance in salary, wages and in status." To industry, however, he promised a reduction in taxes, as well as a firm grasp on the political machinery which, while enriching a ruling minority, has kept Southern per capita wealth lowest in the country.

Talmadge's professed friendship for labor is puzzling, in that he has opposed unions in the past and had the support of certain reactionary business interests. His *Statesman* headlined a statement on the subject "The Laborer Is Worth His Hire." Talmadge said he learned this the hard way while walking between the plow handles down the long rows of cotton and tobacco, season in, season out. Of course he doesn't pledge his support to unions; but to Georgia's backwoods population the distinction is not made clear. These simple-minded folk are alarmed at the fact that Richmond, Va., for the "first time in its history has placed two Negro policemen in its City Police Department." These, of course, will police Richmond's Negro population only. Nonetheless, Talmadge and Georgia's unschooled farm population regard it as the beginning of the "end of White Supremacy" for them.

Whatever may be the prospects for Georgia under Talmadge, it's his technique which should interest those of us who want to know "how" a demagogue gets into office. Even though Robert Thompson, Jr. was in Buffalo and could not possibly help Talmadge's candidacy, Talmadge wrote me cordially as "My dear Friend Thompson," and urged me to "please tell all of your friends to get active in my behalf. . . . With kindest personal regards." Talmadge was on the job twenty-four hours a day.

Shortly after Talmadge's victory in the primary, one of the most brutal murders in Southern history took place near Monroe, 40 miles from Atlanta. In broad daylight a gang of 20 men, armed with guns, and dressed in khaki clothes, dragged out two Negroes, one of them a veteran of the Pacific campaign, and their wives, from a car driven by a white farmer. The leader of the gang was described as a "dignified white man." They pumped sixty bullets into the four Negroes and disappeared. It was "white supremacy" striving to "keep the Negro in his place."

Governor Arnall offered a reward of $10,000 as Georgia and FBI investigators sought to unearth witnesses. They were handicapped because "the best people" as well as the worst, wouldn't talk in fear of retaliation. "Things like that are to be regretted," said Talmadge. Previously he had declared in an interview that "nothing can be gained by giving equal rights to someone with an artificial civilization that has been forced upon him only 150 years ago." The murders boosted Georgia's score to 525 lynchings since 1882. The state is second only to Mississippi. During Talmadge's three terms as Governor fourteen lynchings took place in Georgia.

It "can happen here" when a government is lax and its officials merely "regret" the aftermath of brutality.

In my mail one day came an odd eight-page veterans newspaper called *For the Man Who Came Back*, and published in Chicago by one Dick Nielsen. It started off with an autobiographical article. Adjoining this was a column in which Nielsen said: "I want my government to be run strictly by and for Americans. . . . I am not a dumb-bell. I don't want the people I elect to get the idea I can be pushed around for the sake of satisfying personal or group interests." It was mildly anti-Communist and closed with an innocuous "Veteran's Prayer." It was issued by Plain Facts Publishing Co.

Something about the publication told me there was more to it than was apparent on the surface. On November 9, 1945 I interviewed Dick Nielsen at his home in Chicago. Nielsen was in his early twenties, a fine, clean-cut type with blond hair and blue eyes. He and his brother had just returned from overseas service. Dick had worked as usher at a neighborhood movie. His father was guard in a museum. I asked if he had done any magazine work before.

"Nope," he said. "This is the first time I've worked on such a thing. I've got a friend on the *Herald-American* [Hearst] who does some of the writing."

Nielsen's political facts were off base. "Now take this man Dean Acheson," he said. "He is supposed to be a member of the State Department, but he's a Communist. He went to a Communist school just twenty minutes outside of Washington."

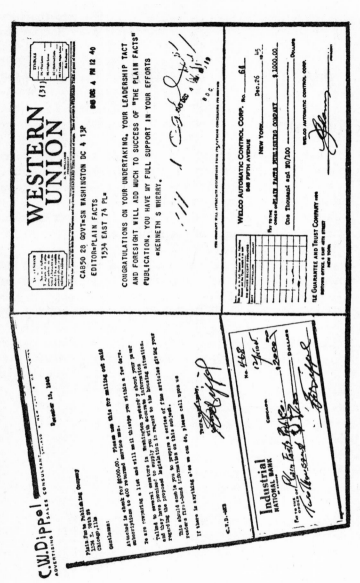

A Senator and two checks backed the efforts of an editorially inexperienced ex-GI to become a big-shot publisher in the anti-labor, super-American movement.

"Which one?" I asked.

"I don't remember, but somebody told me and I know it's true. And take this United Nations business, it won't work either." Tactfully, I asked Nielsen how he knew that. "I've been talking to people who are in a position to know," he answered. Dick impressed me as a nice fellow who didn't know the political score and was parroting someone else's views. Let's take his views on Hitler. "Hitler did a lot of good to Germany," he said earnestly. "But he just overstepped his bounds."

Dick was one of those awfully nice young kids who could be easily exploited. I could see that he was helpless by himself. I wanted to know who was behind him. Nielsen didn't want to say at first, but he finally took me into his confidence.

"I've got a business agent," he said. "The newspaper was his idea. I wouldn't move without him. He got me the $500 for the 10,000 copies we printed of the first issue."

I began to cultivate Nielsen in earnest. I was anxious to meet his "business manager." Nielsen took me further into his confidence by showing me photostatic copies of two checks he had received. My eyes popped when I saw a check for $2,000 from one C. W. Dippel, advertising and sales consultant of Chicago, New York and Washington; and another for $1,000 from the Welco Automatic Control Corporation in New York. Both Dippel and J. Adams, President of Welco, had written him letters directing that the funds be used for subscriptions to veterans.

I obtained photostatic copies of the letters and checks.

I didn't interview Nielsen as Robert Thompson, Jr., or under any of my usual investigational names. I've forgotten the name I used. I remember, though, that it was Germanic and, whoever I was, I came from Cleveland. On parting, I agreed to meet Nielsen the next day in the lobby of the LaSalle Hotel and meet his "business manager."

C. W. Dippel proved to be a short, blond fellow with thick lips, a wisp of a mustache and a mousy manner about him. We had lunch at the LaSalle Hotel, which has since gone up in flames with the loss of many lives. "This country is going Communist. Take these people," Dippel said, pointing to the diners. "They're smug and complacent and don't know what is going on under their noses."

Take the CIO and the PAC—they're Communist. My job is to counteract the work of the PAC."

The General Motors strike was on then and I asked Dippel what he thought of it.

"General Motors and Big Steel are trying to kill two birds with one stone. They want to knock out Truman by discrediting him and kill the unions at the same time."

I thought this remark of Dippel's showed good reasoning.

"My contacts in Washington are perfect," Dippel resumed. "That's not generally known, but I know a lot of big men. I know Senator Wherry personally. I've done some undercover work in connection with the Catholic Church fighting Communism," Dippel said, as I pricked up my ears. "I turned it over to the FBI because they wanted certain information on Communists in Washington." He did not amplify.

Dippel and Nielsen asked me why I was interested in their newspaper.

"Your newspaper looks as though it had possibilities," I said, "and I'd like to work for it. I can sell mass subscriptions for you. I'm a salesman."

"How much commission would you want?" Dippel asked.

"This is how we'll work it." I made up the scheme as I went along. "I'll call on manufacturers in Cleveland. I'll show them the magazine. I'll tell them all about you and your contacts in Washington. They can telephone you and check up personally. I'll try to hit for a minimum of $500 from each businessman. That makes roughly 100 subscriptions to be sent to veterans. Right? I'll collect twenty-five percent commission if that's OK with you."

Dippel had listened carefully. "The commission is OK. How'll you handle the money?"

"I don't want to handle any money," I said. "That's your job. All I do is to make the sale. Checks will be sent in direct to you. You give me my cut out of the money that comes in. How's that for a deal?"

It was agreed that I'd call on Cleveland manufacturers and tell them that the magazine was being published for one purpose: "to counteract the work of the PAC." Dippel gave me a three-page set of instructions outlining his policy and suggesting similar schemes to attract anti-labor money. One paragraph read, referring to the veterans: "We have here a group of millions of young adults who are willing to be led. In my opinion it is very simply a question of who will lead them—the Communists or the sound American business men."

Dippel spoke of getting big money from a Texas oil man and a Houston attorney "who has more money than he knows what to do with." Both had allegedly phoned Dippel for details of his plan. "Money don't mean anything to those fellows," Nielsen put in. "Why, they'll laugh at you if you ask for only $5,000. That's peanuts to them. You gotta talk in terms of hundreds of thousands of dollars."

Here was a young man who had no experience in writing or editorial work, who was shallow politically, but who posed as an expert on complex national politics. The important fact from my point of view is that young Nielsen was being used to grind someone else's axe. There are countless Nielsens throughout the country—impressionable young men whose minds are being bought to serve narrow interests, and not those of America as a whole.

Here is a case study of how a former collaborator of General Moseley, George Deatherage and James True (both Deatherage and True are under indictment for alleged sedition) almost captured the position of Junior Vice-Commander of the Veterans of Foreign Wars at its October, 1945 convention in Chicago. Only the alertness of a young veteran (whose name I've been asked not to reveal) prevented him from making the grade. The abortive attempt came after efforts to select a World War II candidate were deadlocked. One of the veterans insisted that no one be nominated until they had heard from "Colonel Campbell."

"Campbell arrived with a bang," my informant wrote. "He is a stocky fellow, bursting with energy, and looks a lot like Father Coughlin. He was in uniform and bemedaled. He immediately took the rostrum and opened up something like this: 'Forget the colonel stuff, fellows. I'm just one of the boys. Call me Jim. All my friends call me Jim. Now I know you're suspicious of all officers. Well, my record's clean. My boys whom I commanded will tell you I'm a right guy. Ask any of them. . . .'

"Campbell, talking smoothly and with fire, said that he had been in the VFW a long time, and had always been bucking the big boys.

And now, by God, it was time for the World War II men to take over from the old fogies. What was more he, Jim Campbell, had a platform for the veterans. He was willing to lead the fight. He wanted more and more jobs for the veterans . . . even if it was necessary to drive the radicals from the factories and make room for honest-to-goodness vets.

"It was only that one remark which jarred me. Otherwise, the boy sounded good. A regular firebrand. He swept most of the vets off their feet. But I smelled the old herring in Campbell's barrel. A check at the Chicago *Times* that night bolstered my suspicion. I passed around copies of the information. I must say that the next day the vets dropped Campbell like a hot potato when they learned to their dismay his background."

Who is James E. Campbell and why was he dropped "like a hot potato"? The answer is found in his testimony in Volume 5 of the Dies Committee hearings which took place in May, 1939. It is the amazing story of how Campbell received more than $8,000 for "fighting Communism." He used parts of the funds to buy a car and pay off alimony and his creditors. Campbell testified that with the funds he also started to build a house in the Kentucky hinterlands, so that when the "Communist revolution" rolled around he and his wealthy backer could hide in the hills and direct "patriotic" strategy from there.

Campbell's angel was Dudley Pierrepont Gilbert, member of an old New York family and of the Sons of the Revolution. He and five others, including a former president of the New York Produce Exchange, founded the American Nationalists, Inc. to fight "Communism" on a "Park-Avenue" level. Gilbert testified that he was no Jew-baiter, and told how he had resigned from a phony Order of '76 because "they were doing no good; they were doing Jew-baiting but no real job on Communists." Gilbert met Campbell in 1938 in Newport, R. I., the swank summer resort. With Campbell was George Deatherage, a former Klansman, führer of the American Nationalist Confederation, speaker with Fritz Kuhn at Joe McWilliams' "patriotic" rally in 1939, and now under indictment charged with sedition.

Gilbert had served as a buck private and Campbell as a captain in World War I. Campbell was "Americanism" Chairman of the Subversive Activity Investigation Committee of the Reserve Officers

Association. "We got slapped down," Campbell testified, referring to Army authorities who finally stopped his tactics. It didn't discourage Campbell. He convinced Gilbert that he was just the man to help save America. All he needed was funds.

Campbell set up office in Owensboro, Ky., as the Business Engineering Associates. Owensboro banks knew nothing about him because Campbell kept his account in another county. From his New York office Gilbert fed Campbell with hot news of the "revolution" which, Gilbert testified, he expected "before the snow flies"—in 1939. His informant was one George Rice, said to have been a waiter in a New York club of wealthy Jews. Gilbert testified that he wasn't sure if Rice was the informant's real name; he didn't know where Rice lived; he knew nothing of his background. He had seen no credentials, asked for no references. Rice's reports alleging that wealthy New York Jews were engaged in a fantastic and sinister plot to bolshevize America were in no way documented. Gilbert took the mysterious Mr. Rice completely at his word and paid him up to $25 per report. When the Dies Committee asked Gilbert to produce Rice for questioning, Rice couldn't be found.

Gilbert and Campbell were asked why they hadn't reported the alleged plotting to the Department of Justice. They would have been asked for documents, they answered, and they didn't have any. Besides, they didn't want to "dry up" their valuable source of "information." They preferred to handle it in their own vigilante way. How did Rice obtain his information, Campbell was asked. He testified that Rice was supposed to have overheard the plotting while standing "at the door"—*outside* the door—of the secret meeting room. Rice wrote his "reports" in longhand. He phoned Gilbert at unexpected hours and met him in such odd places as the information booth of the Grand Central Station in New York, one of the busiest spots on earth. Gilbert would wait there till Rice tapped him on the shoulder and the two would go off to some secluded spot. Then, Gilbert testified, he would copy Rice's dope in his own handwriting. Either Gilbert destroyed the originals or Rice himself tore them to bits first, then flushed them in a public lavatory.

Gilbert was asked whether he took Rice's reports seriously. Gilbert answered: "I may be a patriotic fool, but I believe it."

After his ordeal with Rice, Gilbert testified, he made typewritten copies of the "music rolls" (reports) and sent them to Campbell for distribution among "high officials" of the leading veterans' groups and other organizations. He also slipped in clippings from *Social Justice* and other "patriotic" stuff which was on hand. Campbell would then touch up the "music rolls," mimeograph and send out the copies to key individuals in veterans' and other groups.

Campbell was a member of the Legion and Post Commander of a VFW post in Kentucky which he helped organize. Before he went into his patriotic work with Gilbert he had headed the Constitutional Protective League. Campbell traveled widely, spreading the bogey of an immediate Communist revolution. But there were times when even Campbell became "discouraged" in his struggles to save America. Gilbert boosted his morale with such letters as the following, which appears on page 3291 of the Dies testimony:

Keep up your courage. Remember those who are finally successful always suffer much before victory. You and I are no exception to that rule. Mussolini was insulted, stoned, and driven from town to town. Hitler was jailed and persecuted for years. It is that very persecution that tries men's souls. It is that very suffering that has welded together the strong type of men that have led Nazi-ism to victory in other countries. The same will be so here. We must win; we will win, because America must live and the Stars and Stripes must wave over every foot of North America from the Panama Canal to the Arctic Circle. Such is our future. You and I are destined to lead America to that greatness. Otherwise we would long ago have been crushed. Long live nationalist America! Let us fight harder than ever.

Among those who received some of the fantastic "music rolls" was General Moseley. Campbell arranged for the General to speak at Nashville, Tenn. Another recipient of the "music rolls" was Homer Capehart, present Senator from Indiana. According to the testimony, a third person to receive the Gilbert-Campbell reports was Felix McWhirter, President of the People's State Bank of Indianapolis, who served in World War II as Security Officer of the Great Lakes Training Station. Apparently influenced by Rice's reports, McWhirter wrote Campbell:

Yours of the 9th this morning received. Is it true that Cordell Hull's wife is part or full-blooded Semite? What do you know of Landon's Semitic connections? What do you know of William Allen White's Semitic connections?

With the help of Campbell, McWhirter brought Moseley to speak in Indianapolis on December 29, 1938. Campbell had the speech printed and sent to "patriots" from coast to coast. William Dudley Pelley picked up the cue and circularized it among his own pro-Nazi following. Howard B. Rand, director of the Anglo-Saxon Federation, also published and distributed the Moseley speech.

For the answers to McWhirter's questions Campbell wrote to Deatherage, who was urging Moseley to become the "Man on Horseback" under whose unified command, Deatherage hoped, nationalists could "fight Communism." Deatherage testified that he was not only in close touch with Campbell but had also "helped" him "financially." In a letter to Campbell, Deatherage wrote:

I believe as you do that it will take military action to get this gang out, and the organization must be built around a propaganda organization now that can in a few hours be turned into a militant fighting force. That's the idea of the boss, also. As far as the program is concerned that is something else, but to my mind we will have fascism, call it what you may, for there can be no solution to this except as a disciplined force under central leadership.

Campbell answered that he, too, thought "this thing has gone so far that there is only one remedy and that is a military action which will put a military court in charge of the United States Federal Government and each State Government."

That was the period when Nazi agents were trying to create terrific division in the United States so that Hitler, while pleading for peace, could initiate his conquest of Europe. Americans innocently fell for the technique, and many believed that Hitler actually wanted peace. One of those innocently duped was General Moseley.* In January, 1939 he wrote Campbell:

* In June, 1946 I asked McWhirter if he were still associated with Campbell. I received no answer. To my similar query, Moseley answered on June 16: "I have always tried to make it very clear that I never had any political connections or ambitions. In speaking, I made a practice of explaining that I belonged to no organization and was not affiliated with any political party. I have not changed now. Mr. McWhirter wrote asking me to speak in Indianapolis. This was about two years before Pearl Harbor. I have had no other communication from him since about July, 1939. You did not ask about Mr. Deatherage. I know nothing of him or where he may be. I am not in touch with him directly or indirectly."

I am sure you listened to Mr. Hitler with a great deal of interest. While we do not agree with him in many things, some of his remarks were reassuring and confirming. He pointed out how ridiculous it is to talk of Germany's attacking America. He also had several very appropriate remarks to say about the Jews and their international intrigues.

This, in brief, is the story of the campaign of Gilbert, Campbell, Inc., to "save America." It isn't fantastic at all. It's going on in modified form today. I have cited it to show how the powers of fear and hatred of Communism may infect some of our prominent citizens, who certainly do not mean to hurt our country. But they, together with other innocent citizens, may easily be inveigled into questionable schemes under the pretext of fighting Communism.

Immediately after learning of Campbell's attempt to become Junior Vice-Commander of the Veterans of Foreign Wars, I wrote him at Owensboro, Ky., as Robert Thompson, Jr. In a few weeks I received a letter on the stationery of the Industrial and Sales Engineering Co., of Evansville, Ind., Campbell's old stamping ground. It was here, according to Gilbert's testimony, that Campbell's creditors had demanded payment, or else. Indications were that Campbell was doing business at the same old stand. He wrote me on April 2, 1946:

If being in favor of your own country first; if advocating strong National Defense; a firm statesmanlike policy with our Foreign Department; National Leaders who are interested in preserving this country against Communistic Inroads and Radicalism—If demand of all these things and standing for it makes me anything other than a staunch believer in American Nationalism, then I care not what I am called. . . . Our Industrial Engineering work, due to the unsettled conditions in Industry, is taking all the time we have to cope with it.

What is the nature of Campbell's "engineering work"? I've learned that he has established a "Veterans Foundation" dedicated to the "perpetuation of 100 percent Americanism" and to "preserving the Constitution." My last reports state that he was establishing "patriotic" cells in factories in Evansville and was convincing the "right" people that the "American" way was to use coercive measures on "radicals" and "unions." It was the same old Campbell, at the same old divisive game.

The need for vigilance has never been greater than now. From the left, American Communists stand ready to bore their way into middle-of-the-road democratic groups; while from the right, nationalists watch for a chance to inject their poison. Few organizations are immune. Those which think themselves so are often the most unwitting victims. They go along complacently until they suddenly discover that someone within their ranks, or someone from outside influencing those within, has exploited the group for selfish, partisan aims.

This happened to the American War Dads, of Kansas City, Mo. The War Dads are an organization of fathers of sons and daughters who participated in World War I and World War II. Their functions are to "work for a lasting peace, to aid our sons and daughters in their employment needs and their rehabilitation program, to build a better community, a stronger state, a finer nation and a more understanding world." The organization has about 152,000 members and 850 chapters. It's "non-sectarian, non-profit, politically non-partisan." The President is Arch Stafford, retired Omaha oil industrialist, Rotarian and elder of the First Presbyterian Church. President Truman is a "Life Foundation member," according to the October, 1945, issue of *American War Dad*.

War Dads was founded in 1924 by Nat Milgram, Kansas City businessman of the Jewish faith. Milgram is not only respected for his deep humanitarian instincts and abiding interest in youth work, but is also an honorary director of Rockhurst Catholic College. The officers of War Dads seem to be mostly of the Protestant faith, including Masons and Rotarians, although Col. J. J. Griffin, St. Louis banker and one of eight vice-presidents, is a member of the Knights of Columbus and Knights of the Holy Sepulchre by appointment of the Pope. The War Dads membership belongs generally to the middle-class, conservative strata of Americans, comprising small businessmen and leaders in civic and welfare work.

The strength of War Dads lies mainly in the Midwest. They seem, however, to be unduly conscious of religion. Of thirteen officers listed in a booklet, everyone's religion was indicated.

American War Dads have worked hard to make the veteran's personal reconversion easier. They claim credit for amending the income-tax law to exempt for three years the first $2,500 of income earned by a veteran; for getting larger gasoline allowance for GIs on leave; for compelling the War Surplus Administration to remove limitations from purchases by veterans.

But the American War Dads were taken for a grand, rough ride! Here's how. Late in 1945 there appeared a booklet written by one William R. James, called *The Communist Cancer*. It was published by the Forum Press Associates of St. Louis and sold at $1. Who was William R. James? Whether he actually existed or whether the name was a pseudonym was not explained. At any rate, the booklet was irresponsible, smearing as "Communist" such strongly anti-Communist groups as the American Unitarian Association, The Rand School, and the American Civil Liberties Union (which had cleaned out its Communist members long before). Listed as Communist also were the Fellowship of Reconciliation, a pacifist-religious body (which once pleaded that we bombard Germany with peace leaflets, not bombs), and the National Council for the Prevention of War, directed largely by Quakers. Mixed in with liberal groups was a hodgepodge of Communist and Communist-front organizations.

The listing purported to be a guide to current Communist groups; it resembled the list once prepared by the late A. Cloyd Gill, a nationalist who worked closely with Kamp. Gill was found mysteriously dead in the Constitutional Educational League office, slumped over a desk, in April, 1943. William R. James listed as apparently current Communist groups many which were knocked out of business long before Pearl Harbor. It was, at best, a distorted and hysterical misrepresentation of a serious national problem which needs sober and mature countermeasures. We'll never get rid of Communism by shouting at it.

Suddenly, in the spring of 1946, James' booklet appeared rubber-stamped "Compliments of American War Dads." In May the rubber stamping had changed to a *printed* phrase: "Distributed by War Dads." The James book had undergone a thorough overhauling for its War Dads edition. All hostile references to John L. Lewis had been removed. A preface appeared, by H. Roe Bartle, National Executive Director of the War Dads. Col. John J. Griffin was named as Chairman of the Americanism Committee. The book was priced at fifty cents. The author, William R. James, remained a mysterious figure.

A number of other changes made it an insidious propaganda document and gave American War Dads a complexion which I had never before suspected it of having. Quoting an unnamed "authoritative and unusually reliable source," it charged with allegedly "Communist entrenched leadership" the American Veterans Committee, the Friends of Democracy and others equally anti-Communist. As an employee of the Friends of Democracy for six years, I know from intimate observation that the Friends of Democracy is anything but Communist, except, of course, in the eyes of the nationalist demagogues and their better-dressed, better-spoken party-line followers. The Friends of Democracy was strongly interventionist during the Hitler-Stalin pact. Its national director is a Missouri-bred preacher and a registered Republican of the Wendell Willkie tradition. The Friends of Democracy has openly denounced Communism. Two of its staff members served as lieutenants with Army Intelligence, after the most thorough examination of their political views. Would I have been allowed to lecture before Army audiences if there were a taint of Communism anywhere?

The War Dads booklet nowhere declared its opposition to Naziism or Fascism. It nowhere denounced American nationalists. While asserting that Communism is "eating its way toward the vitals" of the American system, it made no mention of nationalist hate-mongers who are corroding our national structure. By way of explanation the jacket lamely declared:

Our campaign is designed to drive all political isms except Americanism from the horizon of these United States, but at the moment, the American War Dads will center its thought, attention and leadership on the menace of Communism.

Reports persist in St. Louis—where the booklet has been on sale—that *sub rosa,* Coughlinite-type "patriots" have reached the ears of certain American War Dads officials and frightened them into believing that Communism is the one and only menace.

Had I been aware of the Coughlinite germs I should have started my investigations long ago. I had given the War Dads a clean bill. In their literature of the past few years I had found no labor-baiting or even Red-baiting. I knew that Upton Close and his former radio sponsor, James Scott Kemper, were members, but they did not formulate policy. And I was aware that in July, 1943 the War Dads' official organ belittled the late President Roosevelt as "the great almsgiver of all time." Regardless of their merit, its other expressions of opinion were moderate. I looked upon War Dads as a clean-handed organization until, in the closing weeks of this manuscript, they issued James' fantastic booklet.

On July 2 I wrote President Stafford a long letter asking for information on the identity of William R. James, the source of the funds and other pertinent data. I sent carbon copies to four other officials. By July 8 I heard from Nat Milgram, as follows:

I am very much disturbed at the booklet being distributed by Col. Griffith [Griffin]. . . . After making an investigation, I find that at the January meeting, permission was granted said Col. Griffith [Griffin] to fight Communism. I have made it known to Mr. Bartle . . . that I object

Kansas City 6, Mo.

My dear Mr. Carlson: July 13, 1946

National Vice President Griffin at the January meeting presented a copy of the pamphlet under the title of "Communist Cancer." Copies were distributed, material carefully analyzed by members of the national board and it was there agreed that this pamphlet, if authentic, merited distribution. The National Council thus gave to Colonel Griffin permission to circulate the book in St. Louis with funds which Colonel Griffin was to secure from friends and associates in his community.

The action of the national board stood as herein presented until the next meeting of the National Council of the American War Dads which was held May 25 and 26, at which time the National Council, again by unanimous action, instructed that no further distribution of the pamphlet referred to as the "Communist Cancer" should be distributed or any other like material be circulated with the endorsement of the American War Dads until the national convention by its action should so decree.

Very truly yours,

H. Roe Bartle

The official finger of the War Dads points to Colonel John J. Griffin as responsible for the publication of the wild-shooting booklet, *The Communist Cancer.*

to this literature being sent out under our name, for it seems to be something deeper than just the fight of Communism as such.

I can assure you that the money is not coming out of the National Council but is being paid for by parties unknown to me. . . . After our convention [in September, 1946] I doubt very much that any more of this literature will be sent out sponsored by the American War Dads. . . . Personally, I would be listed as a Communist, too, according to this pamphlet, for I contribute to Rev. Birkhead.

A few days later H. Roe Bartle wrote me stating that in January members of the National Council had "carefully analyzed" the early edition of *The Communist Cancer* and "agreed that this pamphlet, if authentic, merited distribution. The National Council thus gave to Colonel Griffin permission to circulate the book in St. Louis with funds which Colonel Griffin was to secure from friends and associates in his community." Bartle added that a National Council meeting on May 25 and 26 had prohibited by "unanimous action" the further distribution of *The Communist Cancer* "until the [forthcoming] national convention should so decree."

Despite the apparent May decision of the National Council, I had written for, paid for, and received four copies of *The Communist Cancer* late in June, 1946. I used two different undercover names in order to obtain this evidence. Both envelopes carried the return address of the War Dads office in Kansas City. Two of the booklets were mailed from Kansas City and were overprinted "Distributed by American War Dads." The bill which accompanied the two others read: "American War Dads Distribution Center, St. Louis," and bore the post office box of the Forum Press Associates. These copies were rubber-stamped "Compliments of American War Dads."

Another development had not been explained at the time when this book went to press. It was the publication of excerpts from my letter to President Arch Stafford, copies of which I sent to Col. Griffin and three other officials, in a monthly sheet, *Today's World*, published in St. Louis by one Tom Finan, Jr. Its contents were totally unrepresentative of the activities of War Dads. Styling itself a "News Magazine Written and Published by Catholic Laymen," it made the outlandish claim that "almost single-handedly, the Catholic Church is now waging a world-wide battle against the onrushing tide of atheistic Communism." *Today's World* set itself up as a Knight girding on the armor and doing battle on behalf of God and Country.

The first three issues (June, July, and August, 1946) railed against real and alleged Communist activity in true Coughlinite fashion. It saw Communism as the *only* enemy threatening Christianity and Democracy. On the heels of a staunch defense of Spanish Nazi Franco was an attack on Quentin Reynolds as an "ardent advocate of subversive groups." The June issue promoted a campaign being conducted by the Knights of Columbus of St. Louis. In a quoted interview, the Missouri State Deputy of the Knights of Columbus bewailed the alleged refusal of the New York *Times*, St. Louis *Post-Dispatch*, and Washington *Post* to run Knights of Columbus ads in defense of Franco and the Franco régime. A blistering attack on "three well-known Communists . . . Cohen, Levy and Cohen," started in June, was continued in July, when Finan, in a screeching statement, welcomed a libel suit by "Cohen, Levy and Cohen."

The impression created by the glaring and repetitious headlines was that only those bearing Jewish names were Communists. Whether this was intentional or not cannot be established, and no charge is made of the use of the Nazi device, also employed by Father Coughlin, of associating Jewry with Communism. Perhaps that criticism had been levelled by others, for an editorial self-consciously entitled "Are We Anti-Labor, Anti-Semitic?" loudly denied both charges. Next to the editorial was a column portraying Franco as a "hero."

Finan then trained his guns on me. My cordial letters to War Dad officials were perverted to "Carlson Threatens War Dads." Finan devoted more than five columns to a strained attempt to "prove" that I was "Communist." His reasoning was pathetic. The smear page also denounced Walter Winchell, Rev. Birkhead and the Anti-Defamation League (a Jewish research-defense organization) as Communist. All this was the usual rot and distortion. What interested me most, however, were the excerpts from my letter.

How did this letter find its way into the Coughlinite sheet? Who sent it? On August 21, Mr. Bartle assured me that neither he nor Mr. Stafford referred my letters "to anyone."

Another discovery was that the July and August issues carried a column, "*Spotlight News Letter*," "Compiled from Authoritative Sources by the Forum Press Associates." This caused me to speculate on the links between *Today's World* and the Forum Press Associates. Were the Associates, in fact, an outpost of the men behind *Today's World?* The contents of the column were strikingly similar to the drivel in *The Communist Cancer*. I think I've learned enough about the publishers of *The Communist Cancer* and *Today's World* to bolster my impression that they are backed by Coughlinite, unrepresentative Catholic "laymen." They are aping the followers of Father Coughlin who sought to achieve self-respect by identifying themselves with a great religious order, much in the manner in which American Communists assume for themselves the role of defenders of "Democracy."

I believe that American War Dads can do a lot of good. They mean well and their membership is loyally American. It would be tragic to see a group of 152,000 Americans flounder because of sinister nationalist scheming somewhere in its ranks, which would be the surest way of splitting the organization. It would not surprise me to learn that that was the intent of the scheme. Should War Dads split between pro- and anti-Coughlinite propaganda factions, the nationalist element would have performed its destructive work and started the War Dads on the road to disintegration.

Nationalist, like Communist, influence can creep into any group or organization which, even while desperately trying to keep a middle course, may swing at the instigation of a hidden nationalist agent. If it can happen to an organization it can, in a larger sense, happen to a nation which is not on guard.

The instances I have cited are merely illustrative. In themselves they are little more than straws in the wind, showing the nationalist pattern and its implicit danger to our democracy. It's significant, however, that from these seemingly unrelated episodes, a central pattern emerges for nationalist action. Basic in that program is a plan to dull one's reasoning faculty by arousing the passions. The demagogues work through direct incitements to hate. The subtler nationalist works through the implanting of doubts, suspicions and fears. After World War I, when Russia was flat on its back, when there were only a few hundred Bolsheviks here and labor was wobbly, the synthetic bogey of "Bolshevism" was conjured up from coast to coast. The same thing is happening again today, incited by the same sinister anti-democratic forces, the same greedy, totalitarian-minded racketeers in profits and patriotism.

Working according to a well-knit, long-range plan, a hierarchy of like-minded, like-souled, democracy-hating nationalists *can* bring about the conditions for the enthronement of extreme nationalism here. One may or may not be able to place his finger on such a hierarchy and the details of its carefully nurtured plot to undermine democracy. One may or may not prove the existence of the plot through an interception of documents. One may or may not learn of the technical details in the performance, transmitted by secret couriers. Did the Nazi hierarchy depend upon native German fascists in Hungary, France, Austria, Norway, Belgium and Spain? That was often unnecessary. There were Quislings everywhere. The fascist mind is the same everywhere. One need not always see the blueprint to be convinced that the conspiracy exists.

By the same token, one may read in the press of the actors against democracy, related and unrelated, and interpret their common ultimate goal—the betrayal of the cause of democracy. For the moment, forget hirelings like Gerald Smith. Look for democracy's would-be assassins among the topmost branches of international intrigue.

Events are doubtless more conducive to nationalist reaction in 1946 than in 1919. Russia is powerful. Labor is better organized. Militant Americans express themselves more articulately. The terrific concentration of our productive resources in the hands of monopolists who wield private government is frightening. We have gone through a tragic depression which made cynics of many. The most brutal war in history has shaken the faith of others in God and humanity; it has brutalized some. These are factors which can be exploited by demagogues and plotters against democracy.

No time has been set. No definite leader has been chosen. These are details. This is the period of laying the groundwork for the nationalist revolution. A law case is won and a successful book written only after intensive research and preparation. By the same token, the nationalist groundwork may take years to lay down, for America is big, its people are heterogeneous and there are many crosscurrents of opinion to be neutralized and redirected. But nationalism, if it should come, will do so with the unstoppable suddenness of Pearl Harbor. It may be achieved overnight. And this time there will be no democratic base of operations from which to attack the enemy. For the enemy will be in our midst, coursing through the blood stream of America.

Those who feel that I may be overstating the case, because Hitler is dead and the Germans are a defeated power, may be convinced by Spruille Braden, Assistant Secretary of State. Speaking at Clark University on May 26, 1946, Mr. Braden warned:

Make no mistake, our great military triumph has not killed the ideologies of Nazism and Fascism, any more than the Prussian militarism of the Junkers was killed by our victory in the first World War. The Nazi and Fascist doctrines survive. Their adherents are simply biding time until, in the complacency that follows victory, we allow them to gather their forces in secret once more, toward the day when they may again renew their attempt on human liberty.

When respectable and innocent organizations like the American War Dads can be sucked in by Coughlinite-brand propaganda, then something fearful has happened to the sturdy American mind. It has lost its balance and suffered in judgment. It has deviated from its path of serving the veteran and country and turned to propagandizing. Of course it all came wrapped in patriotic colors. Of course it came in the name of anti-Communism. Of course it was sugar-coated. The sugar-coated pill contains the nationalist germ.

Was it not Schicklgruber who rose to power through the dominant cry of anti-Communism? Didn't the masses and the classes believe in his promise to save Germany from Red ruin? Aren't some of us falling for the same line? In our zeal against Communism, through fear and hysteria, aren't we letting the nationalist paranoia creep upon us—as happened in Germany? Must Americans, who pride themselves on their shrewdness and common sense, allow themselves to be led by the counterparts of the Nazi nationalists who led Germany to her doom? Must we be equally blind and let it "happen here"?

CHAPTER FIFTEEN

"What Can I Do for Democracy?"

> Some of them [Christian Fronters] used to come to my church.
> So one Sunday I said in my sermons: "I have no right to inter-
> fere with your freedom of speech. . . . But as your priest, let
> me say this. You are not going to preach hate from the street
> corners on Friday nights and come to my church Sunday morn-
> ings. Either you come to church or you go to your street meet-
> ings. . . ." That sermon ended the Christian Front meetings.
>
> *Father George B. Ford, Corpus Christi Church*

PRESERVING DEMOCRACY is essentially a community job—including
the community of states and nations. But it must begin with the
individual before being carried through on the community scale. It
isn't necessary to be pompous and make a show of it. It isn't necessary to tell others about it. Doing one's part for democracy can be a
very simple and quiet experience—but dramatic.

Here's what a young mother did:

Mrs. Helen Bell, born Helen Foy, is as Irish as Father Flanagan
of Boys' Town. In June, 1944 Helen lived in a rough section of up-
town New York. A fairly tough neighborhood, but a lot of decent
people lived among the rowdies. Rents were low and the young
mother lived in a tiny one-room basement apartment with Rose Ann,
nicknamed Stuffings, who was thirteen months old and went around
in bare feet when I saw her. Helen's husband, Melvin, was Chief
Petty Officer in the Coast Guard. Melvin had five brothers in the
service.

"Melvin didn't go through five invasions for the right of anti-
Semites to beat up little kids and call them dirty Jews," his wife once
said.

Helen was referring to a neighbor whom she saw slap fourteen-
year-old Emmanuel Witty and curse him obscenely as a Jew. Judge

369

Anna Kross, according to Tom O'Connor's story in *PM,* committed the neighbor to Bellevue Hospital for observation in June, 1944. Helen testified against her and because of it she received threatening notes. One of them was sent by special delivery: "You get out of court you Jew-lover or you will go back South with less than you came here with." It was signed with a cryptic symbol.

Before that someone threw a rock through Helen's living-room window; her landlady told her to get out; unprintable curses came from a vile old vixen down the block. Helen related: "One woman told me I should be ashamed to say I was Catholic and Irish. I told her she should be ashamed to act like they do in Germany. Another lady said I was a Communist. And a Jewish lady across the street told me not to go to court and testify, that she wouldn't go, even though she's Jewish, because you just stick your neck out and get in trouble."

"I don't see why I should be afraid of them," the young mother told me in an interview. "I just look straight at them when I go by. There are a lot of good people with us and God is on our side. If more people would fight such ignorance, I think we'd win."

Helen's courage is traceable to her schooling by the Children of Mary Sodality. "Father Kane of St. Francis de Sales Church preached that we should all be tolerant of each other, all races and all religions," she explained. "Then my father—he's a bartender and a member of the Knights of Columbus—was here the day the woman beat up Manny, and he said I ought to do what I could because if these Nazis got the upper hand here they'd be persecuting everyone, and not stop with the Jews."

This is all there is to the story of a good Christian and a good American, except that Helen summed up her philosophy with these simple words: "How did I get my ideas against prejudice? Oh, I just figured things out. If we've had to fight a war against hate in Germany, I don't see any use in letting it start over here. I mean people beating people up and cussing them just because they're Jews. I don't see what the use would be in our boys giving their lives, if that was the way it turned out."

Here's what a priest can do:

Thirty blocks from Helen's home is the parish and school of one of the greatest Catholic clergymen in the United States. He is only a humble priest of the Church, but he has few peers in the wholesome practice of true Christianity. He is Father George B. Ford of the Corpus Christi Church. Father Ford's parochial school is "progressive" in a Catholic sense. Pupils learn that the best training for living in a democracy comes through consciously acting in a democratic way. The practical application of Christian teachings is the heart of the school's philosophy.

While Father Ford was advisor to Catholic students at Columbia University, he asked me to speak to his students. I found them an unusually bright and well-informed group. I always look forward to my meetings with Father Ford. I enjoy hearing his anecdotes of his experiences in inter-racial, inter-faith, inter-cultural work and in his constant rounds of democratic activity. He is associated with Freedom House, the Conference of Christians and Jews, and many liberal non-Catholic organizations.

Father Ford's account of how he got rid of the Christian Front goons who held street meetings around the corner from his parish is direct and simple:

"Some of them used to come to my church," Father Ford said with candor. "So one Sunday I said in my sermons: 'I have no right to interfere with your freedom of speech. In our Democracy you have the right to express your love or hate for anyone you please. There is no law against it. But as your priest, let me say this. You are not going to preach hate from the street corners on Friday nights and come to my church Sunday mornings. Either you come to church or you go to your street meetings. Be consistent in your hates and leave Christ out of it.' That sermon," said Father Ford, "ended the Christian Front meetings."

"The only way I know to be a Christian," Father Ford remarked dryly at dinner one day, "is to practice Christianity."

In Boston, in 1943, a wave of beatings of innocent Jews by Christian Front hoodlums brought the city a wave of humiliating publicity, until public opinion rose up in wrath. *Here, then, is what an aroused community can do to clean up bigotry in its back yard:*

Governor Leverett Saltonstall established the Governor's Committee for Racial and Religious Understanding, of which Mrs. Mildred H. Mahoney became the spark-plug. Boston's Catholic and Protestant clergymen busied themselves with long-delayed sermons on

Christian ethics. Mass meetings by civic, labor, and inter-faith groups were held. Most newspapers fell into line and publicized an ugly situation which had long been ignored.

Governor Saltonstall changed police commissioners and put an end to the negligence of those cops who had somehow always arrived just too late to nab Christian Front goons and had blamed the battered victims instead. "Our men can handle riots if they occur," said Deputy Police Superintendent Thomas S. J. Kavanaugh. "What we would like to know is what makes people intolerant." Through a series of courses held at police headquarters and later at Harvard University, Boston police were given the rudiments of inter-cultural education, including how to recognize prejudice and what to do about it. Such well known educators as Professor Gordon W. Allport of Harvard and Professor John Mahoney of Boston University were among the instructors. Within a month the number of beatings had dropped sharply.

One reason why reforms were delayed in Boston was because newspapers, except for the *Christian Science Monitor,* with a Boston circulation of only 15,000 well-behaved readers, hushed up hooliganism. Coughlinite readers gravitated to the *Post,* with the largest morning circulation, which seemed primarily interested in crime news.

My exposé in *Under Cover* of Boston's fascists and the hate-swamp its Fronters had created, helped dramatize a bad situation and aroused certain Bostonians against me. In the fall of 1943, at the request of the Treasury Department, I addressed a war bond rally in Cambridge with Edna Ferber, Van Wyck Brooks and Roy Chapman Andrews. The DAR, Legion and Rotary Club participated in the program.

At about 11 o'clock in the evening, as I was leaving the building after the rally, a woman on the sidewalk shouted, "Who is paying your expenses out here, you Communist?" She was identified as Miss Marie M. Ballem of Winthrop, Mass., who headed the Boston wing of the Coughlinite "Mothers" organization. With her was Miss Alice M. Billings, another "Mothers" member who is now a Terminiello henchwoman. Without answering Miss Ballem I stepped into a waiting car. The next day the *Post* burst out with the sensational and distorted headline: "WOMEN YELL 'YOU RED' AT BOND RALLY; JOHN CARLSON FLEES FROM ATTACK IN

CAMBRIDGE." The *Post* slighted the impressive total of war bonds sold and played up the stunt of the Coughlinite pair.

Boston, however, also has staunch fighters for democracy. *Here's what an organization can do:* The Frances Sweeney Committee was founded by Frances Sweeney, a fighting Irish lady whose untimely death in 1943 comforted only the Christian Fronters who had tormented her and called her a Communist. It was my privilege to know and work with Frances. She was posthumously awarded the Pope Leo XIII Medal by the Sheil School for Social Studies in Chicago.

Frances fought the hate-mongers the direct way. "A fascist," she said, "is anyone who hates the common man. A fascist can be a statesman or a soldier or a minister or a Catholic priest. To see fascists as Germans only is to lose sight of the great danger that exists right in our midst." She collared churchmen and civic leaders and persuaded them to join in protest. A one-woman crusader, Frances did more effective work at minimum expense than certain well-heeled Boston sectarian groups. Father Ford, a close friend of hers, said: "Frances Sweeney was a totalitarian in the acceptance and practice of religion and democracy. Frances personified the individual ablaze with a missionary fervor for democracy."

Miss Sweeney's special interest was Father Curran, who spoke often in Boston. Here's Frances at her best, writing with the incisive logic of a crusader who will accept no compromise:

It is very bewildering for a small "d" democrat like me to see a Roman Catholic priest, with diocesan permission, arouse his audience to "wild applause, whistling and stamping" as he attacked our Allies . . . on the eve of the invasion of Europe. It is very difficult to discount him as a lone clerical dissenter when he is pictured in the Boston *Herald* of March 22nd with Father J. F. X. Murphy, S.J., of Boston College, and two other priests. It is a strange paradox to see a priest who has called our government "Communistic" go unchallenged when a Notre Dame lay professor, Francis McMahon, was discharged for calling a foreign dictator, Francisco Franco, a Fascist.

The work of Frances' Committee is being carried on minus her personal fire, but with equal effectiveness, by Mary Fitzgerald and Isabel Currier. The Committee is affiliated with the Friends of Democracy.

The Massachusetts Legislature has enacted a Race Libel Law "penalizing the libel of groups of persons because of race, color or religion." The measure prohibits the distribution in Massachusetts by mail, or through sale, of hate-inciting literature. Infraction is punishable by a fine of $1,000. The law has proven psychologically effective. Boston Fronters fear to issue hate-inciting literature for consumption in Massachusetts. Nothing prevents their sending it outside the state, however, or receiving it from other states.

In Cleveland, unlike Boston, one newspaper, the *Press,* has won country-wide recognition for its vigorous policy against nationalists. Eugene Segal, its undercover reporter, has dug up much original material and has done an effective job against hate-mongers.

Partly as a result of articles in the *Press* and the fine work of former Mayor (now Governor) Frank J. Lausche of Cleveland, the city has passed an ordinance prohibiting the circulation of "anonymous printed matter inciting racial or religious hatred." The law demands that the printer or sponsor of the leaflet insert his or her name "in a conspicuous place." Violators are subject to a fine of up to $500. The bill was introduced jointly by a Catholic, a Protestant, a Jew and a Negro. Albert A. Woldman, Assistant Director of Law, wrote me that the measure had been endorsed by the American Legion, the Joint Veterans Commission and civic, inter-racial and sectarian organizations. Only Mrs. Stanley and her gang of United Mothers of America opposed it. Woldman added:

Up to date no case has arisen to test this ordinance in Cleveland. I am quite certain, however, that its very existence has had a salutary and deterrent effect and has caused persons and organizations who in the past have distributed anonymous hate literature to "stop, look and listen." . . . The ordinance has been adopted in modified form by several other cities.

The Cleveland law doesn't curtail freedom of expression. It merely makes publishers responsible to the community. Moran continues to issue his hate-inciting magazine, *Police.* The Mothers continue with their meetings and their vicious whispering and lying campaigns. But Cleveland citizens, like alert Bostonians, are conscious of the hate-mongers in their midst and are trying to fight them by legal and democratic methods. That's what wide-awake voters and law-enforcement agencies can do.

Here's what a school principal can do:

Mr. Ralph W. Haller is principal of Andrew Jackson High School in St. Albans, Queens County, N. Y., where Coughlinites and Klansmen are found in considerable numbers. It was here that the Citizens of Queens United for Democracy met on the night when Kurt Mertig, Elmhurst, Maertz, Kister and Mrs. Brown staged their hate fest. When reports of increased prejudice on the part of students reached Mr. Haller, he warned bluntly that whoever was caught insulting the race, religion or national background of a fellow pupil would be denied his diploma. "I consider such activities totally in contradiction to everything that the America of today stands for, or the America which we hope to have tomorrow," he said. The psychological impact of Mr. Haller's declaration solved a delicate situation firmly and effectively.

Here's what a board of education has done:

Springfield, Mass., is a typical American city of 165,000. Forty percent of the people are Yankee Protestants. There are large groups of Irish, French, Canadian, Italian and Polish extraction, and smaller minorities of Armenian-Americans, Jews, German-Americans and Negroes. Thirteen years ago Dr. John Granrud, Superintendent of Springfield schools, abolished a ruling limiting the number of Catholic teachers to ten percent. From then on, he announced, teachers would be hired on the basis of merit exclusively. Granrud appointed a board of four Catholic and four Protestant principals to carry out the policy. The whole city of Springfield has learned to like it.

In the Springfield schools, children are not made to feel ashamed of being the sons and daughters of immigrants. On the contrary, they are encouraged to share their rich heritage. A little Armenian girl brings some of her mother's unusual lacework, and displays it with New England pewter and the beautiful candleholders used in Jewish rituals. All are masterpieces of creative minds and cultures. The development of false superiority complexes is discouraged.

One of Springfield's schools is located next door to a parochial school. The Sister Superior and the Protestant school principal get along so well that their students visit each other's assemblies. In 1943 a Negro boy was editor of the trade-school paper. The

O'Rourkes, Potowskis, Papadopouloses, Steinbergs and Simpsons get along famously in Springfield.

In educational circles this system of training in mutual appreciation of cultures has become known as the Springfield Plan. A steady march of teachers and other educators visit Springfield to see it in action. "Actually it's not a plan at all," one teacher said. "It's a state of mind." Another teacher observed profoundly, "You don't have to teach these children tolerance. Our job is to keep them the way they are." It's true. A child is born without hates or prejudices. He acquires them first from his parents. Democracy—or the lack of it—in a child's make-up—begins at home. The genesis of most hate and bigotry was summed up by a participant in the National Parent-Teacher Education Conference on May 3, 1946:

It is unusual for children to adopt and live by feelings toward other races and religious faiths which are at variance with those held by their parents. An ounce of example in doing, set by parents and teachers, is worth a pound of lectures, courses and study groups.

Here is what an American of the Jewish faith can do:

Early in June, 1946 I asked Mort Levy, Buffalo, N. Y., Legionnaire, if he knew one young nationalist prominently connected with the Buffalo Christian Youth League, who had sponsored a meeting for Frederick Kister. Mort knew the young man's family. He is their tailor. "His folks are wild against him for going around with the Gerald Smith crowd," Mort wrote. "They are a respectable Catholic family, very devout." Mort Levy set out to help this boy. He got in touch with him, then wrote me:

Right now —— is out of employment so I'm going to try and see if I can't swing him over to our side. You see, I think I can place him where he can work days, go to school at night, whereby he can further his ambition to become a big shot. He is supposed to have friends among our enemies who up to now have done nothing for him except to take his few pennies away from him. We Jews want to show them we are not as bad or as black as we are painted. . . .

An executive of one of our large oil companies . . . promised me a job for this chap. Yep, a Jewish boy taking a Catholic boy and getting him a job with an oil company owned jointly by a Catholic and a Protestant.

In the inter-faith and inter-cultural fields, three organizations whose work I know personally are doing excellent work.

The Council Against Intolerance (17 East 42nd St., New York, N. Y.) is directed by James Waterman Wise. Working mainly through schools, it has a broad program to combat prejudice. The U.S. Army ordered 5,000 copies of its magnificent color poster, "America—A Nation of One People from Many Countries." The Detroit Board of Education asked for 7,500 copies of its magazine *American Unity*. Literature is sent free on request. With its limited funds, the Council is doing an excellent job for democracy on a front where many prejudices unfortunately start.

Mr. Wise's books, graphically describing the contributions of America's cultural minorities, deserve to be read by all advocates of "white supremacy" and others similarly afflicted.

The National Conference of Christians and Jews (300 Fourth Ave., New York, N. Y.) is directed by Dr. Everett W. Clinchy. It was organized for "justice, amity, understanding and cooperation among Protestants, Catholics and Jews" in America. Its program was presented to Army bases around the world. With branches throughout the country, the Conference reaches many Americans through extensive use of radio, literature and public speakers. In July, 1946, Dr. Clinchy called upon leaders in religion, education, veterans' organizations, labor, business, fraternal and civic organizations, youth agencies, police, press and radio to work together on a community program to crush the subversive trend.

"Take this hate movement seriously," he pleaded. "Do not laugh it off as the Germans did, no matter how comic or ineffectual it seems."

The Common Council for American Unity (the Willkie Memorial Building, New York, N. Y.) is doing splendid work among America's foreign language speaking groups "to unite Americans of all backgrounds, colors and creeds in support of a vigorous all-inclusive democracy." Read Lewis is its director. For a quarter century the Council has devoted itself to aiding the integration and adjustment of immigrants to America. More than 22,000,000 Americans today have a mother tongue other than English. For these the Council maintains an extensive foreign-language press and adult radio educational program, in the face of a restricted budget. Its inter-group Education Department and photo service help in the combating of prejudice. *Common Ground* is its informative magazine.

Jointly with the Willkie Memorial of Freedom House, the Council has established an annual award of a round-the-world-trip, patterned on Willkie's historic flight in 1942, for the American whose work best typifies Willkie's idea of One World. Norman Corwin, radio dramatist, received the first award in 1946.

Detroit has made a start toward easing its racial tensions by the establishment of the Inter-Racial Committee. It's essentially a "study" rather than an action group at present, and its work is limited by a small appropriation. But it's at least a start in the right direction.

More ambitious is the New Jersey Good-Will Commission, composed of civic, YMCA, church, school and other organizations devoted to a program of inter-American good will. It places particular emphasis on its work among school children and uses regularly the material of the Council Against Intolerance. Among its many concrete achievements was the placement of many Negroes, Catholics (particularly Italians) and Jews in certain war plants where they had formerly been denied employment solely because of their national, racial and religious backgrounds. The Commission's Inter-Racial Committee specializes in the "lessening of racial tensions, and preventing conflicts between white and Negro groups."

As an individual American one can:

1. Join a democratic group, when convinced that it's a truly democratic organization. Organized democratic workers can stamp out by the force of public opinion the intolerance spread by organized hate-mongers and their political counterparts. When anti-democratic elements begin operations in a community, democratic groups can expose them and stop or retard a spreading conflagration.

2. Express oneself vigorously in speaking and writing. Don't fight for democracy by half-hearted measures. Write your Congressman and your newspaper. Build up public opinion *for* democracy.

3. Broaden one's horizon by remembering the relation between a program of full employment and home-front tranquillity. Jobs and security for employees and employers alike mean a happy society in which neither the left-wing nor the right-wing extremist can thrive. On the other hand, unemployment and economic chaos will play into the hands of the nationalist and radical messiahs.

4. Oppose discrimination, regardless of whether or not it applies to you personally. If the full benefits of democracy are denied to one, they may some day be denied to all. The Constitution was intended to serve all our people at all times. The security of the Protestant rests upon the security he gives the Catholic and Jew. Willkie's principle of One World applies even more to the concept of One Nation. A hurt administered to one group will injure the nation as a whole.

5. Fight greed. In New York recently the proprietors of a famous chain of high-priced restaurants were convicted of a plot to defraud the U.S. Treasury Department of several million dollars. Besides their enormous profits, the owners kept double books, defrauded the government of taxes, and raided the petty cash. Greed causes many of our troubles: black markets, religious, political and labor racketeering, public corruption, monopolistic abuses.

What can the veteran, the worker and the unorganized American do?

They can band together and keep undesirable Congressmen out of office. In July, 1946 they did just that in Montana and eliminated Wheeler from the primaries. Everyone thought Wheeler would win. He had the open endorsement of President Truman and of AFL leader William Green, and the tacit OK of John L. Lewis. The hierarchy of the American Legion and the Veterans of Foreign Wars backed him. Montana's major newspapers and radio stations were on his side. Wheeler had the cooperation of a former Dies Committee investigator who tried to embarrass his opponent, Leif Erickson, by an "investigation" and also called on those who had contributed to Erickson's campaign. It was a gentle method of discouraging financial support. Wheeler had everything on his side—except the confidence of his people.

Wheeler unleashed his entire bag of tricks. He declared that "Jewish" money was pouring into his opponent's campaign (Erickson, the winner, spent less than $12,000). Only Communists opposed him, Wheeler said, after which he damned *PM*, which sells only a few copies on the newsstands and 40 copies by subscription in *all* of Montana (as of July, 1946, according to *PM*).

Here's the inside picture of how Wheeler lost. State AFL workers bolted against the dictates of Green. They quietly campaigned and voted for Erickson. Many of Lewis' miners did the same. Legionnaires and VFW members also bolted and worked for Erickson. The CIO-PAC, which was all out for Erickson at the outset, threw in its full force. These were the elements which spelled defeat for Wheeler. A committee of "Farmers, workers, veterans" known as Vets Against Wheeler Club, pooled their dollars and bought advertisements in the smaller newspapers denouncing Wheeler, and listing their reasons.

They pointed to his isolationist record, to his America First Committee connections, his vote against Lend-Lease, against the increase in Navy and Army appropriations. They pointed out that in the "declaration of war with Japan or Germany, Wheeler did NOT vote." The advertisements fired the humble folks of Montana. They blared Wheeler's postwar record. They told how Wheeler had opposed the Full Employment and the FEPC Bills, as well as our participation in the United Nations. The advertisements concluded: "Senator Wheeler offers no program for the period ahead—only more of the same old isolationism and obstructionism."

It was gratifying to know that *Under Cover* played a share in Wheeler's defeat, as it did in the defeat of ex-Senator Gerald P. Nye and others. I had interviewed Wheeler in 1943 and exposed him as a ringleader of the pre-Pearl Harbor isolationist appeasers and defeatists. Excerpts from *Under Cover* were circulated during the campaign. Wheeler denounced the book in blistering terms, merely referring to it as "that book." It was Senator Wheeler who, in 1943, apparently tried to intimidate me by introducing a Senate resolution to investigate me. I challenged Wheeler to go through with it, but nothing happened, except that the attempt at smearing back-fired in Wheeler's own face, three years later—thanks to the common sense of the great common people of Montana.

In Athens, McMinn County, Tennessee, veterans resorted to bullets in order to win an honest count of the ballots they had cast in the 1946 primaries elections. The fracas started when GI poll watchers were beaten, detained and even jailed by henchmen of the county machine who were alarmed at the strength of a fusion ticket of ex-GI's. The rotten machine had hired some 300 "special deputies" to act as poll watchers and keep "law and order" throughout Athens. When they transferred the ballot boxes to the Athens jail in order to "count" them in leisurely fashion, the GI's seized several of the opposition and held them as hostages. Then they milled around the jail, a mob 1,000 strong, augmented by non-veteran Athenians, demanding the release of the ballot boxes and an honest count. The local sheriff threatened to shoot to kill. The mob defied him.

From then there was real fighting with the ex-GI's holding the upper hand. After a wild night of gunfire, sweating, cussing and incidental violence, the GI's finally set off a charge of dynamite and blew off the jail porch. The sheriff and his special deputies surrendered. A number of casualties were hospitalized. Miraculously, there were no deaths. Later, when the votes were honestly counted, the GI ticket candidates also won the Battle of Ballots.

One shudders to think at the consequences of "direct action" by a bilious mob, at the hands of a Bilboite—or whenever a mob of ex-soldiers can be aroused sufficiently by a demagogue of the Left or Right to take the law into their own hands and slug it out with brass-knuckles or bullets.

The lesson of Athens is a sobering one for post-war Americans. It drives home the potency of organized mass veteran action. The tough sheriff and his squad seemed comparatively powerless when faced with the superior discipline and young fighting fervor of the ex-GI's. The police chief was in hiding during the melee. But although a clean political slate has now been established in McMinn County and the Battle of Athens had its salutary effect on adjoining counties, to say nothing of a veteran clean-up move in Arkansas, nonetheless the flouting of the democratic process and

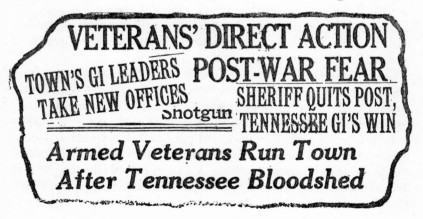

the resort to vigilantism—albeit in a "good cause"—is a perilous double-edged sword which might cleave democracy in two.

There is a democratic way of attaining a square deal for veterans. In New York a group of veterans known as Veterans for Better Government has been formed. It declares:

Internal reform all too often is brought about only by a national emergency. We have faith in the American ideals. This faith was conspicuous on the battlefield. We must now transform this faith into a civic conscience. We have a responsibility which we must assume in order to further the ideals for which we fought. This goal can be attained by the traditional American way, the intelligent use of the ballot.

To combat the hate poison of the nationalists, Americans must get over their feelings of timidity. The "hatriot" crew is brutal, outspoken, arrogant and bullying in its tactics. A bully respects and understands only a counter-force. Cajoling Hitler, and appeasing him at Munich, got the democracies nowhere. Not until they had mobilized and the liberating Allied Armies were marshalled in battle was the score settled with the Nazis. The same principle of democratic forces mobilized to fight by legal methods will win against the enemies on the home front.

The psychological make-up of the nationalist bully was symbolized by the number of goons who followed me at the Madison Square Garden meeting. Nationalists fear the show of strength— whether it's a strong book or a strong denunciation by a person in authority. I do not advocate a strong punch in the face, because it's neither lawful nor democratic and it defeats its own end. But within all legal limits I recommend without reservation a strong treatment of America's home-grown fascists.

Governor Arnall's powerful offensive against the Klan was a magnificent display of courage. It requires the highest nerve for a Southern political figure to oppose the Klan at the moment of its resurgence. If our Attorney General, the chief of the Federal Bureau of Investigation, and other respected public officials would denounce by *name* the Smiths and Smythes of our nation, those "patriots" would never get beyond first base. A case in point is the magnificent declaration on September 8, 1944 by Supreme Court Justice Frank Murphy:

The Jewish problem has struck me as being a Christian problem and an American problem. We've got to be sure that the Nazi revolution doesn't win any phase of this war. Hitler unloosed anti-Semitism as a prelude to the destruction of all liberty. He seized newspapers, closed labor unions, then stifled Catholic and Protestant churches. Niemoeller languishes in a concentration camp because he refused to accept deification of the state.

The rash of anti-Negro violence in the South, the flouting of the civil rights of American citizens, have brought the clamor: "Why isn't the Government doing something about it?" The Department of Justice is often singled out as the object of attack. On August 15 Tom Clark gave this explanation:

As Attorney General, I have caused to be investigated all cases which might imply violations of the civil liberties statutes. Federal action in most of these cases hangs upon a very thin thread of law. It is like trying to fight a modern atomic war with a Civil War musket. However, we have been unsuccessful in halting some displays of mob violence. The time has come when Congress may have to pass legislation to insure to all citizens the guarantees under the Constitution.

It seems ironical to have to wait for Congress to pass laws in order to invoke the Constitution against lynching and terror. A few Southern states such as Virginia have statutes making participants in a lynching party accountable to a murder charge. If laws are the immediate need, let's have them—followed by other counter measures similar to those undertaken by Boston, and projected on a state-wide and national basis. If we are dedicated to a democratic order, let's truly practice democracy and not be hypocritical about it.

Timidity pervades many newspapers and magazines which avoid "controversial" subjects if the controversy is on behalf of the little people and would therefore be resented by certain big advertisers. Certain household magazines, for example, refuse to accept "controversial" articles, but *Woman's Home Companion* thrives on a vigorous editorial policy. Its exposé, "The Mother Racket," by Patricia Lochridge, helped give the Mothers hate movement a severe, although temporary, setback. Some publications give the pretext of fearing libel suits. Nuisance libel actions may undoubtedly be filed by publicity seekers, but at the same time they have the certain advantage of dramatizing the pro-democratic fight. Suing for alleged libel is a favorite nationalist device for throttling criticism.

In prewar France, shysters were employed by French fascists to stifle political opposition. These political lawyers sued for libel, for while a libel suit is pending the defendant may not comment further on the plaintiff without injury to his defense.

In the same way, monopoly corporations have stifled independent inventors owning valuable patents by suing them on the grounds that the invention violates their own exclusive patents. Court action can be an effective weapon for the suppression of truth and freedom of speech. Those who come to court with dirty hands, however, eventually lose out, as did Gerald Smith and Merwin K. Hart. Smith sued Walter Winchell and Detroit radio station WXYZ. When he failed to show up for the case the judge threw it out. Hart sued the Friends of Democracy for $1,000,000 for alleged injury to his alleged "patriotism." He withdrew the suit on the condition that the Friends of Democracy wouldn't publicize his action.

Permanent results against hate cannot be achieved unless the hate-mongers are placed constantly on the defensive and exposed by a democratic process of assault. Their brazenness will submit to no other method. Hate cannot be coddled. It must be treated by measures more vigorous than a hush-hush policy and a cringing on the part of an editor or publisher lest it "offend" reader or advertiser. One cannot fight for democracy merely by writing nice editorials. It's a field job and not necessarily a desk job.

Such a committee as the present House Committee to Investigate Un-American Activities is almost worthless in exposing the enemies of democracy. Despite its hounding of the Communists almost exclusively, it's doing a sloppy job and playing directly into their hands. The "investigation" of William Z. Foster and other Communist officials was a farce. On another front, the mission of the Committee seems to be to smear as Communist many fine and democratic organizations and individuals who are doing a much better job of fighting Communism. Rankin suggested, for instance, that the Common Council for American Unity was probably a Communist front. With fine disregard for the facts, Rankin denounced as "Communist" the Socialist-minded but nonetheless anti-Communist Veterans League of America.

Almost anyone who works for inter-racial, inter-faith or better inter-cultural relations is likely to be branded a Communist by Rankin. This is the formula adopted by the Terminiellos, Winrods and other leaders of the nationalist movement. The Committee, however, is the Communists' greatest publicity getter. It is doing as good a job in this respect as Father Coughlin, whose screaming accusations against innocent Americans earned him the wrath of most other decent Americans.

Witch-hunting and newspaper headlines cannot effectively remove the danger of Communism in America. The Rankin Committee, therefore, is rendering a disservice to the American people. The scope of its present investigations is revealed in a report released in June, 1946 summarizing its activities. This document is a hodgepodge of witch-hunting and such statements as the following blast at Army Orientation Fact Sheet No. 64:

The War Department sought to teach that any person who claimed to be any one or all of the following was a fascist, or was likely to become a fascist very shortly: "100 percent American, anti-Jew, anti-Negro, anti-Labor, anti-foreign born, anti-Catholic." It should be noted that if a person is anti-American, or anti-Gentile, or anti-white man, under the Army teachings he is quite all right, but the article goes on to say that if he is "anti-British, anti-Soviet, anti-French, or anti-United Nations," he is definitely a suspicious character.

Finally, the Rankin Committee falsely brands Fact Sheet No. 64 as one of "the dirtiest blots on the history of the War Department." Upon a careful analysis of the document I regard the Committee's conclusions as completely unwarranted. The document attempted to show how GIs could recognize fascist propaganda and what they could do about it. In clear, bold language it traced the development of fascism in Germany and Italy, re-told the consequences, and speculated on the forms it might take in America if the dreams of Axis propagandists came true. It recommended effective countermeasures. In other parts Fact Sheet 64 stated: "Fascism cannot tolerate such religious and ethical concepts as 'brotherhood of man.' The only way to prevent fascism from getting hold in America is by making our democracy work."

On the last page were excerpts from the Soviet Constitution, in

an apparent effort to inform the GI about an important military
ally and promote better Army morale. The publication gave the
non-political-minded GI some solid facts which are denied to him
in other publications. It tried to stimulate his thinking and give
him a moral and intelligent basis for answering the all-important
query: "What am I fighting for?" Many a battle has been won or
lost on the strength of that conviction.*

The Committee's criticism differs in no essential from that of Mrs.
Dilling, who called the Army Orientation courses "traitorous" and
their originators "war criminals of the lowest and most treasonable
order." Rankin's name-calling technique, of course, is liberally used
in the report. It hints that the orientation program was Communist-
led and "subversive." For this type of cold-blooded propaganda the
permanent Congressional Committee received an additional appropriation of $75,000 in May, 1946.

About half of the sloppy 74-page report is devoted to an exposé
of the American Committee for Spanish Freedom. This leftist group
is portrayed as the hub of a Communist plot against the U.S.A.
Reproductions of several form letters, one of them signed by Albert
Einstein, and numerous clippings from the *Daily Worker,* are offered as documentary evidence. One could have gotten this "evidence" merely by reading the *Daily Worker* at five cents a day.

The ballyhoo report ends with the reproduction of a radio speech
by former Commander Edward T. McCaffrey of the Catholic War
Veterans in which, with understandable fervor, he denounces Professor Laski. Despite the merits of McCaffrey's emotional portrayal
of Laski, Franco and the Catholic Church, his speech hardly falls
into the category of testimony and evidence, and has no place in a
document supposedly dealing only with facts.

What is Rankin doing about the nationalist hate-mongers? He
has conveniently ignored them. Early in 1946 Rankin "investigated"
Gerald L. K. Smith. It was a pleasant afternoon session in which
Rankin asked Smith leading questions and gave the Detroit rabble-

* Fact Sheet No. 64 deserves wide circulation. To school teachers, students,
clergymen, politicians, business men and others, copies will be sent at the
actual cost of reprinting, handling and mailing the pamphlet. Also available are
selected passages from the writings of Bishop Bernard J. Shiel and Eric Johnston. These provide enlightening reading and serve as helpful guides to the
propaganda barrage bombarding the American mind. For information write:
Friends of Democracy, 137 East 57th Street, New York 22, N. Y.

rouser the opportunity to use the Committee as a national forum. No attempt was made to learn about Smith's financing, to trace his connections with Maertz and other pro-Nazi propagandists. No effort was made to show that a course of extreme nationalism inevitably incites to revolution, that the call to action "at the right time" may lead to explosive demonstrations.

As to the Klan, on May 26, 1946 Representative Gerald W. Landis, a member of the Committee, stated, "Our investigators are going down there [Georgia] to see what's behind the revival." Landis spoke without Rankin's authority, for Rankin rushed back from Mississippi and on May 27 issued a statement which showed who bossed the Committee. Reports of an investigation of the Klan, Rankin said, were "without foundation." His Committee was "not called upon to interfere" in Georgia's affairs.

When Rev. Harvey Springer called on Rankin personally, in May, 1946, Rankin received him cordially and said, "Rev. Springer is a Christian minister." Rankin and the co-Rankinites have placed themselves in the position of "thought-police," frequently censuring Americans for their opinions. When Gerald Smith wanted the "Communists" investigated in "Hollywood, the Moscow of America," which allegedly was "raping America," he simply rushed down to Rankin, with a handful of petitions. Rankin promptly issued a manifesto that Hollywood would be investigated. Nothing happened, of course. It just kept the pot boiling and at the same time drew the proverbial red-herring across the trail of nationalists. This was the pattern in pre-Hitler Germany.

Americans want an honest and thorough investigation of the American Communist Party and its ramifications so that we may learn, without prejudice, how Communists and Communist front groups are hurting America. The Rankin Committee at present seems poorly qualified to do an effective job. Those who expect the Committee to investigate the Klan and the other anti-Semitic, anti-Catholic, anti-Negro, anti-democratic, hate-mongering groups will be disappointed. Small wonder, for Rankin himself has openly expressed some of those un-American prejudices.

Before the Committee can undertake a thorough investigation of nationalist bigots it must clean house by starting with Rankin. There can be no investigation of organized hate when a hate-monger wields the bull whip. There can be no impartial investigation of subversive postwar activity, so long as the effective leader of the Committee is seemingly partial to the Kluxers and other nationalist elements in American life and politics. Hate-mongers do not trample on hate. We cannot fight for democracy with un-democratic weapons.

Indications are that the Rankin Committee may carry witch-hunting even further than the old Dies Committee, which, at least, had several fine, outspoken Americans on it. Representative Herman P. Eberharter, from Pittsburgh, was one of these. When Dies began to call me a Communist I visited Mr. Eberharter and voluntarily submitted to a "private" hearing. I invited him to grill me with questions. I brought *documents* to show my impartial opposition to Communism and Fascism. I remained with Mr. Eberharter for more than an hour. After the meeting I prepared an autobiographical statement which Mr. Eberharter, to my eternal gratitude, placed in the *Congressional Record.*

I make an issue of the Committee to Investigate Un-American Activities because it can promote extreme nationalism by refusing to recognize it as a creeping menace. It publicizes and dignifies Communism. Whereas they should be a guide to democratic and anti-democratic groups, I regard the Committee's declarations so far as futile. Except by the nationalist fringers, Hearst paper readers, die-hard businessmen and Russo-phobes, the Committee is seemingly held in little respect. The Hon. John S. Wood of Georgia is officially its chairman, with Representative Rankin a mere member. Yet one hardly hears of Wood or other members of the Committee. In Wood's instance perhaps this is just as well; he has subtly defended the Klan: "The threats and intimidations of the Klan are an old American custom—just like illegal whiskey making."

Some of the blame rests on the chief counsel of the Committee, Ernie Adamson. He achieved almost Rankin-like eminence when on January 29, 1946 he wrote the Veterans Against Discrimination, in New York, the following silly letter:

Several of your circulars have been sent to us and I note you refer to democracy several times. I wonder if you are sufficiently familiar with the History of the United States to be aware that this country was not organized as a democracy, and that Section 4 of Article 4 of the Constitution reads in part as follows: "The United States shall guarantee to every state in this union a republican form of government."

Is it your purpose to ask for an amendment of the Constitution or do you propose to conduct a propaganda campaign against the administration of the provisions of the Constitution?

Nationalists often use the we-are-a-Republic-not-a-democracy line as an oblique way of denouncing democracy, which, of course, is supposed to be both Jewish and Communist. I make no charge that Adamson is an extreme nationalist or believes their propaganda line. I merely point out the parallel between the hate-mongers who propagate slurs on democracy and the counsel of an important Congressional Committee who volunteers letters which at least propagate the picayune notion that we are not, and were never intended to be, a democracy. Must one gather that Mr. Adamson's political growth stopped the year "Section 4 of Article 4 of the Constitution" was enacted? At best, Adamson's line gives further aid and comfort to the nationalists in their campaign for slurring democracy, and claiming some public officials as members of their own fraternity.

The security of our democratic system rests upon our ability to keep the affairs of our country directed by all for the benefit of all the people of our nation. No minority must ever be permitted to gain control, directly or through its "front" organizations. Such control will immediately upset the balance of democracy.

Minority control takes various forms.

Dictation can come from a minority of inter-locking giant trusts and monopoly-seeking interests. It can come from a bloc of legally elected officials who may suddenly and at the "right time," declare themselves the "law," as happened in Argentina. Entrenched religious minorities can work in conjunction with either or both of the first two groups. Dictation can arise through labor unions that gain control over government. In a crisis it might come about through officials appointed to maintain "law and order" who refused to relinquish their power even though the "emergency" was over. Any such coalition of irresponsible minority interests can, in favorable circumstances, bring about the decay and collapse of democratic government. In America, some of the groups mentioned have already carried such coalition beyond the primary stage and are developing their programs further.

The antidote is to keep the roots nourishing democracy well

diversified, keep the variegated pattern and zealously guard our precious freedoms of speech, of assembly, of press, of protest in order to expose instantly the advances of any anti-democratic coalition. Democracy must continue to feed through its various cultural, religious and social roots. The minute government became all "labor," "Catholic," "Protestant," it would cease to be American.

To be watched closely is the attempt of some minorities to gain a bridgehead in certain Federal agencies. Our police and sheriffs' forces must be guarded against infiltration by extremists of the Right. (Leftists have little influence among the usually highly conservative and long-entrenched officers of our investigational and law-enforcing agencies, who are often too occupied with their duties to become aware of the need for social and political progress.) For these gentlemen, systematic and thorough schooling with long-range objectives and patterned after the manner of Boston police may prove extremely helpful to the cause of democracy.

Our task for the future is to restore the teamwork which converted America from a trackless wilderness to potentially the greatest power for good on earth. "Allied teamwork," said General Eisenhower, "extending through all the services, has again demonstrated the ability to overcome the most adverse kind of conditions in defeating the enemy." It was teamwork on the home front which kept a continuous stream of supplies flowing from factory to firing line— teamwork of capital and labor, teamwork between the white-collared worker who made the blueprints and the blue-shirted white man who carried out orders and the fellows at his side whose skins were darker, or more yellow. Teamwork won the war.

Exceptional teamwork produced the atomic bomb. In charge of the research was an American of the Jewish faith, Dr. J. Robert Oppenheimer. Refugees from Europe of all faiths worked side by side with old-stock Americans.

Let's go back a few years. It was teamwork which built us into an industrial giant. There were discrimination and injustice, but there was also teamwork among the Irish immigrants who helped build the railroads, the Italians who laid many of our highways, and the immigrants from middle Europe who stoked the furnaces and blazing ovens; between Anglo-Saxons with short names and citizens with jawbreaking names and faces toughened by toiling in their adopted country. America was built on a common faith in the eternal promise of our country.

In the early twenties a new doctrine of world rebellion was born. Let Hitler himself speak from purgatory: "The place of artillery in trench warfare will in the future be taken by revolutionary propaganda. The enemy must be demoralized and ready to capitulate before military action can even be thought of." For the first time in history, psychological warfare became the twin arm of the military. One of the strongest forces in human relations is that of hate based upon fear. Hitler, through his agents and unpaid dupes, exploited it to the full here. During the present century, from both the extreme right and the left, hate has been organized with scientific thoroughness. Now it threatens to destroy the capacity for teamwork that has made America great.

The tragedy of postwar America is like that of a bomber crew of men from all parts of our country, men of different faiths and national backgrounds, who had fought together, together shot down enemy attackers, and together cussed at their bellyful of blood and sweat. Then, suddenly, something happened to break up the combination. The fatal germs of fear and hate entered and split up the good teamwork, turning the crew into squabbling factions, each obstinate and self-centered, telling the others what better men they were because of their jobs, races, religions, names and colors.

We have seen how one nation, through this hysterical mass fear and hate, could be stampeded into accepting a monstrous führer and a monstrous regime. Hitler is dead, but experiences and investigations reported on in this book may serve to show how his brood carries on. His converts are alive. Hitler's heritage was passed on to the Homer Maertzes, the Gerald Smiths and their ilk, and they are of his faith. Nationalists of their kind kept the torch of hate smouldering throughout the war years. And the smouldering fires are now breaking into red-white-blue flames. That's why the returning GI hears the same type of propaganda in America he heard from Axis Sally and Tokyo Rose.

As an American, I wanted to know why and how hysterical demagogues, fear-mongers and hate-peddlers were trying to make cowards and bullies of us all, parading the illusory "threat" of various "enemies" who will supposedly conquer us. Such a cleverly induced psychosis can perfectly well, at the "right time" and under the "right conditions," spread with the speed of a prairie fire from mind to mind, sweeping away our American system and its ideals overnight.

Crude and fanatical as many of them are, we should be concerned about those among us who are injecting the element of fear into our national outlook: fear of change, fear of World War III, fear of another "depression," fear of attack by an enemy overseas. This artificially induced fear is as un-American as bigotry. From the Boston Tea Party down to the Japanese surrender, our tradition has never been one of fear, but a bold tradition of raw strength, exploration, creation and imagination. Those who fear, fear change. And those who fear change are a drag on progress. Fear paralyzes the mental processes and can make men helpless in the hands of the spell-binding demagogue and bogus patriot.

Those who breed fear, breed hate, and the breeders of fear and hate are in themselves un-American, regardless of who they are!

Founded by peoples of more than fifty cultural strains and a dozen religious faiths who refused to be intimidated by European tyrants, America has been enriched and vitalized beyond any other nation. This explains our resourcefulness and our strength. Why, then, should Americans fear today? Surely we shall not let a wave of hysteria sweep our land and divert us from the task of reconstruction which can make the postwar era the greatest in our annals.

Which way will the veterans go? Let us trust that no self-seeking group will succeed in massing any veterans' bloc behind it. The ex-GI is, in a sense, America—not all of it, to be sure, yet such a vital amalgam that whichever way the bulk of the GIs—and with them their families—turn, in that way America may remain for generations to come. I believe that the vast and still partly unharnessed brain power and strength of the homecoming youth of America will continue to serve democracy as a whole, not the interests of any special group. There is plenty to do and plenty for all in America's postwar century. It belongs to us.

An immediate postwar period is usually among the darkest in a nation's history. Famine, friction and distress are everywhere born of war, the revolutionary upheaval of human society. Nationalists yammer that the future must bring world fascism, Communists preach the inevitability of a socialist brand of authoritarianism and seek to apply the pressure now, while the world economy is dislocated. America need not swing either way.

There *is* a middle road. We have travelled on it for many years. It has lately become rough in spots, but I still regard it as more worthwhile traveling than any other side road to the Left or the Right. If once the road is cleared of the road hogs, the onrushing reckless drivers, and the oldsters driving in '29 jalopies, I believe we can make it last without reconstructing the whole thing.

I have better reasons than most to be cynical about democracy. My job has taken me deep into the ranks of organized sabotage. I continue to meet the most incorrigible, hate-scarred fanatics in America. Despite the sordidness of the world I visit, my faith in the American people remains unshaken. Far from regarding the American system as the blind alley bogus patriots would have us believe it is, I regard it as our highway to a more abundant future.

I have no alternative from this point on but to keep on fighting for the promise of the New World which fanatical extremists from abroad and their American satellites have sought to destroy. I am confident that America will meet the challenge and win. That has always been our performance in history.

Geographical Fever Chart

Index